MAY 30 1977	DATE DUE		DEC 1 4 1988
OCT 1 0 1977	FEB. 27 1979	APR 21 1981	JAN 1 0 1989
NOV 2 8 1977	MAR 16 1979	JUL 21 1981	FEB 2 8 1989
JAN 3 1978	APR 17 1979	AUG -4 1981	MAY 2 3 1989
FEB 1 8 1978	MAY 19 1979	FEB -9 1982	AUG 2 2 1989
MAR 10 1978		MAR 16 1982	MAR 1 0 1992
MAR 15 1978	JUL -6 1979	AUG 17	MAY 8 1992
MAR 31 1978	JAN 28 1980	MAR 8 1983	OCT 2 6 1993
	APR 22 1980	JUN 3 83	FEB 2 2 1994
APR 18 1978	MAY -6 1980	JUL 8 1986	DEC 1 5 1995
MAY 13 1978	MAY 27 1980	AUG 2 6 1986	
MAY 30 1978	JUL 15 1980	NOV 2 2 1988	

THE
MINOR PROPHETS

THE
MINOR
PROPHETS

✠

Charles L. Feinberg

❧ ❧ ❧
❧ ❧ ❧

MOODY PRESS
CHICAGO

Formerly published in the series
The Major Messages of the Minor Prophets
in five volumes:

*Hosea: God's Love for Israel
Joel, Amos, and Obadiah*

Copyright 1948 by
Charles Lee Feinberg

*Jonah, Micah, and Nahum
Habakkuk, Zephaniah, Haggai, and Malachi*

Copyright 1951 by
Charles Lee Feinberg

Zechariah: Israel's Comfort and Glory

Copyright 1952 by
Charles Lee Feinberg

Moody Press Combined Edition, 1976

Library of Congress Cataloging in Publication Data

Feinberg, Charles Lee.
　The minor prophets.

　Formerly published in the series: The Major messages of the
minor prophets, c1948-c1952.
　Includes indexes.
　CONTENTS: Hosea: God's love for Israel.—Joel, Amos, and
Obadiah.—Jonah, Micah, and Nahum.—Habakkuk, Zephaniah,
Haggai, and Malachi. [etc.]
　1. Bible. O.T. Minor prophets—Commentaries. I. Title.

BS1560.F4　　　1976　　　229'.9'066　　　75-44088

ISBN 0-8024-5306-4

Printed in the United States of America

CONTENTS

FOREWORD

THE DECISION of Moody Press to bring out in a compact, single volume the fine series originally published by the American Board of Missions to the Jews (1948-1952) will surely be welcomed and appreciated by Bible students all over the English speaking world. Dr. Charles Feinberg displayed in those five small paperbacks an unusual combination of gifts which made for outstanding excellence in the teaching of Christian laymen who have a sincere love of the Bible. His profound knowledge of biblical Hebrew, dating back to his early training for the rabbinate, combined with a complete command of New Testament Greek, qualify him for a thoroughgoing study of Holy Scripture in the original languages. As a conscientious scholar he is well acquainted with the views of other biblical experts of nondispensational persuasion, and he is always careful to treat them fairly, despite his basic personal commitment to dispensationalism. This means that almost every premillennialist reader will find his expositions helpful and enriching, even though there may be some minor areas of disagreement in details. But in matters pertaining to the historical setting and cultural framework within which the twelve minor prophets received their messages from the Lord, no well-informed biblical scholar could find fault with Dr. Feinberg's treatment of the data.

In addition to his competence in linguistics, history, and biblical theology, the author displays in this volume a mastery of the art of communication. His language is lucid and clear and conveys the message of Scripture in a simple but persuasive manner that the mind can grasp and the heart can respond to. Even the more difficult and controversial matters of interpretation (such as the immorality of Hosea's wife, Gomer, and the ethical problem of his marrying her) are handled in a satisfying and convincing way, in terms which the average readers can easily understand. Quite enviable is his talent for treating such matters with both adequacy and brevity.

Along with the succinct lucidity, Dr. Feinberg displays a warm interest and concern for the spiritual growth of his readers. Quite frequently he proceeds from interpretation to exhortation, urging upon them the duty

7

of embracing the revealed will of God with true faith and love, so that it will make a real difference in their lives.

Dr. Feinberg displays a fine sense of balance in handling matters of dispute as they arise in the more controversial positions of the minor prophets. For example, in Joel 1 he states, "There are men who have taken the position that the chapter deals solely with the locust plague; others maintain just as firmly that the passage is entirely future. Both views are extreme. As a matter of fact, Joel starts with the situation then existing in the land after the havoc of the locust plague and then goes on to picture the dreadful Day of Jehovah yet future, but imminent." Or again, in connection with the passage in Joel 2 that is quoted by Peter at Pentecost in Acts 2:16-20, he comments, "We cannot take the position that only a portion of the prophecy was meant to be fulfilled at all, because this would work havoc with Bible prophecy. . . . The best position to take is that Peter used Joel's prophecy as an illustration of what was transpiring in his day and not as a fulfillment of this prediction. In short, Peter saw in the events of his day proof that God would yet completely bring to pass all that Joel prophesied. Joel's prophecy, then, was prefilled; it is yet (as the Old Testament passages on the outpouring of the Spirit show) to be fulfilled." Some of us might phrase it a little differently, affirming that part of Joel's prophecy was certainly fulfilled at Pentecost and part of it is yet to be fulfilled in the last days; but Dr. Feinberg's choice of the term *prefilled* minimizes the cleavage between his view and ours. I might add that I have used his larger commentary of Zechariah,[1] one of the most difficult of the prophetic books, in connection with evening school classes for laymen and found it to be very helpful for my students. His interpretation of the intriguing symbolism of the prophet's visions is lucid and convincing and gives respectful attention to views from which he personally dissents. The discussion will be found in a somewhat briefer form in this survey of the entire twelve prophets.

GLEASON L. ARCHER
Trinity Evangelical Divinity School

---

1. Charles Lee Feinberg, *God Remembers* (Wheaton, Ill.: Van Kampen, 1950).

PREFACE

ONE OF THE LITERARY INEPTITUDES of the centuries is the popular name given to the last twelve books of the Old Testament, namely, the Minor Prophets. The impression often gained is that these books are of minor importance. A better designation for them is that which the rabbis employed, that is, the Twelve. The Hebrew canon divided the prophetic books into Former Prophets (Joshua, Judges, Samuel, and Kings) and Latter Prophets (Isaiah, Jeremiah, Ezekiel, and the Twelve). The Twelve were known from ancient times as the smaller prophets because of their relative size compared with Isaiah, Jeremiah, and Ezekiel. They formed one book to insure against loss of any of the books.

The human authors lived, labored, and wrote from the ninth to the fifth centuries BC. Their messages, which are of major significance, contain the dominant themes of the prophetic Scriptures concerning the Messiah, Israel, the nations, and the earthly Kingdom of the Lord. Their times belong in the era of the Assyrian Empire, the Babylonian period, and the postcaptivity centuries. Arrangement, however, is not strictly according to chronological order.

The material contained in this commentary first appeared in five volumes (1947-1952) through the encouragement of the late Dr. Joseph Hoffman Cohn, General Secretary of the American Board of Missions to the Jews, Inc. During the more than a quarter of a century since the original publication of these volumes many expressions of appreciation have come, for which we are grateful to God. Now through the suggestion of Dr. Daniel Fuchs, President and successor to Dr. Cohn, the studies are published in one volume.

The reader will notice that the vast literature on the twelve prophets in the languages of Europe and the Near East is not presented. This is intentional because the expositions have primarily in view the laity to whom English is the native tongue. All the studies have been carried through on the basis of the original Hebrew.

9

It remains only to thank the staff of the Moody Press for their usual helpfulness and cooperation in seeing the volume through to publication. We commend the work to God for His glory and for the dissemination of the truth to Jews and Gentiles, as well as to the household of faith.

CHARLES LEE FEINBERG
Dean Emeritus
Professor of Semitics and Old Testament
Talbot Theological Seminary

PART I

HOSEA
God's Love for Israel

THE MATERIAL incorporated in Part I appeared from January 1945 to May 1946 as "Studies in Hosea" in *The Chosen People,* missionary publication of the American Board of Missions to the Jews, Inc. By request these articles are now being published in permanent form.

The writer has written this commentary on the book of Hosea with the general Christian reader in mind, in order to awaken a scriptural and lasting love for God's chosen people, Israel, and to arouse to a missionary zeal on behalf of their salvation. For this reason, although standard works on the minor prophets have been carefully consulted, we have not deemed it necessary to burden the reader with citations in footnotes. The Hebrew text has been before us throughout the writing, and we trust each position taken can be substantiated from the original.

The writer has been richly repaid in spiritual blessing in pursuing these studies in the Word of God and has rejoiced that God has seen fit to make them a blessing to others. If these pages will be used of God to turn many more hearts to Israel in her sad plight in these epoch-making days in order for us to make known to them their Messiah, the Lord Jesus Christ, we shall be grateful to God.

1

HOSEA, THE PROPHET

THE MAN

THE BOOK OF HOSEA itself is our sole source of information for the life and ministry of the prophet. His name, occurring in the Bible as Hosea, Joshua, and Jesus, means salvation. He was a contemporary of the Judean prophets Isaiah and Micah (cp. Ho 1:1 with Is 1:1 and Mic 1:1). Whereas the ministry of the latter two prophets was directed to the Southern Kingdom of Judah, the labors of Hosea were centered in the main upon the Northern Kingdom of Israel, founded by Jeroboam the son of Nebat.

Our prophet ministered during the reigns of Uzziah, Jotham, Ahaz, and Hezekiah of Judah, and during that of Jeroboam II, son of Joash of Israel. A comparison of dates will reveal that Hosea long outlived Jeroboam II. However, it is far from necessary to hold that he ministered from the first year of Uzziah's reign to the last of Hezekiah's, a period of about a century. (We must remember that Jotham's reign overlaps Uzziah's, his father, who was a leper; the illness of the latter made imperative a coregency, 2 Ki 15:5.) The prophet probably prophesied somewhat over a half-century, some maintaining seventy or even eighty years.

DOMESTIC LIFE

The home life of no prophet is told forth more fully than that of Hosea, because therein lay the message of God to His people, as we shall see later. Both the wife of Hosea and his children were signs and prophecies to Israel, Judah, and the coming reunited nation. If Isaiah could say, "Behold, I and the children whom Jehovah hath given me are for signs and for wonders in Israel from Jehovah of hosts, who dwelleth in mount Zion" (Is 8:18), Hosea could say as much with equal right. Because this fact has been overlooked, all too often the force of the message of the book has been dissipated by symbolizing the transactions recorded. The message was real because the acts noted were actually lived out in the life of the prophet.

13

HIS MESSAGE

Chapters 1 to 3 form a distinct section of the book, giving the prophet's own domestic experiences. In chapters 4 to 14, we are given the prophetic discourses proper. Amos had preached repentance to lead Israel back to God; Hosea preaches love. Amos had told forth the unapproachable righteousness of God; Hosea, the unfailing love of God. Our prophet presents the Lord as the God of the loving heart. Someone has well said, "He is the first prophet of Grace, Israel's earliest Evangelist." Just as Luke presents the prodigal son, so Hosea portrays the prodigal wife. Nowhere in the whole range of God's revelation do we find more beautiful words of love than in Hosea 2:14-16; 6:1-4; 11:1-4, 8, 9; 14:4-8.

HIS TIMES

Every prophet's message, in order to be understood properly, must be studied against the background of his times. Hosea lived in a time of outward prosperity. Uzziah's reign was marked by repeated successful wars, increased building projects in the land, the multiplication of fortifications, and the promotion of agriculture (see 2 Ch 26). The kings who followed him, though not to the same degree, prospered also. As for Jeroboam II, he recovered (2 Ki 14:25) for Israel a larger sphere of rule than it had ever enjoyed since the disruption of the Solomonic kingdom, annexing even Damascus, which had been lost already in Solomon's day (1 Ki 11:24).

In spite of the prospering of God, the people substituted outward forms (see Is 1 and 58) for the inward reality; they were committing all manner of sin; and they were in great moral and spiritual decline. Jeshurun had waxed fat and kicked (Deu 32:15). Against this low spiritual state the prophet Hosea, as well as his contemporaries, inveighed.

THE INTRODUCTORY WORD

The first three chapters of the book give us a kind of summary of the whole message of the prophet and are introductory in character. (For the sake of space we shall omit the text of the prophecy, but the reader must have it at hand in order to get the most out of the study.) Hosea begins his prophecy by dating it. Though a prophet of Israel, he marks his message by the names of Judean kings for the most part, because the promises of God were centered in the line of David.

The first word from God to the prophet was an order for him to marry a woman who would later become a harlot. This command of God to the prophet has been the occasion of much discussion and disagreement. It is held that if this were literally so, God was enjoining upon Hosea an unseemly: not to say sinful deed. This line of reasoning is difficult to understand, because the prophet could not become personally defiled just because he married a woman who later proved to be a harlot, or rather an adulteress, for her crimes are committed after she is married. It is only when the transaction is seen in its literal character as pointing to the relationship existing between God and Israel, that the full meaning of the prophet can be grasped.

In other words, God chose Israel and brought her into a most blessed relationship with Himself, likened to the marriage bond, and while in this state she committed harlotry. Her sin is explained as departing from the Lord. Just as harlotry and adultery, sins of the deepest dye and utterly abhorrent, are the result of infidelity, so spiritual harlotry (a case where the physical is transferred into the realm of the spiritual, as many times in Scripture) is the outcome of spiritual defection from God. God had entered into an eternal covenant with Abraham and desired to be bound to His people. But in all fitness He expected His people to remember their bond to Him. This they did not do, and God portrays their infidelity to Him through the domestic life of the prophet. (See Ps 73:27. Any good concordance will show the reader how many times the natural figure of harlotry is transferred to the spiritual realm. It will be illuminating to see how many times God's messengers use this comparison.)

Need we say how much the heart of the prophet was wounded over the shameful conduct of his wife? Of how much greater wounding was the conduct of Israel toward God? The children of Gomer are called "children of whoredom," not because they were not the children of Hosea. Nor were they some already begotten but rather those yet to be born. In other words, the marriage of the prophet was normally to issue in children, who are so named ("children of whoredom") because their mother was unfaithful in marriage. The mother represents Israel corporately, while the children speak of the nation individually, although the transaction in the home of Hosea was literal and historical.

THE CHILDREN AS SIGNS

The first child of this union of the prophet and Gomer, the daughter of Diblaim, was a son. God commanded his name to be called Jezreel, for in a short time God was to avenge the blood of Jezreel upon the house of Jehu, and was to bring an end to the kingdom of the house of Israel. What did God mean by the name? The long, sad story of Jezreel begins back in the days of vacillating and weak Ahab and his wicked and designing wife, Jezebel (1 Ki 21). Naboth the Jezreelite, who owned a vineyard near the palace of Ahab, was murdered through the infamous plotting of

Jezebel in order to dispossess him of his father's heritage. For this atrocity God pronounced doom upon Ahab, Jezebel, and their descendants, this doom to overtake them in Jezreel in the very place where Naboth was slain. The sentence on Ahab was executed first, when he fought at Ramoth-gilead (1 Ki 22); then the blow fell upon Jezebel and Jehoram through Jehu the son of Jehoshaphat the son of Nimshi (2 Ki 9).

Jehu was the instrument of God to execute His judgment upon the house of Ahab. But he came to the throne through dastardly crimes of bloodguiltiness (2 Ki 9:14 and following). True, his act was commended (2 Ki 10:30), for it was such in itself, but later events showed the motivating causes in Jehu's life had been pride and ambition. The prophet Hosea's pronouncement had point here, for Jeroboam II then reigning was of Jehu's house. God would not only visit that house because it had gone into idolatry, but all Israel with the destruction of their kingdom because of their gross departure from the Lord.

A DISTINCTION WITH A DIFFERENCE

We must digress here for a moment, because a great governing principle of God is here being enunciated. It is clear that although Jehu was the instrument of God for a visitation upon punishment-deserving Ahab and his dynasty, nevertheless God required it of him because his own heart was not right and because he had personal ambitions contrary to the mind of God. Can we not learn a lesson here with regard to Israel and the nations of the earth? Though God prophesied the Egyptian bondage and it was in a sense a chastisement upon Jacob's seed because they left the land of blessing, nevertheless God judged the Egyptians for their oppression of His people.

It is clear from the prophet Habakkuk that Israel was ripe for judgment because of evil on every hand, and God foretold that the Babylonians would be that instrument of visitation. But the same prophet reveals the wrath of God upon these enemies of Israel, because they were not executing the will of God in their acts, but were directed of their own wicked hearts. No man, Hitler or any other, can oppress God's people with selfish motives and expect reward from God because they claim to be instruments in the hands of God. God requires truth in the inward parts, and He wants such in the hearts of others as well as Israel. Some one has well said, "So awful a thing is it, to be the instrument of God in punishing or reproving others, if we do not, by His grace, keep our own hearts and hands pure from sin." No nation nor individual has accomplished it thus far, so the safest path and the one with the approval of wisdom upon it, is to lay no violent hand upon Israel under any condition or circumstance.

THE FULFILLMENT

Though the Northern Kingdom was prospering at the time and all seemed well, Hosea forewarned of the end of Jehu's dynasty and the destruction of the Northern Kingdom with its military power in the valley of Jezreel, verse 5. These events took place, though at least forty years apart, just as foretold. (See 2 Ki 15:8-12 and chap. 18.) The valley of Jezreel is the great plain of Esdraelon in central Palestine. Hosea lived to see this prophecy realized in Shalmaneser's victory at Beth-arbel (10:14). It was the last dread admonition from God before the fall of Samaria.

NOT PITIED

The second child of Hosea and Gomer was called Lo-ruhamah, "not compassionated or pitied." The word in the original expresses great depths of love and tenderness. The hour for Israel, the Northern Kingdom, has struck and her punishment is inevitable. She is ripe for judgment and it draws on apace. But God promises at the same time that His wrath will not go forth against Judah at the same hour. For them He had reserved mercy yet, a deliverance to be brought about by no human agency, but solely by the power of God. The defeat of Sennacherib before Jerusalem at the end of the eighth century BC, when 185,000 were slain by the Angel of Jehovah in one night (see 2 Ki 19 and Is 37), was a glorious fulfillment of this prediction, but the prophecies of all the prophets are luminous with promises of the future complete deliverance (physical) and salvation (spiritual) of Israel.

NOT MY PEOPLE

When Lo-ruhamah had been weaned (in the East this takes place two or even three years after birth), the wife of the prophet conceived and bore him a second son, Lo-ammi. God was thus saying to Israel they were not His people and He was no longer their God. How can this be true? Has God scrapped His unconditional covenant with Abraham? Does not Paul still call Israel "His [i.e., God's] people" in Romans 11:1? The difficulty is resolved if we realize that the Abrahamic covenant stands fast and sure, no matter what Israel does. First and last it is an unconditional covenant. This makes Abraham's seed always God's chosen people. But they must be in obedience and following the will of the Lord before they can have this experimentally realized in their lives. When they depart from the way of the Lord and are dealt with by God in chastisement, they appear for all intents and purposes to be "Not My People," Lo-ammi. When they return to God through Christ in a coming day, they will be in fact what they have always been in the counsels of God.

This same principle is seen to operate with the believer in Christ today, whether from Israel or from the Gentiles. Through faith in Christ and His finished work on Calvary, any soul, Jew or Gentile, is born again of the Spirit of God unto eternal life. However, that child of God can possibly live in lack of separation from the world and appear as though he knew nothing of the Father care of God and enjoy none of the blessings of intimacy with the heart of God.

For this reason, Paul exhorts the Christians of Corinth to separate from the world so that God may be their Father and they may be His sons and daughters (2 Co 6:14-18). But were they not already such, for they were believers? Yes, but Paul wants them to realize in daily experience what they are in actual standing before God. The situation is similar with regard to Israel, and we stress this great truth, because there is so much error abroad on this vital feature of God's relationship to Israel. In short, Israel, having lightly esteemed the privilege she sustains toward God (a veritable Gomer), will not enjoy the blessing and reality of it. The patriarchal blessings and promises are never abrogated, for Israel nationally is "beloved for the fathers' sake" even while they are enemies of the gospel for the sake of the Gentiles (Ro 11:28-29).

PROMISE OF BLESSING

Just as no other prophet pronounces doom alone upon Israel without a promise of future blessing, so Hosea follows his dark predictions with words of great comfort. In verses 1:10 through 2:1 the prophet promises five great blessings to Israel: (1) *national increase* (1:10*a*); (2) *national conversion* (1:10*b*); (3) *national reunion* (1:11*a*); (4) *national leadership* (1:11*b*); (5) *national restoration* (2:1). In view of the unspeakable decimation of Israel in Europe through the Nazi criminals, the promise of national increase is a bright hope indeed.

Do the words not remind one of the very assurance given to Abraham of a great progeny? Not only so, but they will then live up to their heritage, by His grace, as sons of the living God. See Romans 9:25 and 1 Peter 2:10 where the expression is applied to both redeemed Gentiles and Jews, because they stand alike before God in grace. The reunion of the divided nation will manifest the restored favor of God to His people. (See Eze 37:15-23.) The one head over them will be their glorious Messiah King, David's greater Son, in whom they shall trust. (Cp. Ho 3:5; Jer 23:1-5; Eze 34:23; 37:15.)

Their going up from the land has been interpreted as their going up to Esdraelon to the battle which will be decisively victorious for them, but it is perhaps better to see in the prediction the going up of the people from all parts of the land to celebrate their solemn feasts. (Of the many references see Is 2:1-4; Zec 14.) "Great shall be the day of Jezreel" for in that day God will in Christ rout the enemy once for all when Israel's Messiah stands upon the Mount of Olives to espouse their cause in person. Then will they be Ammi (My People) and Ruhamah (Pitied). Thus all three names have reappeared, but now in blessing.

THE BLIGHT OF DISOBEDIENCE

In verses 2 to 13 of chapter 2, we have the declaration of God concerning the judgment to fall upon Israel for her many sins. God disowns Israel: this is the valley of Achor. In the latter part of the chapter (vv. 14-23) the blessings of obedience and restoration are set forth. God reclaims Israel: this is the door of hope (see 2:15 which is the key of the entire chapter).

Those addressed in verse 2 are Israel, not the children of the prophet. Israel as a whole is viewed as the mother; the children are the individual members of the nation. The purpose of such a distinction is to bring upon the mother the reproach she merits for her sinful acts and to dissuade her from her continued unfaithfulness.

Throughout the passage by means of the physical figures employed, the enormity and heinousness of the spiritual defection of Israel from the Lord are more clearly seen. The brazenness of her infidelity is pictured by the words "her whoredoms from her face." God never glosses over sin. This is a distinctive feature of the Bible that differentiates it from all other books, ancient and modern. It never palliates sin regardless of who is involved in it. Hence, Israel must bear the bitter pain and blight for her spiritual whoredoms and adulteries. The warning is that she will be deprived of all subsistence and all earthly possessions. All this is brought out under the picture of nakedness (see Eze 16:4), desolation, waste, and death by thirst. Here we have an intimation of the coming captivity to Assyria for the Northern Kingdom, but it is not yet specifically stated.

THE SHAME OF INFIDELITY

As an unabashed harlot, Israel has declared her intention of pursuing her "lovers" (the idols of her pagan worship) in order to receive her bread, water (necessities of food), wool, flax (necessities of clothing), oil, and drinks (luxuries). The time of prosperity in Israel, a gracious manifestation of the love of God, was taken by them as a benefit from the worthless gods they were worshiping.

The prophet thunders in the name of God, "She did not know that I gave her the grain, and the new wine, and the oil, and multiplied unto her silver and gold, which they use for Baal" (v. 8). Note the emphasis on "my" in verse 5: Israel took these bounties as rightfully belonging to her. But in verse 9 they are shown to be actually God's, for He claims them by a reiterated "my." For a comparable case see Jeremiah 44:15-23 where Israel again attributes the benefits of God to her worship of vain idols. No words could bring out more forcefully the insanity of idol worship; such service so befogs and darkens the mind that the beneficences of God are credited to senseless vanities which profit not. (See Ro 1.)

RETRIBUTION FROM GOD

Because of this festering cancer in Israel's spiritual life, God will hem her in on every side, so that she shall be separated from her paramours. She will pursue her lovers relentlessly but will not find them. Her disappointment will be so keen, that she will desire to return to her true and "first husband." She will be deprived of grain, new wine, wool, and flax: a depression of real proportions will be her lot. God will lay her bare before her lovers to her shame. Yea, more, God will remove every occasion of joy and gladness from her; her feasts, her new moons, her sabbaths, and her solemn assemblies. At these times her consorting with idolatry found its fullest expression instead of being times for honoring God.

For this desecration of the things of God, He will lay waste the land as a forest and multiply against them the beasts of the field. The "days of the Baalim" wherein Israel forgot God will all be visited upon her. The prophet thus, in vivid and unmistakable language, outlines the curse and blight of Israel's disobedience; nakedness, waste, hunger, thirst, shame, sadness, loneliness, and desolation will be her sad portion.

THE BLESSINGS OF OBEDIENCE

Again, Hosea will not close this prophecy until he has told forth the future blessings and glories in store for Israel when in obedience to the revealed will of God. In that day God will bring Israel into the wilderness, that is, alone and will speak to her heart. From this face-to-face meeting with the Lord, Israel's valley of Achor, valley of troubling, will be turned into a door of hope.

The mention of the valley of Achor is another of Hosea's frequent uses of past events in the history of Israel. It reminds us of the entering of Israel into the land of Canaan in the days of Joshua. Through faith, the Lord had given glorious victory over Jericho. But Achan had taken of the accursed booty of the city, which had been strictly forbidden of God. The result of this sin was the defeat of Israel at Ai. After Achan and his house had been found out and stoned, then the Lord gave success to their campaign against Ai. Thus Achan's sin was turned into blessing by the opening up of the land through the defeat of Ai. See Joshua 7:24-26; also Isaiah 65:10, where the valley of Achor becomes a place for herds to lie down.

In similar manner, when Israel has owned her sin and put it from her in truth, there will be restoration. The valley of Achor will thus be changed into a door of hope. The Lord will restore and more the years that the cankerworm hath eaten. Even the very names of the Baalim (the idols of Baal) will be removed from Israel. They shall call God Ishi (my husband) and not Baali (my lord or master). Affection is implied in the first, while rule is expressed by the second. But even more, the word *Baal* must go now because of its evil connotations and the sins committed in Baal worship.

MULTIPLIED MERCY

In the hour of return to the Lord, Israel will have all creation in subjection to her. The beasts of the field, the birds of the heavens, and the creeping things of the earth will have the restraint of God upon them, so that Israel may dwell in safety. The bow, the sword, and battle will be no more. As Micah prophesied, every man shall sit under his own vine and fig tree, and none shall make them afraid (Mic 4:4).

Best of all, however, will be the new relationship into which Israel shall be brought. There will be a renewal of the marriage vows. Thrice does God say to Israel that He will betroth her unto Himself: (1) forever; (2) in righteousness, justice, lovingkindness, and mercies; (3) in faithfulness. (Vv. 19 and 20 of chap. 2 are recited by every orthodox Israelite as he places the phylacteries on the middle finger of his left hand.) The word used for "betroth" (*'aras*, to woo a virgin) speaks volumes of the grace of God that blots out sin. Israel is no longer seen as a harlot or an adulteress, but, mind you, as an unsullied virgin. She is seen as though she had never sinned. Compare this to 2 Corinthians 11:2 of the Church in spite of all her failings. For Israel see also the remarkable statement in Numbers 23:21 and the gracious designation in Deuteronomy 32:15 (Jeshurun means, as a diminutive, "little upright one").

Then the earth will yield her fruit, and the land shall be prosperous once more. This is given under the figure of personification in verses 21 and 22, as though the heavens asked the Lord to be permitted to rain refreshing showers upon the earth to give grain, new wine, and oil. The answer of God will be in the affirmative, and Israel shall be sown of the Lord, Jezreel. (See Mic 5:7 and Is 37:31.) Finally, the promise is that Lo-ruhamah shall be Ruhamah and Lo-ammi shall be Ammi. A cycle is thus completed. Every curse shall be not only averted, but turned into blessing. For our summary of the blessings upon Israel we see: (1) comfort—verse 14; (2) fruitfulness of the land—verses 15, 21, 22; (3) removal of idolatry—verse 17 (Zec 13:2); (4) restoration of nature's glory—verse 18 (Is 35); (5) safety in the land—verse 18; (6) mercy of the Lord in His restored favor—verse 23; and (7) national conversion—verses 19, 20, 23. Truly the valley of Achor shall be the door of hope!

2

THE IMPORTANCE OF THE PROPHECY

THOUGH THE THIRD CHAPTER of Hosea consists of but eighty-one words in the original Hebrew, it rightfully takes its place among the greatest prophetic pronouncements in the whole revelation of God. The expression, *"multum in parvo"* (much in little space), is certainly true of this passage. With skillful and quick lines, the prophet, through the Spirit of God, paints for us the complete picture of Israel's national history. The fourth verse of the chapter is one of the surest proofs of the divine origin of prophecy and the Bible in general. This chapter has been likened to the eleventh chapter of Romans, because here, as there, God makes large disclosures of His plans and dealings, past, present, and future, with Israel, His chosen. The temptation is great upon us to quote the chapter in its entirety, but we refrain because of the imperative to conserve space. But we must insist upon its being open before the reader as he peruses these lines; nothing, absolutely nothing, that we can say about these lines and verses of Scripture is comparable to the passage itself.

ISRAEL'S PAST

In verses 1-3 we have the act which was literally carried out in the life of the prophet; in verses 4 and 5 the import and intention of the transaction are clearly set forth. Throughout the second chapter of our prophecy, the picture of Gomer in the home of Hosea had broadened out into the message of warning and blessing for all Israel. Now the prophet comes back to the individual and personal relationship that was set up at the outset of the book. God speaks directly to the prophet and tells him to love again that woman who, though beloved of her husband, had become an adulteress. Specifically, this is to portray the boundless love of God for Israel. But Gomer, so exalted and elevated by the position of being the wife of the prophet and partaking of his undivided love, has so wretchedly debased herself that she must be bought back, as though from the slave mart. And what a paltry price is hers! When once bought back, she is solemnly requested to be no man's wife again and the prophet will assume a similar position toward her. Since all this is a miniature of God's dealings with Israel, we may directly apply these acts to historical events. Immediately three distinct features emerge: first, relationship to Israel; second, unfaithfulness of Israel; third, God's love for Israel.

RELATIONSHIP TO ISRAEL

It is impossible to read the Old Testament with any degree of understanding without being struck very early in the record with the fact that God had willingly and sovereignly entered into certain binding relationships with Israel. God had taken her to Himself by His redemption of her from Egypt and by His entrance into covenant relationship with her. (See Ex 4:22 and Amos 3:1-2.)

The relationship was and is inward, sacred, indissoluble. It is exactly pictured by the marriage between the prophet and Gomer. Never has God forgotten this time of entering into covenant relationship. Hear Jeremiah say: "I remember for thee the kindness of thy youth, the love of thine espousals; how thou wentest after me in the wilderness, in a land that was not sown" (Jer 2:2). Do you realize what God is saying here and what marvelous grace He is displaying? Unmentioned are the facts that Israel was under galling bondage in Egypt, that she groaned and sighed to the Lord in her pitiful plight, that she rebelled throughout the time of the wilderness. The picture is that God was delighted with Israel's love, the love of betrothal, and to think that she would go with the Lord even though it be through a wilderness! God's eye sweeps away in love all the secondary features of the picture and centers His thought upon the glorious fact that Israel became His.

UNFAITHFULNESS OF ISRAEL

But the wife of the prophet became an adulteress. What shame, what public disgrace, what burning anguish to the sensitive heart of the prophet! Ah, but no worse than the wife of Jehovah consorting with other gods and loving cakes of raisins. These cakes of raisins are explained by Jeremiah 7:18 and 44:19 as parts of a ceremony in honor of the queen of heaven; they speak of open worship of the idols of the day. What shame and open scandal this was in the eyes of God can be gleaned only faintly from the counterpart on the human scale in the life of the prophet.

To what depths this led Gomer is clear from the price to be paid for her redemption. Fifteen pieces of silver. The price of a common slave was thirty pieces of silver according to Exodus 21:32. She had lowered herself to such a plane where she was worth but half the price of a common slave. The homer and *lethech* of barley speak of her utter worthlessness, for this was the food of animals. Nothing so undoes man altogether and ruins him completely as defection from the Lord. It is no less than high treason against high heaven.

GOD'S LOVE FOR ISRAEL

God never enjoined upon Hosea a task of which He could not be a partaker, when He bade the prophet to love "a woman beloved of her friend." For God's love for Israel has no relationship to time; it is timeless and constant. When we read that Gomer was beloved of her friend, this does not indicate the love of a paramour. The Revised Standard Version (RSV) margin is probably correct in translating the word as "husband." The word indicates the tenderness of her treatment at his hands, leaving her all the more inexcusable in her action.

Notice that the first verse of this chapter uses the word "love" four times. The verse can almost be set out in a mathematical proportion: as the love of God has ever been toward Israel, though she has loved idols rather than God, so the love of Hosea is to be toward Gomer, though she has loved strangers rather than her lawful husband. Just as Gomer still retains the love of the prophet, Israel is beloved of God. Israel is engraven on the hands of God (Is 49:14-16); she is the apple of His eye (Zec 2:8). And even after centuries of disobedience on the part of His people, God could rebuke accusing Satan with the all-prevailing answer that He had chosen Jerusalem (Zec 3:2).

ISRAEL'S PRESENT

Neither Gomer's nor Israel's past is a thing of glory, but the end of the story is not yet. Israel's present condition is sketched for us in verse 4. This has been her condition since she chose Caesar to rule over her in preference to the Christ of God. Every detail, and there is much of it here, is amazing in its accuracy until we realize it is God who is speaking, the One who knows the end from the beginning.

This verse, mark you, gives the lie squarely to all such vaporizings as the one labelled Anglo-Israelism. The conditions set forth here have not been the portion of England and cannot be twisted into such a meaning. The condition is anomalous; it defies all categories. No wonder the great German philosopher, Hegel, an ardent student of the philosophy of history, said of the history of Israel: "It is a dark, troublesome enigma to me. I am not able to understand it. It does not fit in with any of our categories. It is a riddle." Just as Gomer was placed in the position where she no longer consorted with her former paramours and yet was not in full fellowship in marriage—a truly strange condition—so Israel is throughout this age in a position where she is neither idolatrous nor enjoying the fellowship of God in a worship pleasing to Him.

WITHOUT—WITHOUT—WITHOUT

For many days, and these many days answer to those of Gomer's, Israel is to be without a king, without a prince, without sacrifice, without pillar, without ephod, and without teraphim. What does this mean?

It signifies, first of all, that the nation will be without civil polity; they shall have neither king nor prince. After the Babylonian captivity and the death of Zedekiah, the last king of Judah, the people of Israel knew no longer a king in their midst. (The Hasmonean dynasty scarcely offers a parallel to the pre-Exilic dynasties.) But they did have princes, such as Zerubbabel, the son of Shealtiel, as is clear from his genealogy. In this age, since the death of Israel's Messiah, who came as King of the Jews, Israel has known neither king nor prince. It has been said: "No one of their own nation has been able to gather them together or become their king."

Second, they shall be without God's appointed sacrifice. There is no Temple, for the land on which the Temple is, is not theirs; there is no high priest, for there are no genealogies extant to prove it; there is no sacrifice, for there are no duly constituted priests to perform it and the one sacrifice in Christ has been completed once for all: there is no atonement, because there is no blood of sacrifice in their religious ceremonies.

Third, and probably most remarkable of all, they shall be without idolatry. Natural inference would lead us to believe that if Israel, when she had the true worship of God, turned repeatedly to idolatry, she would most assuredly do so when without the true worship. But no, the prophet is not telling the story by human inference but through divine revelation. Says Hosea, though Israel shall be without a religious center and ritual, yet she will not turn to idolatry. Israel, through the centuries of her dispersion, will have none of idol pillar (the obelisk) nor lying teraphim. Though Israel has lost distinctive national features—king, prince, and with these the occupation of all the land as well—and religious features, such as sacrifice and ephod, yet the marvel is that Israel abides! Covetous and vacillating Balaam spoke better than he knew when he said, "Lo, it is a people that dwelleth alone, And shall not be reckoned among the nations" (Num 23:9).

ISRAEL'S FUTURE

At this point there are those who would have us believe that the tale has been told. That is the end for Israel. If so, we do well to cast the Bible from us as a vile and worthless thing, not to be depended upon in any particular. If this condition is the end for Israel, then why did Hosea not close his prophecy at this point? Why does he lead us to believe there is an "afterward" for Israel? Why? Yes, he may well do so, for there is a tomorrow for Israel, an afterward for the despised, criticized, and ostracized people of God. Notice the three marks of time: "many days," "afterward," and "in the latter days," which are of vital importance here as elsewhere in prophetic Scriptures.

Here are the three elements in Israel's future: return, seek, and come with fear. Verse 1 told us that Israel turned to other gods; this verse tells us she will return to the true God. (See Deu 4:30-31; 30:1.) She will not need to be sought, but through God's grace will seek Jehovah her God. Note the important truth in Hosea 5:15. The seeking will be to her God and "David their king" in the person of His greater Son, the Lord Jesus Christ. Remarkable to state, the Targum of Jonathan says, "This is the King Messiah." (Cp. Jer 30:9; Eze 34:23; 37:24.) They will come with fear (reverential awe mingled with joy; see Is 60:5 for the same verb) unto His blessing and salvation. How could God's love for Israel eventuate otherwise? God's love outlives Israel's, just as Hosea's outlived Gomer's. May God shed abroad this divine love for Israel in our hearts that she may know Him!

THE SECOND PART OF THE PROPHECY

Chapter 4 of Hosea introduces the rest of the book and contains a summary of the prophet's messages. The chapters of this portion give in minute and vivid details what was set forth in broad outline and under the picture of a domestic scene in chapters 1, 2, and 3. The section does not lend itself easily to division, because its parts form one long indictment from God on the morally corrupt, politically decaying, and spiritually bankrupt nation. At the very outset we are confronted with the attention-arresting word: "Hear!" (This is repeated in 5:1.) The whole nation is in view with particular emphasis on the Northern Kingdom of Israel. Note how repeatedly Ephraim (i.e., Israel, which was so called because Ephraim was its most populous tribe) appears at the head of these chapters, Hosea 4:1 to the end of the book.

BILL OF PARTICULARS

Chapter 4 is to the book of Hosea what chapter 1 of the book of Isaiah is to that prophecy. Here, as there, we have God's arraignment of

His people. As in regular court procedure we are aroused to attention with the words: "Hear the word of Jehovah!" (See Is 1:2.) Then follows the bill of particulars, charge upon charge of devastating character. God has a lawsuit, a controversy, with His people. The land is bereft of truth, goodness, and the knowledge of God, and full of swearing, lying, killing, stealing, committing adultery, and bloodshed.

Notice how many infractions of the Ten Commandments are here laid to the people's charge. Such departures from God bring with them sure judgment from Him, so the land has languished and mourned. Even the beasts of the field, the birds of the heavens, and the fishes of the sea have experienced thereby the displeasure of God. Man's sin works havoc even upon lower creation. Is it not so in the war-torn world of today? Man has great capacities not only for bringing about his own ruin, but that of those about him as well.

We are reminded too that it is not man who is indicting the sin of the people, but it is God. He admonishes that He has the matter well in hand and expects no man to meddle with it. The people need this warning because they have long since become adept at striving with their priests. This reveals their insubmission to the revealed will of God, for they had displayed the highest insolence in contending with the God-appointed teachers of the people. Deuteronomy 17:12 shows the gravity of such action. But whether it was people, priest, or prophet, the charges were valid against all. The prophet and priest had set shameful examples: they were drunken, sensual, rejecting God and His claims, lovers of formality in worship, and devoid of spirituality. The sentence of the Judge is clear: "I will destroy thy mother [i.e., the nation itself]!"

LACK OF KNOWLEDGE

The cause of the trouble is stated as lack of knowledge, but only because they have already rejected the knowledge given them. In this the priests, their teachers, were the chief offenders for they had misled the people of God. Rejecting the knowledge and will of God, Israel could no longer fill the priestly office, so they are deposed from their noble position. God sets Israel aside for a time from her priestly calling (Ex 19:6), to which she will be reinstated in the future according to the prophecy of Zechariah 3. And all this defection of the people came not because they had not been previously prospered of God. On the contrary, prosperity had the opposite effect that it should have had. The more they were multiplied, the more they sinned against the Lord. Consequently, such glory as they had would be turned into shame.

"LIKE PEOPLE, LIKE PRIEST"

The accusation of Hosea against the priests of the day is extremely grave. He charges that the priests delighted in the sins of the people and had their hearts set on the people's iniquity, because it brought them revenues in fines and sin offerings. They had a vested interest in the continued sin of Israel. The priest and the people were equally bad; the one corresponded to the other exactly. The people were no less culpable than the priest, nor was he less blameworthy than they. He conformed his life to their ways and they, viewing the godless conduct of their teachers, found an example they delighted to follow as well as confirmation for their own deeds. The priests reaped a harvest in a corrupted and misled people. Both were equally to be punished for their ways. What they had would not satisfy them, and they would know no real increase. (For a strikingly analogous situation see Hag 1:5-6.)

DEPTHS OF MORAL CORRUPTION

Not desiring to retain the knowledge of God, the people were given over to work every kind of moral uncleanness. It is the same lot which befell the heathen nations as recorded in chapter 1 of Romans. Occupation with a lifeless ritual ultimately led the people into idolatry and every unclean practice. Their stock and their staff, with every senseless idol, became their oracle and source of counsel. Blindness and a spirit of error settled down upon them.

The soul-destroying abominations of the Canaanites, for which the awful curse of God was pronounced against them unto extinction, became the practice and daily routine of God's highly favored people. They conformed to the unwholesome practices about them instead of inveighing with holy zeal and fervor against them. With these idolatrous rituals, all manner of physical impurity was bound up. Such pollution spreads as a cancerous growth, and soon the womankind of the nation became corrupt. The collapse of the nation and its accompanying ruin became inevitable.

Faithlessness toward God always results in faithlessness to the most sacred ties of earth. If God be not honored in the life, man can expect to fare no better. Defection from God brings with it disaster in the social and home life of a nation. Against these conditions Isaiah also inveighed. (See Is 3:16-26.)

EPHRAIM JOINED TO IDOLS

Thus far in chapter 4 the prophet has been rebuking the entire nation. Now he turns for a moment to direct a special word to Judah. The inference would seem to be that Judah, the Southern Kingdom and the center of the Davidic dynasty, was more loyal to God than Israel in the north. Judah is strongly exhorted not to follow in the wicked ways of Israel. To Israel's idolatrous feasts at Gilgal and Beth-aven she is not to make a pilgrimage.

These were noted shrines of the ten tribes. Gilgal had been the seat of a school of the prophets in the time of the prophet Elisha (2 Ki 2:1 and 4:38), but Hosea speaks of it in his prophecy as the place of idol worship (9:15; 12:11). Beth-aven, a city east of Bethel, is singled out rather than Bethel for a significant reason. The prophet is showing that the people had exchanged Bethel ("house of God") for Beth-aven ("house of vanity"). God says to Judah, "Keep away!" Judah is warned to separate herself from the God-dishonoring practices of Israel, where they mingled oaths in the name of Jehovah with their service to idols.

The prophet is all the more eager that Judah heed the warning because Israel, acting like a stubborn heifer, did not. The prophet's designations of Israel are anything but falsely flattering to her, for he calls Ephraim a silly dove (7:11) and a cake not turned (7:8). But an intractable, balking heifer brings out clearly her distaste of godly restraint. For this God will feed them as a lamb in a large place. This has often been understood to mean that God will let them have their desire: He will allow them free rein for their wayward propensities. They can wander now like sheep on a large plain, not knowing that such dispersal will work their own ruin. Such an interpretation does not do justice to the fact that God is going to feed them as a lamb is fed.

Another alternative is to take the words as irony: if Israel is so stubborn, then God will feed her as a lamb, will He not? This is rather forced. The best solution is to take the last clause as a question: since Israel is so refractory, how can God now feed them as a lamb in a large place? Isaiah 30:23 shows that the expression is used in a good sense and not of punishment.

How far Ephraim has departed from following the Lord is clear from the heart-rending cry of the prophet: "Ephraim is joined to idols; let him alone!" Ephraim is so bound up with idols that he will not be severed from them. The word rendered "joined" is the one employed in speaking of binding with spells. The Northern Kingdom is held by idolatry as though under a spell, bewitched by it and utterly helpless in himself to extricate himself. He has so wholly given himself, mated himself, to his senseless idols, that only judgment remains. He must now learn the full bitterness of his deeds by costly experience. "Let him alone!" Such was the extreme to which ungodliness had brought Israel. The very pleasures in which she had so long delighted herself will become utterly distasteful to her. Their drinks and drinking bouts will become tasteless, spoiled. The leaders of the nation, called "shields," for they were to be the defenders of the populace, are as corrupt as the lower classes of society. The devastating leaven of idolatry with its attendant immoralities has worked its way from highest in society to the lowest. What can be the only outcome? The scourge of the Assyrian tempest will yet sweep them away, idols, people, prophet, priest, and leaders.

3

"I KNOW EPHRAIM"

CHAPTERS 5 and 6 of the prophecy of Hosea bring vividly to us the destruction and ruin to which the sin and rebellion of Ephraim and Judah have led them. So full is the cup of iniquity of God's people that the servant of God must reprove, rebuke, and exhort by varied means. God would win back His own by loving entreaty before the hour of doom. The passage now before us, as the previous chapters, runs the gamut of Israel's history from the then present hour when Hosea proclaimed to her the word of the Lord, until that day when, restored and obedient, she will in truth know the favor of God toward her.

With a threefold exhortation to hear, Hosea addresses himself to the priests, the people, and the royal court. The judgment of God is toward them all. The sin of idolatry like a venom had infected high and low alike. Those who were constituted the judges of God's people were now to be judged by Him for their unfaithfulness to His truth and will. Mizpah in the east of the land and Tabor in the west were made places of a snare and trap where the people were enticed to worship idols in the high places. In short, instead of protecting the people from delusions that would lead them from the worship of the Lord, the leaders were the very ones who went forth as hunters to ensnare them from following the Lord.

So wholly have they given themselves over to this revolting from the Lord, that they have gone to all excesses. And all this in spite of the repeated admonitions and rebukes of the Lord through His messenger. If Ephraim considers that the Lord does not see or is unmindful of his ways, He reminds him: "I know Ephraim!" All things are open and always clear to Him with whom we have to do. He may hope to hide his defilement from others or deceive himself concerning it, but the Lord reminds him that He knows the fact and extent of his pollution.

GOD WITHDRAWS HIMSELF

The evil power of the Israelites' ungodly habits is having its way, for their deeds will not permit them to turn to the Lord. They are held by them as in a vice. Like a spirit of drunkenness or the spirit of stupor so has the spirit of whoredom, of spiritual defection, settled upon the people. They have become spiritually darkened, therefore, and know not Jehovah.

Note the contrast between verse 3 and verse 4: God says He knows Ephraim, but Ephraim does not know Him. Instead of the warnings of God bringing about deep searchings of heart and turning back to the Lord, Israel has become unbearably proud. Pride is always out of place and is so often meant to conceal other errors. But the very arrogance of Israel, fed by the outward prosperity of the land, will testify against the people in the hour of national decline and ruin. Pride ever goes before a fall, so both Ephraim and Judah are headed for a fall.

Now, driven by slavish fear, they seek the Lord to sacrifice to Him of their flocks and herds. But He knows the true condition of their hearts, and will not be found of them. He has withdrawn Himself from them. Not finding the root of the matter in them, He will not be satisfied with outward acts and observances. He must have truth, sincerity, in the inward parts. They have not realized the enormity of their sin. They have dealt treacherously (the figure is one of the marriage bond between God and Israel) against the Lord, and the generation that they have reared knows not the Lord.

Thus, apostasy was perpetuating itself in their midst and the fear of the Lord in the highest sense was not known. In a short time they and their possessions will be overtaken by destruction and the scourge.

THE INVASION BY THE ENEMY

At long last the predicted judgment of God falls upon the people. The invasion of the land by the Assyrian hosts is portrayed before the very eyes of the people. The coming of the enemy's forces is announced in a call to defend the land by shouting and sending the alarm broadcast through the land.

The danger will threaten Benjamin also, a part of the Southern Kingdom which adjoined on the territory of the northern tribes, for Gibeah, Ramah, and Beth-aven are all cities of Benjamin. The old battlecry will be raised, "After thee, O Benjamin!" Evidently the enemy will make a clean sweep of the kingdom of Ephraim and endanger the southern tribes as well. This is "the day of rebuke" and chastisement concerning which they had been repeatedly warned.

It is not now a matter of a conditional threat which may be averted. No, God has made known that which shall surely be. There is no hope now for a stay of sentence, for the people are thoroughly impenitent. The princes of Judah, no better than their brothers of the Northern Kingdom, have placed themselves on the plane of the commonest thieves in the land—those that remove the landmark. The rights of others mean nothing to them. The outrage of Ahab against Naboth had been committed again and again since the first attempt had achieved its object. For this God's wrath will be poured out upon them as a flood. Ephraim and his ruling house will be oppressed and crushed by the judgment of God, because he obeyed the command of man, that command of Jeroboam who called upon Israel to worship the golden calves at Dan and Bethel.

In the hour of visitation God has become to Ephraim as a moth and to Judah as rottenness. Both kingdoms are falling to pieces and cannot maintain themselves any longer. In the hour of their stringency, instead of looking to God, both looked to man. Foolishly they turned to the king of Assyria who had no concern for their interests and was to be the final scourge in the hand of God to carry away Ephraim into captivity.

But Judah was not without fault, for she also sought after the help of the Assyrian power, who is here designated by a nickname, according to the opinion of some. (See Is 7:17-19.) Neither the arm of the Assyrian monarch nor any other human agency will avail to heal the wound of God's people, for He Himself will tear and rend them as an irresistible and rapacious lion. When He carries off the prey, none will be able to withstand Him or deliver from His hand. (Cp. Ps 50:22.)

RETURNING TO THE LORD

But is there no further word of comfort or bright hope for the future of the stricken people? Is it a wounding at the hand of the Lord without remedy? The Lord gives the blessed word of assurance. He foretells that He will go away until His people acknowledge their offence and seek Him with their whole heart. In the hour of their affliction they will seek God diligently.

What is the meaning of these words? They have been taken to mean that, following out the figure of the tearing lion, God will withdraw Himself and His favor, just as a lion goes off to his lair with the prey. If the prophecy means only this, then the latter part of verse 15 of chapter 5 has very little meaning, if any at all. The passage may be understood to refer to the withdrawal of God's protection and favor to His people in the time of the past captivities, and then the seeking of Him on the part of the godly (e.g., Daniel, Ezra, and Nehemiah) in the time of their affliction in exile.

But the prediction of Hosea is much more forceful if we understand the prophet to be looking, by the spirit of prophecy, into the far distant future for Israel. He sees beyond both the Assyrian captivity for Ephraim and the Babylonian captivity for Judah, as well as the final worldwide dispersion of the whole nation, to the time when the relationship between God and His people will be righted.

When in the fullness of time God sent forth His Son, He came unto His own and they who were His own received Him not. They would not have Him as King, but preferred Caesar. Therefore, He went and returned to His place. And what a place had been prepared for Him, at the right hand of the Father! (See Ps 110:1.) There the blessed Son of David and rightful King of Israel remains until Israel in penitence acknowledges the offence in rejecting Him and delivering Him to the Romans. In that hour she will seek His face, not the plans and panaceas of men. It will be an hour of affliction, the day and time of Jacob's trouble (Jer 30:1-7), when she will with all earnestness seek the Lord.

How true a picture does this short verse give of the events in Israel's history from the time of His first coming until the hour of His second coming, when she shall greet Him who comes in the name of the Lord. It is the same hour of which Zechariah speaks (12:10-14) when he prophesies that upon Israel will the spirit of grace and supplications be poured out, and they shall look upon Him whom they have pierced, with great smitings of heart and mourning for their national calamity and ingratitude to the Shepherd of Israel.

Not only is the fact of the Israelites' return stated, but the very words which they shall employ at that time are stated at the beginning of chapter 6. (The division of chapters is unfortunate, because 6:1 and 5:15 are inseparably linked together.) Now they recognize who it is that has wounded them so grievously and who it is that can heal them. The figure is carried over from the previous chapter where God is pictured as a lion in His fury against Israel. Man can wound and tear and smite, but he is powerless to bind up and heal. This the Lord alone can accomplish, and He will do it speedily, "on the third day." Then will the national pulse begin to beat again and they will live before Him.

The great prophecy of Ezekiel in chapter 37 is in point here. There Israel is pictured as dry bones in the midst of a valley. She is dead nationally and seemingly without any hope. But by the omnipotent word of God, bone joins bone, sinews appear upon the bones, skin covers bone and sinew, and breath is breathed into the bodies. The result is an exceedingly great army, a worldwide cemetery come alive! It will be life from the dead (Ro 11:15). And where life is there must be growth. This Israel will know also as, knowing the Lord, she shall go on to know Him more fully, after He has gone forth to her as the morning after the dark night of calamity and heartache. Then God will no longer be to her as a moth or as rottenness or as a lion, but as the fruitgiving rain in its appointed season, refreshing and blessing.

CONTINUED LOVING ENTREATY

But we have been looking at a picture of Israel's future blessedness and restoration; Hosea had need to turn to the crying spiritual need of his hour as well. God lovingly entreats and asks Ephraim and Judah what more He could do for them than He has done in blessing and warning, in order to turn their hearts to Him. If their hearts do incline them toward God, it is only for a passing moment and is gone as soon as the dew before the morning sun. Their desires to do good are shallow and cannot abide. For this reason God has had to send His messengers with harsh and stern warnings to hew them and slay them, so that when the judgment does fall, it will be clear who has sent it upon them.

Nor need they suppose that sacrifice and burnt offerings would suffice for their need. The natural man, when once he has been aroused to the sadness of his plight, seeks to remedy matters by recourse to outward forms and observances. He becomes more diligent in pursuing his self-conceived remedy. But the Lord, as Samuel made clear to Saul (1 Sa 15:22), has delight in heart piety and knowledge of Himself rather than in mere external forms.

Some men have inferred from such a passage as this, together with Isaiah 1:11-20; Micah 6:6-8; Jeremiah 7:21-26; and others, that God never desired the sacrificial system in Israel. This is surely a shortsighted view, for God Himself instituted the Levitical system in Israel, as is clear from the books of Moses. What God is requiring is something deeper than the mere routine of sacrifice-bringing and sacrifice-offering. It is easy to substitute the visible for the real. The Lord would have godliness first and foremost. Instead they have been found to be covenant-breakers, shedders of blood and workers of iniquity. Their priests have exceeded all bounds in banding themselves together into companies to murder men in the way, as do robbers. Nor is Judah guiltless in these matters; for her a harvest of punishment is ripening also.

WHAT SHALL I DO UNTO THEE?

God tenderly asked this of both Ephraim and Judah, but only after He had granted them token upon token of His blessing. It is not inappropriate to ask ourselves, as we think of Israel today, "What have I done for thee?" Will our hearts convict us of our neglect of their souls? True, Hosea pictured God as withdrawing Himself from them in that day for purposes of judgment, but in this day of grace He is nigh unto all that call upon

Him. The promise is still valid that whosoever does call upon Him shall be saved. This is the age of grace for the world and for Israel as well. May Israel hear the message of life in Christ through our prayers and our interest while it is yet called day!

DEPTHS OF SIN

In chapter 6 there is stated the desire of God to heal Israel of their spiritual ills, but in chapter 7 it is noted that when effort to do so is put into effect it is repeatedly frustrated by the sin of the people. Every repeated attempt to redeem Israel only disclosed more of her sinfulness. Search as He might, God could not discover repentance in His people. Their condemning sin was idolatry.

All Israel is at fault but the Northern Kingdom is especially pointed out in "Ephraim" and "Samaria." Infidelity and unfaithfulness toward God have resulted in violence and danger to man. The thief does his work within the home and a troop of robbers plunders without. The entire social fabric is insecure when men turn their backs upon God and rush headlong to their own destruction. Israel was beyond hope of human recovery.

Moreover, the tragedy of it all is this: she does not realize that God takes account of every deed. Her misdeeds have hedged her in. Every act of hers, regardless of what she thought, was patent and manifest to God. It has been well said that secret sin on earth is open scandal in heaven. Our secret sins are set in the light of His countenance. (See Ps 90:8.) Each stroke of the pen of the prophet paints the picture in more vivid and lurid colors. The rulers found real delight in the unrighteousness of the people. They encouraged each other in sin. Whatever was approved by those in power was the rule of life for the masses. Both king and princes misruled and lowered their high offices by finding pleasure in the ungodliness of the people. How could God's hand be stayed from judgment under such circumstances?

OUTBROKEN WICKEDNESS

But the end was not yet. The portrait which Hosea now paints of Israel sickens the heart as it reveals the extremes to which she went in her iniquities. The prophet with one fell swoop denounces all the people as adulterers. They were habitually such, as the Hebrew word shows.

The sin here is not of spiritual defection from the Lord but the sin of adultery in the moral realm, as the figure of the oven reveals. They were surfeited with forbidden desires and passions. They were like an oven which, though heated by the baker, has its flame kept down until the baker has completed his work of kneading and leavening the dough. Their evil lusts, already set on fire, although kept under the form of calm respectability, were merely awaiting the opportunity to break forth in the most hideous deeds of immorality. Even the day of the king, probably his birthday or the anniversary of his coronation, was the occasion for riot and excess. The princes made themselves sick with wine, and the king acted the part of a buffoon. All power of self-restraint and respectability was gone. Their heart, like a perennial source, was continually storing up sin. Note the threefold mention of an oven in verses 4, 6, and 7.

Sin rebounded upon those who first instigated it. The judges, that is, their kings, were devoured by the streams of influence for evil which they kept loose by their example and sponsorship. The prophet declares that all their kings had fallen. More specifically, he is speaking of the murders of Zachariah, Shallum, Menahem, Pekahiah, and Pekah. The kingdom of the north had not been set up in the will of God, and remained unstable and without fixedness throughout its history. Read the record and note how many kings were murdered. By the time of the Assyrian captivity, the Northern Kingdom had undergone nine changes since the disruption of the Solomonic kingdom. There was none among them that called upon God. There was not one godly king who ruled in Ephraim. What an indictment!

"A CAKE NOT TURNED"

The characterizations with which Hosea designates Ephraim now are famous, but not in the least complimentary to them. First of all, Ephraim forgot the great principle of separation which God repeatedly sought to inculcate in the hearts of the people of Israel. (See Ex 34:12-16 especially.) They mixed themselves among the peoples, the heathen nations about them. God always denounces mixture. (Cp. Deu 22:10-11; the mixed multitude of Egypt in Ex 16 and Num 11; and 2 Co 6:17-18.)

Carrying out the figure of mixing, the prophet Hosea calls Ephraim a cake not turned. The cake referred to was a sort of pancake (circular). Among all classes in the East, especially where haste is a factor, a cake is used which is baked on hot stones. The matter of importance is to turn the cake at the right moment. If not, the cake is burned to a cinder on one side and raw and doughy on the other. In Israel the outward performance was done to a nicety, but the inward indifference to the things of God was rawness itself.

It is easy for us all to become like a cake unturned. We may have much of doctrine and little of deed, much of creed and little of conduct, much of belief and little of behavior, much of principle and little of practice, much of orthodoxy and little of orthopraxy. We may have much of Israel in every prophetic address or Bible conference, but nowhere in our hearts or our missionary endeavors and gifts. Do you not know that, though you support and sustain a hundred missionaries to the heathen Gentile nations of the world and yet have none to Israel, that your missionary program is a cake not turned? It must be to Jew and Gentile unless we care not that we are charged as an unturned soppy cake.

Poor Ephraim was in such a sad predicament and yet knew it not. Sin makes us senseless. Strangers were devouring the strength of the land, and yet Ephraim was unaware of it. As a matter of fact the kings of Syria and Assyria exacted tribute from the land. The signs of age and oncoming decline are there, but he does not realize how serious his condition really is. There are decline and decadence, but he does not appear to be aware of them. Ephraim reminds us of Samson who knew not that the Spirit had departed from him, insensible to his plight. And in the midst of it all, there was unbearable pride on the part of Ephraim. He was convicted by his pride, but it was difficult to make an impression upon his heart. Turning to the Lord in faith was farthest from his thoughts.

"A SILLY DOVE"

Hosea uses another illustration drawn from nature to characterize Ephraim in his sin. He is like a silly dove without understanding (lit., without a heart). An Eastern proverb says, "There is nothing more simple than a dove." A silly dove listens to every beck and call, uncertainly flying to and fro. Such a dove has no affection for its benefactor. Ephraim had been flitting back and forth between the two powerful nations of the day—Egypt and Assyria. The object was to play one off against the other in order to maintain that elusive state called "the balance of power." Neither one of them really had Ephraim's interests at heart, and in the final analysis neither one of them could help Israel. But God's people looked to every human agency, and ignored and disregarded God.

Nevertheless, the Lord has no intention of allowing Israel to go on about her silly way. He warns her that He will spread His net upon her and bring her down as the birds of the heavens.

How is this to be understood? Some take it that the Lord loves her too much to let her go, so He spreads His net upon her. That the Lord loves her is evident enough throughout this book of prophecy, as well as the entire Word of God, but God's love does not preclude His chastening of His own. Indeed, His own come in for repeated chastenings now (as they did then) to show His love and His desire for purer gold.

The remainder of verse 12 shows that the spreading of God's net over her is in chastisement. He will hem in her ways and hold her down. This is no new principle to the people of Israel, for they have heard it again and again. That punishment followed disobedience had been stated repeatedly by Moses, by the prophets, and by Hosea himself. Here we have the first woe of the prophecy (the only other one in Hosea being 9:12). Their wanderings from the Lord result in their destruction. When the Lord would redeem them, they spoke lies against Him, as if God could not or would not deliver them. How man repays God's efforts of love to redeem him!

"A DECEITFUL BOW"

In the midst of their terrifying chastisements the people do not pray unto the Lord as their only resort, but they howl upon their beds. Their howls did not bespeak their repentance and faith. They howled their misery because of the sting of God's chastisements and not because of grief over their evil ways. Their distresses occupied their minds and not the heinousness of their sins before God. Their gatherings together are not for the glory of God but that they might be profited in grain and new wine. They were bent on rebellion against the moral Governor of the universe. The strength given them of God they have treacherously used against Him. And it is not that they have not changed, but it was never for God. They were a deceitful bow; no matter how well aimed, they always went astray of the mark. They could never be depended upon to strike true to the aim. Since they would not return to God, they must yet experience greater chastisements from the hand of God. They shall be ridiculed by the very ones (Egypt) upon whom they depended for help. Since their tongues were employed unguardedly, the tongues of others, their enemies, would be used against them.

"O EPHRAIM!"

How revealing and cutting the designations are whereby God speaks of Ephraim: a cake not turned, a silly dove, and a deceitful bow! Has God cast off all care for His wayward people? Need there be any doubt in our minds on this score? Hear Hosea as he echoes the plaintive cry of God's broken heart: "How shall I give thee up, O Ephraim?" (11:8). God has not given them up and will not. He is even now sending messengers of love to them to win them to the Saviour, the Lord Jesus Christ, who died for them.

THE TERRIFYING ALARM

Throughout the prophecy of Hosea thus far he has repeatedly inveighed against the sin of Israel in every form. The eighth chapter is no exception to his purpose, that is, by every means of entreaty and fore-warning to draw her back from the awful pit of destruction toward which she is so precipitously rushing. The emphasis in this chapter is on the continued violation of the commands of God's Law. Such continuance in ill-doing can only issue in the devastating judgment of God.

Hosea begins with two short and pointed blasts as is clear from the abruptness of speech: "The trumpet to thy mouth!" "As an eagle against the house of Jehovah!" The watchman is to put the trumpet to his mouth to warn the people of the oncoming invasion. The blow will fall as swiftly and suddenly as the eagle in its flight. Its objective will be the house of Jehovah, the whole people of Israel. (Cp. 9:8-15 and Zec 9:8.)

The remainder of the chapter now outlines for us in specific charges the five causes for the coming judgment here predicted: (1) transgression of the covenant and trespass against God's Law, verse 1; (2) setting up kings and princes without God's direction, verse 4; (3) idolatry, verses 4, 5, and 6; (4) the sin of seeking help from Assyria, verse 9; and (5) idolatrous and sinful altars, verse 11. God's covenant and Law may be lightly regarded by man, but He regards every infraction of either with greatest displeasure. He is the covenant-keeping God and can require nothing less than com-plete obedience in His people. This they were loath to give Him, but He could not alter His righteous requirements.

In the midst of their distress they cry to God as One whom they know, but it is not in sincerity and truth. They plead their knowledge of God (how many in the Church today are doing the same and their declaration is taken at face value), but they do not know Him. (See Is 29:13 and Mt 7:21-22.) When will men realize that with God empty profession goes for naught? Though Israel cries in the hour of agony that she knows God, He says she has cast off that which is good and the enemy shall pursue her. In verse 2 we have Israel's pleading before God, but in verse 3 is to be found her true condition and the divine retribution for it.

THE BLASTING SIN

The root of the sin in the Northern Kingdom was the sin of setting up kings and princes without the authority of God; He did not approve, order, nor sanction it. True, the disruption of the Solomonic kingdom had been announced to Jeroboam the son of Nebat by God's prophet, Ahijah (1 Ki 11:30 and following verses), but this does not mean that God approved it. Cities make laws in view of traffic violations, but they do not approve such infractions. Then, too, there was the fact of the many dethronements and murders in the Israelite kingdom. (Cp. 7:7.) Surely this was not of God. Nor was their subsequent departure into idolatry pleasing to the Lord.

One sin led to another. Note how her departure from the Davidic dynasty is bound up with her departure into idolatry. God can no more forget His covenant with David to give him a perpetual dynasty than He can forget the Abrahamic covenant, for the two covenants are inseparably linked. God is aroused to wrath at the setting aside of either. Idolatry thus became the cause of her destruction. She had broken grievously the first commandment given upon Mt. Sinai and only the judgment of God remained now for her. She made images of silver and gold to her own cutting off. The most damning sin of all is idolatry. The last injunction of the apostle John in his first epistle is to the effect that the children of God are to heed well that they keep themselves from idolatry (1 Jn 5:21).

When we realize, too, that God regards covetousness as idolatry, we can see more clearly how real is the temptation against which the Word of God warns us. (See Col 3:5.)

Samaria is addressed for all Israel and is assured that God's anger is kindled against them for their idolatry, the calf of Samaria. Hosea asks them pointedly and fearlessly how long it will be until they attain to innocency, how long before they will be able to bear innocency; for they are incapable of a godly walk before the Lord untainted with the pollution of idol worship. The idol was but the work of a man and no God at all; the calf and its worship began with them and not with God.

How senseless idolatry is, Isaiah, a contemporary of the prophet Hosea, has shown with consummate skill and sarcasm in his prophecy (44:9-20). But such miserable substitutes for the true and living, loving, and righteous God must pass away, and the perpetrators of such grievous sin must be visited with the sore displeasure and stored-up wrath of God. Sowing the wind they reap the whirlwind. They cannot turn back the law of the harvest: if they sow they must reap. They cannot reverse the law of uniformity: if they sow the wind, senseless, heartless, vain, and empty worship, they must reap in kind. They cannot abrogate the law of multiplication: though they sow but the wind, it will bring forth the abundant harvest of the whirlwind which shall sweep them away with all their defiance of God and His Law (cp. 10:12). The result is they have no standing grain; all their hopes and prospects come to naught. There was no fruitage anywhere. But if there should be the semblance of fruitage, even that will be swept away by the invading army. The shadow of Assyria, the strangers of verse 7, is already falling across their path.

ISRAEL SWALLOWED UP

When God chose Israel to bring glory and praise to His name among the nations of the earth, He intended her to keep herself separate from the world. This design of God, Israel did not follow out, and by her mingling with the nations she became swallowed up. She lost her reason for existence; she became as a utensil for which no one had use. The disintegrating forces had so wrought and corrupted that even to the nations Israel was worthless, let alone a delight to the heart of God. Nothing so demoralizes us and renders us useless as continuance in opposition to the revealed will of God for us and our lives.

In the face of repeated warnings Israel, like a stubborn and obdurate mule, had gone to Assyria for help and alliances. This was the folly of Menahem when he went to Pul of Assyria to establish him on his throne. (See 5:13; 7:11; also 2 Ki 15:19.) For this disobedience Israel was placed under tribute to the Assyrian power.

What a sad picture is presented to us of Israel running to and fro, seeking aid from every quarter but from God, and all this "alone by himself." This has been true through the ages: Israel abides alone, despite the many protestations of loyalty on the part of its worldly friends. (Cp. Num 23:9).

Ephraim, like Gomer the daughter of Diblaim in the life of Hosea, had hired lovers. But though the lovers appear won over to the cause of Israel, God will gather them against Israel for judgment instead of a help to Israel as she had so desired. The end thereof for Israel will be a diminishing and a groaning under the heavy yoke and tribute of the Assyrian king, the king of those princes who were subservient to the Assyrian domination. On Assyrian inscriptions we find the boast of their kings that they were king of kings, as Nebuchadnezzar was designated by God in Daniel 2:37. Far worse, then, than the fact that the harvest of Israel shall be swallowed up is the threat and warning (which was fulfilled with sad literalism) that Israel herself would be swallowed up.

GOD FORGOTTEN

Because Ephraim, in direct contravention of God's explicit command (read carefully Deu 12:5, 6, 13, 14), multiplied altars throughout the land by which he sinned against God, those very altars were deceptive and seducing forces to draw him on into further and more aggravated sin. Sin often becomes its own punishment. (Cp. Is 1:31.)

And it was not as though there was neither law nor precept to guide him in such matters, for he had the multiplied statutes, ordinances, and judgments of the Lord by which he was to order his religious life. But these he counted as a strange thing, as though not at all applicable to him. Even when he does offer offerings to the Lord, he has in mind ultimately how much profit he may get from the eating of the flesh of the sacrifices. Like the sons of Eli the priest (1 Sa 2:12-17), he was only concerned for his own satisfaction. (See Zec 7:4-5.)

Hence, God could not accept these offerings with favor, and for the perversion of His appointed way of approach to Himself He must of necessity visit the people's sins upon them. The warning of the return to Egypt was more than a figure of speech, for Israelites fled there to escape from the Assyrians when they overthrew the Northern Kingdom about 722 BC. (For the same condition in Judah when they took with them the prophet Jeremiah, see Jer 42-44.)

Throughout our reading of this chapter and others in this prophecy we keep asking ourselves, "But why all this? Why? Why?" The answer is simply: Israel has forgotten her Maker! How could this be possible? She had followed her own way so long and had left God out of her reckoning so consistently that she had ultimately forgotten God, her Maker. It was as though He did not exist. He was not in all her thoughts. Is it possible? It is all too possible and fearfully actual. How unspeakably sad to build temples to idols and fortified cities for the dependence upon the flesh and neglect the only source of help and hope in God. In this both Israel and Judah were implicated. Fire upon their cities and palaces was fulfilled by Sennacherib invading the land; Jerusalem alone was exempt. (See 2 Ki 18:13 and following verses.)

"Rejoice Not, O Israel"

Chapter 9 of Hosea is full not only of the rebuke of the Lord against His sinning and wayward people, but also of the definite features of their coming catastrophic judgment. The elements of that judgment were (1) the death of joy, verses 1 and 2; (2) exile from their land, verses 3 to 6; (3) the loss of spiritual discernment, verses 7 to 9; (4) a declining birth rate, verses 10-16; and (5) casting out, verse 17.

Since joy is not the portion of the soul away from God, the prophet Hosea enjoins Israel not to rejoice unto exultation like other peoples. The rejoicing in view is evidently that over harvest as the rest of the verse clearly indicates. Israel at this time was enjoying a period of prosperity and luxury, rejoicing in the benefits God had given but unmindful of the Giver.

The hire spoken of here is that of a harlot, from paramour to mistress, here from the idol to its senseless worshiper.

The fruits given Israel were attributed to the idols and that with great abandon, on every threshing floor. Blessings abused are withdrawn by God. The earth, with its grain and product of the vine, will disappoint Israel in her expectations of increase. She will lose the harvest through captivity, for she shall not continue to dwell in Jehovah's land. (See Deu 30:17-18.) She will return to Egypt, because she resorted to her ancient enemy against the will of God. In exile and banishment, she will be sent back there against her own will.

Some students of this passage would take Egypt here as standing typically for Assyria who is throughout the prophecy the rod of God's wrath (5:13; 10:6, 14) and, in view of 11:5, that Israel will not return to Egypt, but have Assyria as king. But compare Deuteronomy 28:68 and Hosea 8:13. Moreover, she shall eat unclean food in Assyria. Contrast Daniel in Daniel 1:8. Israel has done this in her own land, contrary to God's will, by eating in the idol feasts. Now through necessity or compulsion she would have to eat such in a foreign land for her sustenance. That which she had done willingly and willfully in transgressing the Law of God, she would be compelled to do habitually in a manner which placed her on a plane with the heathen nations surrounding her.

The wine offerings would cease also. These were poured out in relation to the burnt offerings. (See Ex 29:38-41; Num 28:3-9.) This was both a daily and Sabbath practice. According to Numbers 15:8-10 they were connected with the peace offerings also. Hosea is foretelling that all their public sacrifices shall cease (3:4). And because the appointed means of approach to God will be lacking, the people themselves will not be pleasing to God.

This is the condition of Israel this hour—not pleasing to God, because the reconciliation brought about through Christ's sacrifice she has not yet received by faith. (See Ro 10:1-4.) Should she attempt sacrifice to God out of the land, it would not only be unacceptable to God, but a source of pollution and defilement, as the bread of mourners. All that was in the same tent or house with the dead was unclean for seven days (Num 19:14). She will use such sacrifices for her own appetite, but it will not be accepted by the Lord.

"WHAT WILL YE DO?"

When scattered among the nations and exiled from her beloved land, what will wandering Israel do in the day of solemn assembly and in the day of Jehovah's feast? These were times of festal joy which commemorated acts of God's goodness to Israel. When shut out from His service,

these times will be seasons of deeper gloom and sorrow because of God's
withdrawal of blessing (Cp. 2:11).

Fleeing from the destruction by Assyria, she had escaped to Egypt—a
surer source of destruction. Egypt would gather the people up for common and wholesale burial. None will escape. Memphis was at this time
the capital of Egypt and a favorite burial place of the Egyptians. The
mention of the nettles and thorns completes the picture of complete and
utter desolation. The false prophets had lyingly said that the days of
visitation and recompense would not come, but they have inevitably, in-
exorably, and irresistibly come. Israel now knows by experience what she
would not formerly receive by faith.

The men of unbelief had called the true prophet and servant of the
Lord a fool and the man of the spirit (that is, the one possessing the Holy
Spirit to prophesy) mad. It was so even with our Lord Jesus (Jn 10:20).
The root and cause of Israel's calamities was the abundance of her iniquity
and the greatness of her hatred of God. See John 15:25 for the baseless
hatred against Christ. First, the ungodly *disregard* God, then they *disobey*
God (when His will is made known to them), and finally they *despise*
God (when He chastens and judges them).

The eighth verse of our chapter is admittedly very difficult. The probable meaning is that Ephraim was a watchman with God, that is, the
whole nation as helped and sustained by God, in fellowship with Him
and in accord with His purposes. Thus God had made him to the other
nations, but by sin he had become a snare instead of a support.

The prophet pointed out here is specifically the false prophet who
seduced the people of God and was the very embodiment of hatred in
God's house. They have gone the full extent of corruption.

The reference to the days of Gibeah is another of the many references
to the past history of Israel which are brought forward to teach the people
the disastrous character of sin. Hosea is referring to the time when Benjamin (Judg 19 and following chapters) championed the outrage against
the concubine of the Levite—an incident that brings out glaringly a period
of spiritual decline in Israel second to none. All of Benjamin but 600
men perished at that time. Though bearing long with him, God will
finally visit Ephraim with the threatened judgment.

"LIKE GRAPES IN THE WILDERNESS"

In the midst of a scene of judgment and dire prophecies of woe, the
tender heart of God goes back to the days of Israel's earliest history, as it
did so often (see Jer 2:1-3). The Lord remembers how He first found
Israel like grapes in the wilderness. The thought is that she was pleasant

to Him, such as grapes would be to one finding them in the wilderness. She was also like the first-ripe figs, the sweetness of which was proverbial, because of their freshness and because of the long abstinence from them during the nonproductive season. (Note Is 28:4.)

God speaks of Israel as being both pleasant and rich in His eyes, but soon she corrupted herself and the gifts of God. For His care over her at that time, see Deuteronomy 32:10. How did she corrupt herself? She committed the abominations of Baal-peor. This was the stumbling block advised by Balaam to Balak; when the prophet could not curse Israel, he gave counsel how to corrupt her. (Cp. Num 25:1-5.) The people separated themselves, became Nazirites, not to God, but to the shame of Baal-peor with its vile and sensuous practices connected with its idolatry. The result was that they became abominable like their loves. (See Ps 115:8.) It has been well said that man "makes his god in his own image and likeness, the essence and concentration of his own bad passions, and then conforms himself to the likeness, not of God, but of what was most evil in himself." Therefore, the glory of Ephraim was to depart as a bird.

Hosea, as no other writer of ancient times, traces the results of national immorality and sin in a declining population. Their honor, their glory, their position of privilege will be taken from them by God. The name Ephraim which means fruitfulness (Gen 41:52; 48:19) would no longer be their glory for God would take away conception, birth, and child.

Absolute cutting off of all offspring is not meant, as is clear from verse 12, where we see that they do bring up some children, but the number of children shall be greatly reduced. (Cp. Deu 28:58-62.) The climax of all their woes and calamities is that God will depart from them. Ephraim's location was beautiful (see Is 28:1) : God would make him glorious as Tyre. But though he be rich and his situation enviable, childlessness awaited them all.

"WHAT WILT THOU GIVE?"

Since so much misery awaits the Israelites' children, the prophet is constrained to pray that they may have no children—a mercy which would spare them greater grief.

Gilgal was the center where their wickedness was manifest. The place of so many of God's blessings had been turned into the scene of idol worship. When God says He hated them, the expression manifests the height of His displeasure. In driving them out of His house, He expels them from the land altogether. (Cp. 8:1 for the same use of "house.")

"I will love them no more" is a national judgment which did not preclude mercy to individuals and has a definite time element in mind. After their chastisement, God will take them back into fullest fellowship. In this same prophecy (14:4) Hosea predicts: "I will love them freely." But since for the time all their princes, their rulers, had followed in the way of Jeroboam the son of Nebat, they had opened the floodgates of God's wrath against them. Ephraim was to be smitten like a tree (v. 13). The withering of the root meant no hope for future fruitfulness. Not only would their offspring be cut off, but they themselves were appointed to be wanderers among the nations, because they would not hearken to the Lord.

IS IT NOTHING TO YOU?

When we realize that Israel's songs and hymns are in the minor key, we understand how fully has entered into the nation's experience the force of the injunction not to rejoice. How can they rejoice when they are not pleasing Him? When they have no appointed way of approach? When so many have not heard of the all-sufficient and all-fulfilling sacrifice of the Messiah of Israel? Is it nothing to us that such is the plight of God's people Israel?

4

MULTIPLIED ALTARS

LIKE A SKILLFUL and experienced physician, the prophet Hosea keeps probing at the core of Israel's sin, namely, her idolatry. The prophet again uses a figure drawn from nature to describe the people of God. Israel is a luxuriant vine. The King James Version reads "empty vine," but both usage as well as the remainder of the first verse decide in favor of the rendering "luxuriant vine." The thought is that the vine empties out, pours out itself in fruit, is widespread.

To the superficial observer, the people were rich and prosperous under Jehoash and Jeroboam II and lacked for nothing. (For the metaphor of the vine, see Ps 80:8 and following verses; Is 5:1-7, especially v. 7 where the explanation is given of the figure employed; Jer 2:21; and Eze 17:6.) However, the more God prospered them, the more they misused His bounties, praising the idols with sacrifices on idolatrous altars. (See 8:11 of our prophecy.) For every blessing from God the people gave glory and worship to the idols. The root of all their failure and sin was that their heart was divided.

The divided heart and the halting between two opinions characterized Israel in Elijah's day (1 Ki 18:21) and made him cry out for wholeheartedness and whole-souledness for God. How great is the need for this exhortation in our own day among the Church of our Lord, is only too well known. We have need to pray with the psalmist: "Unite my heart to fear thy name" (Ps 86:11).

As a result of her spiritual defection from the Lord, Israel is found guilty; and her altars and pillars will be swept away by the judgment of God's hand. The threat is vivid, for the word translated "smite" actually means "break the neck." In the midst of their chastisements, the sad people will utter their words of discouragement and despair, lamenting the loss of their king. They will be deprived of their king, for he will be cut off. (Note vv. 7 and 15 of this chapter.) And it will not be as though they were ignorant of the cause of their calamity; they themselves will admit

49

it has come upon them because they have not feared and obeyed the Lord.
They had cast off their heavenly King, so they were shorn of their earthly
king. But on further and deeper reflection they conclude with the question, "What can the king do for us, since God is against us?" They realize
now that against the omnipotent and sovereign God no human devices or
personalities can avail.

DEPARTED GLORY

Among their failings was the fault of speaking words, mere words, just
so much talking. In just such a day do we live with our innumerable
books, magazines, forums, and radio and television broadcasts with their
news, views, and blues. Talk, talk, talk, words no end. And when this is
committed in the realm of the spiritual and as between nations it has
disastrous effects.

Israel swore falsely in making covenants. It has been suggested that
reference is made to her breaking faith with Shalmaneser (2 Ki 17:4) to
make an agreement with So of Egypt. In all her dealings she perpetrated
injustices and inequities, so that justice and judgment went forth perverted. (For the same truth see Amos 5:7 and 6:12.) The issue was like a
deadly poison, hemlock, in the furrows of the field.

Once more the prophet turns to the blighting and all-destroying sin of
idolatry. Samaria's inhabitants, instead of resting securely in their dependence upon their images, will be in terror because of what they see transpiring to their godlings. The calves are connected with Beth-aven, a name
substituted for Bethel in derision (see 4:15, where the house of God has
been changed to the house of vanity and sin). Far from their idols helping
them, they will be concerned and afraid for their idols. Hosea calls them
the people of the calf and not the people of God, and their priests are the
priests of the calf and not priests of the Most High God.

The priests will feel the loss of the idols most when they are taken into
captivity, because they had previously rejoiced over the gain derived from
them. The glory of the idols spoken of here is evidently the worship accorded the idols. The glory will truly have departed from Ephraim, and
"Ichabod" will be written large over the Northern Kingdom.

It is clear that the idols will not escape the scourge which shall befall
the ten tribes, for they will be carried into captivity to Assyria, a manifest
proof of their helplessness and worthlessness. (Cp. Is 46:1-2, for the same
picture of the utter uselessness and burdensomeness of idols in time of
trial and captivity.)

When the full weight of God's visitation is upon Israel, she will be
ashamed of that counsel which Jeroboam the son of Nebat took in estab-

lishing a separate kingdom from Judah and especially in introducing the calf worship.

The idols are helpless, the people and priests are also, but what of the king, that mighty arm of defence of the people? The king of Samaria will be cut off as foam, or better, as the twigs or straw, upon the water. He will be as a light, empty, and worthless thing. Such was Hoshea who was swept away to Assyria. The shrines of the idols—the high places which are designated as the sin of Israel—will be demolished.

The mention of the thorn and thistle completes the picture of the desolation of the land and the cessation of the sin of idolatry. With their national life destroyed, object of their trust (the idols) carried away, their political structure in ruins with the cutting off of the king, the people find themselves in the very depths of despair. They seek to escape that which to them is worse than death. They cry to the mountains to cover them and to the hills to fall on them. What tragic end to godless lives! It is the keynote for the future despair that will grip men's hearts in the hour of great tribulation and anguish. (See Lk 23:30 and Rev 6:16.)

Idolatry, as all sin, carried within it the seeds of Israel's undoing. To depart from the living God into senseless idol worship is to court certain and fearful catastrophe. It is always a fearful thing to fall into the hands of the living God, for our God is a consuming fire in His vindication of His holiness and righteousness.

GIBEAH REMEMBERED AGAIN

In verse 9 we have brought before us again the sinful days of Gibeah. (See 5:8 and 9:9.) The account in the book of Judges reveals that Benjamin was the chief perpetrator of the offence there recorded, but all Israel was in sin, not only Benjamin, because at first all the tribes were smitten in battle before Benjamin. In any event what was true of Benjamin was typical of the whole nation, and thus Hosea pronounces upon it. But though smitten twice, the people were avenging God's righteous Law, so they stood against Benjamin.

It is not that they stood persisting in their sin, as some would interpret it, but rather the remaining tribes stood their ground and did not perish then. The battle against the children of iniquity did not overtake them then, but it will now. Though God spared them then, He will not do so now. The battle in Gibeah where God judged the Gibeonite children of iniquity will be a token of the more grievous visitation upon the entire Northern Kingdom for their continued sin.

When God desires to vindicate His righteousness, in that hour His chastisement will fall upon the ungodly ones. Just as all the tribes were gathered together against Benjamin, so all peoples, the foreign invaders, will be assembled against the ten tribes.

And the cause is that they have been bound to their two transgressions. Some suggest that the two transgressions are those of Jeremiah 2:13 where Israel has forsaken the Lord, the fountain of living waters, and hewed out cisterns, broken cisterns, which can hold no water. But in keeping with the context, which keeps reiterating the heinous sin of idolatry, we would rather understand it as the two calves of Bethel and Dan.

In the past, Israel as a trained heifer had accustomed herself to pleasant and profitable labor. Treading out the grain was easier than plowing or harrowing. In threshing, the beast was allowed to eat at will (Deu 25:4) and thus Israel waxed fat and kicked. (Cp. Deu 32:15.) We have thus a picture of Israel's prosperity and self-indulgence heretofore. Treading out the grain is more enjoyable from every standpoint, but the harder tasks of plowing and harrowing will be Ephraim's, because now the yoke will be put upon him. Not only will there be a yoke upon the neck, but a rider on the back as well, namely, the Assyrian invader.

Hosea had warned them before that God would hedge up Israel's way and hem them in; this is another confirmation of the same intention. But the Northern Kingdom will not be alone in this; judgment will extend to Judah also for he is not faultless. Both will share the judgment of God, given here under the figure of plowing and breaking the clods. How clearly the prophet sets before them and us the discerning truth that sin does not liberate but rather confines and restricts and ultimately robs one of freedom.

WHAT KIND OF SOWING?

Now the word from God for the only time in this chapter pleads with Israel to turn from her evil ways. She is exhorted to return and escape judgment. In three pointed entreaties she is besought to sow to herself for righteousness, as the objective, to reap according to kindness, after the measure of the grace of God, and to break up the fallow ground, in removing her idols and sinful practices.

She had been sowing contrary to the will of God and reaping a harvest of God's displeasure, rebuke, and judgment; now let her sow to the glory of God and remove the spiritual obstacles, so that she might reap a bountiful harvest of God's blessing, prospering, and joy. For her, the time has long arrived when she should be seeking the Lord and not idols, in order that He might come and teach her righteousness.

Both the King James Version (KJV) and the American Standard Version (ASV) translate the latter part of verse 12 poorly. It is not that He will come "and rain righteousness upon you," although this does fit into the picture of yoking the heifer, plowing, sowing, harrowing, and reaping. But the Hebrew word is rarely translated "rain"; the idiom of "teach" is frequent. Besides, the remainder of the construction does not lend itself properly to the translation of the English versions. The coming of the Lord is surely the promise of the coming of the Messiah in blessedness to instruct His people in the way of God and to obtain for them salvation, both temporal and spiritual.

The injunction to sow after God's pattern is all the more necessary in view of the fact that the people had been plowing wickedness and reaping iniquity. In plowing wickedness they were at pains to cultivate sin. When they reaped iniquity they were proving again the truth of the law of the harvest: as a man soweth, so shall he also reap. Indeed, they were eating the fruit of lies: instead of promoting the welfare and prosperity of the kingdom of Israel by their deeds as they had hoped, they were succeeding only in bringing about its downfall and utter ruin. The fruit of their false worship they would find to be bitterness itself. For their trust was in their way, not God's. God's curse is pronounced upon the man that trusts in man and makes flesh his arm (Jer 17:5).

How easily the hearts of men rest upon carnal reliances instead of upon the mighty arm of the omnipotent God. But Ephraim's mighty men will not help him when the tumult of war arises among them. There was no unity to mold them together, so they are called by the prophet "peoples," rather than "people." Their every fortification will be brought low, as Shalman destroyed Beth-arbel in battle.

Undoubtedly, Shalman stands here as a contraction for the familiar Shalmaneser. (See 2 Ki 17:3.) Shalmaneser is a compound Assyrian name, and the part in common with other Assyrian names, such as Tiglath-pileser and Shar-ezer, is omitted. History has not yet given us information concerning a devastation of Beth-arbel by Shalmaneser, but the statement of Hosea is none the less true.

The Beth-arbel under discussion is a city in Galilee which the Greeks called Arbela. Here we have a fulfillment of Hosea's own prophecy (1:5). As an example of the extreme cruelty and barbarity of that destruction by Shalmaneser, a similar fate now awaiting Israel, the prophet states that in that battle the mother was dashed in pieces with her children. This practice was widespread and was followed by the Syrians (2 Ki 8:12); Assyrians (here and 13:16); Medes (Is 13:16); and the Babylonians (Ps 137:8-9).

The calf at Bethel will be the cause of a similar visitation from God upon Ephraim, because of the wickedness of his wickedness, as the original reads. Early, quickly, and irrevocably the king of Israel would be utterly cut off, and the kingdom of Israel with him. After Hoshea, the Northern Kingdom would never know another king apart from the Davidic line; the royal office was completely abolished in the ten tribes with the Assyrian captivity. The throne of the Northern Kingdom has never been restored to this day and never will be. And all this calamity they had brought upon themselves. Ultimately it would not be God nor the Assyrian who would bring this catastrophe upon Israel, but Bethel with its sins.

I LOVED ISRAEL

In the first ten chapters of the prophecy of Hosea, the emphasis has been on the disobedience of God's people and the inevitable judgment as a consequence, although passages are not lacking that speak with detail of the blessings and glories that await a repentant and believing remnant in Israel in the days to come. The dominant note and chord in the last four chapters of the book is the love of God.

It is held by some that in the alternating speeches of these chapters, it is the Lord whose speeches are burdened and freighted with love, while the messages of the prophet reveal a sense of the sin and unworthiness of God's people. Such a position cannot ultimately be valid, because the Lord speaks throughout whether in the first person or in the third person.

When God would speak of His infinite love for the nation Israel, He shows that it had its beginning when they were being formed into a nation through the fiery crucible of Egyptian bondage. From her earliest history God loved Israel; He says so. And nowhere in the Bible do we read that God has to explain this love or defend it, as though to apologize for it. He loves sovereignly with boundless love, and loves because He loves.

This love motivated God to liberate His people from Egyptian slavery. They are called not only "child," but "my son" as well. (See Ex 4:22.) This bespeaks a covenant relationship, which can never be dissolved. They are to this hour beloved of God for the Father's sake (Ro 11:28).

If we turn to the New Testament we find this passage is quoted in Matthew 2:15 of our Lord Jesus Christ. Who was wrong? Hosea or Matthew? Neither, for both were moved by the same Spirit to give us an inerrant record. Hosea calls Israel "my son" and Matthew calls the Lord Jesus "my son." The answer is to be found in the wonderful way in which Christ identifies Himself with His people, so that His position is theirs and His relationship is theirs.

More than once Israel and the Messiah are viewed together, as though to form a composite picture. Read Isaiah 49:3 for an example. In that passage Isaiah is giving us the second of the Servant Songs leading up to the climax in Isaiah 53. He has been speaking clearly of the Messiah and then calls Him "Israel." We do well to remember that the Messiah and Israel are inseparably and eternally bound together in the bundle of life in the Lord our God.

Because of this relationship into which God has brought Israel with Himself, it might be supposed that she would be all the more devoted and obedient to Him. Sad to say, the very opposite was the case. The more the prophets and emissaries from the Lord called the people of God to paths of righteousness and blessing, the more they departed from the truth of God. Sad commentary is this on the manner in which man ever repays the gracious outpourings of God's heart to him. The departure of Israel from the pleadings of the prophets was not to something or someone better but to the senseless Baalim and the graven images. But God's love, never founded upon nor grounded in man's merit or goodness, persisted in following His disobedient people. After all, no earthly parent gives up his child because of disobedience, nor will God, though the sin of idolatry is more grievous than the human mind can ever comprehend.

Never was a human parent so sinned against as was God, yet He taught Ephraim to take his first steps. Just as a father teaches a child to walk and bears with it in all its stumbling, awkward ways, God tenderly and solicitously taught Israel how to walk. When the child becomes weary of its first strenuous attempts, the father is quick to note and take the child in his arms again. Such is the picture of the exceedingly loving treatment that Israel has been accorded of the Lord. But all the while she knew not that the Lord had healed her. How hard is it when love is unrecognized and unrequited.

Recently during a period of ministry in San Antonio, Texas, after one of the services a young mother came struggling with her large child on a pillow to the front of the church. The child was now four and absolutely helpless, even to feed herself. She could scarcely swallow. Each day the mother was required to feed the child for six hours. I need not tell you how broken-hearted was this mother over the plight of her child who could not respond to her love, though in true Christian submission she thanked God for this burden that drew her closer to God for fuller support.

What pathos in the word, "But they knew not that I healed them." During their wilderness journeys and murmurings the people did not realize that their Father was their Physician as well, the great Jehovah Rapha. (See Ex 15:26.) Such treatment as God bestowed upon them (Deu 1:31) was more than even Moses, with his great love for his people, was able to manifest. (Note Num 11:12.)

One of the most beautiful expressions in the Bible of God's love is found in Hosea 11:4. He drew (not dragged, drove, or pulled) them with cords of a man. Such bands as those by which men lead children, not such as oxen are led by, did God employ in attracting His people to Him. Though they struggled against God and were refractory, He did not drive them as beasts, but with bands of love He drew them. God knows there is more power in love than in force, so He delights to use the best way.

We are told that Napoleon the Great on the Island of St. Helena said to General Bertrand, "I tell you, Bertrand, I know men; and I tell you that Jesus Christ is not a man . . . Everything about him amazes me. His spirit overawes me, and his will confounds me. There is no possible comparison between him and any other being in the world. He is truly a being by himself . . . His birth, and the history of his life, the profoundness of his doctrine . . . his gospel . . . his empire, his march across the ages—all this is to me a wonder, an insoluble mystery . . . Though I come near and examine closely, all is above me, great with a greatness that overwhelms me . . . Alexander, Caesar, Charlemagne, and myself founded empires. But on what did the creations of our genius rest? On force. Jesus Christ alone founded his empire on love; and at this hour millions would die for him."

The power of love, the love of God, is incalculable. As a husband woos his bride, so with the bands of love God repeatedly drew Israel to His heart. Moreover, He was the lightener of her burdens and the source of her nourishment. The lifting of the yoke is a figure of the herdsman caring for his cattle. The cattle come home in the evening after the labor of the day, and he lifts the yoke, freeing their jaws, to feed them. All this is a fit picture of God's dealings with Israel in freeing her from Egyptian bondage and feeding her in the wilderness. He did it though they questioned faithlessly, "Can God prepare a table in the wilderness?"

THE ASSYRIAN SCOURGE

God's love may be and is limitless, but it can never overlook sin or dismiss it lightly. Sin is ever dire and serious business with God. He never palliates it nor compromises with it. His purpose is ever to exterminate it root and branch. Therefore, Israel is to be visited with the Assyrian invader.

The statement that the nation would not return to Egypt seems to contradict passages like 8:13 and 9:3 in this book. Egypt in those cases, however, stands typically for a land of bondage, that is, Egypt-like bondage. Whenever they returned to Egypt it was to get help against Assyria (7:11) as they had done (2 Ki 17:4) in pleading to King So, after rebelling

against Assyria, to whom they paid tribute since Menahem (2 Ki 15:19).
They will be unable to go to Egypt, because they will be captive in Assyria.
The prophet Hosea tells them plainly that they will not return to Egypt
to which they looked and upon which they were depending, but would
rather have an Assyrian king over them whom they would not desire.
Since they did not want God as their king, they would have the Assyrian
as king. Because of their refusal to turn unto the Lord, the sword will rage
against their cities, consuming and destroying on every hand.

And to such a pass had their own counsels brought them. Instead of
delivering them, their counsels, ill-founded and ill-advised, were the cause
of their destruction. Nor is the spiritual condition of the people a temporary or accidental phenomenon: they were bent on backsliding from the
Lord, literally, they "are hung to it." So engrossed were they with their
backsliding ways, that no matter how the servants of God called them back
to Him that is on high (7:16), they were not of a mind to exalt Him.

"HOW SHALL I GIVE THEE UP?"

Again, such conduct against the living God must be visited with His
righteous wrath and condemnation. But God never delights in judgment,
which is His strange work, but takes pleasure in mercy and favor. True,
Israel is worthy of punishment but God's love must be reckoned with as
well. Therefore, He cries out from the innermost recesses of His blessed
being, "How shall I give thee up, Ephraim? how shall I cast thee off,
Israel?"

This verse has been said to be the greatest passage in the book. It may
well vie for that honor. If God says He loved them from the very beginning, from a child, how much greater must be His love for them after so
many centuries of gracious dealings with them? He finds it impossible to
give them up, though they have revolted against Him. His love is now in
the form of compassion, because in their unworthiness they need His love
all the more. How our children as they grow older entwine themselves
about our hearts! So did Ephraim about the heart of God. He could not
bring Himself to the place where He would cast him off wholly, as He did
with Admah and Zeboim (Deu 29:23), the wicked cities of the plain
which were completely overthrown with Sodom and Gomorrah.

Actually, God is saying they are as wicked and guilty as these cities, de-
serving of the severest punishment, but His love is kindled for them. Let
us not forget that God did chasten them for their waywardness, although
He could not give them up altogether.

Samuel Rutherford's grand hymn is right: "O Christ, He is the Fountain, The deep, sweet well of love." His love and His compassions are

kindled when He thinks of Israel. He is determined that He will not execute the fierceness of His anger; mercy rejoices over judgment. Ephraim will not suffer the same irrevocable fate of the cities of the plain. For the Lord is God and not man, who executes his unappeased wrath under great provocation. God will not enter the city as a foe as in the days of Sodom.

The reason God's mercy triumphs so signally is the remnant among God's people. They will seek and walk after the Lord (see 3:4-5). Apostasy in Israel, even in the darkest days of her history, is never complete and universal; there is always a remnant among the people. To these godly ones God roars like a lion, His summons to gather His dispersed ones from their dispersion. It will be a voice of majesty and awe that will call the wandering ones back. They, on their part, will come trembling in eagerness and glad anticipation. The place of their origin will be specifically the west, as well as from Egypt and Assyria.

This was not true in the Assyrian or Babylonian exiles, but has been true ever since the dispersion by the Romans. What is meant, then, is a regathering from all the world as the prophet Isaiah also confirms (Is 11:11). From all these places they will come flying in haste as a dove (no longer the silly dove of 7:11), to be resettled in their own land by the Lord, never to be uprooted again.

EPHRAIM FALSE AND JUDAH FAITHFUL

In the Hebrew, verse 12 of chapter 11 is verse 1 of the next chapter. Perhaps it is better placed at the end of our present chapter. The prophet would show that Ephraim now is not in the condition just described. In fact, he is heaping up falsehood, principally that of idolatry, on every hand. Instead of compassing the Lord with his love and faithfulness, he was intent on surrounding Him, as it were, with lying.

Such was the condition of Ephraim, but with Judah it was otherwise. Decline with her was slower than with Israel. She was at least outwardly faithful, adhering to God's appointed king of the Davidic line and maintaining the Aaronic priesthood with its sacrifice. The word *yet* implies that Judah would yet turn from God also, but for the present, she formed a contrast to the condition of Ephraim, sunk in deep apostasy.

FEEDING ON WIND

At the end of the eleventh chapter, Hosea charged Ephraim with compassing the Lord about with falsehood and deceit. Now the prophet would show that Israel has been as faithless and covenant-breaking with men. It has ever been thus in the history of man: the attitude taken toward God determines the attitude toward man.

Ephraim has been feeding on wind—scant nourishment to say the least—
and following after the east wind. Feeding on wind is a vivid description
for pursuit of empty and vain things which are without profit. The east
wind is the sirocco which comes from the desert east of Palestine, a dry,
scorching, devastating wind. The northern tribes were continually resorting to lies, which would ultimately issue in their desolation, in their
dealings with both Assyria and Egypt. They were ever playing off one
power against the other, the old and yet ever new game of power politics.
In order to maintain that illusive state, called "the balance of power" in
our day, they made a covenant with Assyria (5:13; 7:11) and then sought
after the help of Egypt as well. (See 2 Ki 17:4; Is 30:6; 57:9.) Palestine
was famed for its oil (Deu 8:8; Eze 27:17) which it exported to Tyre;
now it is sent to Egypt for whatever aid they could render the decaying
and declining Israelite kingdom.

But Judah is not without fault in the matter. The Lord has somewhat
against her also. (Cp. 4:1 and Mic 6:2.) Judah has gone into idolatry
under the reign of Ahaz, as is clear from 2 Kings 16:3, 10-16. Therefore,
the judgment of God must fall upon the whole nation called here by the
name of Jacob.

JACOB THE PRINCE WITH GOD

Those who have interpreted the account of the life of Jacob in the book
of Genesis in such a manner that no good thing could be said of him, will
find it difficult to understand the words of Hosea concerning the illustrious
patriarch, with whose name God links His own—"the God of Jacob." It is
easily discernible in the life of Jacob that he ever sought spiritual blessings
throughout his life. He may have sought them before the appointed time
or in the energy of the flesh, but he did long for the things of the Spirit
of God and the spiritual life. This is undeniable.

The nation is now reminded of the experiences of Jacob. There is all
contrast here. Jacob ever sought the favor of the Lord even in weakness
and falteringly; but they have no desire for the paths of the Lord. Even
in his mother's womb Jacob sought after the blessing of the firstborn
(Gen 25:22-26), and in his manhood he was willing to wrestle all night
with the Angel of Jehovah for it. There he obtained it (Gen 32:24-32).
His strength lay in his conscious weakness: that of his thigh being out
of joint (2 Co 12:9-10). When Jacob could no longer wrestle, he resorted
to weeping and supplication, thus prevailing with God and receiving the
exalted honor of being named "Israel," prince with God. The weeping is
not mentioned in Genesis, but the supplication is. Thus, Hosea would

show that Jacob, having striven after the blessing of God from his mother's womb, was granted it by God in his manhood.

How unlike him were his descendants in the days of the prophet. Whereas Jacob prevailed with God, they were mastered by idols. God found Jacob at Bethel (first, when on the journey to Aram, Gen 28:11-19, and second, on his return, Gen 35:1), but that was the very place which they had turned into a place of idol worship. At Bethel Jacob sought to purge his household of all idolatry (see Gen 35); at the same sanctuary they had set up defiling worship and practices.

God extended His grace to the patriarch in that day and would extend it to his progeny in Hosea's day by virtue of His character revealed in His unchangeable, faith-keeping name, I AM. This is God's memorial name, that which distinguishes Him from all worthless gods. (See Ps 135:13 and Is 42:8). Therefore, in view of God's dealings with their great ancestor and the grace extended to him, they are exhorted to turn to the Lord—to keep kindness and justice, including duties to man; and wait for their God, comprising duties to God. The order is the same as that in Micah 6:8.

EPHRAIM THE CANAANITE

With a sudden blast, as it were, the prophet nicknames his mercenary contemporaries "Canaan." The word translated "merchant" in the KJV and rendered "trafficker" in the ASV is the Hebrew word "Canaan."

The Canaanites or Phoenicians were the great merchants of the time (Is 23:11 and Eze 17:4). They were known for their grasping, cheating ways. Even Homer, the great Greek poet, designated the Phoenicians as "money-lovers." Ephraim is now likened to them. He uses the balances of deceit (secret fraud) and loves to oppress (outbroken violence). Thus they were continually in violation of the clear commandments of the Law of God through Moses. (Cp. Lev 19:36; Deu 25:13-16.)

Did Ephraim sense his wrong? Did he make amends therefor? On the contrary, the more he prospered in his godless ways, the more he assumed that all was well between God and him. Ephraim reasoned that his very success was proof that nothing was amiss and that the prophets were in error who denounced his sin. The Preacher spoke truthfully when he said, "Because sentence against an evil work is not executed speedily, therefore the heart of the sons of men is fully set in them to do evil" (Ec 8:11). Ephraim was confident of his integrity; he boasted that no one could find iniquity in him to be labelled sin.

How easy it is to feel that God is surely pleased with us, merely because we are outwardly prospered of the Lord. Prosperity is not enough, for is it not the goodness of God that leads us to repentance, to reconsider our ways before Him? Ephraim felt certain that no one could find iniquity in him, but to God all was open and naked.

MULTIPLIED MERCIES

Nor was God now dealing with a people with whom He had no dealings heretofore. These are the very people whom He led forth from the land of Egypt with great and trying judgments upon Egypt and their gods, with the drying up of the Red Sea, with the pillar of cloud by day and the pillar of fire by night, with manna from heaven for the wilderness trek, and with water brought forth from the rock. Mercy upon mercy and grace upon grace had been showered upon them. How could they deal so with their gracious God? And yet, as though to reveal to them the unchanging character of their God, He predicts that He will yet make them to dwell in tents as in the days of the solemn feast.

This word has been differently understood by interpreters of the Scripture. There are those who understand the prophet to be foretelling that God will again make Ephraim a people without commercial prosperity, returned to the plane of nomadic life, or that God will so judge them that they will lose their homes. Others hold that the dwelling in tents is not a threat but another manifestation of that mercy which brought Israel out of the land of Egypt. Instead of casting them off, God will extend them further grace.

Surely the latter view is the correct one. We must remember that the days of the solemn feast, the Feast of Passover, the Feast of Weeks, and the Feast of Tabernacles, were all times of rejoicing. (Note Deu 16:13-17.) The season of dwelling in tents was particularly a joyful one, because the harvest had been gathered and God's care was so manifest to all. This prophecy was actually fulfilled on the return from Babylon (Neh 8:17; notice there the word about gladness) but only in a measure.

There is a time yet future when Israel will truly and fully enter into the joys of the Feast of Tabernacles, namely, in the millennial age. (See Zec 14:16-19, also Rev 7:15-17; mark here also how the emphasis on joy predominates, for every tear is wiped away.) How the grace of God shines out in all its undimmed luster when we can read promises like these immediately after words of arrogant sinfulness on the part of sinning Ephraim.

Moreover, God had shown in times past other tokens of His favor. He had given His message to prophets for the calling of His people. These should have brought them back to the Lord from whom they had wandered. And not only so, but the Lord had employed through His servants visions and similitudes, couching His message in terms that would be readily grasped and obeyed. God tried every means to reach their heart. By various methods God sought to win back His people, just as through Hosea God begins with the analogy in the life of Hosea himself, then by rebuke, then by prediction of coming judgment, and by promises of blessing and joy for the godly among them. Through any one of these various methods they could well have discerned the will of God for them. But their hearts were bent on following their own ways.

BLOODGUILTINESS OF EPHRAIM

The prophet comes to the core of the matter with a direct question: "Is Gilead iniquity?" To ask the question is to answer it. Gilead is altogether false, because it was permeated with idolatry. Reference here is to Mizpeh-gilead (6:8; Judg 11:29), which was representative of the land beyond Jordan.

But Gilgal, typical of the region west of the Jordan, is no better, for they sacrificed bullocks to strange gods. To what are their altars to be likened? They are as heaps, just as numerous as piles of stones cleared from a field, and just as fruitless, harmful, and displeasing. (For the seat of idolatry in Gilgal see 4:15 and 9:15.)

Again the prophet turns to Jacob to rebuke them by the life of their ancestor. He had to flee to the field of Aram. This is the region between the Tigris and Euphrates Rivers, called Mesopotamia. He was a fugitive, oppressed, and made to do arduous labor. In spite of all this he kept firm faith in the Lord. (Some have suggested that Jacob in fleeing had in mind fleeing from marriage with an idolatress, such as Esau married. But the text requires no such elaboration.)

He is brought before them as example again, in that during hours of hardships he trusted in the Lord. The mention of the service for a wife may be meant to remind of the trickery that Laban played on Jacob. Despite this, Jacob's faith did not waver in the Lord. But what was the case with Israel, his descendants? God brought them up out of Egypt in a manner never accomplished before then and never duplicated since. You, however, who have been delivered from such bondage, will not follow the Lord.

Instead of all this care calling forth the gratitude of the people of God, they provoked God to anger more bitterly. The Hebrew expression states that they provoked God to anger with bitterness itself. For this there must be and there will be judgment. God will not remove the bloodguiltiness of Ephraim from him; it will abide upon him until the penalty is carried out. God will requite his idol worship; the punishment for his idolatry

God will visit upon him. The Lord is still spoken of as "his Lord." Though God chasten him sore, He will not disown Ephraim.

EPHRAIM'S IDOLATRY AGAIN

The thought with which the twelfth chapter closed is continued in the thirteenth chapter. The prophet recalls the days past when Ephraim was honored in the nation. When he spoke, all trembled; men had respect for his power and prestige. One can hardly read the history of the twelve tribes without noting how prominent was the position of Ephraim. He was truly exalted in Israel, respectfully feared. But when he gave himself over to the worship of Baal under Ahab (see 1 Ki 16:31), he died. His power was destroyed and broken. He died spiritually with consequent political decline.

The infection has grown and Ephraim has multiplied idols to himself according to his own devisings. All the ingenuity and skill at his command he employed in making the worthless images, nothing more than the work of men's hands. Those who make the idols encourage those who sacrifice to pay homage to the vain images. The kiss was the act of homage in the East, whether on the hand, foot, knees, or shoulder of the idol. The act of homage is transferred to natural objects (toward which the hand was kissed) and even God. Compare 1 Kings 19:18 (idols); Psalm 2:12 (God the Son); and Job 31:26-27 (natural objects).

Worshiping such transitory creatures as idols, Ephraim is doomed to pass away also. He is likened to the morning cloud, the dew, the chaff, and the smoke of the chimney. All these have one property or quality in common: transitoriness. The cloud of the morning may seem to be full of permanence and promise, but it is gone before the oncoming day. The dew that is so heavy in the East will be gone in an hour under the sun's hot rays. The chaff, when they winnowed, was carried away in a moment from the threshing floor when the whirlwind caught it. The custom was to throw in the air both the chaff and the grain, the latter falling to the floor again while the former was carried off (cp. Ps 1:4). The smoke which comes up in billows and spreads itself, having no substance nor body, is soon dissipated. So fleeting is Ephraim. Idolatry has been his ruin.

GOD'S WARNINGS

It was not that Ephraim had insufficient knowledge of God. He had known that the Lord had brought him out of Egyptian bondage. At that time He made it plain that the Jews were to have no other gods beside Him; He alone is their Saviour. (Note also Is 45:21.) God cared for them and provided for them in the weary journeyings of the wilderness. There was no reason for their departure from the Lord, but no sooner were they filled with the bounty of the Lord than they forgot the living God in the pride of their hearts. As so often before and since, prosperity brought with it pride and forgetfulness of the Lord and His goodness.

They may forget God but He has not forgotten them nor their ingratitude. He will be to them as a lion, a leopard, a bear, and a wild beast. Hosea had foretold already that God would be as a lion to His people (5:14). As a crouching leopard He would watch by the way to pounce upon them. He would meet them as a bear robbed of her whelps. Under such conditions she is savage indeed. (Cp. 2 Sa 17:8.)

It has been pointed out that here we have the four beasts of Daniel chapter seven which are mentioned long after Hosea's time. There where they have sinned God will devour them as a lioness. He will tear their pericardium, in order to penetrate to the heart. The warnings are clear and it requires only the willing and obedient heart to follow in the way of the Lord.

BANE AND BLESSING

Israel's destruction stems from the fact that the people are against the Lord, their only true help. Of course, they had conceived that kings and princes were a great asset to them. Now God asks them how their kings and princes can save them from the calamities that yet await them. They had been cleaving to those who could not help them and forsaking the Lord who alone could succor them.

The reference to the people's request for a king is an allusion to the nation's demand in the time of Samuel (1 Sa 8:4-9). In answer to their desire God gave them a king in His anger and took him away in His wrath. What a summary to describe the monarchy in Israel! The statement is not only true of Saul (1 Sa 15:22-23; 16:1), but of Jeroboam's dynasty as well (1 Ki 15:25-27; 2 Ki 15:30).

The iniquity of Ephraim is bound up; his sin is stored up. The case is closed and the evidence is all in hand. Divine retribution is certain. By a bold and vivid figure Hosea shows that, when Israel could be delivered by pangs of penitence, she ought not to court disaster by deferring that liberating hour. The sorrows or pangs of a travailing woman are sudden and violent. If these pangs do not perform their purpose, they issue in death. So with God's chastisements: if they do not result in the repentance of the sinner, they lead to his undoing.

Israel is likened to the mother upon whom the pangs come suddenly; then she is compared to the child whose birth means relief for mother and child. The fourteenth verse has been understood by some to be a continuation of the threat of the Lord; by others it is taken to be a glorious promise. We understand it in the latter sense and conceive the connection to be after this manner: Hosea has been speaking about a situation which could easily, and often does, issue in death (see v. 13). Now the Lord promises the death of death itself. Grace shines through in the midst of words of judgment. The Lord, who has threatened to appear as lion, bear, and other ferocious beasts, will appear as Redeemer from Sheol and death, to those who trust Him. In the midst of proclamation of doom, God foretells that He has future purposes of mercy and redemption. The question form is the best rendering of the verse. The New Testament (1 Co 15:55) takes the passage as a promise and in question form for emphasis.

When the Lord says repentance is hid from His eyes, He does not mean that He will pay no attention to repentant hearts. This is contrary to the whole teaching of the Bible. He does mean that He has determined not to repent of these purposes just stated in the promise. Of these purposes in grace He will never repent; such repentance is far from His thoughts. God declares that He will not change His purpose of executing His promise to Israel should she return to Him. (Cp. Ro 11:29).

FINAL JUDGMENT

What the scorching east wind does to fruit, the Assyrian, the chastening rod of the Lord, will perform upon Ephraim in spite of his fruitfulness. The Assyrian Shalmaneser is presented here under the figure of the east wind. There is a play upon the thought of fruitfulness, for such is the meaning of Ephraim's name. The hot and parching wind will dry up the springs and fountains, and the enemy will take all the nation's treasures as spoil.

The chapter closes with the solemn pronouncement that Samaria will experience to the full the retribution of God upon her sins. Rebellion against God can no more be countenanced than treason among men. The ruthless Assyrian would regard neither child, nor woman, nor motherhood (see 10:14; 2 Ki 15:16; Is 13:16; Amos 1:13).

LONG-AWAITED REPENTANCE

In many ways the last chapter of Hosea is the most beautiful in the entire prophecy and forms a fitting close to the series of prophetic discourses. The chapter is reminiscent of truths contained in chapter 2. The great billows of condemnation and denunciation have lashed themselves against Israel (especially the closing word in 13:16, which forms verse 1 of chapter 14 in the original text); now God speaks tenderly in grace. Grace shines through the threatening clouds at last.

The main exhortation of all the prophets is repeated here once more: "O Israel, return unto Jehovah thy God." The entreaty expresses great longing on God's part that His people may do so, and that without delay. Their fall has been through their own sin, but now there is a new day ahead of them. They are told to take with them words and return to the Lord not sacrifices nor gifts but true penitence. God wants word of penitence, prayer, and confession.

In thus returning they beseech the Lord to remove all their iniquity and accept the contriteness of their hearts. Instead of bullocks on altars the praise from their lips will be the choicest of all offerings to God. (See Ps 69:30-31 and Heb 13:15.) Then will the people's entire hope and dependence be in the Lord. They will recognize the impotence of Assyria to help them, though they had sought after them time after time. They will recognize also that the horse is vain for safety, so they will no longer look to Egypt for cavalry. (Cp. Deu 17:16.) Nor will they resort to the idols which are but the work of their hands. Neither in Assyria, nor in Egypt, nor in idols will they find mercy, but in the Lord God Himself, full of tender mercies and loving-kindness, who has mercy upon the fatherless, the unprotected, and the needy.

UNTOLD BLESSING

This portion of the passage contains a mountain-like accumulation of promises from the Lord. Repeatedly He says, "I will . . . I will . . . I will." You and I dare not say He will not. He promises first that He will heal their backsliding. Those who had been backsliding (11:7) did not come away from such experiences without injury. On the contrary, they were deeply wounded. God promises to be their great spiritual Healer, the true Jehovah Rapha. He will love them freely, without a cause in themselves, apart from and regardless of any merit or demerit of theirs, namely, from a very necessity of His being. The floodgates of His love will be opened, and, thank God, it will overwhelm them. His anger will no longer need to be spent upon them. God will be as dew unto Israel, reminding us of the copious dews which mean so much to the productivity of the soil.

This is the third mention of dew in the book of Hosea. In 6:4 it had reference to the goodness of Israel which barely came into existence before it vanished away; in 13:3 it spoke of the transitory character of the whole Northern Kingdom, soon to be swept away in the Assyrian invasion; here it is a figure for God's invigorating and fructifying power in the life of Israel, whereby the people of God will bring forth fruitage unto Him. They will yet take root downward and bear fruit upward, filling the face of the whole earth with fruit.

Israel shall then blossom as the lily, known both for its purity and pro-ductivity. A lily is one of the most productive plants, for it is said that one root can produce as many as fifty bulbs. Though it is able to multiply itself, it has no depth of root and soon fades. But Israel shall cast forth her roots as Lebanon. The cedars of Lebanon are proverbial for firmness and durability. They spoke of the cedars of Lebanon much as we do today of the Rock of Gibraltar.

Pure as the lily and durable as the cedar, Israel will also be as fruitful and beautiful as the ever-green olive-tree. Her scent will be that of a well-wooded and well-planted stretch of land. Lebanon with its aromatic plants and fragrant flowers can alone describe the fragrance that will be the por-tion of the Lord's own in that day. Those who dwell under the shadow of the Lord, those who have taken refuge in Him (cp. Is 4:6), will return to their land, be fruitful as the grain and the vine. They will no more bring forth wild grapes (Is 5:2), but their fragrance will be as the wine of Lebanon. The grapes of Lebanon have been likened in size to plums.

Ephraim, that Ephraim who was so joined and bound up in idols, will have no more to do with idols. He will cast them from him once for all because he is yielded, has responded to God. He will now regard God alone, occupied with contemplation of the Lord. Like a green fir tree (this designation cannot be of the Lord Himself as some would have it), Ephra-im will render fruit unto God. Now fruit for God will be found in Israel; before this the fruit was for Ephraim alone. Note "his fruit" in 10:1. In Ephraim the fruit of godliness will be seen.

THE FINAL WORD

The last verse is the epilogue to the whole prophecy. The one wise as unto the Lord and prudent before God will understand these things. All the ways of the Lord will be seen as right. The just will delight to walk in them, but transgressors will fall because of them to their own ruin. All prophecy is given to induce a godly walk in conformity with the will of God. This does not always result because the same sun that melts the wax hardens the clay. How blessed it is to have the heart submissive to learn of the ways of the Lord, then to follow in them diligently to our blessing and that of countless others. The transgressor, who finds no delight in the revealed ways of the Lord, will find the purpose of God will condemn him in the hour of judgment.

"I WILL LOVE THEM FREELY"

How this refrain sings itself into the very heart of the child of God! God has loved Israel; He does love them now; He will love them freely.

In grace all His promises will be fulfilled to them. But future promises for the nation Israel do not avail for the individual Israelite now. He is no more saved because of them than the Gentile. He must *now* accept the Lord Jesus Christ as his Messiah and Saviour, to be saved. Such is the path of obedience and such is the path of unspeakable blessing.

Part II

JOEL, AMOS, AND OBADIAH

To

PAUL DAVID,

LOIS ANNE,

and

JOHN SAMUEL,

God's gifts of great love, this section
is lovingly dedicated by their father.

THE PURPOSE of the writer is the same in this section as in the previous one, namely, to inculcate in Christian hearts from the Word of God a love for God's own people Israel, and to encourage the widespread preaching among them of the Gospel of their Messiah, the Lord Jesus Christ.

The words that have come to us concerning encouragement and blessing received through these studies have led us to hope that God may make them a source of similar refreshing to a wider group of the Lord's people. If it be so, we shall give thanks to God.

5

JOEL

THE DAY OF THE LORD

THE LOCUST PLAGUE AND DAY OF JEHOVAH

THE PROPHET AND HIS TIMES

JOEL, a name borne by many in the Old Testament, means "Jehovah is God." A few have suggested that this prophet was the son of the prophet Samuel (cp. 1 Sa 8:2), but the Scripture here is clear that the Joel of the prophecy was the son of Pethuel, of whom we know nothing further.

In contrast to the fullness of detail given in relation to the life of the prophet Hosea, practically nothing is known of the personal history of Joel. From the prophecy itself we may gather that he was a prophet of Judah and that he probably prophesied in Jerusalem. Note the references to the sanctuary in Jerusalem in 1:9, 13, 14; 2:15.

Joel was probably one of the earliest of the minor prophets. Compare the quotation of Joel 3:16 in Amos 1:2 and that of Joel 3:18 in Amos 9:13. The sins denounced by Amos and Hosea are not mentioned here, nor is the sin of idolatry touched upon at all.

There is difference of opinion among students of the book as to whether the first part of the book is to be taken as a literal locust plague or to be understood allegorically (i.e., figuratively of some future judgment). We must decide for the literal view. An actual locust plague had devastated the land. There are no hints in the text itself that the prophet is using an allegory. The picture given in the prophecy of the locusts is true to their manner of action and to the results of their blighting invasions: the disappearance of the vegetation in the fields; the eating of the bark of woody plants together with the roots under the ground; their swarms darkening the sun; their compact march in military manner; the wind-like noise of their movements; and the munching sounds accompanying their eating.

71

The prophecy begins with a terse statement containing the fact of the divine revelation and the recipient of it. One need only compare this superscription with that of Hosea or Isaiah in order to see the difference in detail. For this reason we cannot speak dogmatically as to the time of the ministry of Joel. The prophet calls upon the old men especially to recall whether they have known of any visitation in their time or in that of their predecessors similar to the locust plague which has devastated the land by successive swarms of locusts. This judgment could not be paralleled in the memory of any contemporary of the prophet. Because of the unheard of character of the destruction the word concerning it is to be passed on from generation to generation. Thus is the unprecedented character of the calamity vividly brought before us. It had never occurred on this wise before.

The four names in verse 4, meaning literally, the gnawer, the swarmer or multiplier, the licker, and the consumer or devourer, have been taken to mean either four types of locusts or four stages of growth in the case of one locust. (Note that the KJV and the ASV translate these Hebrew words alike.) Neither view is tenable, for the prophet uses the common word for locust (*'arbeh*) and then gives three poetic equivalents.

What the prophet means to convey is this: in the successive swarms of the locusts what one portion of them left the other portion devoured. Notice the number four in the matter of judgments in Jeremiah 15:3 and Ezekiel 14:21. Some Hebrew commentators have tried to relate the four names to the four empires in Daniel 2 and 7. Nothing in the text warrants such allegorical treatment. Furthermore, we have only to compare Joel 1:3 with Exodus 10:2, 6, and Deuteronomy 28:38-42 to realize the literal import of the words of the prophecy.

Locusts have rightly been called "the incarnation of hunger." They have been known to devour over an area of almost ninety miles every green herb and every blade of grass, so that the ground gave the appearance of having been scorched by fire. The locusts have a "scorched-earth policy" of their own. Joel's description of the plague has been confirmed by many accounts of locust devastations.

THE FEARSOME PLAGUE

The drunkards are first called upon to awake out of the stupefying effect of their intoxication with wine. (Cp. Is 5:11, 22, 23; 24:7-9; 28:7, 8; and Amos 6:1-6 for drunkenness in the land.) The drunkard, who is known for his song and raucous laughter, is to weep, because his delightsome vine has been destroyed by the locust plague. Note the different mournings in this chapter: (1) the drunkards, verse 5; (2) the nation under the figure of a virgin, verse 8; (3) the priests, verse 9; (4) the land, verse 10; and (5) the farmers and vinedressers, verse 11.

The locusts are now represented under the figure of an invading nation, because of their great numbers and the completeness of the desolating work. That the locusts are compared to a nation is no reason to infer that the plague was not a literal one. See Proverbs 30:25-27 where ants are pictured as a people along with locusts who are said to have no king over them.

The teeth of the locust are likened to those of a lion and a lioness, because the two jaws of the locust have saw-like teeth like the eye teeth of the lion and lioness. Both the locust and the lion are most destructive in their ravages. (Cp. Revelation 9:7-8.) The extent of the desolation is clear from the word concerning the vine, the fig tree, and all branches. The barks of the trees were gone, and the branches were withered. And all this desolation had been done to God's own land, wherefore He calls them "my vine" and "my fig tree."

DESOLATION EVERYWHERE

The prophet thus far has noted in general terms only the vast reach of the catastrophe. Now he fills in the picture with well-chosen details. The accuracy of the delineation is beyond question. God's people Israel, under the figure of a young virgin who has lost her bridegroom in death, are exhorted to lament for the calamity that has come upon them.

Why this bitterest of all weeping? Because the offerings of the house of the Lord (the meal offering being dependent upon the fruit of the field and the drink offering being dependent upon the produce of the vine) were cut off. Even the worship of God's house was affected by the desolation. What ravages sin can introduce into every realm of life! No greater catastrophe in the spiritual and religious sphere could have overtaken them. This meant practically the setting aside of the covenant relationship between God and His people. Mark you, we said the setting aside of that relationship and not the annulment of it.

No wonder then that the priests of the Lord gave themselves to mourning. Desolation touched everything: the field, the grain, the vine, the olive tree, the wheat, the barley, the fig tree, the pomegranate tree, the palm tree, the apple tree, all the trees; in short, everything had undergone the blighting effect of the locust scourge. All joy was gone because the harvest and vintage were denied them. (See Is 9:4 and Ps 4:7 for the joy of the harvest and vintage.) The gravity of the situation is brought home to us by the accumulation of words describing ruin and desolation: *cut off* in verse 9; *laid waste, mourneth, is destroyed, dried up,* and *languisheth* in verse 10; *is perished* in verse 11; *withered, languisheth,* and *withered away* in verse 12. It was no usual locust plague about which Joel was writing.

The Spirit of God through the prophet now instructs the people of God as to the way of return and blessing. Though the priests were mourning (v. 9) because of the interruption of the ceremonial life of the people, the Lord calls them to a girding with sackcloth, a wailing, and a lamenting that will bespeak their turning to the Lord with repentant hearts.

The visitation of the locusts came not upon the land because the Lord delighted in judgment. He does not willingly afflict the children of men, but by chastisements, often severe but always purposeful, He would bring them back from their evil ways and from the pit of destruction. God is still the God of His people; note the use in verse 13 of "my God" and then "your God." The spiritual leaders of the nation are to proclaim and set aside a fast, convene a public gathering of all the inhabitants of the land, especially the elders who are to set the example, and then to cry mightily unto the Lord for His restoring grace. Since the judgment and calamity have been public, the humiliation and repentance must be also. God delights in prayer and heart piety, and eagerly hearkens to the supplications of His people.

TOKEN OF THE DAY OF JEHOVAH

Though the plague be literal and the prophet bewails the destruction wrought thereby, yet the plague in its literal sense does not exhaust the intent of the Lord. It points ahead to the coming great visitation of the day of Jehovah. This day is mentioned in 1:15; 2:1, 11, 31; and 3:14. Because the day of Jehovah looms so large in prophetic Scriptures, we define it and its relation to other days designated in the Word of God.

In 1 Corinthians 4:3 Paul speaks of "man's day" (see ASV margin). The day here spoken of is that in which we live, when man has sway and governs on the earth. To represent this rule God gave Nebuchadnezzar a dream of an image of a *man* (Dan 2). This day will come to an end, as far as the Church is concerned, with the "day of Christ" which is the rapture. (See Phil 1:6.)

After the rapture "the day of Jehovah" begins. It comprises the time of the Great Tribulation on earth, the seventieth week of Daniel 9:27, and the time of the rule of the Messiah of Israel over them in Jerusalem on the throne of David. (See not only the Scriptures noted above in Joel, but

Amos 5:18; Zep 1:14—2:2 together with Is 2:1-21 among many Scriptures throughout the prophetic books.)

At the termination of the day of Jehovah, the "day of God" will begin. In that day the elements will melt with fervent heat and the new heavens and the new earth will result. This day lasts throughout eternity when God is all and in all. (Cp. 1 Co 15:28.)

We have purposely elaborated upon these vital days, because the theme of the prophecy of Joel is The Day of Jehovah. With this truth in mind, we can readily discern how the locust plague serves as a harbinger or foreshadowing of the coming Day of Jehovah. Joel rightly views it with alarm. The then present judgment spoke clearly of the future terrifying day of judgment. The words *destruction* and *Almighty* are a play on words (lit., "shod" and "Shaddai"). Not only does the land suffer, but the beasts, the cattle, and the flocks of sheep suffer as well. Animals suffer with man, and especially so because of the drought that attended the plague. The unrelieved drought which affected the brooks and the pastures was as a fire consuming what the locusts may not have touched. The animals cannot pray, so the prophet, voicing his own desire toward the Lord in this crisis and setting an example for all (v. 14), intercedes for all.

THE OUTPOURED SPIRIT

THE IMPENDING DAY OF JEHOVAH

Just as the prophet Joel in the first chapter of the prophecy turned the minds of his contemporaries, who were filled with the sense of calamity because of the ruin wrought by the locust plague, from the visitation of the moment to a far worse judgment from the Lord, so he does throughout the second chapter of the book. There are men who have taken the position that the chapter deals solely with the locust plague; others maintain just as firmly that the passage is entirely future. Both views are extreme. As a matter of fact, Joel starts with the situation then existing in the land after the havoc of the locust plague and then goes on to picture the dreadful Day of Jehovah yet future, but imminent.

"SOUND AN ALARM!"

It was the duty of the priests in Israel to blow the trumpets on specific occasions. (See Num 10:1, 2, 9.) The Lord is here calling upon them to blow the trumpet of alarm from God's holy mountain, from the place of His sanctuary and the center of their worship. Why? What was the threatening calamity? The Day of Jehovah was at hand.

Here we have an elaboration of the prediction in 1:15. The locust visitation was a clear indication of what events were yet in store for Israel in the imminent Day of Jehovah. Why this day, this time of judgment, is so terror-inspiring is now set forth by Joel. It is a day of darkness, gloominess, and thick clouds. Darkness is a figure in Scripture for misery and distress. (Note in this connection such passages as Is 8:22; 60:2; Jer 13:16; Amos 5:18; and Zep 1:15-16.) The figure is a most telling one because locust swarms by their density do obscure the light of the sun.

Some students of the passage have found it difficult to take the words "as the dawn spread upon the mountains" to refer to the darkness just mentioned, because of the evident contrast between light and darkness. For this reason it has been suggested that the comparison with the dawn be taken with the following words concerning the great and strong people. But this explanation is not wholly necessary. The points of comparison are these: just as the dawn is sudden and widespread, so will the darkness of the Day of Jehovah be. What great and strong people the prophet is alluding to can be discerned from the latter part of the verse where it is clearly stated that there never has been the like nor will there be in the future.

We have proof here that an ordinary, or even extraordinary plague of locusts is not the final and ultimate fulfillment of this prophecy. The Spirit of God through the prophet is pointing to an unparalleled foe of the people of God who will in a coming day inflict greater desolation than did the locust plague. Who is this enemy? With many other students of the book we understand it to be the Assyrian power of the future, the northern power of the last days. Study carefully Isaiah 10 and Daniel 11.

DESTRUCTION ON THE MARCH

The record now paints for us an eye-witness account of what ruin the drought and the locusts accomplished in the land. The drought was as a consuming fire that leaves all scorched in its trail, and with the locusts what was as the Garden of Eden before they descended upon the land, was now nothing more than a desolate wilderness. Nothing escapes the devastating blight.

Now follows an accurate description of locusts in their march, an account unexcelled in all the realm of literature. The locusts are likened first of all to horses; in fact the head of the locust is so like that of a horse that the Italians call it *cavalette* (little horse) and the Germans speak of locusts as *Heupferde* (hay horses). They not only look like horses but they have the speed of the war-horse. (Cp. Job 39:20.) And noise accompanies all their movements, noise as when chariots jostle in their running, noise as when fire licks up the dried stubble, noise as when a strong host is being mustered for the conflict.

The noise of the wings of the locusts in motion and of their hind legs strikes terror in every heart. In the life of every member of the nation this visitation will long linger in memory. The locusts are as tireless in their running as mighty men of war; they appear to have their regulated phalanxes like an army on the march (see Pr 30:27); they are adept at scaling walls; as though directed by a master mind, they do not break their ranks; no one thrusts another out of his place. All is in turmoil and in confusion at their onslaught. The heavenly bodies themselves are darkened by the thick masses of locusts flying under the whole expanse of the heavens. Destruction is literally on the march, for as thieves the locusts seek out what they may devour. But the Lord Himself is in all this as well. He utters His voice—the thunderstorm—before His great army of locusts. They are His army in a real sense because they are both powerful and numerous. One of the laws of Mohammed reads: "Ye shall not kill the locusts, for they are the army of God Almighty." The command of God is being executed by His instruments.

If this be so terrible that man can scarce abide it, how much less will he be able to do so in the hour when God's fullest judgments will be upon a Christ-rejecting and God-dishonoring world, in the Day of Jehovah? Here we find one of the great principles of God's dealing with man throughout his history: God only inflicts punishment after great provocation, and when He does so, it is meant to draw man back from further and more severe visitations of the wrath of God. The plague of locusts was severe, but it could not approximate the devastation to be wrought in that time known as the Day of Jehovah. Says God: "From the lesser learn the greater and be warned."

THE CALL TO REPENT

What grace God offers them! Even at that late hour it was possible to repent and turn to the Lord, thus averting further disaster. God calls for a time of deep exercise of heart and spirit, a time of fasting, a time of brokenness of heart before Him. Because it is ever so easy to substitute the external for the real, to be lost in the round of outward show, God exhorts them to rend their hearts and not their garments.

The rending of garments on occasions of great mourning is recorded early in the Scriptures (see Gen 37:29, 34; also 1 Sa 4:12; 1 Ki 21:27; and Is 37:2). It was meant to convey that broken and rent condition of the heart of the mourner. Because the sign often replaces the reality, God through the prophet enjoins a true and genuine contrition of heart. All such action before God is based upon the fact of God's wonderful character, for He is gracious beyond words and ready to forgive. God is always more willing to bless than to blast, to pardon than to punish, to win by love than to wound by lashing. So there is always the possibility of God's displeasure being turned into His favor, when His people come low before Him. God has no delight in the death of the wicked, but that he turn from the evil of his ways and live. (Note the case of the Ninevites in Jon 3:9.) Upon true repentance God will restore to them plentiful harvests. The meal offering and the drink offering, both dependent upon the harvest of the field and vineyard, had ceased because of the drought and the plague, but will now be available to repentant Israel. (See 1:9, 13, 16.)

"CALL A SOLEMN ASSEMBLY"

Again the priests are called upon to blow the trumpet in Zion. The first trumpet (cp. Joel 2:1 and Num 10:5) was to sound an alarm; the second trumpet (2:15 and Num 10:10) was to call a convocation in Israel to gather the people to the sanctuary of the Lord. To this assembly all are to come, old men, infants, children, even the bridegroom and the bride who ordinarily are exempt from all public obligation (Deu 20:7; 24:5). All are guilty, so all must humble themselves before God. Personal, individual joys are to give way to the interests of the entire community.

The priests, the ministers of God, are to assume their rightful places of responsibility and lead the people in their penitent crying unto the Lord. The very words are indicated which are to be spoken: "Spare thy people, O Jehovah, and give not thy heritage to reproach, that the nations should rule over them."

Can you conceive of the blessing with which these words are fraught? How such attitude of heart lays bare the mighty arm of God on behalf of His people. Would that the Church of the living God were aroused throughout its length and breadth to pray that such turning to God may be realized in our day among the dry bones of the house of Israel. The very ends of the earth would feel the impact of such a turning of Israel to God. In apostolic days it was simply stated that men from among Israel with the message of God turned the world upside down; flaming evangelists from among Israel today can have no less of the power of God at their disposal now. All too long have the nations of the earth trodden Israel under foot with seeming impunity. Because God has not rent the heavens and come down visibly on their behalf, the hearts of God-defying nations have been hardened to continue their domination of Israel and to cry, "Where is their God?" But the hour of God's prophetic clock cannot be far off when Israel shall turn in penitence to the living God from whom they have grievously strayed, and God will requite the nations in their bosom fully for the havoc they have wrought upon the heritage of the Lord and the woundings they have perpetrated upon the apple of His eye. Then they will know the answer of their ridicule of the omnipotent God as though He were helpless to aid His own and as though He were unmindful of the covenant relationship which He has brought into being between Himself and Israel.

THE ANSWER OF GOD

When the faintest cry of the penitent is uttered, it does not escape the ear of the Lord. His zeal and His jealousy on behalf of His people are aroused and He goes forth to bless them unstintingly. He remembers the wounds of His land and He heals them. He is mindful of the sorrows of His people, and He graciously solaces them. The grain, the new wine, and the oil, long withheld because of their sin, will be restored; the land will give its produce and they will be abundantly satisfied. God will remove their reproach among the nations, and He will exalt them as head of the nations.

In that conclusion of the day of Jehovah, the Lord will utterly rout the army of the invading Assyrian, the army of the northern power. (Literal locusts, mark you, would scarcely be called "the northern army.") The land barren and desolate is Arabia, the eastern sea is the Dead Sea, and the western sea is the Mediterranean. In short, the army will be divided and completely annihilated. All this will come upon the enemy because he has exalted himself in his pride. See the book of Nahum concerning the pride of the Assyrian, also Zechariah 10:11.

REJOICING AND RESTORATION

The Assyrian enemy may attempt great things, but the Lord will truly accomplish great things for His people. That land and people which languished, mourned, and wept shall have its sorrow turned to joy.

First of all, the land is told to rejoice and be glad (v. 21). Its desolate condition was vividly portrayed in the first chapter (see vv. 17 and 19). Then the beasts of the field are called upon to put away their fears, for now there will be pasture and the fruit of the tree and vine. Formerly they had panted for lack of water and food (cp. 1:18-20). Finally, in the climaxing word the children of Zion are to rejoice in the Lord (note 1:16). First there will be temporal blessings and then additional spiritual blessings. God will give them the former and latter rain in due and proper measure, that amount necessary where the drought had prevailed.

It is of great interest to the student of the Word of God to know that the rains have increased in Palestine within recent years, but the grand fulfillment is yet future when Israel turns to the Lord. Once the rains are no longer withheld there will be plentiful harvests of wheat, wine, and oil. The very losses sustained through the locust plague will be restored and more. The years that the locusts have eaten will be forgotten in the new bounties. The locust plague did not last for years, but one such devastation could have results for years. The locusts were God's great army which He personally had sent. There will be the enjoyment of God's bounty now that Israel is reconciled to her God, and she will be satisfied. God will be praised by His people and they shall never suffer shame again. They shall never be put to shame. Verses 26 and 27 end with the same words because God would give fullest assurance of the truth stated. In verse 26 it is used of temporal benefits; in verse 27, of spiritual benefits. God is the sole and only necessary guarantee that all these will be accomplished.

NEVER PUT TO SHAME

God in the midst of Israel in blessing: is not this the goal of all His dealings with them? And what provision He has made for this very thing in the gift of His Son to be their Messiah and Saviour from sin. How can we stand idly by without letting them know of this Saviour and Lord? How can they hear without a preacher? How can God receive His rightful praise from redeemed hearts in Israel except they hear and believe the message of the Gospel of Christ? In all this plan God has a place, a real place, for you and me. May we be quick to see it and ready to obey.

THE OUTPOURING OF THE SPIRIT

Verses 28 through 32 form chapter 3 in the Hebrew text; and chapter 3 in the English translations is chapter 4 in the original. No one will be inclined to doubt that the disclosure of truth in 2:28-32 is of sufficient importance to warrant its appearing in a separate chapter. Sad to say, this vital passage (with its New Testament counterpart in Ac 2) has been grossly misunderstood and made to teach what was never intended.

Note the time indicated in the passage. The events set forth here are placed chronologically in that time designated as "afterward." What does that time mean? We find it in Hosea 3:5 and there it is coupled with "in the latter days." The prophet is speaking of the latter days for Israel, a period which covers both the Tribulation period and the reign of the Messiah which follows it. (Cp. carefully Is 2:2, and Peter's words in Ac

2:17.) At that time God will pour out His Spirit, the blessed Holy Spirit, upon all flesh.

Several truths are implied here: (1) the figure employed is taken from the analogy of the rain (see 2:23) ; (2) the pouring out reveals the Spirit is from above; and (3) the Spirit is given in abundance. The outpouring of the Spirit is to be upon all flesh. It will be universal in character and scope. But does this mean universal for all Israel or for all mankind generally?

Expositors of the passage are divided, some holding to one position and others holding to the other positon just as positively. No one, however, will deny, from the context and the prophetic teaching of other portions of the Old Testament, that all Israel surely is included. Differences of age (young and old) , sex (sons and daughters) , or position (servants and handmaids) will constitute no barrier nor hindrance to this gift of the Spirit.

There is no recorded case in the Old Testament where the gift of prophecy was granted to a slave. In the latter days, however, the fond desire of Moses (Num 11:29) will be realized. The dreams, visions, and prophecy spoken of here are the three modes mentioned in Numbers 12:6. Note that verse 29 reiterates the same truth given in verse 28: "I will pour out my Spirit." The time element is also repeated.

We must not think that this is the first mention of an outpouring of the Spirit of God upon Israel in the Old Testament prophetic books. (See Is 32:15; 44:3, 4; Eze 36:27, 28; 37:14; 39:29; and Zec 12:10.) But that day will mean wrath and judgment upon the unbelieving. God will perform mighty transformations both in heaven and on earth. The sun and the moon will be affected; blood and fire (as in Ex 7:17 and 9:24) and pillars of smoke (as in Ex 19:18) will be visible. It will be the great and fearful day of Jehovah.

Nevertheless, the outpouring of the Spirit will result in salvation. There will be those who call upon the Lord unto physical deliverance and whom the Lord will call unto spiritual salvation. Notice the twofold use of the thought of calling: (1) calling on God (this means salvation; see Ro 10:13) and (2) God calling them. God has foretold that there would be an escaped remnant (cp. Ob 17 as well as Zec 14:1-5) and these will be a blessing to the whole earth.

THE FULFILLMENT OF THE PROPHECY

At this point it is in place to ask whether Joel's prophecy has been fulfilled in Acts 2. At the outset it must be made clear that it is incorrect to say there is no connection between the two passages. Peter distinctly states that he is referring to the prediction of Joel. However, that fact alone does not constitute a fulfillment. In the first place, the customary formula for a fulfilled prophecy is entirely lacking in Acts 2:16. And even more telling is the fact that much of Joel's prophecy, even as quoted in Acts 2:19-20, was not fulfilled at that time. We cannot take the position that only a portion of the prophecy was meant to be fulfilled at all, because this would work havoc with Bible prophecy. God predicts and He can perform just what He predicted. The best position to take is that Peter used Joel's prophecy as an illustration of what was transpiring in his day and not as a fulfillment of this prediction. In short, Peter saw in the events of his day proof that God would yet completely bring to pass all that Joel prophesied. Joel's prophecy, then, was prefilled; it is yet (as the Old Testament passages on the outpouring of the Spirit show) to be fulfilled.

THE JUDGMENT OF ALL NATIONS

No prophet of the Old Testament has a more important revelation of the end times than the one now before us in the third chapter. How gracious of God to let us know the exact time of these happenings. They will take place when the Lord Himself returns the captivity of Judah and Jerusalem. The return of Israel to the land will never be fully accomplished until the Lord does it by His omnipotent power. (Note Jer 23:1-8.)

At the time of God's regathering of Israel to the land, He will gather all nations into the Valley of Jehoshaphat to judgment. The prophet evidently has in mind the historical narrative in 2 Chronicles 20. Tradition has assigned the judgment to the Kidron Valley; though this tradition is only from Eusebius' time (fourth century AD on), there are those who believe it to be correct. The site indicated must be in or near Jerusalem. The method of God's gathering of the nations to the judgment is set forth in verses 9-12 of chapter 3. (Cp. also Zec 12:1-3, 9; 14:2-4; Is 29:1-8.)

One of the most important features of the judgment is the basis of it: the nations will be judged for God's people and for His heritage Israel. Read carefully Matthew 25:31-46 and note the words *my brethren*. The same judgment is in view in both passages. Without doubt our Lord Jesus Christ had this passage in mind when He concluded His marvelous Olivet discourse.

The great sin of the nations—all will be involved in it in the time of Jacob's trouble (Jer 30:7)—is that against Israel. Little do the nations realize how they incur the wrath of God when they lay violent hands upon His heritage and the plant of His choosing. He will not suffer it always. Joel shows the day of reckoning has come because Israel was scattered among the nations; their land was divided; they were sold to indulge the vilest passions—a night of revelry or debauchery. Josephus, the historian, tells us (see *The Wars of the Jews,* Book VI, chap. 9, par. 2; also his *Antiquities,* Book XII, chap. 7, par. 3; and 1 Mac 3:41; 2 Mac 8:11, 25) that in the Roman wars the enemy chose out of the Jews "the tallest and most beautiful, and reserved them for the triumph; and as for the rest of the multitude that were above seventeen years old, he put them into bonds; and sent them to the Egyptian mines . . . those that were under seventeen years of age were sold for slaves." Such indignities and worse have been perpetrated upon God's people in our own generation, and the end is not yet. Will God visit with judgment for these? Be certain that He will.

DIVINE RETRIBUTION

The Lord through His prophet now addresses Tyre and Sidon as representative of all the land of Phoenicia. Do they think they can fare differently from all the rest? Do they not realize that they injure God in the person of His people? All the grievances committed upon God's people, He considers as done to Himself. If men think they can strike at God, He will show them that swiftly and speedily divine retribution will overtake and overwhelm them. God will not keep His silence for ever.

The prophet recalls the plundering of Judah and Jerusalem by the Philistines and the Arabians in the time of Jehoram (2 Ch 21:16-17). The very ones sold afar off will God use to bring about His judgment upon His and their foes. Instead of the children of Judah being sold for sport or profit, the sons and daughters of their enemies will be sold into the hand of the people of Israel who in turn will sell the enemy into the hand of a nation afar off. The fate which they planned for Israel will rebound upon the head of Israel's godless adversaries.

THE ARMIES MUSTERED

God calls upon the nations to prepare for war; this is the method whereby He brings the nations to their deserved judgment. The word *prepare* is literally "sanctify"; that is, by sacrifices and appropriate rites and ceremonies. (See 1 Sa 7:8-9 and Jer 6:4.) This is to be war to the finish. To that end let all the nations muster and mobilize their manpower to the very hilt. Let them come fully equipped and accoutered. In order that no man lack proper weapons let every tool used for peaceful pursuits, the plowshares and the pruning-hooks, be beaten into swords and spears. (Who of us will soon forget the preview of this in World War II when we had our "scrap drives"?)

So great will be the desire to destroy God's people that even the weak will fancy himself to be strong. What an assemblage that will be! The nations will be banded together and confederate as never before (see Ps 2:1-3). In the midst of the scene which passes before the prophet's vision he prays that God's mighty ones (His hosts) may come down, in contradistinction to the supposed "mighty ones" of verse 9.

Now the whole theme is summarized for us in verse 12. The nations are seen as bestirring themselves to the white heat of wrath against Israel; their objective is the Valley of Jehoshaphat (how appropriately is it thus named: "Jehovah judges"); and there they (the nations) will meet the blessed King of Israel, their Protector through all ages, and their Champion in their darkest and blackest hour, the Lord Jesus Christ, who will sit ready to judge once and for all the accumulated sins of the nations against Israel. Fearful day that will be, and the nations will as easily escape it as they can cause the sun to cease shining in the heavens.

Just as the Lord speaks to the nations in verse 12, so He commands His agents of judgment. The judgment is described under the double figure of the harvest and the vintage. The harvest is ripe, and the winepress and vats are full to overflowing. What this means is stated in literal language: "for their wickedness is great." This judgment is referred to in Isaiah 63:1 and prominently in Revelation 14:14-20. Terrific will be the impact when God's mighty ones meet the mighty ones of the nations in mortal and final combat.

The issue will not hang in doubt; it is all clearly stated beforehand. The lifeblood of the nations will drench the soil of the earth. How unspeakably sad that the nations will not learn the lesson regarding God's people, the Jews, before it is too late! Remember that this is not a caprice with God, for the wickedness of the nations is insufferably great.

"MULTITUDES IN THE VALLEY OF DECISION"

But the story is so ponderous that it must be told out further. The prophet sees the nations assembled in innumerable hosts in the valley where God (not they) will make His decision. The repetition of the word *multitudes* is meant to show how innumerable they are. As far as the eye can possibly see, the hosts of the peoples of the earth are drawn up in array—a great sea of surging humanity. The valley of decision defines more clearly the Valley of Jehoshaphat. There the words of decision: "Come, ye blessed of my Father" and "Depart, ye cursed" (learn here the literalness of the words of Gen 12:1-3), will be uttered with the voice of the mighty Son of God, voice as the sound of many waters. Heaven and earth will feel the force of this judgment, and the Lord Himself will be roused up as a lion.

Indeed, the Lion of the tribe of Judah will utter His voice from Zion and Jerusalem. Creation will resound at the voice of Him who in that hour will be the refuge of His people and a stronghold to the children of Israel. The Lord will dwell in Zion and all will be holiness for God's people. (Cp. Ps 132:13-14.) No strangers will pass through her any more to plunder, to destroy, or to pollute. When they do come, it will be to worship the Lord of hosts. (Zec 8:20-23.)

BLESSINGS ON JUDAH

The judgment on the nations, however, is never meant to be an end in itself. Through it God means to bring blessing to His people Israel. Joel concludes now with words of promise for God's downtrodden ones. Even the mountains and hills (ordinarily the least productive of all soil) will flourish abundantly. Water will be present in great supply; a perennial fountain will furnish all the water needed. The Valley of Shittim, on the border between Moab and Israel beyond Jordan, known for its dryness, will be well watered. Egypt and Edom, representative of all Israel's enemies (that such is the case can be readily seen from the "all" of verses 2, 11, and 12), will be made a desolation forever. But Judah and Jerusalem shall abide eternally. God's people will remain, and by judging the nations the Lord will wipe away the blood-guiltiness of the nations in their persecution of God's people. (Note vv. 19-21.)

HOW FAR AWAY?

As we meditate on this marvelous disclosure in God's Word, we are driven to the question, How far off can it be? Not very far!

6

AMOS

THE RIGHTEOUSNESS OF GOD

ORACLES AGAINST THE NATIONS

THE MESSENGER OF GOD

Amos, whose name occurs nowhere else in the Old Testament outside of his prophecy, was born in the Southern Kingdom of Judah in Tekoa. He was not the son of a prophet (see 7:14-15) nor a prophet from his birth (cp. Jer 1:5), but was a herdsman, a sheep-tender, and a cultivator of sycamore trees. He was not of a family of rank, wealth, or influence, but given to the pastoral life in the rugged regions of Tekoa, which lay twelve miles southeast of Jerusalem and six miles south of Bethlehem. His figures and images, beautiful and abundant, are drawn from rustic life. His book is characterized by beauty of expression and loftiness of thought.

He was a contemporary of Hosea and, although born in Judah, was sent by God to prophesy to the Northern Kingdom of Israel at Bethel, its religious center. While Hosea emphasizes the love of God in the midst of His judgments, Amos sets forth the majesty and uncompromising righteousness of God against sinners. His prophetic messages and visions are (with the exception of the last) of a threatening nature. They are directed against the low moral condition of the people and especially against their apostasy from the Lord to the worship of idols.

THE TIME OF HIS MINISTRY

The days of Uzziah in Judah and Jeroboam II in Israel were marked by great prosperity, in fact, the most prosperous for the Northern Kingdom. Israel was at the height of her power under this king. The period was one of great wealth, luxury, arrogance, carnal security, oppression of the poor, moral decay, and formal worship. The moral declension and spiritual degradation of the people were appalling.

86

Amos foretold chastisement from the Lord but did not name the foreign invader—Assyria—to be the scourge of the Lord. Though verse 1 of this prophecy mentions Uzziah, it is clear that the object of the prophecy is Israel in particular.

The time of the message is dated as two years before the earthquake. Earthquakes are not uncommon in Palestine, but this must have been of unusual severity for it is mentioned more than two centuries after this by Zechariah (14:4-5). Josephus the historian claims the earthquake took place when Uzziah tried to assume priestly functions (2 Ch 26:16-23), but this is without proof and useless for the purpose of dating the event. We have no means of ascertaining the time of this terrifying visitation in nature, a warning in itself of the judgment yet to overtake them.

ROARING FROM ZION

Amos relates his message immediately to that of Joel by declaring that the Lord will roar as a lion from Zion (cp. Joel 3:16). The roaring of the Lord is here against Israel; in Joel it is for Israel against her enemies. When the lion roars, he leaps on the prey. Judgment is about to fall upon Israel. The pastures of the shepherds in the south and the top of Carmel in the north are mentioned as comprising the whole land in this stroke of judgment. Carmel is the great promontory on the Mediterranean Sea, rich in pastures, oliveyards, and vineyards. (See Is 35:2.) If Carmel withers, how great will be the desolation elsewhere? The withering is not of drought alone, but destruction in general is meant.

JUDGMENT ON SYRIA

The prophets Isaiah, Jeremiah, and Ezekiel also have prophecies against foreign nations, but they place such oracles after the indictments against God's own people Israel. Amos reverses the order, and we shall see the wisdom of the arrangement in due course.

Judgment will fall first upon Damascus, the capital city of Syria. The nations chosen, representative of a larger number as we know from other prophetic passages, are those noted for their oppression of Israel. Those are mentioned last as a sort of climax (Edom, Ammon, Moab) who were related to Israel. The expression, "for three transgression . . . yea, for four," which occurs with each announcement of punishment (giving an intended impression of uniformity) does not have in mind a mathematical enumeration. These nations are being visited not for three or even four transgressions, but for an incalculable number. The expression means the measure of iniquity is full and wrath must fall upon the wicked. The punishment cannot be turned away: it is inevitable; it is irrevocable.

How had the Syrians filled up the measure of their iniquities against God's people, Israel? They had threshed Gilead with iron threshing instruments. Gilead was the territory east of the Jordan belonging to the tribes of Reuben, Gad, and the half tribe of Manasseh, a region especially open to attack from Syria on the north. The atrocity mentioned here—the tearing and mangling of bodies with iron threshing sledges—was perpetrated by the Syrian king, Hazael of Damascus, in his oppression of Israel under Jehu and Jehoahaz. (Note 2 Ki 10:32, 33; 13:3-7.)

The prophets of Scripture are the inspired commentators on the historical events of the Word of God. In each case the punishment is set forth as fire, that of war and destruction. (See Jer 49:27.) Hazael and Ben-hadad were two of the most grievous oppressors of Israel. The Ben-hadad referred to may possibly be both Syrians of that name, but probably the son of Hazael (2 Ki 13:3) is meant rather than the Ben-hadad who was slain by Hazael (2 Ki 8:7, 15). Breaking the bar meant the breaking of the gate of the city and the consequent entrance of the besieging enemy. The Valley of Aven is probably the present day Bekaa, between Lebanon and Antilibanus, of which Heliopolis (Baalbek) was the most important city. Beth Eden is a district near Haran, and Kir is an Assyrian province on the banks of the river of the same name. The judgment predicted here came through the Assyrian Tiglath-pileser who drove the Syrians to Kir (2 Ki 16:9). Thus Syria was to be visited for her cruelties to Israel, and especially would the blow fall upon Damascus, that renowned city of which the Arabs have said: "If there is a garden of Eden on earth, it is Damascus; and if in Heaven, Damascus is like it on earth."

DOOM OF PHILISTIA

In Amos 1, the reference to Gaza includes all Philistia, as is clear from the mention of Ashdod, Ashkelon, and Ekron in verse 8. Gath is omitted from the mention of the cities of the Philistine Pentapolis probably because it had already been destroyed by King Uzziah (2 Ch 26:6). The sin of the Philistines was that they took an entire captivity, leaving no one, and delivered them up to Edom, probably Israel's most inveterate enemy. Wholesale expatriation of an entire region, and not the exiling of a few war captives, is meant. Some understand it was for commercial purposes.

If we compare this passage with Joel 3, we shall see that the matter was accomplished after this manner: the Philistines sold a portion of prisoners to the Edomites and the remainder to the Phoenicians who in turn sold them to the Greeks. Then, as now, it seemed highly profitable to the enemies of Israel to make merchandise of the people of God.

What historical events are alluded to here? It has been suggested that these cruelties took place in the reign of King Ahaz when the Philistines invaded the cities of the lowland and the south of Judah. (See 2 Ch 28:18.) It is more probable that the prophet is referring to the invasion of Judah by the Philistines in the reign of Jehoram (2 Ch 21:16). Decimation of the population of Philistia will be the answer of God for these misdeeds. Turning His hand against Ekron speaks of His visiting them again with the same judgment.

WRATH UPON PHOENICIA

The prophecy against Tyre is meant for all Phoenicia. The crime in this instance is the same as that of the Philistines—the selling of prisoners of war as slaves. The Phoenicians were known as a great commercial people and must have disposed of the prisoners of war to more than one nation. The prisoners may have been taken in the course of the wars of Israel with Hazael and Ben-hadad of Syria, from whom the Phoenicians could have obtained them.

These transactions were all the more grievous when perpetrated by the Tyrians, because there had been a brotherly covenant of long standing between King Hiram of Tyre and David and Solomon. (Note carefully 2 Sa 5:11; 1 Ki 5:2-6, 15-18; 9:11-14.) Moreover, no king of Israel or Judah ever made war upon Phoenicia. The judgment announced in verse 10 was made good when parts of Tyre were burned with missiles of the Chaldeans under Nebuchadnezzar.

PUNISHMENT FOR AMMON

The Ammonites, also related to Israel, had attacked Jabesh-gilead under Nahash. (Compare 1 Sa 11:1.) They also joined the Chaldeans in their invasion of Judah for plunder (2 Ki 24:2). But the atrocities touched upon in verse 13 are not mentioned in the Old Testament historical accounts. They were carried out for the purpose of expansion. It is the new but ever old cry of extermination for expansion, for *Lebensraum*, as the Germans call it.

The tables will be turned and Ammon will be the object of the foreign invader. Rabbah (Deu 3:11), the capital city, called by the Greeks Philadelphia after Ptolemy Philadelphus of Egypt and now known as Amman, will be visited by invasion and captivity. (See Jer 49:3.) What a refutation is a chapter like this to the contention that Israel's God was considered a tribal or national God. He is Lord of all the earth as the Scriptures maintain throughout.

HANDS OFF ISRAEL!

Chapter 1 speaks with divine eloquence of the danger involved in touching Israel, the apple of God's eye, for harm. God has not only reproved kings for their sakes (Ps 105:14) but nations as well, as this portion of His Word so amply attests. Is it not patent that the Word of God contains its own authentication of the promise of God that He would curse him that cursed the seed of Abraham? What a commentary is this chapter, with many others which could be added here, on the faithfulness of God to carry out every word He has ever uttered. Remember also that the other portion of the promise is still true as well: God blesses those who bless Abraham's seed.

THE SINS OF ISRAEL

INDIGNATION AGAINST MOAB

The second chapter of Amos' prophecy carries on the word of condemnation against the nations which was begun in the first chapter. The indignation of God is now stated to be against Moab. The climaxing sin of this nation was the burning of the bones of the king of Edom into lime. Vengeance was poured out even upon the dead. It reveals a spirit of revenge which will not stop even at death.

This incident is not recorded in the historical books of the Old Testament. It has been suggested, and it is probable, that it took place at the time of the war between Jehoram of Israel and Jehoshaphat of Judah, with the king of Edom, against the Moabites. (See 2 Ki 3:26-27.) For such a display of unrestrained wrath, God will visit Moab with the fire of destruction. Kerioth, one of the prominent cities of Moab, will find her palaces consumed by fire. (Cp. Is 15:1; Jer 48:24, 41, 45.) The death of Moab with tumult, shouting, and the sound of the trumpet, as well as the cutting off of the judge and princes, was realized when Nebuchadnezzar completely subjugated Moab; from that time it no longer existed as a nation.

SINS OF JUDAH

The nations are punished for sins against the laws of nature, conscience, and natural feeling; Judah and Israel are visited because they sinned against the revealed will of God. (Note the important truths set forth in Ro 2:12, 14, 15.) Verses 4 and 5 of Amos 2 are directed against Judah, while the remainder of the book of Amos is addressed to Israel. God is not partial, so even His people, when guilty, must be judged.

The cycle of prophecies was meant to end with the people of God. They had what the heathen nations never had—the Law of the Lord in the commandments of Moses. But they paid no heed to it and cast it from them, failing utterly to keep the righteous statutes given therein. They engaged themselves with lies, their false idols, which led them farther astray from the way of God's choice. (Note Ps 40:4 and Jer 16:19-20.)

Bad example has a way of perpetuating itself, so we find that the fathers of Amos' contemporaries also followed in their day the same worthless idols. Preceding generations were guilty of the same sins. The judgment pronounced in each case is that of fire (1:4, 7, 10, 12, 14; 2:2, 5). The palaces of Jerusalem were devoured by fire when the hosts of Nebuchadnezzar captured the city in 586 BC.

TRANSGRESSIONS OF ISRAEL

The iniquities of Israel are now set forth in all their heinous details. God cannot gloss over the failures and sins of Israel, if she is to realize the gravity of her spiritual decline and turn in true penitence to the Lord from whom she has so grievously revolted. The Scriptures tell us that he who oppresses or mocks the poor reproaches His Maker (Pr 14:31; 17:5), and God surely espouses the cause of His poor and righteous ones.

In Israel, because of the insatiable greed of unrighteous judges, the one who had a righteous cause was condemned by the judge for the sake of a bribe. This violated the clear prohibition of Deuteronomy 16:19 and other passages. For the paltriest sum, even a pair of shoes, the tribunals of that day could be bought (see also 8:6). The sin of despising the poor is mentioned several times in this prophetic book: 2:6, 7; 4:1; 5:11; and 8:6.

The ungodly are further said to pant after the dust of the earth on the head of the poor. What does this mean? Various have been the explanations of this part of the verse. It has been suggested that the prophet is saying that the wicked bring the poor so low by oppression that the latter cast dust on their heads in mourning. For this custom in mourning, widespread throughout the East, note 2 Samuel 1:2 and Job 2:12 among others. Another view is that the ungodly tread the poor in the dust of the earth under their feet. Still others think the creditors begrudged the poor even the dust which they, as mourners, cast on their heads. Probably the first position is the best; that is, the unrighteous cannot rest until they have brought the poor down to the very depths of sorrow. And because the meek are not forward in presenting and maintaining their just case, they are taken advantage of and their cause is perverted. (Cp. Is 10:2.)

Their greed is accompanied by unbridled lust. Father and son go to the same maiden, probably one of the prostitutes attached to idol temples, such as that of the goddess Astarte. Invariably spiritual departure from the Lord is followed by moral departure as well. The result is, whether by intent or not, that the holy name of the Lord is profaned. God is disgraced in the vile actions of His people. (See 2 Sa 12:14.)

As children of God in this wicked world, we are exhorted of God, since we have named the name of Christ, to depart from iniquity (2 Ti 2:19). We either grace the grace that saved us or we disgrace the grace that saved us.

But Amos has not concluded his indictment of the guilty ones in the Northern Kingdom of Israel. He appears to have left the worst for last as a kind of climax. The wicked were laying themselves down beside every altar upon clothes taken in pledge. The outer garment is meant. Exodus 22:25-27 and Deuteronomy 24:12-13 commanded that this be returned before sunset, so that the poor could have it as his covering for the cool night. They not only refuse to return the garment but lie on it themselves and that in idol temples (I so understand the words *every altar*, for this could hardly refer to the central temple of God in Palestine).

The dastardly character of this sin (or rather several sins compounded) grows on one the more it is contemplated. When those who know the light commit sin, they often go to greater extremes than those who know not God at all. Light rejected ever results in greater night. The wine which these revelers drink in their idolatrous and obscene feasts to their god (not "God") has been bought with the money which they procured through unjust fines. Oppression was rampant and they were speeding on to judgment at the hands of an infinitely righteous and holy God.

GOD'S FORMER MERCIES

To bring out by marked contrast their base ingratitude to the Lord, Amos enumerates some of the gracious benefits which Israel has received at the hand of the Lord. The benefits of God to Israel are in themselves accusations against the nation for their sins. Rebellious though they were, the Lord had destroyed the Amorite (Jos 24:8) before them.

The Amorites were the most powerful of all the nations inhabiting the land of Canaan, and in this verse they probably stand representatively for all. (Note how this nation is singled out repeatedly in Gen 15:16; 48:22; Deu 1:20; Jos 7:7.) The description given of them is vivid—tall as the cedars and strong as the oaks—and shows that the report of the unbelieving spies was right as far as outward appearances were concerned. (See Num 13:22, 32, 33.) Their trouble was that they reckoned not on the power of God, as did faithful Caleb and Joshua. Though the enemies were giants in stature, God destroyed both their fruits and their roots, in a word, utterly. For the same figure compare Ezekiel 17:9 and Malachi 4:1.

Moreover, the destruction of the enemy in the land had been preceded by the favor of God in liberating the nation from Egyptian slavery and in preserving them for forty years through the wilderness wastes (Ps 44:3). To climax all these bounties, God raised up of their sons, when dwelling in the land, those who were to bear the message of His will to the nation, the prophets, and He gave of their young men to be Nazirites. (See Num 6.) God had done all to provide for their instruction in the truth and in His will and for the maintenance of purity and holiness of life in the nation.

Though the vow of the Nazirite was of one's free will, yet it is said that God raised them up because the desire and impulse to such action came from Him. In these men, young men at that, God gave Israel extraordinary examples of purity and complete dedication to the Lord.

Now the prophet turns and asks in point-blank manner: "Is it not even thus?" "Will you dare to deny or dispute this?" Did Israel delight in these mercies of God and render the Lord grateful service? The Word of God gives the devastating answer: they tempted the Nazirite to breach of his holy vow and to unfaithfulness and sought to silence the message of the prophet of God. Compare 7:12-14 (Amos experienced this very thing in his own ministry) and Jeremiah 11:21. Could brazenness and defiance extend further? No. So Amos foretells the hour of their visitation.

INESCAPABLE JUDGMENT

The opinion has been given that verses 13 to 15 tell of a destructive earthquake. The visitation is to be war as is clear from the actions pictured in the remaining verses of the chapter. Not all verses in either the Old or New Testaments are as easy of translation as they appear in our versions. Does verse 13 in the original speak of Israel being pressed under the Lord as a cart is pressed that is full of sheaves? Or is it the Lord who is pressed under them in that manner? (See the ASV margin for the latter.) Surely it is the first view, for the second would give an inelegant picture of the Lord, to say the least. The thought of the verse is that Israel has been running the gamut of sin in departing from the Lord; she has owned and obeyed no check or restraint to her wayward life. Now God will press her down in her place; He will hem her way in so that she will not be able to escape. The swift, the strong, and the mighty will be helpless before the judgment of the Lord. Flight, force, and deliverance will fail these men in the hour of need. The trained bowman, the foot soldier, and the horseman (all these indicate, incidentally, that the scourge is that of war) will find their prowess unavailing in this calamity. Even the bravest among the mighty will be able to save only his life. In short, none will escape the Assyrian army when they come to carry out God's purposes of judgment upon His sinful people. The rod of God's anger will fall and no one will be able to evade it in that fearful day.

"IS IT NOT EVEN THUS?"

If the prophecies of Amos thus far reveal anything, they show clearly that their central message is this: there is no turning back of the judgment of God after His repeated offers of grace and blessing are spurned or refused. And this is true today. It is rightly called the day and age of grace, for the evident reason that God is offering graciously eternal life and glory to those in Israel and throughout the world who will trust the Lord Jesus Christ for their salvation. Apart from God's offer there is only the hopeless doom of perdition.

PRIVILEGE AND RESPONSIBILITY

GOD'S CHOICE OF ISRAEL

Amos directs his prophecies primarily, but not exclusively, to Israel, the Northern Kingdom, as did the prophet Hosea. The third chapter begins with the call, "Hear this word." (For the same expression see 4:1; 5:1; also note 3:13.) All Israel, the whole family that God brought up from Egypt, is addressed, though Ephraim is especially in view.

What is the message of surpassing importance that both parts of the nation must hear? God says that of all the families on the earth (note the contrast with "family" of v. 1) He has known only His people Israel. To know them in the sense of this passage is to choose them, to set them apart for His own purposes. God took them to be His people and accorded them special privileges for testimony. (Read carefully such passages as Ps 1:6; 144:3; and Jn 10:14 for this meaning of *know*. For the special choice of Israel, see such passages as Ex 19:5; Deu 4:20; 7:6; Ps 147:19 20.) We may have expected the prophet to declare that, because God has chosen Israel, He will overlook their failures and sins. The unknowing and the unbelieving often accuse God of such partial dealings with His people Israel, as though He could deny His holy character no matter who is involved. The Word of God states the opposite of man's inferences: because God has taken Israel into a place of intimacy with Himself, He will all the more assuredly visit upon her head all her iniquities.

Nowhere in the Bible is a more vital and basic principle enunciated. The prophet is saying that punishment is commensurate with privilege. Of the one to whom much is given, much is expected. Judgment must begin at the house of God (1 Pe 4:17). The nearer we are to the Lord in relationship, the more is faithfulness required of us. Even the laxness of other believers can never be our standard.

The prophet thunders against his people that the choice of God was never meant as a cloak for wickedness. Because God had chosen the Church in New Testament times to be His channel of blessing through this age of grace, did not preclude His visiting wickedness with judgment when it manifested itself. See the case of Ananias and Sapphira in Acts 5:1-11. The angels of heaven who sinned against the greatest light have no redemption provided for them at all (2 Pe 2:4 and Jude 6). Great is the blessing of nearness to God, but great also is the responsibility of living in conformity with such light.

JUDGMENT FOLLOWS SIN

In verses 3 to 8 the prophet establishes his right to announce the judgment of God on his contemporaries. The aim of this series of seven questions is to show the people the relation between the prophet's utterances and the events of the day. In the natural world, the realm of nature, nothing happens by accident or chance; so in the sphere of God's dealings there is always a cause for every effect.

The first question is: Can two people walk together except they appoint a specified time and place, agreeable to both? When we see two walking together, it is taken for granted that they have had a previous arrangement and are of like mind. The former fact is the effect, while the latter is the cause. Transferred into the realm of Israel's spiritual condition, God asks how He can walk with Israel and look in favor upon her when she is walking in sin. At one time God walked with her (Jer 3:14) because they were agreed, but now the ways of Israel and the way of the Lord are so diverse that there can be no fellowship between them.

The second question is: does a lion roar in the forest when he has caught nothing? Amos knew well the habits of the lion and understood the lion's roar to mean that the prey had been caught. In like manner God threatens only (Joel 3:16; Amos 1:2) when He is preparing to punish. The same thought is expressed by a different figure in Matthew 24:28.

A related question is: will the young lion (who remains in his lair) cry out of his den, if the old lion has taken nothing? As a matter of fact, when the old lion approaches with the prey, the young lion is aroused. The underlying truth is that, if Israel's sins did not merit and call forth judgment, the prophet would not be crying out against her. The threatening predictions of the prophet are the effect, while the cause is the sinful state of the nation.

The next question is just as pointed: will a snare spring up from the ground where it has been placed without something having been caught in it? So the instruments of God's judgment will find their object, because they have gone in the way of their sin. The first clause in verse 5 states the same question as the latter part but from a slightly different viewpoint. The answer is exactly the same in both instances, and in both cases the prophet still has sinning Israel in mind.

A hint that the trumpet of war will yet be blown in the land is given in the following question: will the trumpet be blown in a city and the people not be afraid? The nation was well acquainted with the trumpet for festal gatherings (Num 10:2, 7; Joel 2:15) as well as that for warfare (Num 10:9; Joel 2:1). And who was it that would not be filled with fear and forebodings when the alarm for the war was sounded? Who among Israel should not fear now when Amos is sounding the alarm of the approach of God's swift instruments of visitation?

The last question in the series has suffered much from misinterpretations. It has been made to teach that God is the cause of evil, that is, moral evil. Such a position runs counter to all the teachings of the Scriptures. (Note Ja 1:13, 17.) The query is: does evil befall a city without the hand of the Lord being in it? The difficulty has arisen (as in so many other cases) because of a failure to recognize that the word *evil* has more than one meaning depending upon its use. Here it does not mean moral evil, but calamity. (Study carefully Gen 19:19; 44:34; Ex 32:14; Is 45:7; and Eze 7:5.) In short, God is the One who brings your trials and calamities upon you for your sins.

The secrets of His dealings He reveals to His servants the prophets; thus they can speak forth the mind and purpose of God. God warned Noah of the flood; He told Abraham of the destruction of Sodom and Gomorrah (mark Gen 18:17 with Jn 15:15); He forewarned Joseph of the seven years of famine; and so with His servants down through the centuries of Israel's history. Even our Lord Jesus warned the apostles of the coming desolation of Jerusalem (Lk 21:20-24).

Just as surely as there is fear when the lion roars, then, there must be prophesying when the Lord Jehovah speaks. The prophet cannot but prophesy. He must obey God no matter how the people react to his message. Amos prophesied, as did all the prophets of God, because he was impelled by divine constraint to do it. What surer authority did the prophet need? None, because he had the authority for his message from the omnipotent God Himself.

OPPRESSIONS OF SAMARIA

The Lord now addresses Himself to His prophets that they may spread this word upon the palaces of Ashdod and of Egypt. It was not only customary in the East to assemble on the flat roofs of the houses, but from that vantage point, especially the highest roofs of the palaces, the invitation could go out broadcast through all the land.

The nations are bidden to come together upon the mountains of Samaria to behold what tumults and oppressions are to be found in that city. Ashdod stands here as representative for all of Philistia. Samaria was built on one mountain (1 Ki 16:24), but there were other mountains surrounding the city. From these mountains surrounding Samaria, men could see what was transpiring within the city. If these pagan nations steeped in idolatry condemn Israel, then how much more the righteous God?

The great tumults were occasioned by the oppression of the poor. See Isaiah 5:7 for the same truth. The sad part of it all is that the people no longer know to do right; sin has blinded their ability to discern (Jer 4:22). It was so long since they had done good, that they were out of practice. Sin's blinding power is only too real, as all know who have been enlightened by the Spirit of God.

The palaces of Samaria were full of those things gained by violence and robbery. (Note Pr 10:2.) The punishment is now stated in abrupt and vivid language: "An enemy, round about the land." The abruptness of the text brings out the idea of suddenness and presents the threat in bolder relief. Those very palaces which stored up plunder (see v. 10) will in turn be plundered. Men's sins carry with them their own dire punishments. The fulfillment of all this warning is found in 2 Kings 17:5.

Yet in wrath God remembers mercy, so He rescues from the destruction a small remnant—likened here to two legs or a piece of an ear—of all that are living in ease in Samaria. The picture is that of a shepherd trying to save from the devouring lion even the most insignificant parts of the sheep, because of the shepherd's love for his own sheep. Only such a small part will remain of those who are living in extravagance and luxury (note also 6:1, 4) in the capital city.

The corner of the couch or the divan is the most comfortable and is the place of honor. The mention of silken cushions, made of costly stuffs, adds to the picture of careless self-indulgence. There is the possibility of reading the last part of verse 12 as "and in Damascus on a bed." The reason is that the same letters are employed in the original to spell *damask* or the material, or the city of Damascus. The name of the city would then be parallel in thought to Samaria. But how did the people of the northern tribes get to Damascus? It is suggested that at the time of the Assyrian invasion, the city was in the power of the Israelites, already conquered by Jeroboam II, as stated in 2 Kings 14:28. After the city had been taken by

the Northern Kingdom, probably many residents of the northern tribes
went there to live.

THE DAY OF VISITATION

The same ones as in verse 9 are called upon to testify against the house
of Jacob, all twelve tribes. Mark the accumulation of names for God in
order to bring out the solemnity of the declaration and the assurance of its
fulfillment. The altars of Bethel, which were supposed to be a refuge for
them, would be the first to suffer from God's visitation. The golden calves
are here in view. (See 1 Ki 12:32; 13:2.) Amos, like Hosea, traces all their
calamity to their departure into idolatry. With idolatry cut off, their own
personal home life will also be destroyed. The winter houses and the
summer houses (of the nobility and rich as well as of the royalty) together
with many houses will be brought to a sad end. Homes, sumptuously dec-
orated with walls, doors, and ceilings of inlaid ivory, will suffer the same
fate as the rest. For Ahab's house of ivory see 1 Kings 22:39; also Psalm
45:8. Prosperity abused and misused can only issue in utter and irreparable loss.

PREPARE, O ISRAEL!

"YE KINE OF BASHAN"

The fourth chapter of Amos' prophecy begins with the same call to
hear which we met in the previous chapter. The address is now directed
to the kine of Bashan.

Bashan is that territory east of the Jordan River between Mount Her-
mon and the mountains of Gilead. The kine of Bashan were noted for
their well-fed and strong condition, for the pastures of this region were
lush. (Cp. Deu 32:14; Ps 22:12; and Eze 39:18.)

Some students of this passage think, although feminine forms of expression are used here, that the nobles of Samaria are meant by the
prophet. They hold that the feminine is employed only to show the
effeminacy of the aristocracy of the land. We prefer to see, with many
others, the luxury-loving and extravagant women of the capital of Samaria in this reference. Such a usage is not contrary to prophetic Scriptures. See Isaiah's denunciation of the wanton women of Zion in Isaiah
3:16-26, as well as 32:9-13. That land is not far from the judgment of
God whose womanhood is degraded, and such was Samaria in the days of
our prophet.

In order to enjoy their luxuries these women oppressed and crushed the
poor. The form of expression used shows this was their habitual action.
Their lords, that is, their husbands (Gen 18:12), they continually urged

to provide them with the needs for their drunken revelries and debaucheries. Mark how oppression and idolatry (see v. 4) go hand in hand. Because of such contempt for the will of God and because of the profanation of His name, He swore by His holiness (for He can swear by no greater) that they would be carried off into exile.

This deportation is given under the figure of a fisherman catching fish with fishhooks. They will be helpless and completely at the mercy of their captors. Captives were led by their conquerors by a hook through the nose. See 2 Kings 19:28 and 2 Chronicles 33:11 (note the margin of the ASV for this verse); also Jeremiah 16:16; Ezekiel 29:4; and Habakkuk 1:15.

The residue mentioned in this passage refers to what is left over from the taking away with hooks, not the posterity of the prophet's contemporaries. In the siege of the city the women, driven as cattle, will go out at the breaches of the city walls, broken open by the enemy. Each one will go straight before her, not allowed by the enemy to turn to either side and rushing headlong to escape the terror and death in the city.

The latter part of verse 3 is admittedly very obscure. The difficulty arises from the fact that a word is used (the Hebrew *haharmonah*) which occurs nowhere else in the Old Testament. This accounts for the numerous and varied views presented for the explanation of the passage. Suggested translations are "the Rimmon image," "Hadadrimmon," "the mountains of Armenia," "the mountains of Monah," or "palace." With so little evidence upon which to proceed and with such variety of opinions, we do well to avoid dogmatism on this point. Probably what is meant is that in order to facilitate their flight from the enemy they will cast themselves into a certain land or district which they hope will afford them the necessary refuge for the hour. More than this we cannot say, except to add that most recent biblical atlases know nothing of a site called Harmon. The thought of the prophet, however, is quite clear: exile will be the portion of the pleasure-loving, poor-oppressing, unfeeling women of Samaria.

MISDIRECTED ZEAL

Amos turns now from solemn declaration to biting and bitter irony. He invites the whole of the kingdom, not merely the women, to come to Bethel and transgress and to frequent Gilgal and multiply transgression. On the very surface it is evident that the words are ironical, because nowhere in the Bible does God reveal Himself as countenancing sin or inviting to it.

Bethel and Gilgal are specifically mentioned because of the manner in which they had perverted the places of most sacred memories to the nation. (See Gen 35 and Jos 5:1-9.) Verses 4 and 5 give a true picture of the way in which the people adhered to their idol practices and yet were careful in keeping certain appointments ordained by the Law of Moses. They were bringing their sacrifices every morning as the Law had commanded (Num 28:3-4). They were adhering to the letter, while transgressing it by their calf-worship. God is here giving them up to their own idolatrous worship.

They were also paying their tithes every three years (not every three days as the ASV suggests), conforming in this also to the regulations of the Law. (Cp. Deu 14:28; 26:12.)

There are those who understand the next exhortation to offer a sacrifice of thanksgiving of that which is leavened as contrary to the precepts of the Mosaic law. A study of the Levitical regulations will show that frankincense was laid on the meal offering (Lev 2:1, 2, 8), as commanded here, and that leavened bread was commanded to be offered with the sacrifice of thanksgiving (Lev 7:12-13). Thus far all that has been stated shows they were unusually meticulous in the carrying out of the details of the laws for worship. True, their proclamation and publishing of freewill offerings (see Mt 6:2) savors of self-will in their worship, for he states definitely that such pleased them. They were intent on ultimately pleasing themselves instead of God (so in Zec 7:5, 6).

But the emphasis is scarcely on these shortcomings. The words are meant to convey that everything was outwardly in order and done according to law, yet in the doing of them they were multiplying transgression. Why? Because at the same time they were steeped in all the debasing forms of idol worship. God is not pleased with the divided heart, with the limping between two opinions. He is the only God and brooks no rival in worship. Thus, though they were going through the rounds of worship, they were sinning because their hearts were not wholly unto the Lord. (See Eze 20:39 and Mt 23:32.)

GOD'S JUDGMENTS UNHEEDED

Since their gifts to God were so displeasing to Him, He gives them chastisements in return. The list of chastisements recorded in verses 6 to 11 reveals not only the obstinacy and sinfulness of Israel, but the unremitting and exhaustless love of God. It is a love that will not let the loved one go. And the punishments were all intended to prevent greater chastisements. Yet at the end of each visitation it is stated that they had not returned to the Lord in spite of all His dealings. Note the repetition of "yet have ye not returned unto me, saith Jehovah" in verses 6, 8, 9, 10, 11.

We are reminded in this recital of Isaiah 9:13; Jeremiah 5:3; and Hosea 7:10.

The repetition by Amos marks the persistent opposition, bringing out forcefully their stubbornness and impenitence. The first calamity was famine which is described vividly as cleanness of teeth and want of bread. God had taken away the material necessities of life to bring them to their senses and to set aright the spiritualities of life. There is no need to seek for a historical confirmation of this in the historical books of the Old Testament, because God did this more than once. One example is to be found in 2 Kings 8:1. Though they hungered, yet they sought not the Lord in repentance and faith.

The second visitation was drought. God withheld rain three months before the time of harvest. This is disastrous. Reference is made to the latter rain of the spring which is so vital for the development of the corn and the grain for a bountiful harvest. But the withholding was not universal: it rained on one city and not upon another. This was purposeful to show that the giving or withholding was not by chance, but by the sovereign act and choice of God. Scarcity of water compelled the inhabitants of the cities visited by drought to go long distances for the necessary water to carry on life.

Another stroke of judgment was the blasting and mildew, the very judgments predicted in Deuteronomy 28:22 for disobedience to the Law of God. Blasting is the effect of the withering east wind from the dry desert. Note Genesis 41:6. In the mildew (from excessive drought, not moisture) the ears became yellow without grain.

To climax this a locust plague devoured vineyards, fig trees, and olive trees (cp. Deu 28:39-40, 42). Life was undoubtedly being made unbearable from the physical standpoint alone, but the impenitent heart stores up for itself wrath unto the day of judgment. See Revelation 16:21 for the effect of the judgments of the Great Tribulation upon defiant hearts. The sad refrain continues that for all this they did not return to the Lord. Like Pharaoh of old they steeled their hearts the harder against the wooings of God.

Next, the plague after the manner of Egypt, where it was native, was sent upon them (Deu 28:27, 60). And the choice of the manhood of the nation was slain in prolonged and recurring warfare; their boasted cavalry was carried away into exile. So great was the number of the slain on the battlefields that their unburied corpses filled the air with stench. Surely they would turn to the Lord by this time, but the record states that they continued in their obdurate disobedience to the Lord.

Last, Amos recalls that they underwent overturnings and desolations comparable only to God's overthrow of the wicked cities of Sodom and Gomorrah. Some think reference is made to the earthquake of 1:1, but the information at hand is insufficient to decide definitely. Probably what is meant is a summary of all the previous visitations. (Cp. Is 1:9.) So trying were the inflictions of the Lord's hand that the people narrowly escaped complete destruction. (See Zec 3:2 and 1 Co 2:15.)

For the fifth and last time, Amos notes that even so the people were not minded to return to the Lord.

THE COMING CALAMITY

Now the prophet is prepared to declare to Israel the consequences of such opposition to the Lord and His will. Because all the previous chastisements did not produce in them the fruits of repentance and faith, God says, "Thus will I do unto thee, O Israel." But the prophet never states what the punishment is to be! The undefined character and uncertainty connected with the coming calamity make the fear and apprehension all the greater. Since they did not heed God's providential warnings, they must now meet Him face to face. It will not be indirectly by way of His judgments, but directly, person to person.

Some interpreters understand this warning to mean that they are to prepare to encounter God as their enemy and not for the purpose of reconciliation. Although this is surely a possible meaning, a probable explanation is that the prophet is holding out to them the last and final warning. They had better get ready to meet God Himself, not His judgments, and give Him an answer for their impenitence. Who this God is that they are to meet is set forth in majestic terms. He is the omnipotent Creator, forming the mountains and creating the wind; He is the omniscient God who knows every thought of man; He is the ruler over all nature who can turn the morning light in due course into darkness; and He, the mighty Lord God of hosts, is the sovereign over all the places of the earth. The five participles of the original bring out the majesty of God as constantly operative in His created universe of matter and man. This is the Mighty God whom Israel must be ready to meet!

EXHORTATION TO REPENTANCE
DIRGE OVER ISRAEL

There is a note of finality about the conclusion of the fourth chapter which would cause one to believe that all was over for Israel. But this chapter shows that in the midst of warnings, God, in His infinite love, holds out the brightest promises for obedience and faith.

The fifth chapter begins with a lamentation over the ruin of Israel.

Amos views the Northern Kingdom as though the stroke of judgment from God had already overtaken the ungodly. The ruin is complete. The virgin Israel is fallen with no prospect of recovery; there is no one to whom she can look to aid her in her present plight. She is addressed as virgin, not because of the beauty of the land nor because of her hitherto unconquered condition (see Is 23:12), but because this is customary prophetic usage in personifying countries or states. (Note Is 47:1.)

We must beware that we do not misinterpret the word concerning Israel's rising no more. The statement has its emphasis in relation to the exile of Israel and not for the indefinite future ages, because this would deny the restoration of Israel (mark carefully Is 27:6), a glorious return of God's people abundantly attested in all the prophetic writings, as well in the New Testament as in the Old.

The invasion of the Assyrian will be costly in human life; only a tenth will be spared. This prophecy and others throughout Amos and the other prophetic books of the Old Testament show how literally God meant the warnings of Deuteronomy 28. Compare Deuteronomy 28:62 with verse 3 of chapter 5. We have described for us, then, the utterly prostrate and helpless condition to which the Northern Kingdom was to be reduced by the Assyrian foe.

EXHORTATION TO SEEK THE LORD

Before the judgment falls there is still an opportunity for repentance and restoration. God is loath to close the door of grace and mercy. In Noah's day He waited (Gen 6:3; 1 Pe 3:20) one hundred and twenty years before He shut the door (Gen 7:16). Let us not be impatient with the patience of God if He tarries for the lost among Israel that they too may be saved to make up the Body of Christ with us.

The prophet's words are short (two words in the original) but freighted with blessing for those who would hear. The exhortation to seek recurs in verse 5 (in the negative), 6, and 14. Again and again the love of God calls His wayward ones. It is the Lord they must seek and not the places of idolatrous worship—Bethel, Gilgal, and Beersheba.

The first two cities have been before us in the previous chapter (v. 4) to which are added Beersheba, hallowed by memories of the past (especially Abraham, Gen 21:33) but now a place to which pilgrimages were made for the worship of idols. (See 8:14 of this prophecy.) Since this town was about twenty-five miles south of Hebron, one can get an inkling of the territory that had to be covered to reach this spot. Amos testifies that to seek after these idol shrines is to pursue that which is to come to nought.

Again the call is repeated to seek the Lord and live; otherwise, the Lord would break forth as fire (we saw how often this was the judgment in the first chapters of this book) upon the house of Joseph. God is likened to fire in Isaiah 10:17; Lamentations 2:3; and Hebrews 12:29. The house of Joseph is a less frequent name for the ten tribes whose most important tribe was Ephraim, the son of Joseph (Ob 18; Zec 10:6).

Of the many guilty ones in the kingdom, the unrighteous judges are singled out, for they have turned justice into wormwood (6:12), that which is bitterly wrong. Justice is sweet, but injustice is bitter, obnoxious, and injurious. By their acts they have cast righteousness to the ground. Now, in contrast to their unjust ways they are reminded to consider Him, the righteous Judge, who is also the omnipotent Lord. He is altogether sovereign in nature: the Pleiades and Orion (well-known constellations appearing in Job 9:9; 38:31) are the work of His hands; He brings about the changes from day to night and vice versa; the floods (with a possible allusion to the Flood of Noah's day) are in His control. He also can bring sudden and irreparable destruction upon ungodly men and their carnal reliances. It is Jehovah with whom they have to do.

THE EVIL TIME IN SAMARIA

The unjust judges of Samaria have grievously sinned against the Lord, for they are denounced once more. In the gate, the public place of assembly where tribunals were held, they hated such as reproved their ungodly ways and despised anyone who spoke uprightly. The poor were trampled under foot and had to pay for justice if they were to obtain it. They used taxes from the poor (possibly they took interest too, which was forbidden) on themselves, instead of returning it to the needy who could ill afford to pay it. As a result they, the judges, were able to have homes of hewn stone which were costly dwellings (Is 9:10), for houses were usually made of sun-dried bricks.

But ill-gotten gain is never enjoyed and short-lived at the best. They would not dwell in their fine homes and would not enjoy the fruit of the vineyards they had planted. (See Deu 28:30, 39.) In the time of Israel's glorious restoration the reverse will be true (Is 65:21-22). The transgressions and sins of the unrighteous and bribed judges are called manifold and mighty. How God hates unjust judges! The times were so evil that it seemed the better part of prudence to keep silent concerning these outrages. Those who were wise spiritually knew that protests under such conditions could only make matters worse.

ENTREATY TO REPENTANCE

Yet again Amos beseeches them to seek good and not evil, so that they might live. Then would God be with them indeed, and not as they were falsely comforting themselves on the presence of God with them. Their claim was empty pretense based on the fact that outwardly they continued in the worship of the Lord. They are counselled to hate evil, love good, and do justice, so that the Lord may display His grace to the remnant of Joseph. Although Hazael and Benhadad had wrought great havoc in the Northern Kingdom (2 Ki 10:32-33; 13:3, 7), yet in the time of Joash and Jeroboam II all the conquered territory had been retaken, so that the kingdom was not at all restricted in extent. (Note 2 Ki 13:23-25; 14:26-28.)

This cannot refer to the ten tribes, then, in the time of Jeroboam II. The reference is to the coming judgment in which Israel will be reduced to a remnant. Isaiah speaks of the remnant from Judah in 6:13. For thoughts similar to those in verses 14 and 15 of chapter 5, see Isaiah 1:16-17.

THE BLOW HAS FALLEN

The judgment implied in verse 15 is now stated. In the light of verses 7, 10, 12, and because God knew that they would not repent, He proclaims the visitation. The combination of the names of God in verse 16 is unusual.

The mourning will be universal: in the country and field as well as in the city, death will strike. The city dweller will find the dead in all the streets, and the farmer will be called from the field to mourn for someone dead in his home. The professional mourners, who for hire displayed excessive grief (Jer 9:17-19), would find ample employment. The death wail will even penetrate the vineyards where ordinarily only the sound of rejoicing is heard. God would pass through the land. (Cp. Ex 12:12.) In Egypt it was a miraculous infliction of punishment; here in Israel it will be by the hand of the Assyrian.

THE DAY OF THE LORD

Amos now turns to those who desire the day of the Lord and pronounces woe upon them. There are some who see in this group scoffers (Is 5:19; Jer 17:15) who defiantly dare the Lord to do His worst. While this is certainly a possible explanation of the passage, we prefer to see here those who speak piously in the midst of their wicked actions. They are self-deceived hypocrites. In the midst of all their sin they still desired the Day of the Lord, because they thought the day would mean glory and victory and deliverance for all Israel regardless of their heart relationship to God. The prophet explains that the Day of the Lord is a time of darkness for the wicked (Joel 2:2) and not one of bright hope.

They had completely misconceived the nature of the Day of Jehovah. In any event judgment is inescapable. When they seek the Day of the Lord as an escape from their present troubles, they are going from one danger to a worse one. Amos in his rustic way pictures one escaping a disaster and then another, only to fall into a third and fatal one. The man who safely escape the lion does so only to be met by a bear whom he evades only to be mortally bitten by a serpent in the crevice of the wall in his own home when he leans to catch his breath. Inevitable doom, and no bright prospect, will be the portion of the ungodly in that time.

VAIN WORSHIP AND GOD'S SENTENCE

If they still expect their worship to stand them in good stead, they are deceived, for God hates and despises every detail of it. The divine abhorrence and disgust are emphatically expressed by the different terms showing God's vehement displeasure. We are reminded of a similar indictment of Israel's worship in Isaiah 1:10. It is not, let it be remembered, that God had not instituted the sacrificial ritual, but He could not abide it when the heart was not right. All the feasts, the solemn assemblies, the burnt offerings, the meal offerings, and the peace offerings roused the wrath of God. He commands them to remove the noise of their songs, a contemptuous appraisal of the songs played at the festivals by the Levites in the Temple worship when the sacrifices were offered (1 Ch 16:40-42; 23:5).

The worship at Bethel imitated that at Jerusalem in every important feature. They are advised to incorporate in their spiritual life those ele, ments so sorely needed—justice and righteousness. In abundant and perennial measure they are to find their place in the spiritual life stream of the nation; only then will God be satisfied. See 1 Samuel 15:22; Psalm 66:18; Hosea 6:6; and Micah 6:8 for this vital truth.

Among the most difficult verses in the prophecy of Amos are verses 25 and 26 of chapter 5, and they have been interpreted in various ways. Good men are divided as to the answer to the question in verse 25: some say the answer expected is an affirmative one, while others claim it is negative. In this controversy the record in the books of Moses must be decisive. There we find (see Ex 24:4, 6; Num 7; 19) that Israel very definitely and on more than one occasion offered sacrifices and offerings to God in the wilderness. It may be true that, once the generation in the wilderness was sentenced to die, they did so only half-heartedly or even intermittently, yet we cannot give a negative answer to the question of Amos. Says the prophet: "Yes, you did offer to the Lord, and yet you have borne the images also which you made of your gods." Thus Amos is charging Israel with observing the ritual of the Mosaic law at the same time that they followed idols, just as the contemporaries of the prophet in the Northern Kingdom were doing.

Israel from time immemorial had given herself to idolatry, and hoped at the same time that God would be pleased with her perfunctory round of ritual in the Temple. The two things were incompatible in Moses' time as they were in Amos' day. Their calf worship at Dan and Bethel was only the emergence of the idolatry of the calf in the wilderness. God's judicial sentence on this spiritual monstrosity is exile. The whole kingdom was to go into captivity beyond Damascus, clearly a reference to Assyria.

"AT EASE IN ZION"

WOE TO THE GODLESS LEADERS

Amos 6 begins with a "woe" which relates this portion to the woe pronounced in 5:18. It is pronounced upon those who are at ease in Zion. They are resting in a false security engendered by a heartless ritual and worship which they blindly believe will satisfy God. Thus they live in a reckless and careless manner.

What was true of those living in Zion was equally applicable to those who considered themselves secure in the mountain of Samaria. Nature had wonderfully endowed the city of Samaria with fortifications, indeed, of such a character that the Assyrian king could not take it before three years of siege (2 Ki 17:5-6). Both parts of the nation, Judah and Israel, are here in view, although the latter is emphasized in what follows.

"At ease in Zion"—what a vivid designation for those who are indifferent while in a place of privilege and rich blessing! The indictment of Amos is laid at the door of the notable leaders of the nation which is here designated as the chief of the nations. Their nation held a privileged and exalted position as the peculiar and chosen people of the Lord. To the godless and careless heads of this chosen nation, the people of Israel came for justice, help, and for the settlement of their controversies. The people come to their leaders, but they have a care only for self-indulgence, ease, and revelry.

The prophet now tells them to consider carefully Calneh, which was built by Nimrod in the land of Shinar (Gen 10:10; Is 10:9; and probably Eze 27:23) on the east bank of the Tigris River, although some identify it with Kullani, a few miles from Arpad; Hamath, the chief city of Syria which was situated on the Orontes River, later called Epiphania; and Gath, the principal city of Philistia.

Why are these cities pointed out by the prophet? We know that they were cities of spiritual corruption, but the prophet does not emphasize this fact. Some think the verse is understandable only if these kingdoms were on the decline. For Gath we are directed to 1:8 where it is not even mentioned among the cities that comprise Philistia. Calneh, too, is said to have lost its independence early and have been annexed to the Assyrian Empire. Hamath was subdued by Jeroboam II (2 Ki 14:25) and then by Assyria (2 Ki 18:34). These could not ward off the enemy, then how do you expect to? If they experienced the' judgment of God for their heathen ways, how can guilty Judah and Israel escape similar chastisement from the Lord? All about her God's people could see warning signs in the fate of other godless nations. See Nahum 3:8.

While such a view is entirely possible, we believe the prophet is probably pointing to the aforementioned nations and asking whether they (the nations) were better than these kingdoms (Judah and Israel)? The answer is negative, for none of the surrounding nations was comparable to Israel. Amos shows that she is rightly called the chief of the nations, because she is not lacking in greatness to any of the prosperous nations about her, in fact, excels them. Their border was not greater than that of the people of God. The prophet says, Look at these others and see just how favored (chief) you are.

LUXURY AND SIN

Being chief of the nations, how did Israel respond to the favor and blessing of God? With aversion and with desire to avoid the wrath of God she put far away the evil day, the day of God's punishment for her evil deeds (cp. Eze 12:22, 27). When men disregard the day of God's reckoning, they always feel free to indulge themselves in all manner of violence. So it was in Israel. Note Ecclesiastes 8:11 for this important truth.

The violence was manifested most clearly by the sitting of the unjust judges in judgment. While these judges were harsh in judging others, they were soft, indulgent, and licentious. Stretching themselves full length (so the original) on beds inlaid with ivory, they feasted to their hearts' content on the choicest and fattest of meats. Self-indulgence was given free rein. Here was extravagant and careless living in the midst of oppression and poverty. Indulgence of every appetite was the order of the day. And what would revelling be without song and wine? In Samaria they were not lacking either. Their songs were idle songs; they were mere nonsense. The drunkard is known by his song.

The ungodly leaders in Israel devised instruments of music for their special occasions and feastings. In this they were paralleling the genius of David, the great master musician of Israel. His ability was directed toward the praise of God; theirs was employed to celebrate the impious revelries in which they were engaged. David honored God with his music; they dishonored both God and man. Music which is degrading is a sure sign of an incipient national decline.

The hours of debauchery would not be complete if wine did not find its place among the celebrants. The regular cups were insufficient for their insatiable appetites, so they drank wine from bowls. It is the same word as for the bowls used for sacrificial purposes to catch the blood and then sprinkle it (Num 7:13). When they should have been sitting in sackcloth and ashes over the affliction of their people, that is, the low spiritual condition of the kingdom, they were anointing themselves with the most costly oils instead. In time of mourning (see 2 Sa 14:2) anointing was suspended.

CAPTIVITY FORETOLD

Those who were first in prominence and sin will be the first in punishment and captivity. Going with the first captives will make their shame all the more conspicuous. The revelry, the discordant noises and screeching, of the carousers will pass away. The Lord swears by Himself (cp. 4:2) that, because He abhors and hates the excellency of Jacob and his palaces, He will deliver over the entire city with all it possesses to the hand of the enemy. In Hosea 5:5 the word translated here "excellency" means pride or arrogance; in Amos 8:7 it clearly refers to God Himself as the object of Israel's glorying. In our text here it must refer, as being parallel to palaces, to the sanctuary and all that constituted the glory of the nation Israel. See Psalm 47:4 and Ezekiel 24:21.

The palaces, which were places of corruption and storehouses of plunder from the poor (3:10, 15), would suffer the stroke of God also. In the next two verses we are given a vivid picture of the plague such as usually followed war in the East, as elsewhere even to modern times. The prophet desires to show the comprehensive sweep of the judgment, so he assumes a house in which ten men live, and states that they shall all die. The number is a round number (Lev 26:26; Zec 8:23) but indicates a large house. What a fearful contrast, then, do we have here to the conditions portrayed in verses 4 to 6 of this chapter. There we have pictured for us luxury, licentiousness, and indifference, while here we have fear, stark tragedy, and universal death. How widespread the plague will be is noted for us in verse 10. When one's next of kin, to whom the duty of burial belonged, would come to carry the corpse out of the house to burn it, he would find but one remaining out of the ten who lived there formerly. And that last surviving one hidden away in the innermost recesses of the houses fearfully awaiting the hour when the plague would carry him away also.

In ancient Israel, in accordance with the words of Genesis 3:19, burial was the accepted method of disposal of the dead. In this the New Testament doctrine of the body concurs. Hence cremation was considered wrong and not countenanced (see Amos 2:1). But when God's judgment falls upon His people, there will be so many dead that they will not bury but burn them. The cases here and 1 Samuel 31:12 are exceptional cases. Here cremation is resorted to in order to prevent contagion; in 1 Samuel it was done to obviate further dishonor of the bodies of Saul and his sons by the Philistines.

When asked if there are others alive, the remaining occupant of the house will say there is none. Immediately he will be told to hold his peace for fear he would mention the name of the Lord in announcing the death of the others in the household, or in praising God for his own deliverance. Punishment will so work fear and despair in them all that they will refrain from even the mention of the name of the Lord (which should be their sole refuge in such an hour) lest further wrath come upon them.

By the command of the Lord both the great house and the small house will be smitten. From early times it has been suggested that the great house refers to the kingdom of the ten tribes and the small house to the kingdom of the two tribes. Although it is true that the Assyrians did break up the first and begin the work of destruction in the second, it is better to see here a reference to the judgment of God which will touch the homes of the rich and poor alike. (See 3:15.)

FALSE CONFIDENCE

Amos would now show how impossible it is for them in their sinful state to expect the protection, prospering, or blessing of God. Taking a figure from the realm of the rustic, he asks whether it is customary for horses to run upon a rock, or whether oxen are used there to plow. This is no more possible than that their evil deeds should issue in their blessing. How can they expect the favor of the Lord at the very time they are committing deeds displeasing to God? It is as absurd as trying to run horses on rocks.

Those who have delighted in unjust judgment, turning justice and righteousness into gall and wormwood, have prided themselves in and boasted themselves of that which is truly nothing, namely, their boasted strength. They have vaunted themselves that they have gotten them horns (a figure in Scripture for power, which it is to a number of animals) by their own strength. To what is the reference made? We have doubtless a reference to the military resources of Jeroboam II in which the kingdom of Israel was vainly trusting. Theirs was a false security doomed to catastrophe.

Again Amos foretells the coming of the nation which is the rod of God's chastisement for Israel, namely, Assyria, but the name is not given. The Assyrian army will do an effective work on Israel for they will smite the kingdom in its entire extent, from the entrance of Hamath, the pass between the Lebanons, to the brook of the Arabah, the Kidron. The latter was the southern boundary of the ten tribes, and falls into the Dead Sea south of Jericho. The prophet began the chapter with the pronouncement of woe, and concludes it with the execution of that woe.

GOD'S WORD AND MAN'S OPPOSITION

THE VISION OF THE LOCUSTS

Chapter 7 begins the third division of the book: (1) oracles of judgment on the nations, chapters 1 and 2; (2) threatening prophecies on Israel, chapters 3 to 6; and (3) a series of five visions of judgment, concluding with ultimate blessing. The first four visions have practically the same introductory formula. (See 7:1, 4, 7, and 8:1.)

Some students of this prophecy understand these visions to speak figuratively of the three invasions of the Assyrians under Pul, Tiglath-pileser, and finally Shalmaneser. But the form of the visions and the context would lead us to take the visions as representing actual occurrences in the corporate life of Israel. Nor are the judgments portrayed in the first two visions prospective; they are better considered as actual and taking place in the time and hour in which Amos was prophesying and ministering.

Amos was shown the Lord as He was forming locusts to plague the land after the king's mowings at the beginning of the shooting up of the latter growth. This is not necessarily the same plague mentioned in chapter 4, for locust are plagues frequent in Palestine, occurring about every seven years. The king's mowings evidently refer to the tribute which the people paid to the king from the first harvest. (Cp. 1 Ki 4:7 and 18:5.)

In Palestine two crops a year were usual. Since the first mowings were the king's, the people depended of necessity upon the second crop for their own sustenance, and it was this harvest which was threatened by the locust plague sent by God. God uses nature in His moral government of His people for their correction.

The language of verse 2 would appear to preclude the conclusion that the locusts here speak of an invading army as they do in the prophecy of Joel; however, some do so interpret it.

When the locusts had consumed all the grass of the land, the prophet betook himself to intercessory prayer. Prayer alone could divert the disaster, and the man of God prays that the people may be forgiven. Else how could the nation, helpless and enfeebled, hope to endure in its insignificant condition? We need not wonder. at the extreme condition in which Israel is portrayed in this verse for a locust plague is a calamity of great proportions. Amos pleads in such a way as to touch the heart of God with the plight of His people, and He is entreated for them. The prophets were ever touched with the need of God's people. Note Isaiah 51:19; also Psalm 106:44-45. At the intercession of Amos the Lord repented Himself and stayed the plague. Prayer had made it possible for God justly to spare Israel in answer to it.

Many have wondered how it could ever be said that God repents (Num 23:19; Ja 1:17), but it is more in the way of the language of appearance. We must remember that God ever works in accordance with His infinite holiness and righteousness. When sin is present God must condemn and punish it; when prayer and the grace of God operate to provide a way of escape, then God spares. In each case He is working in the strictest conformity with His known holiness. Thus it was in answer to trusting prayer, God said He would not allow the plague to ravage any longer. Only eternity will reveal fully how much in the plan of God has been wrought through consistent and persistent prayer for the salvation of souls in Israel and throughout the world.

THE VISION OF THE FIRE

When Israel continued in her sinful ways though she had been spared in the grace of God, He determined to send upon her another visitation.

In the second vision, Amos sees the Lord calling fire into His service in order to punish His people. The fire referred to is doubtless drought. (See 4:6-11.) (In the early part of the prophecy it had reference to war, as in 1:4 and succeeding passages.) The drought was so severe that it is represented as devouring the great deep, a designation for the ocean which feeds the earth with springs of water. (Cp. Gen 7:11; 49:25; Is 51:10.) The land also, that is, the portion of Israel, was threatened (Mic 2:4).

This grievous stroke calls forth the prayer of Amos once more, and he beseeches the Lord to cease because of the miserable condition of Israel. Again the Lord, who loves to be entreated of His own and for His own, heard and removed the distress. Thus Amos would show that the Lord was not bent on destroying Israel, but on turning her from her evil ways by disciplinary judgments. How well these threatenings achieved their objective we shall see in the next vision.

THE VISION OF THE PLUMB LINE

In the last vision of this chapter, Amos is shown the Lord as He stands beside (or over) a wall made by a plumb line, that is, a perpendicular wall. In His hand He has a plumb line which is clearly to be put to use to test how true and straight the wall is. Just as the builder uses the plumb line for testing, God will exercise His unerring standard to test the spiritual integrity of His people.

The Scriptures reveal that the plumb line was employed not only in building houses, but in destroying as well. In this passage the Lord has destruction in mind as is clear from verses 8 and 9. (Note carefully 2 Ki 21:13; Is 28:17; 34:11; Lam 2:8.) The plumb line is set in the midst of Israel, not merely on the circumference of the nation. This will be a thoroughgoing judgment, and the Lord warns that He will not again pass by, forgive, them. There is no intercession from the prophet here, for the patience of God is at an end. Now nothing can stay the oncoming catastrophe. More than once the intercession of the prophet had averted the blow from the Lord's hand, but that hour was passed.

We next learn of what the judgment will consist: the high places will be made desolate, the sanctuaries will be destroyed, and the house of Jeroboam will be cut off by the sword.

The high places were the groves where idols were worshiped, and the sanctuaries are those set up originally by Jeroboam the son of Nebat at Dan and Bethel. The name Isaac is used here instead of Israel as a name for the ten tribes.

Both the false worship and the ungodly monarchy in Israel will be swept away. Amos does not declare that Jeroboam will perish by the sword (which was not true; see 2 Ki 14:23-29), but that God would rise against the house of Jeroboam with the sword which was fulfilled in the assassination of his son Zechariah by Shallum (2 Ki 15:8-10). In the next generation the name of Jeroboam was cut off. How sure are the mercies of God and how certain are His judgments!

FALSE PRIEST VERSUS GOD'S PROPHET

Such straightforward proclamation of the will and purpose of God is ever displeasing to the unregenerate and ungodly man. And so it was in the day of Amos. The Word of God did not go unchallenged. Amaziah, who was the high priest at the sanctuary of the golden calf in Bethel, accused the prophet before Jeroboam. Note the particulars of his indictment: first, he claims that Amos has conspired against the king himself, implying others were with the prophet in a plot; second, that the conspiracy was being perpetrated in the very midst of the house of Israel, at the religious center of the kingdom at Bethel; lastly, that the land could not suffer the prophesying of Amos.

Ungodly Amaziah begins with the baseless charge of treason and concludes with the alarming word that revolution or sedition may result from the prophet's words. It was an unintentional testimony to the power of God's Word when it comes to convict or correct, or indeed at any time. Political expediency in every age dishonors and opposes the testimony of the truth. Note Elijah (1 Ki 18:17); Jeremiah (Jer 37:13-15); our Lord Jesus (Jn 19:12); the disciples (Jn 11:48-50); and Paul (Ac 17:6-7).

In verse 11 we have the manner in which a hireling and timeserver can twist the simple words of a servant of God. Amaziah distorts the words of Amos so that they appear to be a personal charge against the king.

There is no mention of any action of the king against the prophet. The false priest omits the basis of the threat, the hope held out by the prophet for the people in the event of repentance (5:4, 6), and the prophet's own intercession for the kingdom.

Now Amaziah addresses himself to Amos and calling him seer with contemptuous reference to his visions, advises the prophet to flee to his own country in Judah and there prophesy for his living, his bread. He insinuated that Amos ministered for the sake of his livelihood. The king's priest was himself a hireling and intimates that God's prophet is also.

He further enjoins upon Amos that he prophesy no more at Bethel, because it was a royal sanctuary and royal residence (1 Ki 12:28). Manmade religion cannot abide the truth of God. Mark that Amaziah does not call Bethel and its sanctuary the house or sanctuary of God. It is the king's. Unwittingly he truthfully lays bare the human origin of the entire worship of the Israelite kingdom begun by Jeroboam I and carried on by his godless successors. Amos is told (2:12) that his ministry at Bethel must be discontinued, because the city was the seat of the religion of the kingdom as well as one of the king's residences.

AMOS' DEFENCE AND ISRAEL'S DOOM

Amos' only defence, and altogether adequate it is too, is a simple statement of how God called His servant to the work of the prophet. Amos denies that he is a professional prophet or that he was taught in the schools of the prophets where young men were trained for instructing the nation (1 Sa 19:24). He was pursuing his humble occupation as a herdsman and dresser of sycamore trees when God's unmistakable call came to him to prophesy to Israel. His word and his authority were not his own, but derived directly from God. (See Gal 1:1; also 2 Sa 7:8, where we have similar words in the case of David's call to the royal office.) In short, Amos is saying he must obey God rather than man (Ac 5:29).

Note the contrasts in verse 11: "thus Amos saith" and in verse 16: "Thou sayest" and in verse 17: "thus saith Jehovah." Amos is pointing out as a true prophet that it matters not what Amaziah says nor what he, Amos, says, but it is all important to hear what God the Lord says. No man's opposition can stay the mighty onsweep of the majestic Word of God. One of the early Christian writers said: "Heaven thundered and commanded him to prophesy; the frog croaked in answer out of his marsh, *prophesy no more.*"

Instead of Amaziah's harangue against Amos stopping the mouth of the prophet, it brought the judgment nearer home. The prophecy now names him individually. In the invasion of the land by the enemy, the wife of the false priest would be publicly ravished; his sons and daughters would be slain; his land would be portioned out; and he himself would die in an unclean land (Assyria) whither Israel would be carried captive. With this final prophecy Amos shows the dire consequences of opposition to the truth on individual and nation alike. It is a fearful thing to set one's self against the truth of God. If man tries to silence it, it cries out the louder.

FAMINE OF GOD'S WORD

THE VISION OF THE BASKET OF FRUIT

At the beginning of the eighth chapter of Amos, we have the fourth vision in the series shown the prophet by the Lord. The vision of the plumb line showed the certainty of the coming judgment; this vision reveals the nearness of that visitation.

The prophet sees a basket of ripe fruit, and the Lord explains that this indicates Israel is ripe for judgment. Just as the gathering of fruit marked the end of the harvest, so Israel had come to the end of her national existence. Since the providential dealings of the Lord, His threatenings, His promises, and His early chastenings had not issued in true penitence, the hour for judgment had arrived for the Northern Kingdom.

There is a forceful play on words in this vision: "summer fruit" (*qayits*) and "end" (*qets*). (See Joel 3:13 and Eze 7:2, 3, 6.)

The words "I will not again pass by them," meaning that the Lord will not again forgive them, resume the thought of judgment in Amos' prophecies, interrupted by the accusation and opposition of Amaziah. (Cp. 7:8.) Because the same Hebrew word is sometimes translated "temple" and at other times "palace," students of verse 3 have differed as to which songs are referred to, whether those of the Temple or those of the palace. Both are referred to in this book—temple songs in 5:23 and songs in the palace in 6:5 and probably 8:10. The important feature is that they will not be silenced merely, but will be changed into howlings and wailing because of the ravages of death on every hand. The dead bodies will be so numerous that they will be cast forth in every place in an indiscriminate manner. While occupied thus they are commanded to silence: "Hush!" It is the same charge to silence as in 6:10; it is an exhortation to submit beneath the severity of the judgment of God. The grief is so great that words are utterly useless. Why resort to words when the slaughter is so vast that the customary rites of burial cannot be performed? Truly, Israel was ripe for judgment and that stroke was not far off.

WARNINGS TO THE OPPRESSORS OF THE POOR

Amos now directs a scathing rebuke against those who enrich themselves at the expense of the poor. If they could, they would swallow up the needy (2:6-7) and cause them to cease from the land altogether. (See Is 5:8.) Their covetous spirits took the joy out of the feasts and sabbaths because, although they observed them in a perfunctory way, they were continually thinking only of the end of these sacred days when they could give themselves again to their relentless pursuit of material gain.

The new moon was a holy day on which business and trade were not transacted. The sabbath, of course, was a day on which such pursuits could not be carried on. (Cp. Num 10:10; 28:11; 2 Ki 4:23; and Neh 10:31; 13:15-18.) The mention of new moon and sabbath is another indication in this book that, while the people were keeping the rounds of idol worship, they were practising the appointments of the Mosaic law as well.

Those who have no real piety have no honesty either. Thus we find these oppressors not giving the proper weight in food, while they increase the price. (In those days money was weighed out: Jer 32:9.) The Law had forbidden both these dishonest practices. (See Deu 25:13-16.) Every transaction was marked by fraud and dishonesty. The poor were ultimately reduced to slavery. For the least amount the needy had to sell themselves into slavery. Leviticus 25:39 prohibited such dealings. And that which an honest dealer throws away, the refuse of the wheat, they sold. Grievous as these conditions are, they are not without parallel many times over in our own day. The Scriptures indicate that similar conditions will prevail in Christendom before the return of the Lord. (Note Ja 5:1-6.)

THE COMPREHENSIVE JUDGMENT

As the prophet begins to describe the many-sided judgment on the people of God, he states the fearful truth that the Lord has sworn by the excellency of Jacob, that is, by Himself (as in 4:2 and 6:8), that He will never forget any of their works. They had heaped up sins unto the day of wrath, and God was mindful of every one of them committed. Only God's glorious provision in grace can blot out the memory of any sin before the Lord. So great will be the impact of the judgment from the Lord that the land will tremble, all the inhabitants of the land will mourn, and the land itself will rise and sink like the Nile, the river of Egypt.

Some understand the verse to be speaking of an earthquake, but the thought is rather that the land will shake from the weight of the judgment it is called upon to bear.

The same concept recurs in 9:5, but there it is introduced to show the omnipotence of God. In that same day of chastisement the sun will go down at noon, and the earth will be darkened in a clear day. It has been suggested that the reference is to an eclipse of the sun. This could hardly be a description of an eclipse even from the viewpoint of the language of appearance. Could this be an allusion to the terrible Day of the Lord? A comparison of this passage with Joel 2:2; 3:15; and Matthew 24:29-30 will readily show that such phenomena will take place in the day of tribulation and judgment.

But many epoch-making events in the Bible have their foreshadowings in previous historical events, and this may be just such an instance. For example, this expression is employed when one is destroyed in the midst of prosperity. It is a metaphorical setting forth of the change from prosperity to extreme adversity. Not only will earth and heavens be affected by the comprehensive judgment, but all the inhabitants of the land. The feasts in Israel were always occasions for great joy and rejoicing, but now they shall be turned into mourning and their songs into weeping. (See Ho 2:11.) Sackcloth on all loins (Eze 7:18) and baldness on every head (Is 3:24 and Jer 16:6) are alike marks of deepest mourning. Theirs will be as the mourning for an only son, the one in whom the family name was to be perpetuated. Joel 1:8 gives us a related figure, while Jeremiah 6:26 and Zechariah 12:10 have the identical picture. Just as in Egypt of old there was mourning in every house for the dead (Ex 12:30), so similar conditions would now exist in Israel under the heavy judgment of the Lord. Nor will the trouble be a transitory or a temporary one, but a sorrow that would continue on in its bitterness.

FAMINE OF THE WORD OF GOD

Another phase of the judgment of the Lord must be set forth before Amos presents the last vision in the concluding chapter of the prophecy. The distress of the people will be outward and inward, temporal and spiritual. Their spiritual plight is depicted in terms of a famine but not a famine for bread nor thirst for water; rather it will be a famine of hearing the words of the Lord.

What can this mean? The Old Testament Scriptures reveal clearly enough how God in His boundless love for Israel sent her messages through His servants to draw her back into the path of His choosing and into conformity with His will for her. But these prophets and servants were opposed; their messages were scorned; and they were told to cease their ministrations. Now the Lord tells her that, since she despised His Word through the prophets when it was brought to her, she was to know the cessation of all prophetic communication. (Note Eze 7:26 and Mi 3:7.) The Word of the Lord will be withdrawn from her. Like disobedient Saul in the hour of his extremity (1 Sa 28:6), she will seek after the Lord in order to obtain relief from physical distress and consolation for her troubled heart.

This is divine retribution for such opposition to the truth as seen in 7:12-13. Compare also for the same principle of divine dealing Luke 17:22 and John 7:34; 8:21.

How perverse is the nature of man: when he has the Word of God he despises it; when it is withheld he seeks it because of the severity of the chastisement.

The widespread restlessness and dissatisfaction incident upon the Lord's act of judgment are portrayed vividly in verse 12. The distraught people will wander from sea to sea in every direction seeking the Word of God and will not find it. They will reel like a drunkard or the swaying of trees in the wind. The position has been taken that the directions given in this verse refer to the extent of the land of Palestine, that is, from the Mediterranean to the Dead Sea. In view of the indefinite language of the verse and its affinity to such passages as Psalm 72:8 and Zechariah 9:10, probably every quarter of the globe is intended by the prophet. It has been well said: "He that will not when he may, when he will shall have nay." So with Israel in the hour of judgment; she will seek the Word of Jehovah but will not find it.

Of the entire population those are now singled out who are the strongest and the most buoyant with hope—the fair virgins and the young men. But these too will lack all consolation; they shall faint for thirsting after the

Word. If this be true of the young and vigorous (Is 40:30-31), what of the aged and feeble? What is true of them is all the more so for the rest whom they represent.

Finally, Amos assigns once more the reason for the conditions envisioned in verses 11 to 13. In short, they were so taken up with the false gods that they could no longer hear the Word of the true and living God. They had forsaken the Lord and He now forsakes them.

It was their practice to swear in the name of their gods. God had charged them to swear in the name of the Lord (Deu 6:13; 10:20), not in that of other gods (Jos 23:7). By "the sin of Samaria," the golden calf at Bethel is meant. (See 4:4 and Ho 8:5.) The god of Dan was evidently the bull image set up by Jeroboam the son of Nebat (1 Ki 12:29). The way of Beersheba (5:5) was the last of the three oaths made in the names of the three idol sanctuaries.

Swearing in the name of inanimate objects may be strange to us, but not so in the Orient. Muslims are usually accustomed to swearing "by the pilgrimage" to Mecca, as well as in the name of countless other objects that may come to mind at the time of the oath.

All these oaths were after the form which the Lord Himself had instituted: "As the Lord liveth!" It is appropriate for the Lord, because in Him is life and He exists. It is senseless when employed of idols which represent no living entity. Paul's estimate (through the Spirit of God) of idols is the only true one: "We know that no idol is anything in the world" or as a modern translation of the New Testament puts it: "We know that an idol has no real existence" (1 Co 8:4).

The doom upon them for such idolatry is tersely stated; they shall fall and never rise again (see 5:2). The fulfillment of this word began with the dissolution of the kingdom of Israel and continues until her national restoration, which is promised in such passages as Ezekiel 36:22-31 and 37:15-23. The partial fulfillment in the time of the Assyrian captivity points on to the ultimate fulfillment in the period before the visible return of the Lord in glory. Apostate Christendom, as well as guilty Israel, will share this famine in the time of Great Tribulation. Both have turned now from the light of the truth to the darkness of fables.

THE RESTORATION OF ISRAEL

THE VISION OF THE TEMPLE DESTRUCTION

The last chapter of the prophecy of Amos concerns itself with the final and consummating vision, that of the destruction of the Temple. The scene is in the main sanctuary of the Northern Kingdom at Bethel, not at Jerusalem. The Lord Himself directs the judgment and commands that the capitals, the tops of the pillars, be smitten, so that the very thresholds may shake. The blow from the top shatters the sanctuary to its foundations. Both top and bottom are mentioned to show the complete destruction. When the pillars come crashing they will fall on the heads of the crowds of people who are evidently gathered in the Temple on a festival occasion. They would all be buried in the ruins. In case any should escape the crash of the building, they will be slain by the sword.

In this vivid manner does the prophet depict the wrath of God upon all the idolatrous worship of Israel and His summary judgment upon it, a judgment without remedy. Twice the word is given that no one will flee the catastrophe. Verses 2 to 4 expand the last thought in verse 1 that there is no possibility of escape. We are given hypothetical cases of attempts at escape from the judgment and the utter inevitability of their doom.

In words that strongly remind us of Psalm 139:7-10, Amos sets forth the omnipresence of God. Though the doomed one dig into the bowels of the earth, into Sheol, there will the mighty hand of God overtake them; should they attempt to ascend the greatest heights, thence will God bring them low. The same is said of Babylon in Jeremiah 51:53 and of Edom in Obadiah 4. It has been well said, "The grave is not so awful as God." The omnipresence of God is a comforting and sustaining truth to the good but a terror to the wicked when judgment is in view. Even if the fugitives sought to hide themselves in the top of Carmel, it would not avail them against the searching eye of the Lord.

Mount Carmel rises quite suddenly out of the sea to a height of about 1,800 feet. It is claimed that there are some 1,000 caves in Carmel, especially on the west side toward the sea. The mountain is known for its dense forests and large caverns, the latter often serving hermits for shelter.

Not only will these caverns not suffice for concealment from the wrath of the Lord, but the very bottom of the sea will not afford refuge to those who would escape. At the bottom of the sea the Lord will command the sea serpent to bite the culprits. (Cp. Is 27:1.) Just as the great fish obeyed the Lord when He commanded it to swallow a Jonah, so the serpent of the sea will do the Lord's bidding with regard to the sinners in Israel.

Should the ungodly go into captivity before their enemies, that is, voluntarily in order to spare their lives, even there the sword will destroy them. Assyria is again in view, although not named anywhere in the prophecy. Futile and worse will be all attempts to escape the scourge of God's hand in the day of His fearful visitation. The reason is found in the fact that God has set His eyes with fixed purpose upon them, not as formerly for good and blessing, but for evil only. He has purposed and it will stand; He will watch over it to bring it to pass.

THE OMNIPOTENT GOD

Lest any of his hearers falsely comfort himself that the Lord will not or cannot do what He has threatened, Amos majestically sets forth the omnipotence of our God, the Lord Jehovah of hosts. He is the God of all power (see 4:13; 5:8-9; and 8:8). Assuredly, power belongs, not to the atom bomb, but to the Lord. The Lord needs only touch the earth in judgment and it is dissolved. (Cp. Ps 46:6.)

God can cause the earth to rise and sink like the Nile of Egypt, and, since He has framed the heavens and the earth, He is able to bring floods upon the earth. All nature is subservient to Him; only man defies His will. Therefore, as in the past so in the future, God will employ the very forces of nature to judge His ungodly creatures. This is clearly pictured for us throughout the book of Revelation. The prophet Amos is thus asking Israel, "Can you escape such a God?"

SINNERS AND THE REMNANT

Carnal reliance upon their election as the people of God will not avert the wrath of God against Israel. In idolatry they had become like the pagan peoples about them. They had lowered themselves to the plane of the heathen; hence they are like the Ethiopians in the sight of the Lord. This is the strongest denunciation of Israel by the prophet, because he likens her to the heathen.

Amos shows that since God in His providential dealings has shifted and transferred different peoples from their original homes, Israel need not be illusioned by the notion that, since He had brought her out of Egypt into Canaan, she is in such a favored position that she could never be judged severely for her sins. Privileges cannot be pleaded in the interests of salvation and deliverance so long as they are scorned or abused.

The Ethiopians had been taken from their original abode in Arabia and transplanted among the nations in Africa. The Israelites, after four centuries of bondage, were delivered out of Egypt and returned to Canaan. God had brought the Philistines from Caphtor, probably Crete, although the Greek translators of the Old Testament thought it was Cappadocia. (See Gen 10:14; Deu 2:23; Jer 47:4; and Eze 25:16.) According to the Deuteronomy passage, it would appear that this transfer must have taken place even before the exodus of the people of Israel from Egypt.

Finally, the prophet notes that God had transplanted the Syrians from Kir to the regions about Damascus. (Cp. 1:5.) Where, then, was the occasion for Israel to boast or to rely carnally upon her privileged position? Again God is seen as Lord of all the nations as in chapters 1 and 2. And in all of them alike He must punish sins and departures from Himself. So He declares that His eyes are upon the sinful kingdom of Ephraim to destroy it from the face of the earth.

The words *sinful kingdom* are an unusual designation for the Northern Kingdom, and how contrary is this condition to God's ideal for them as stated in Exodus 19:6.

Up to this point in the book of Amos there has been no word to mitigate the sentence of judgment. The prophecy has been singularly free of predictions of future blessing and prosperity. Now the prophet states that, although in all justice and holiness God must destroy forever the Northern Kingdom, He will not utterly destroy the house of Jacob, the name for the whole nation. The reason is given in Jeremiah 31:36. God will not default in His promises to Abraham and his seed. How the last words of verse 8 are to be understood and carried out is set forth in verse 9. God will sift (a vivid word which means "to cause to move to and fro") the house of Israel among all the nations, as grain in a sieve, yet He will not allow the smallest kernel to fall to the ground.

Here we have several noteworthy features. First, it is the Lord who is the moving Agent in all the sifting. The sifting, in the second place, depicts the highly unsettled condition of Israel. Third, the sifting among all the nations reveals the universal dispersion of God's people. Fourth, the chaff and dust will be done away and lost. And finally, the kernels, the true remnant of Israel, will be preserved and delivered. The whole world is one great sieve in which Israel is shaken from one place to another. How vividly and accurately these words describe the condition of Israel, especially since the destruction of Jerusalem by the Romans in AD 70. Yet through it all God has His eye on her to preserve her. Only thus can her preservation in worldwide exile and through agelong persecutions of the most diabolical sort, be explained.

No grain falls to the ground in this sifting of the Lord, but no sinner escapes either. All the sinners of the nation will perish; especially are those singled out who defiantly boasted that the evil judgment would not reach them (see 6:3, the rich oppressors of Samaria). Those who did not believe in a judgment will be made to suffer it.

RESTORATION OF DAVID'S DYNASTY

At the end of Israel's sad dispersion, He had promised to regather them and place over them His own righteous Ruler, the Messiah the Son of David. Amos now foretells this in words of surpassing beauty.

In the latter days of Israel's history the Lord will raise up the tabernacle (actually the hut or booth) of David that is fallen and in ruins; He will repair the breaches and ruins, building it as in the days of old. It is not a magnificent house of which the prophet speaks, but a ruined, fallen hut. This is in marked contrast to the splendid palace which David had erected for himself (2 Sa 5:11-12).

The Davidic dynasty is usually referred to as "the house of David" as in 2 Samuel 3:1; 1 Kings 11:38; and Isaiah 7:2, 13. In Isaiah 16:5 we find the expression "the tent of David." In our Amos passage the low, degraded condition of the Davidic monarchy is meant. Isaiah 11:1 also speaks of the lowly condition of the line of David. On the basis of this verse the rabbis of the Talmud called the Messiah, Bar Naphli ("the son of the fallen"), although Amos does not specifically mention the personal Messiah, only the line from which He was to come.

Through David's Son, the breaches of the Davidic house, the first of which it suffered upon the breaking away of the ten tribes, will be repaired. The Davidic dynasty and kingdom will be restored. And the restoration will be to its most glorious condition in the days of old, that is, in the time of David and Solomon when the kingdom was both undivided and prosperous, enjoying in its full extent the greatest splendor of kingly rule in all the history of Israel.

When Israel has her rightful King on the throne, then she will be the head of the nations. Amos predicts that she will possess the remnant of Edom, as well as all the nations that are called by the name of the Lord. Manifestly the prophet is mentioning Edom as representative of all the nations of the world. Most closely related to Israel, they were the relentless foes of the Lord's people. (See Ob 12.) The remnant that is called by the name of the Lord is equivalent to those designated in Joel 2:32.

The citation of Amos 9:11-12 by James in Acts 15 does not warrant us in holding, as some do, that this prophecy is fulfilled completely in this age of grace. The phrase "in that day" of our text refers to the last days of Israel. The quotation of our verses in Acts 15:16-18 is made with one object in view: to confirm the fact of the conversion of the Gentiles. Hence the quotation gives only the general sense of the Amos passage and does not support the position that the Amos text has in view the Christian Church as its ultimate fulfillment.

When Israel is head of the nations, her land will be abundantly fruitful. The one plowing will overtake the reaper, and the treader of grapes the one sowing seed. The thought is that scarcely is the farmer finished plowing when the seed will be ripe, and hardly will he have completed treading the wine press when he will have to begin the sowing. (Cp. Lev 26:5.) Vintage time will continue to the sowing time because of the abundance of fruit. The mountains are said to drop with sweet wine, because vines are planted on the terraces of mountains. (See Joel 3:18 also.)

Israel will in that day be restored from centuries-long captivity to rebuild her cities and inhabit them with the enjoyment of her vineyards and her gardens. (Cp. Ho 6:11 and 5:11 of this book.) Then Israel will be planted and rooted in her own land (2 Sa 7:10), never more to be plucked up and uprooted from her God-given land. The day of exile, thank God, will be past. Note carefully Isaiah 61:4; 62:8, 9; 65:21-23.

Let us summarize the remarkable prophecy of Amos to be fulfilled in the consummation of Israel's history: (1) the restoration of the Davidic dynasty, verse 11; (2) the supremacy of Israel over the nations, verse 12; (3) the conversion of the nations, verse 12; (4) the fruitfulness of the land, verse 13; (5) the rebuilding of her cities, verse 14; and (6) her permanent settlement in her own land after her return from captivity, verse 15.

WHAT OF THE KERNELS?

God's heart is full of good things in store for Israel. What is the attitude of our hearts toward them? The chaff will be done away during Israel's worldwide sifting, but God has in mind the preservation of the kernels. Even so now God has purposed the calling out from Israel of those called "the remnant according to the election of grace" (Ro 11:5).

7

OBADIAH
DOOM UPON EDOM

God's Wrath on Edom

THE PROPHET AND HIS TIMES

THE PROPHECY OF OBADIAH is the smallest book in the Old Testament, containing a total of twenty-one verses. It is not quoted in the New Testament, yet its message is a vital part of all the prophetic Scriptures. It is written in lucid and forceful language.

Nothing is known of Obadiah but his name which means "servant of Jehovah." A number of men in the Old Testament bore the same name.

There has been great diversity of opinion as to the time of the prophecy. The enmity of Edom for Israel was so unremitting and persistent through the centuries that students of the book find it difficult to assign the book to a specific time. Some estimates have varied as much as approximately six centuries. In all probability Obadiah was a prophet living before the Babylonian exile who foresaw by the Spirit of prophecy the doom of Edom, the greatest enemy of God's people, Israel. Compare Jeremiah 49:7-22 for a later prophecy on the same subject which has many verbal similarities with the prediction now before us.

If Hosea treats of the love of God for Israel, Amos of the righteousness of the Lord, Joel of the Day of Jehovah, Obadiah prophesies of the doom of Edom.

The Edomites came from Esau, the twin brother of Jacob. The book of Genesis outlines in unmistakable language the enmity that existed between these brothers. Their progeny perpetuated this feud. Edom early became a powerful nation. (See Gen 36; Ex 15:15; Num 20:14.) When the Israelites came up from the land of Egypt, the Edomites denied them passage through their land. (Note Num 20:20-21.) However, God commanded Israel to treat Edom as a brother (Deu 23:7-8). Nevertheless, the

hatred of Edom (who well typifies the flesh and its desires with no
thought for the things of the spiritual life) persisted against Israel, as the
Old Testament Scriptures abundantly attest.

Now it is given to Obadiah to pronounce God's message of final doom
upon this incorrigible foe of His people. The prophecy, though centuries
old, has a familiar ring, for it echoes events and deeds of recent years that
have been perpetrated upon the sons of Jacob throughout the world.

THE PRIDE AND FALL OF EDOM

The prophecy begins with the concise statement that it is a supernatural
revelation, a vision, granted to Obadiah; the word of the Lord that came
to him concerned Edom specifically. The prophet and the nation Israel
are made cognizant of the fact that the Lord has sent a messenger among
the nations to stir them up to war against Edom. It is made known to
them by God directly, for He takes His own into His plans for them and
those about them.

It was God's overruling providences that led the Assyrians and then
Nebuchadnezzar with his confederates against Edom. The Lord says of
Edom that He has made him small among the nations and greatly
despised; indeed, He speaks this word to him directly. God's resolution
to do so makes the humiliation as certain as if it had already taken place.
It will be accomplished through the enemies aroused against him.

What causes the fall of Edom? His unbearable pride. His pride and
conceit were nourished by the fact that his land was full of high mountain
fastnesses. He truly dwelt in the clefts of the rock, for the land of Edom
is a rock mountain full of caves and dwellings hewn out of the rock. The
former inhabitants of Mount Seir were cave-dwellers, the Horites (see
Gen 14:6; Deu 2:12, 22). The haughty spirit of Edom evidently stemmed
from his belief that he was invincible and impregnable. No one, he
thought, could bring him down from his lofty habitation. God assures
him that, though he emulate the eagle and though he set his abode
among the very stars, He will cast him down thence. (Cp. Amos 9:2; Is
14:12-20, the fall of Lucifer; Job 39:27-28.) Edom may be inaccessible to
man, but not to God. The greater his pride the more disastrous his fall.

DESTRUCTION AND TREACHERY

The prophet sets forth now the thoroughgoing character of the destruction of the Idumeans. If robbers break in at night, they steal all they
need or can carry away. They do not take all. When grape gatherers
harvest the vintage, they always leave gleanings as a matter of course. The
vineyard is not left completely bare. But, says Obadiah as he interjects an

exclamation of surprise and amazement at the plundered condition of Edom, the land of Esau will be left with nothing. His ruin will be complete. The enemy in seeking plunder will search out the hidden treasures of Edom.

The capital of Edom, Petra, was the great market of the Syrian and Arabian trade where many costly articles were treasured. These will all be looted.

Moreover, his own confederates will deceive him and prevail against him. As a recompense for his treachery, his allies will drive him out into captivity, let alone give him aid in the hour of need. The ones who had in other days enjoyed the bounty, the bread of Edom, will employ treachery to bring about his certain downfall. The Edomites will be able to look to no one for help. By open means or deceptive snares those who were their allies would compass their undoing. Esau will manifest none of that discernment for which he had been renowned. The wise men of the Mount of Esau will be destroyed.

Because of his communication with Babylon and Egypt and because of the information gleaned through the caravans going to and from Europe and India, Edom had gained an enviable reputation for wisdom. Now his wisdom will be withdrawn from him. The wise and powerful men of Teman will be dismayed, because the Lord purposed to slaughter every one in Edom. It was to be a stroke without mitigation. For the wisdom of Teman see Job 4:1 and Jeremiah 49:7.

THE REASONS FOR THE JUDGMENT

Such punishment calls for a presentation of the underlying causes for the wrath of God against Edom. Verses 10 through 14 give us the bill of particulars against this stubborn enemy of Israel. They portray conditions in Israel when Judah was invaded by Nebuchadnezzar.

Edom resorted to violence against his brother Jacob. (Cp. Joel 3:19.) It was directed against Jacob, his twin brother. There were to be two phases to his punishment: (1) a period in which the Edomites were to be a captive people—shame covering them; (2) a time in which they were to become extinct as a people.

They were ultimately reduced by John Hyrcanus of the Maccabean dynasty and lost their national existence under the Romans. They were cut off forever as a nation, though the land would again be populated, as we shall see from the latter part of this prophecy.

When the Chaldeans invaded Judah in later years, Edom, like the enemies of God's people, had assumed an attitude of hostility. Judah's goods were carried off; her cities were entered by force; lots were cast upon

Jerusalem (Joel 3:3) to sell her population into slavery; but Edom knew only hatred for his kin, entering into the calamity as one of the accomplices of the outrages. (For the hatred of Edom in this hour see Ps 137:7; 83:4-6 especially; Eze 35; Jer 49; Is 34 and 63.)

In addition, Edom feasted on his brother's disaster and rejoiced in the destruction of Judah, when she was exiled as an alien from her homeland. Not only did he revel in the calamity of Judah, but he used arrogant language in exultation over his conquered enemy.

The Idumeans went from looks and rejoicings to insults and actions. They assisted in the spoilation of God's people when they were being robbed by the invaders. Finally, they took their stand at the crossway to cut off the retreat of those who wanted to pass through Idumea to Egypt where they were fleeing from the Chaldean hosts, and then delivered them over to the enemy. They surely compounded their outrages against the distressed ones of Jacob. Note the extent of them: (1) violence, verse 10; (2) hostile attitude, verse 11; (3) joy at Israel's calamity, verse 12; (4) boasting in Jacob's time of distress, verse 12; (5) spoiling of God's people, verse 13; (6) prevention of the escape of the fugitives, verse 14; and (7) the betrayal of them into the hand of their enemy, verse 14. Should not the Lord take account of this? His wrath is kindled with reason. Edom has merited his punishment.

THE DAY OF JEHOVAH AT HAND

Dwelling on the theme of God's visitation in wrath, Obadiah is carried on in mind and heart by the Spirit of God to the great Day of Judgment for all nations. In God's reckoning, the Day of the Lord is near for all the nations who have similarly maltreated the people of God. They will, as Edom, be requited in kind. Edom will come in for judgment in the Day of the Lord. As the seed of Esau have held their wild carousals with the conquerors in the captured city of Jerusalem in their time, so shall all these nations drain to the dregs the cup of calamity and wrath of God. (See Jer 25:15-33.)

In so doing they shall be so completely annihilated, that it will be as though they had never existed. The time of this judgment will be just before the establishment of Messiah's kingdom; then the power of Edom will be finally and completely broken. When the last great confederacy against Israel takes place (Zec 12; 14), the Edomites will be among these adversaries of God's people. They will be routed, and Edom will be blotted out as a nation. When other nations, like Assyria and Egypt, are restored and brought into millennial blessing, Edom will have been utterly destroyed. Edom, representative of the flesh and the carnal mind with its enmity against God and His Law, must be irrevocably cut off.

ISRAEL'S SALVATION AND MESSIAH'S KINGDOM

Whereas Edom can expect only destruction in the wind-up of God's prophetic program, Israel awaits a restoration from worldwide captivity. In Mount Zion will be those of Israel who have escaped the rigors and ravages of the centuries of cruel treatment accorded this people of God. They will be resettled upon their own land. Mount Zion, so often polluted by the repeated invasions of the foreigner, will be holy unto the Lord. (Cp. Is 52:1.)

The house of Jacob will then possess their possessions; they will fully occupy those provinces and countries which were theirs in the time of the greatest expansion of the monarchy in Israel. She will no longer be shorn of her possessions. Then Israel, before this the butt of every attack, will be God's instrument in punishing Edom. (Note Is 11:14; Zec 12:6.) The houses of Jacob and Joseph, the reunited kingdoms, will be as fire to stubble when they execute God's wrath in the last days upon an Edom revived in prophetic times for this very judgment. No remnant is specified for Edom from this judgment. All will be cut off. Then Israel will regain the territories that rightfully belong to her.

Those who dwell in the southern portion of Judah will appropriate to themselves Mount Esau; those of the lowlands on the west will gain the land of the Philistines. The territory of the Northern Kingdom will be restored and enjoyed; and Benjamin, loyal to the Davidic dynasty, will expand to the east to Gilead.

We have here a fulfillment of Genesis 28:14. The large number of Israelitish captives in Phoenicia (where they had been sold and from there into Greece) will possess the land to Zarephath, a town between Sidon and Tyre near the shore of the Mediterranean, the Sarepta of Luke 4:26. The Judean captives in Sepharad will gain the cities of the south mentioned in verse 19.

What is the identity of Sepharad? It has never been satisfactorily identified. Conjectures range from Spain (so the Aramaic versions and the rabbis), the Bosphorus (the position held by the Latin translator of the Bible, Jerome), Saparda in southwest Media according to many, Sparta, and Sardis. The important truth is that Judah and Israel respectively will possess the land adjoining them.

And then saviors, deliverers, and rulers, like the early judges in Israel during the days of the theocracy when God ruled His people directly, will ascend Mount Zion to judge, to punish, the Mount of Esau, and the kingdom shall be Jehovah's—blessed consummation. (See Judg 3:9, 15.) These deliverers will exercise authority in the name of the Lord, but ultimate sovereignty will be His alone. (Read carefully Dan 2:44; Zec 14:9; Lk 1:33; Rev 19:6; and especially Ps 22:28 for the wording.)

To recapitulate the salient features of this important prophecy: Obadiah in preexilic days sees by the Spirit of God the culmination of Edom's hatred for Israel in his vicious conduct toward the distraught people in the day of their exile by Nebuchadnezzar.

The prophet traces the sources of this attitude and pictures vividly the features of the punishment of God upon Edom for his attitudes, arrogant speech, and actions.

When is the time of the fulfillment of this prophecy? The fulfillment of the ruin of Edom foretold by Obadiah was begun in the Chaldean period. Edom was laid waste by them (Jer 49 and Eze 35). The Maccabees further subjugated him. The Romans completed his ruin at the time that they destroyed Jerusalem in AD 70.

Through these centuries, we hear nothing of Edom. In the end time and before the gathering of the nations against Jerusalem in the War of Armageddon, Edom will again be on the scene of world history. There is to be revival of many ancient nations. (See Lk 21:29, especially the words "and all the trees.") Then Edom will experience to the full the wrath of God in destruction, the Lord Jesus Christ Himself executing the judgment of God on Edom and his allies (Is 63:1-6). With the wicked nations destroyed and Edom cut off, Israel restored from captivity will possess all the land originally promised by God to Abraham and the Lord will reign over the earth.

PART III

JONAH, MICAH, AND NAHUM

To

KEITH L. BROOKS,

WILLIAM H. ROGERS,

LEONARD SALE-HARRISON,

men of God,

servants of Christ,

lovers of Israel,

this section is respectfully and

affectionately dedicated.

As with the previous two sections in this series, this is designed to meet the real need for material on the much neglected minor prophets, as viewed in their proper setting in relation to Israel. Amazing it is how timely and applicable are the messages of these servants of God for our distraught age. He who would be well balanced in the truth of God must ponder these words of the prophets.

Throughout the studies the Hebrew text has been before the writer. The reader will be soon aware that there are numerous cross-references in the book. These have been diligently compared and carefully gathered and are essential for the study. It cannot be emphasized too strongly that the text of the English Bible must be followed along with the studies for greatest benefit.

It remains for me to express my hearty thanks to Mrs. Franceen Smith, my secretary, for her help in typing the manuscript and in proofreading; and to my wife and my son, Paul, for their assistance also in reading proof.

Never before has Israel stood in greater need of staunch Bible-believing and Bible-loving Christians who will allow their hearts to be moved by God toward His beloved people in their hour of need. May God raise up a host of helpers of Israel (Est 9:3) , and may He be pleased to use these pages in some measure to that end.

8

JONAH
GOD'S LOVE FOR ALL NATIONS

THE DISOBEDIENT PROPHET

THE PROPHET JONAH

NOTHING IS KNOWN of the prophet Jonah apart from this book and the historical statement in 2 Kings 14:25. His name means "dove" and that of his father, "truthful."

The passage in 2 Kings states that King Jeroboam II restored certain territories to Israel according to the prophecy of Jonah. This statement as to the fulfillment of his prophecy does not give us any certain clue as to the time of its utterance nor as to the time of the ministry of Jonah. It has been generally assumed among conservative students of the book to be in the eighth century BC.

The prophet's home was in Gath-hepher which is in Zebulun (Jos 19:13), north of Nazareth in Galilee. (Note the error of the enemies of the Lord Jesus in Jn 7:52.) The book of Jonah itself is sufficient to give us insight into the character and life of the much-discussed and much-scorned prophet.

A RIDICULED BOOK

Disbelief has attacked this book probably more than any other in the Bible. It has been made the butt of ill-advised humor and undeserved ridicule. This book is the great missionary book of the Old Testament. We can judge how important the Jews consider this book when they read it during the solemn hours of the Day of Atonement. When Cyprian, the Christian orator of the third century AD, read the book of the prophet, he was greatly moved, and the book was used of God for his conversion.

Some question has arisen concerning the book because it does contain history and narrative to the practical exclusion of prophecy or prediction.

There is an absence of the usual prophetic discourse. But there are those who realize that the book is among the prophets, not because of the historical events it records, but because the transactions in it are prophecies themselves. As we shall have occasion to see later, the book is a remarkable prophecy of the entire history of the people of Israel, as well as a clear prediction of the resurrection of Christ. (See Mt 12:39-41 and 16:4.)

Ridicule has especially centered around the swallowing of Jonah by the fish and his preservation in it. The root of the difficulty is the denial of the miraculous. But if we exclude the miraculous from our Bibles, how much of it do we have left? And more important, what kind of a God do we have left? It is nothing less than shortsighted unbelief to think that the difficulty is solved by the removal of this miracle from the book of Jonah.

The prophecy is full of miracles. Note these clear miracles in the book: the storm; the selection of Jonah by lot as guilty; the sudden subsiding of the sea; the great fish appearing at the right time; the preservation of Jonah; his ejection from the fish, safe and sound, on shore; the gourd; the worm; the east wind; and greatest of all by all reckonings, the repentance of the entire city of Nineveh.

The book is an integral unit like the human body; cut it where you will and it will bleed. The trusting child of God is not afraid of the miraculous, for his God is the God of the miraculous. And more, this perennial scorn of the miracle of the swallowing of Jonah has served all too long to swallow up the central message of the book which is the love of God for all the world, as we shall see more fully later.

CALL AND DISOBEDIENCE OF JONAH

Those who would designate this prophecy a myth, legend, allegory, or parable cannot explain satisfactorily why the book begins in accepted prophetic style (see Zec 6:9; 8:1; and other instances in the prophetic books). God's word to Jonah was a clear and unmistakable command to go to heathen Nineveh and preach against it because of its grievous wickedness. This is the only case of a prophet being sent to the heathen.

Nineveh, mentioned for the first time in Genesis 10:11, was the ancient capital of the Assyrian Empire on the eastern bank of the Tigris River. It was made the capital of Assyria by Sennacherib and was destroyed by the Medes and Persians in 612 BC. Classical writers inform us that the city, in the shape of a trapezium, was the largest city in the world in that day (cp. 3:2-3; 4:11).

The prophet was commissioned to preach against the city because of its great sin and corruption. (For a similar expression of sin see Gen

18:21; for the wording, note 1 Sa 5:12.) God commanded Jonah to go, but he was of a contrary mind. He fled to Tarshish. The prophets were not mere machines; they had power to resist the will of God. However, this is the only instance on record where a prophet refused to carry out his commission.

Nineveh was east of Palestine, while Tarshish was west. According to the Greek historian, Herodotus, Tarshish was Tartessus in southern Spain. The latest biblical atlases identify it as a Phoenician smelting center in Spain or Sardinia, the name being found in both places. There is no evidence to identify Tarshish with England.

Why did Jonah flee? The answers to this question have been various. It has been suggested that he felt the repentance of the city, if it should do so, would mean the downfall of his own people. Some advance the opinion that he feared the conversion of the Gentiles lest it detract from the privileges of Israel as the chosen people of God. The disobedience of the prophet has been explained as due to pride and bigotry: he could not rejoice that the Lord was going to show grace to a heathen people. It is true that Jonah knew from previous prophecies (see Ho 9:3) that Assyria was to be God's chastening scourge on Israel. In 4:2 the prophet tells us himself what his motive was in fleeing to Tarshish. He refused to go because he was afraid God's message would be successful among them. The heart of man naturally prefers judgment upon other men, rather than the manifestation of God's grace and mercy to them.

How did Jonah expect to flee from the presence of the Lord? He was not ignorant of the omniscience and omnipresence of God (Ps 139:7-12; Jer 23:24), but was fleeing from the land of Israel where the Lord manifestly dwelt in the Temple. (See Gen 4:16 for a similar expression.) Included may be the thought of his escape from or abandonment of the service of the Lord. Joppa, the modern Mediterranean seaport of Jaffa, was used as a harbor as early as the time of Solomon. (Cp. 2 Ch 2:16.) It is interesting indeed that at this same place the apostle Peter needed the vision from heaven to send him forth with the Gospel to the Gentile Cornelius (note Ac 10).

THE STORM

Jonah may flee, but God has not relinquished His sovereignty over nature or His creatures. God sent (lit., "hurled") a mighty wind and tempest on the sea. The winds are His servants (Ps 104:4).

It was gracious of God to seek out His disobedient servant and not to allow him to remain long in his sin. The mariners, accustomed to storms on the Mediterranean, knew this to be no ordinary tempest and were seized with fear. Probably most of the sailors were Phoenicians but from different places and worshiped different gods. In addition to their prayers the men began casting the goods of the ship into the sea to lighten the burden and hence prevent the ship from sinking. The conduct of the sailors throughout appears most commendable, judged from the details that are given us.

While all this fear and consternation and feverish activity were taking place, Jonah, probably from the fatigue of the journey to Joppa and the anxiety preying on his mind, had gone down into one of the recesses of the ship and fallen asleep. It is well known how often sin brings insensibility with it.

What a shame that the prophet of God had to be called to pray by a heathen. How the Muslim with his five times of prayer daily puts us to shame as believers. Are there among us those who remember not to lift their hearts to God once a day?

In all probability Jonah did pray to God, but the storm was not quieted. The men concluded that there must be on board one who was guilty of some great crime, and they decided to cast lots in order to find out the guilty individual.

The casting of lots was not against the will of God. Note the casting of lots with Achan (Jos 7:16), in the division of the land under Joshua (Jos 15:1), in the case of Jonathan's trespass (1 Sa 14:36-42), and in the choosing of Matthias (Ac 1:26). We read: "The lot is cast into the lap; but the whole disposing thereof is of Jehovah" (Pr 16:33). After the descent of the Holy Spirit at Pentecost we do not read of the lot for the believer. The indwelling Spirit now is all sufficient for guidance in the life of every believer, and He does so in accord with the Word of God.

The lot pointed out guilty Jonah. The questions of the mariners did not show that they doubted the lot, but rather that they wanted Jonah himself to confess that of which he was guilty. Jonah's answers are forthright. He declares himself to be a Hebrew (the name of the Israelites among foreigners, Gen 39:14, 17; 40:15) and a worshiper of Jehovah who was Creator of the heaven, the sea, and the dry land. At this reply the sailors were thrown into a panic of fright, for the storm proclaimed the omnipotence of God better than Jonah could. These heathen mariners were more aroused and alarmed by the flagrant disobedience of Jonah than the prophet of God himself was. What a rebuke it should have been to him!

JONAH IN THE SEA

When the sea kept growing more and more tempestuous, the mariners asked Jonah what course of action should be taken. They did not want to mete out a punishment of their own when they realized the power of the God whom Jonah had offended.

The answer of Jonah reveals him in a better light than anywhere else in the entire book. It took real courage to advise them as he did. Note that he did not throw himself into the sea, for there is a vast difference between an awakened conscience and a despairing conscience. Jonah confesses he is worthy of death and is willing to endure the punishment. These are noble words from a true servant of God. He was willing to sacrifice himself to save those about to die. How like our Lord Jesus is this, although our Lord did not bring about the calamity, as Jonah did by his waywardness. But if Jonah's words were noble, the acts of the sailors were also. For the men tried to spare his life. They rowed hard (lit., "to dig through"), putting forth every effort to make land.

But the tempest grew worse. Then the men called upon God not to lay innocent blood to their account. They had more concern for one life than Jonah had for hundreds of thousands in Nineveh. It is clear that although these heathen sailors did not know the Law of God given to Israel, yet they knew that the life of man is precious in the sight of God (Gen 9:5-6). They realized, too, that the lot and the word of the prophet, as well as the storm, were indications of the sovereign will of God in the matter. God had done as it pleased Him. This was discernment of no low order. With the casting of Jonah into the sea, it became calm.

Truly God spares the praying penitent one: the sailors experience this truth now, as Jonah and the city of Nineveh do later. With the cessation of the raging of the sea the mariners again witness the omnipotence of God. In reverential fear of the Lord they offer sacrifice unto Him of that which they have on ship with them and make vows to be performed when they reach their intended destination.

JONAH IN THE FISH

But the Lord is not through dealing with His servant. The Lord prepared a great fish to swallow Jonah. One of the ancient rabbis suggested that this fish was prepared for this purpose at the creation of the world. The Hebrew word means "appoint, order." God arranged it that the fish should be there when Jonah was cast into the sea. The character and dimensions of the fish are of secondary importance for us. More important than the fish is the man! We dare not be side-tracked and lose sight of the principal agent with whom God is here dealing. No natural explanations can account for all the facts in this case. Jonah's preservation in the belly of the fish can only be explained as a miracle. Our Lord Jesus Himself calls it a "sign" in Matthew 12:39.

Though there is not a word of prediction in the first chapter of this book, yet it is full of prophecy concerning Israel. Jonah is a picture of Israel. Israel, like Jonah, was chosen of God to be His people and His witness. (See Deu 14:2 and Eze 20:5.) As Jonah, so Israel was commissioned of God. (Note Is 43:10-12 and 44:8.) Like Jonah, Israel was disobedient to the will of the Lord. (Cp. Ex 32:1-4; Judg 2:11-19; Eze 6:1-5; Mk 7:6-9.) Just as Jonah found himself among men of different nationalities, so Israel in disobedience has been scattered throughout the earth. (Deu 4:27; Eze 12:15.) While Jonah was among the heathen they came to a knowledge of God; while Israel is among the nations the Gentiles come to know the Lord. (Note Ro 11:11.) Jonah was miraculously preserved in the sea monster. Israel has been miraculously preserved in the plan of God through the centuries of exile and dispersion. (See Ho 3:3; Jer 30:11 and 31:35-37.) Truly the book of Jonah is a prophecy of Israel.

THE CHASTENED PROPHET

THE CONDITION OF JONAH

At the close of the first chapter of this book it is recorded that Jonah remained in the belly of the fish which had swallowed him for three days and three night. The sovereign God, who can keep life before birth, can and did keep Jonah in the belly of the fish.

Jonah was in a state of consciousness, though he may not have realized the full extent of his situation. The prophet of God, though disobedient to the command of God when it did not meet his own desires, knew to whom to turn instinctively when in trouble. In the fish he cried out to God in prayer.

There has been much discussion as to the time of the prayer as well as the time of its recording for our edification. The first verse of chapter 2 is clear that Jonah prayed while he was yet imprisoned in the belly of the great fish. He recorded his prayer together with all the events of this prophecy at a time subsequent to his release from the fish and his ministry at Nineveh.

There are those who believe that Jonah actually died in the fish and then was brought back to life. Apparently the desire is to make the picture and type of the resurrection of Christ as nearly identical to the fulfillment or antitype as possible. There is no need to hold this position. The main feature of the narrative laid hold of by our Lord Jesus was the time element. No more needs to be assumed.

Some have doubted that the prophet could have formulated such a prayer to the Lord under the circumstances in which Jonah found himself. This is the argument of unbelief. The Scripture states plainly that Jonah did pray this prayer while in the fish, and so he did. The word *prayed* does not necessarily imply petition or supplication; it can refer to thanksgiving or praise as well.

As the prayer of chapter 2 is read and studied, it is soon seen that we have here not a petition for a future deliverance to be accomplished, but praise for a deliverance already realized. It has been suggested that throughout the prayer, Jonah wavers between the tendency to despair and that of faith which leads him to hope in God's sure deliverance. On the contrary, instead of wavering, the entire prayer breathes the atmosphere of sure deliverance in spite of the recital of the dire circumstances in which the prophet of God was found.

Mark how he makes his prayer to the Lord "his God" (v. 1) and "my God" (v. 6). These expressions show the faith of Jonah in his God. In spite of the fact that he had tried to flee from the Lord, he knew positively that God had not abandoned him and remained now as formerly his trustworthy God. By faith Jonah sees his deliverance granted and thanks God for it before it is actually accomplished.

The chapter is full of reminiscences of passages from the Psalms, and these reveal how well versed Jonah was in the Holy Scriptures and how full his mind and heart were of the Word of God. The Psalms is a book revealing the outpourings of the heart of the godly in times of deepest distress as well as in other experiences of life. The prophet had stored up these words in his heart, and, now in the time of greatest distress, he is able to draw comfort from them. The Scriptures are meant to be the source of comfort and hope to us too as believers in Christ. (See Ro 15:4.)

Jonah had cried to the Lord out of his affliction, and the Lord was ready and willing to answer him. From the belly of Sheol, which was the place and abode of the departed, he had made his prayer, and the Lord had heard. The place to which he had been brought was as though among those who had departed this life, but God heard his cry for help.

His condition would have been sufficiently terrifying if it had been the result of a so-called accident. But Jonah knew his plight was the consequence of disobeying and provoking God. (See Ps 39:9; for similar thoughts, see also Ps 18:4-6; 30:2; and 120:1.) Now the prophet recognizes that God was the source of his chastisement; it was God who had cast him into the sea. The sailors were only executing the punishment God had designed for him.

Paul never called himself a prisoner of Nero or Rome (Eph 3:1; 4:1; 2 Ti 1:8; and Phile 1, 9), but of Jesus Christ. It is blessed to be enabled of God to push beyond circumstances and see the mighty loving hand of God in all the affairs and changes of our lives.

Note also "thy waves and thy billows," which convey the same thought. He describes clearly enough the details of the peril from which God has rescued him. (For the wording compare Ps 42:7, and for a gracious promise of God at such times note Is 43:2.)

THE PRAYER OF JONAH

From verses 4 to 7 we learn of the prayer itself which Jonah uttered in his peril. He felt he was cast out from the special regard and care which God exercises over His own. Now he realized how dire a thing it is to be apart from the presence of the Lord. Though cast off, he would yet in faith look to God. He expected to enjoy in the future the privileges of worship in the Temple at Jerusalem. (See 1 Ki 8:29, 30, 38.)

That Jonah did not confine God's presence to the Temple, as the heathen did with their gods, is clear from his testimony in 1:9. He knew God as Creator of heaven, sea, and earth. (Cp. Ps 31:22 with Jon 2:4.)

The waters raged about him as though to extinguish physical life; the weeds, so abundant at the bottom of the sea, seemed to entangle him. (Note Ps 18:4; 69:1-2.) Jonah had been brought down to the bottoms of the mountains which were thought of as at the bottom of the sea. (See Ps 18:7, 15.) He considered himself cast out of the earth as a habitation, and its bars were shut against him lest he return. Though it appeared to Jonah at the time it happened that this was his permanent lot, yet God had miraculously brought him back from the pit, that is, corruption. This would have been his portion, had God not intervened on his behalf. (See 1 Sa 2:6; Ps 30:3.)

When his soul was overwhelmed, the prophet remembered the Lord. He had seen the hand of God in the storm, in the lots, but in the hour of deepest distress he recognized and remembered God as never before. He found that God is easily entreated by the humble soul. (For references in the Psalms see Ps 5:7; 18:6; 42:6; and 142:3.) Jonah's prayer closes with the full assurance that God has heard. His ear is ever open to the cry of the righteous.

THE GRATITUDE OF JONAH

Through all his harrowing experiences, the prophet of God had learned experimentally one of the greatest of all lessons in the spiritual realm. He had found that those who cleave with zealous regard to lying vanities forsake their own mercy. This is a revealing description not only of idolaters, but of all who place trust in worthless and helpless objects in the place of trust in the living and true God.

The mercy is that which can come from Him alone, hence stands here for God Himself. He is the great Benefactor, the source of all mercies and benefits. David so knew God also (the same word *chesedh*, "mercy," for God is used in Ps 144:2; see also Ps 31:6 and 59:17.)

Jonah would show how deliverance can be looked for only from the Lord. He knew now the condition of the heathen, because in seeking to flee from the Lord, he had also forsaken the only source of mercy. Priceless lesson the prophet had learned, and he is ready to give God the thanks due Him. Grateful for God's interposition on his behalf, Jonah promises the sacrifice of thanksgiving (note Lev 7:12-14) and the performance of his vows, which doubtless included the carrying out of his commission to Nineveh. At the end of chapter 2, we find Jonah in the same position as the mariners in 1:16, offering a sacrifice and making vows. He has come to know as never before that salvation, deliverance, whether of the soul or the body, can come only from the Lord Himself. (For the same truth, see Ps 3:8.)

THE INTERVENTION OF GOD

Now that the chastened servant of the Lord has been brought to the place of yieldedness, the Lord releases His messenger from his prison. In sovereign power the Lord spoke to the fish and it vomited out Jonah on the dry land. God's command to His irrational creatures is more readily obeyed than that to His rational and understanding ones. Would to God that we all, as servants of the living God in Christ, were as willing to obey each word from God, as were the wind, the storm, and the fish of which we read in this so true and so meaningful narrative in the book of Jonah.

In all probability the dry land upon which Jonah was cast was the coast of Palestine near Joppa. According to Jonah's faith so was it unto him: the deliverance he had taken by faith in the belly of the fish is now realized and viewed by sight.

JONAH AND ISRAEL

Just as the events of chapter 1 picture the history of Israel, so does chapter 2 give further details of the type of God's chosen people in the life history of Jonah.

Though Jonah was preserved of the Lord in the belly of the fish, he was at the same time under the chastening hand of God. During her exile among the nations Israel too, though miraculously preserved in spite of the persecutions of Satan's hosts, undergoes the chastening of the Lord.

Deuteronomy 28 is a remarkable portrayal with the greatest of fidelity of the condition of Israel when in worldwide dispersion. She will be oppressed, knowing no ease nor rest for body or soul, life in constant danger and fear. (Read carefully Deu 28:58-68.)

Just as Jonah feared again and again that he was at the end of his physical life, so Israel has been brought to despair of national existence again and again. But God has been faithful to preserve her even in the midst of chastening. True, the Lord has used nations for this chastening, but when it is accomplished God will reckon in judgment with the guilty nations, as He did in the case of Babylon, Assyria, and every other oppressor of His people.

Because of the grievous chastening of the Lord, Jonah cried out in prayer to God. Moses prophesied that Israel would be scattered among all the peoples and then added these important words (Deu 4:29) : "But from thence ye shall seek Jehovah thy God, and thou shalt find him, when thou searchest after him with all thy heart and with all thy soul." In trial and tribulation among the nations Israel will yet cry out to the Lord for His gracious deliverance.

When the prophet Jonah turned to the Lord in truth, the God of truth heard him and restored him to his land. Israel will be restored to the land of her fathers, brought back from the far corners of the globe. That which we see in our day in preliminary stage will be greatly accelerated and facilitated when God sends forth His angels with a great trumpet sound to gather His people from one end of earth to the other. (Cp. Mt 24:31. Read the glowing promises in Jer 16:14-15; 23:7, 8; 33:25, 26; and Eze 28:25-26 and be assured that God will bring every prediction to pass in His own blessed time and hour.)

Just as truly and surely as Israel has been scattered, preserved, chastened, and child-trained, she will be fully restored by the Lord to her own land and heritage, her inalienable right from the Lord. In the very hour when she turns with all the heart and with all the soul to the Lord God, He will turn her captivity, have compassion on her, and will return and gather her from all the peoples whither He had scattered her. (See Deu 30:1-3.)

SALVATION OF THE LORD

Beyond all things else Israel needs to learn today the great pronouncement of the prophet Jonah: "Salvation is of the Lord." The people of Israel know they are in perilous times; they know that hostile forces are arrayed against them on every hand; they know how diabolical the enemy can be in his persecutions. But they do not know that salvation is of the Lord. They are looking for deliverance in the political sphere, hoping

against hope that the nations of the world may be able to solve their problems. They are seeking deliverance in the social sphere, trusting that
education and social culture will curb the hostile desires of their sworn
enemies. They are trying for deliverance in the military sphere, attempt-
ing at long last to take up the cudgel on their own behalf. But these and
a thousand other devices are all unavailing. Deliverance, safety, and
salvation can be Israel's only through the Lord. And this salvation is
imparted through the Person and work of One alone, the Lord Jesus
Christ, the Messiah of Israel.

THE SUCCESSFUL PROPHET

THE RENEWED COMMISSION

The purpose of the Lord in chastening His servant was to make him
more useful for the work to which he had been clearly called. Thus it was
that the call came to Jonah a second time. God in marvellous grace recommissioned His messenger. God gives men a second chance in His
service, as He did with Jonah, Peter, and John Mark. (Let the reader not
misunderstand. We do not say that God gives a second chance to trust
Christ after this earthly life is closed. There is no such teaching in the
Bible.) Thank God, He bears with His erring servants and is willing to
give them the message "the second time."

Jonah is commanded to arise and go to Nineveh with the same message.
God knows the subtleties of Satan: if he does not prevent the preaching of
the truth, he tries the perversion of it. There was to be no changing of
the message in Jonah's preaching.

Nineveh is called "that great city." (See also Jon 4:11 as well as v. 3
of chap. 3.) The city was about sixty miles in circumference. An ancient
writer described Nineveh as 480 stadia in circuit. It was much larger than
Babylon. The walls of Nineveh were one hundred feet high; they were
broad enough to allow three chariots to ride abreast. It had 1,500 lofty
towers. Since there were more than 120,000 children in the city (4:11), it
has been estimated that the city boasted about a million inhabitants. A
more conservative figure is 600,000 population. This was no mean city
and God's blessed heart went out to all the inhabitants in it.

THE OBEDIENT PROPHET

How differently the record reads now! Jonah arose and did exactly as
the Lord bade him. There is ready obedience now in the place of the
former self-will. Jonah is now a living example of mercy received through
repentance. (See Mt 21:28-29.) Would that Jonah had more followers in

his obedience than he has in his flight. Our Lord tells us that he was a sign to the Ninevites (Lk 11:30).

It is known that Ninevites worshiped the fish god, Dagon, part man and part fish. Interestingly enough, "Oannes" (with "I" before it the name spells Jonah in the New Testament) was the name of one of the incarnations of Dagon. Too, there is an Assyrian mound "Nebi Yunas" (the prophet Jonah). The archaeologist Botta associated the two with Nineveh and uncovered the walls of the old city.

As interesting as these historical confirmations are, the center of the narrative is in the person of Jonah himself as he brings God's message. He himself had been saved from death and thus could give the guilty city of Nineveh its needed hope in the Lord Himself. Again the account brings before us the fact that Nineveh was "an exceeding great city" (lit., "great unto God"); it was great to God who is not misled by mere appearances but views all things in their true light. The three days' journey would come to about sixty miles, as we noted above.

As Jonah journeyed into the city he preached his message of warning. No definite distance is necessarily implied here, because we do not know how long Jonah may have stopped at different places.

Scoffers and skeptics have asked how Jonah could have preached to a people whom he did not know and yet have them understand his preaching. He could easily make himself intelligible to the Assyrians. (Note Is 36:11 in this connection.) There was a language of general use then as there is now. The warning of judgment was in itself a word of grace. A forty-day period was being granted them in which to turn to God from their wicked ways. Forty is the number employed in Scripture in relation to testing. (See Gen 7:17, the Flood; Ex 24:18, Moses in the mount; 1 Ki 19:8, Elijah in his flight to Horeb; and Mt 4:2, the temptation of Christ.) The word *overthrown* is the same word used for the destruction of Sodom and Gomorrah. God threatened to turn the city upside down, to destroy it from the very foundations.

THE REPENTANCE OF NINEVEH

Our Lord said Jonah was a sign to the Ninevites. The events recorded in this book had reached the people of Nineveh before the prophet arrived at the capital, hence he was a sign to them. They could see in Jonah that God punishes sin but also spares the sinner on repentance. The sacred record preserves for us only five words of Jonah's message (in the original of 3:4), but it was one of the greatest messages ever preached by man, if not the greatest. Nowhere do we read in the Bible or outside of it that one message from a servant of God was used of God to so great an extent. For the whole city of Nineveh believed God! Nothing remotely approximating this has ever taken place in the history of revivals. Jonah was a sign, but the people did not concern themselves with the prophet. They believed God.

God is honored by such faith, and He honors it by accomplishing much in answer to it. Everyone, old and young alike, all without exception, turned to God and gave evidence of grief over his sins. They fasted and mourned. They must have reasoned, Why should God send a prophet to warn us? If He had wanted to destroy us outright, He would have left us to pursue our sinful ways. Why, too, does He allow us forty days between the pronouncement of the doom and the punishment itself? Surely it is because of God's intended mercy, and His desire is that we avail ourselves of His willingness to forgive us.

This reponse was so spontaneous that no one waited for orders from the king, nor did they consult his pleasure in the matter. But when the message reached his ears (the identity of this king is not known), the king reacted exactly as the people did. There was no delay, no disbelieving the message, but ready compliance with the implication of the message. It called in no uncertain terms for immediate repentance. The people and the king so understood the warning and acted accordingly.

Some explain the general repentance (for this moral miracle in chap. 3 far exceeds in greatness the physical miracle of the swallowing of Jonah by the fish, his preservation, and the disgorging of the prophet recorded in chaps. 1 and 2) on the ground that the nations of the East are given to emotion, that they highly regard soothsaying and oracles, that the occasion of a foreigner preaching with disinterestedness and boldness the sins of the city—all these must have made a profound impression on the people.

The essential fact is that Jonah, coming with a true message from God, has his message authenticated by the power of the Holy Spirit to the hearts of the heathen Ninevites. In the hour of repentance king and people were on the same level. God is interested in the broken and contrite heart, not the royal purple or the pauper's rags.

In verses 7 to 9 we have the decree of the king and his nobles. The fact that the nobles share with the king in the issuing of the decree reveals that there was not an absolute monarchy. (Cp. Dan 6:17.)

Twice in the decree, beast and man are joined. This is not unusual in the East. Ancient historians tell us that the Persians, after the fall of their commander Masistios, clipped the hair of their horses and mules. The draping of horses with black at funeral processions is not unknown even in our time.

Whatever may have been the moving factor in the minds of the Ninevites, the action is based upon a true premise that there is a relationship between man and beast (see Joel 1:18, 20), whereby the latter are drawn into suffering through the sin of man, and hence both long for liberation from the bondage of corruption. (See the significant passage in Ro 8:19-25; also Is 11:6-9; 35:1-10.) If God had overthrown Nineveh, it would have been the doom of the animals of the city as well. (See Ps 36:6-7.) That God has regard for both man and beast is clearly stated in 4:11, the climaxing verse of the whole book.

The royal edict singles out violence along with all their evil way as that of which they are to repent. (Cp. Nah 3:1.) Records of Assyria are catalogs of military campaigns, cruelties, and plunderings. They were all to repent in the hope that the Lord would turn from His fierce anger. (See Joel 2:13-14.)

When the Scriptures speak of God repenting (in view of Num 23:19), it is the language of appearance; the language of accommodation, from the viewpoint of man. The Ninevites felt there was the possibility of God's mercy without any specific assurance for encouragement, therefore the words *who knoweth*.

THE CITY SPARED

When God saw their works and that they had turned from their wickedness, He repented of the punishment He had warned them of and did not do it. They were not deeds of merit, because there is no word of sacrifices or offerings, but only of true repentance and faith toward God.

This is not salvation by works. Reference is made to their repentance in sackcloth and ashes, which showed a change within them. The readiness which marked their actions showed that they were not ripe for judgment. (Note the principle set forth in Jer 18:7-8; see also Ex 32:14.) God is said, after the manner of man's understanding and feeling, to repent when He alters His proposed action or deals in a way not expected from His promises or warnings. The threatened doom in this instance was conditioned on repentance. When that condition was met and fulfilled, God had no need to execute the warning.

From the record there is no doubt that the repentance was genuine (else God would not have spared the city on the show of a spurious turning to Him), but that it was of short duration can be inferred from the prophecies of the book of Nahum, where certain judgment is predicted for Nineveh. Less than a century later, this city was destroyed by God, but the repentance in Jonah's day was genuine, as our Lord stated in Matthew 12:41. Thank God for the power in repentance which releases the power of God to work as He delights. He is much more willing to bless than to judge.

The book thus teaches clearly the efficacy of repentance, first with Jonah and then with the Ninevites.

JONAH: A PICTURE OF ISRAEL

Chapter 3, like the previous chapters, prefigures the dealings of God with His chosen people, Israel. After Jonah's restoration to the Lord and to the land, he was recommissioned of God to preach the message God had intended from the first.

When Israel turns to the Lord, when the veil is removed from the heart, when she cries out in truth to the Lord from the midst of her distresses, the Lord will restore her not only to her own land but also to the commission of witnessing to the Lord.

This commission is stated repeatedly in the Scriptures. (Note Is 43:10, 12.) Israel was to be a priestly nation ministering God's will among the nations (Ex 19:5-6).

This commission will be fulfilled in the future. Men from all nations of the earth will realize that Israel is the repository of the truth of God (Zec 8:20-23). While the nations of the world will be the plowmen and vinedressers in that day, Israel will ultimately accomplish God's will for her as priests of the Lord and ministers of God. (See Is 61:5-6.) In that time Israel, as Jonah of old, will be armed with the message of God for all peoples.

And more, just as Jonah's ministry was gloriously successful in the power of God, so Israel will be used of God to accomplish that which has never been wrought before, the conversion of the world. Paul states it thus: that if the setting aside of Israel nationally has meant the incalculable enrichment and reconciliation of the world, the restoration and recommission of God's people can only mean life from the dead (Ro 11:15). Life from the dead! In what sense? Like Jonah they will return to the Lord as from the dead. There will be a national resurrection (see Eze 37). The world will see a spiritually resurrected nation. Then the message of this people will be empowered of God to turn the nations from spiritual death to spiritual life. It will be life from the dead for them also. What a day of world revival that will be. A nation of Jonahs will be preaching the message of God to a needy and lost world.

OUR MERCIFUL GOD

How comforting and consoling to our redeemed hearts it is to think long and satisfyingly on the mercy of our gracious God. God truly has no pleasure in the death of the wicked, in the perishing of the lost, but that such ones turn from their evil ways and live. But the sad fact is that many know not the mercy of our God in Christ Jesus the Lord unto eternal life. And of whom is this more true than of Israel? Beloved of God, they are the hated of the world and of Satan. Chosen of God, they are the despised and neglected of the nations. Cherished of God, they are the spurned and persecuted of the nations. Is it not high time that now through the mercy shown us they also may obtain mercy? May we all be empowered unto every good work and word on behalf of their salvation.

THE INSTRUCTED PROPHET

THE ANGER OF JONAH

If man, unaided by the Spirit of God, were writing this account, it would probably have concluded with the close of chapter 3. Apparently the climax has been reached with the repentance and sparing of the wicked city of Nineveh. The mercy of God has been displayed, the now obedient prophet of God has been successful in his ministry, and the city of Nineveh is no longer in danger of fearful punishment.

Why does the record not close here? Because there is a yet greater climax, the true goal and objective of the whole book. Because God must teach His servant (and us through him) certain truths about the narrowness of his heart, as well as the boundless greatness of God's own blessed heart.

Amazing as it strikes us each time we read it, the account states that Jonah was exceedingly displeased and very angry. Why was the chastened messenger of God angry? There are those who tell us that the prophet was anxious over his reputation as a prophet. Because his prediction of judgment was not fulfilled, they say, he was afraid that he would be the laughing stock of his countrymen when he returned home. (See Deu 18:21-22.) The reason is rather that set forth in the next verse of chapter 4. Jonah begrudged the heathen Ninevites the abundant mercy of God.

What a contrast we have here between God's attitude toward Nineveh after its repentance and Jonah's attitude to the same city's repentance. He had received pardoning mercy from the Lord on his repentance but was not willing for Nineveh to have the same. We are reminded of the parable of our Lord in Matthew 18:23-35. The human heart is ever the same in all ages. (Cp. Jer 17:9.)

Jonah is like so many today: they feel they could govern God's world much better than He can. Think of it! The prophet of God angry beyond measure because of the pardoning grace of God. He was, like so many of us, more zealous about the judgment of Nineveh than the sparing of it. He assumed he knew better than God the proper course to be followed.

THE PRAYER OF JONAH

The anger of the prophet, however, did not put him outside the position of prayer. It is still a man of God praying but surely not in conformity with the will and plan and heart of the infinite God. This becomes increasingly clear as the chapter proceeds to its majestic close.

As though God were unaware of the movements of Jonah's heart, the prophet explains to the Lord that this was the dominating thought in his mind when the message first came to him in his own country, namely, that God, being gracious, merciful, longsuffering, full of lovingkindness, and ready to stay His hand in judgment upon repentance, would spare the city of Nineveh if she did turn to the Lord. (See Ex 34:6-7; Joel 2:13.)

Without shame Jonah lays bare the motivating impulses of his heart which were so despicable. Man cannot bear the grace of God to others. In his despondency and chagrin he justifies his flight and quarrels with God because He spared Nineveh.

He reminds us of the elder brother in the parable of the prodigal son of Luke 15. They are spiritual twins. So peeved and angry is Jonah that he prays for death. (Compare vv. 8 and 9 also.) In chapter 2 he thanked God for deliverance from death. Here he seeks death as better than life. How contrary are our desires and how unreasonable we are when petulant and peeved. Elijah also requested to die (note 1 Ki 19:4), but it was because of zeal for the glory of the Lord and against idolatry in Israel. Jonah's request is wholly selfish and indefensible.

Note now the exceeding grace of God in dealing with His servant. There are here not only the grace and love of God, but His infinite patience with carping Jonah. There is no word of rebuke or upbraiding or punishment. God tries to draw Jonah out of himself to view his anger and sinful displeasure in their true light. The Lord asks the prophet but one question, whether he was angry with any warrant, justly, rightly. Did he have true and reasonable grounds for his anger? For answer Jonah went outside the city walls and built himself a booth east of the city to see what the ultimate fate of the city would be.

It has been suggested that Jonah took this course of action before the forty days announced by him had elapsed. The rebuke of the prophet by God appears to have more force if we understand it to have taken place after the expiration of the forty days. Jonah had no means of knowing the depth or the reality of the repentance of Nineveh. In view of the greatness of the threat he waited to see whether there might be a change yet in God's purpose concerning the city. In his mental condition of extreme anger he may have thought God meant by His question, "Why do you think you have a right to be angry, when for all you know I may yet destroy the city?" At any rate Jonah did not realize that the booth he made was going to be used of God as a school of discipline to teach him one of the greatest (if not the greatest) lessons in the world.

THE GOURD, THE WORM, THE WIND

After Jonah had built his booth, God caused a gourd to spring up with miraculous rapidity. How tender of God to see to the physical comfort of His servant, even though the latter was completely out of sympathy with God's plan. The gourd was the ricinusplant, the Palma Christi, which is native to India, Palestine, Arabia, Africa, and eastern Europe. It attains a height usually of from eight to ten feet. The plant has large leaves and grows up in a few days, but it is easily withered by any injury to the tender stalk.

Because of this shade afforded him, Jonah was now as exceedingly glad as he was exceedingly angry at the beginning of the chapter. This is the only place in the book where it is said of Jonah that he was glad, and it was a selfish joy over his own comfort.

What book that we know is so faithful in its portrayal of the faults, as well as the virtues, of its chief characters, as is the Bible? By Jonah's exceeding gladness over the gourd, God intends to reveal to him His own great gladness in the repentance and sparing of Nineveh.

The next morning, at the appointment of the Lord, a worm (or the singular may be used collectively for a number) smote the gourd and it withered. Worms can strip the plant of all its foliage in a single night, according to the word of some authorities. The sudden removal of this welcome relief for the prophet would have been bad enough, but to add to his misery, the rising of the blazing sun was accompanied by a sultry east wind sent by God. The scorching heat, which is relaxing in its effect, of this sirocco is proverbial throughout the Old Testament. (See Eze 17:10.) In the midst of his faint condition Jonah pleaded with God for death. Again God asks him if he has a right to be angry because of the gourd. This time the prophet answers with emphasis that he has every right to be angry, even to the point of death.

THE HEART OF GOD

Now that Jonah has stated so vehemently his right to be angry and his desire to die, God is ready to press the lesson of these strange experiences in the life of the prophet. Since the prophet has expressed himself so clearly on his affection for the gourd which afforded him shade and comfort, he can now be shown how he has tried to deny God His strong love for those much more important than the gourd.

From verse 10 it is evident why a plant like the gourd with its rapid growth was chosen to be the object lesson for Jonah. If it had been a plant which grew slowly, he would have had to water it and care for it. In that case the rebuke of the Lord would have lost its force. Oh, the depth of the wisdom of God! God was saying to Jonah: If you became so attached to the gourd, because it served you and gratified your desires—a gourd upon which you expended no thought, no labor, no toil, no sacrifice, no care, no planting, no watering, no tending, no pruning, a gourd of short duration which grows up quickly and as hastily passes away—shall I not permit My love and pity to flow forth unstintingly to multitudes of My creatures, the work of My hands, the crown of all My creative acts, nurtured, fed, provided for by Me, those who will never go out of existence? Was there ever such irresistible logic? And was there ever such boundless love and pity? We know not any.

Note how the greatness of the city of Nineveh is stated. Those who cannot discern between their right hand and their left hand are children; according to some this is at the age of three, while others claim it bespeaks the age of seven. In any event if we assume this class to be one-fifth of the population, there were some 600,000 inhabitants in the city, a city of no mean size even according to modern standards of reckoning.

Besides these, there was also much cattle, a touch of much tenderness showing God cares even for them. They have a form of life which even the gourd does not possess. Here we have set forth God's love for all His creatures, even cattle. If God was willing and ready to spare wicked Sodom for the sake of ten, He surely desired to have pity and spare 120,000 who, though with inborn sin, had not reached the age of discernment and willful sin. How much better it is to fall into the hands of the living God rather than into the hands of man. (See 2 Sa 24:14.)

The seeming abruptness of the close of the book is intentional and much more forceful than if the thought had been carried out in further detail. The true climax of the thought of the prophecy has been reached and the all-important message of the book is left with the reader. The tender voice of God is telling forth the love of God for all the nations, for all His needy creatures.

HOW SHALL HE NOT HAVE PITY?

We dare not leave the words with which the book closes as though they were an afterthought. The key to the book of Jonah is here. Yea, more, the key to the heart of missions is here. This book is the greatest missionary book in the Old Testament, if not in the whole Bible. It is written to reveal the heart of a servant of God whose heart was not touched with the passion of God in missions. Does it strike home?

Are we more interested in our own comfort than the need of multitudes of lost souls in Israel dying in darkness without the knowledge of their Messiah and Saviour, the Lord Jesus Christ? Are we more content to remain with the "gourds," the comforts of home, than to see the message of Christ go out to the ends of the earth to both Jew and Gentile? We may not, as Jonah did, argue with God for His goodness and mercy and love to the benighted souls lost in sin, but if we do not make it possible for them to hear of His grace and power to save to the uttermost, the result is the same, as far as they are concerned.

How shall He not have pity? The main message of the book, its central and dominant theme, is that of the Bible itself. God's love is ever seeking to save those who are rightly doomed to eternal punishment. (See Gen 18:23-33.) Can God—will God—be stayed in His yearning because puny man may find it in his heart to object to the limitless mercy and love of God? The Bible gives the unmistakable answer: He will not be hindered by man's narrowness of heart, but He must from the very necessity of His blessed nature have pity.

How shall He not have pity? If God should not spare, where then would be the hope for any in the world? No generation of men, nor all generations combined, could find a way of escape from the wrath of God, had God not determined to have pity. If all the nations of the earth must find provision for eternal life in the mercy and grace of God in Christ, how else shall Israel be redeemed?

How shall He not have pity? How can God possibly fail to have mercy when He has stated so clearly that He delights to be entreated, that He intends to save Jew and Gentile in answer to faith in the Lord Jesus Christ, that He is rich in grace to all without difference?

How shall He not have pity? Because our eye may be evil in the matter, shall God cease to be good? (See Mt 20:15.) Because we have hedged men about with innumerable distinctions and have placed them in countless categories, shall God become a respecter of persons?

How shall He not have pity? In our Bible we have the outstanding examples of Jonah and Peter (Ac 10) who were loath to take the message of God's love to unsaved Gentiles. Dare we count the number who are loath and negligent to bear the message of saving grace in Christ to the lost sheep of the house of Israel? Thank God forever more, He does have pity! But do we?

9

MICAH
WRATH UPON SAMARIA AND JERUSALEM

Judgment on Judah's Cities

THE MESSENGER OF GOD

MICAH'S NAME means "Who is like Jehovah?" Practically nothing is known of the prophet besides the town of his residence and the time and place of his ministry. He came from a small town called Moresheth-gath, about twenty miles southwest of Jerusalem. Eusebius and Jerome quote a tradition which placed the site not far to the east of Eleutheropolis.

The prophet was a Judean by birth; he prophesied in Jerusalem; and he was a younger contemporary of Isaiah. (Cp. Is 1:1 with Mic 1:1.) There are passages in Micah parallel to some in Isaiah, especially Micah 4:1-5 with Isaiah 2:2-4. He has been confused, because of identity of name, with Micaiah the son of Imlah (1 Ki 22:8) who ministered in the reign of Ahab. As a contemporary of Isaiah, Hosea, and Amos, he labored in the latter half of the eighth century BC. No kings of the Northern Kingdom of Israel are mentioned by the prophet; only prophets in Israel make mention of kings of Israel.

Micah is quoted by Jeremiah (Jer 26:18-19) and by our Lord Jesus Christ (quoting Mic 7:6 in Mt 10:35-36).

The prophecy of Micah divides easily into three divisions: chapters 1 and 2; chapters 3 to 5; and chapters 6 and 7. Each division is marked by the words, *"Hear ye"* (see 1:2; 3:1; and 6:1). Each of the divisions of the book begins with the rebuke for sin, the announcement of judgment, and the promise of blessing in the Messiah.

THE LORD'S COMING IN JUDGMENT

If the message of the book of Jonah be God's love to all nations, then Micah's concerns judgment upon Samaria and Jerusalem. The prophecies

153

of this book are especially to the capital cities as the centers influencing the whole nation. Verses 1 and 5 of chapter 1 indicate that both the Northern and the Southern Kingdoms are in view.

The Lord is revealed immediately as Judge. The call to hear is addressed in 1:2 to all peoples; in 3:1 to the heads of Jacob and rulers of the house of Israel; and in 3:5 to the false prophets.

The first summons to hear is directed not to Israel alone, but to all the nations. They are to be not judges but witnesses of God's judgment. It is the Lord speaking from heaven and testifying against His people Israel. (For similar expressions see Deu 31:28; 32:1; Is 1:2.)

The prophet pictures the Lord coming forth from heaven and treading upon the high places, the mountains, of the earth. The imagery is taken from the action of earthquakes and volcanoes. (Cp. Judg 5:4; Ps 18:7-10; 50:3; 68:8; 97:5; Is 64:1-2; and Hab 3:5.) The judgment of the Lord is seen as reducing the earth to chaos. The historical events signified here were Shalmaneser's destruction of the Northern Kingdom, the invasion by Sennacherib, and Nebuchadnezzar's invasion.

THE DESTRUCTION OF SAMARIA

Micah now states directly what the cause of God's visitation was: the transgression of Jacob and the sins of the house of Israel. The wrath of God was to fall on the entire nation, because they were all involved. To bring out the culprits all the more clearly the prophet asks what (lit., who) is the cause of the sin in Israel. The answer reveals that the capitals were the seats of corruption in both the Northern and Southern Kingdoms. Samaria and Jerusalem are the core of the pollution. The reformation of the godly king Hezekiah in the fifth year of his reign had not taken place yet.

The high places were places on mountains and hills where altars were erected for sacrifice to idols (2 Ki 12:3; 14:4; and Eze 6:6).

The destruction of Samaria by the Assyrians is now set forth. The beautiful city will become nothing more than a heap of stones. It will be so completely laid waste that the region will return to tillage. The site was probably a vineyard originally (1 Ki 16:24). The stones of the city (see 3:12) in turn will be poured down from the top of the hill on which the city was built, into the valley which the capital of Samaria overlooked. In short, the sumptuous city will be destroyed to the very foundations. What the Assyrians began was fulfilled by John Hyrcanus (Josephus, *Antiquities*. xii. 28. 1). In the overthrow of the city all her images will be beaten to pieces and all the love gifts given to the gods will be consumed by fire.

The hire of a harlot spoken of in verse 7 refers to the payment given a harlot or temple prostitute as among the Phoenicians (Deu 23:18; Ho 9:1; and Is 23:17). Here the word evidently means the images, as well as gifts, set up in the temples of the idols by those who believed they had received benefits from the worthless god. These hires would probably be used again by the heathen for their idols. Terrible indeed are the wages of sin, and Samaria was to receive her portion in full measure.

THE STROKE FALLS ON JUDAH

Having graphically described the doom of Samaria, the prophet of God now directs his words and predictions of the kingdom of Judah. He tells how the judgment affects him personally. His grief is real: he laments and wails, going about naked (a sign of mourning, 2 Sa 15:30). His wailing is likened to that of jackals because of their howl; his lamentation is compared to that of ostriches because of their mournful noise. (See Job 30:29 in his deep grief.) The sorrow of the prophet is all the greater, because the judgment does not stop with Samaria. It spreads over all the land and engulfs Judah as well. The stroke causes an incurable wound because it reaches to the very heart of the nation, even to Jerusalem. The same Assyrian power that reduced Samaria and the Northern Kingdom was to threaten Judah and Jerusalem also. (See further Is 10 and 36.) Companions in sin are doomed to be companions in judgment. It is a solemn spiritual truth that we all do well to heed.

DOOM ON MANY CITIES

From verse 9 on we have foretold the effects of the invasion of Sennacherib and his siege of Jerusalem. The ending verse of chapter 1 would appear to carry on the truth of Judah's judgment to the time of the Babylonian captivity. The towns of Judah which were to experience the scourge of the Assyrian invasion are listed and each has its judgment predicted in words that play on the name of the city.

The first towns mentioned are in the hill country of Judah. The enemy is traveling from Samaria to Jerusalem. The next towns are in the immediate vicinity of Jerusalem; then are named the places in the Judean lowland adjacent to the Philistine country. The capital, mark you, is not declared as destroyed.

Micah exhorts, first of all, that the people keep the news of the desolation of the land from the Philistine city of Gath. Judah's woe is to be kept from the knowledge of the Philistine enemies of Israel, because the prophet fears the vengeful rejoicing of the foes of God's people. (Cp. for the identical exhortation 2 Sa 1:20.) Indeed, the people are told not to weep at all. Some have translated "weep not in Acco" which was a maritime city in Asher, called Ptolemais, between Carmel and Tyre. But the original will scarcely bear out this translation. The Canaanites were not driven out of this city (Judg 1:31), and it never came into the possession of Israel.

As a sign of mourning (Jos 7:6), Micah rolled himself in the dust at Bethleaphrah ("house of dust"). The site of this town is not known. Thus the people are informed that in their own territory they were to lament their plight. The inhabitants of Shaphir (site unknown) were to go into captivity in the midst of shame and nakedness; the people of Zaanan (site uncertain) would not go forth to battle because they would be besieged (Jos 6:1); and the town of Beth-ezel with its lamentation would not permit them to linger there in their flight, being unable to provide them with refuge. The inhabitants of Maroth (lit., "bitter-town"; identity unknown) will look in vain for tidings of good, because the enemy flood will reach to the very gate of Jerusalem (see v. 9). Their hopes will be sorely disappointed.

The call comes now to the well-known defended town of Lachish to take to flight (Is 36:2). The reason given for the stroke of judgment on Lachish is that it first introduced idolatry in Judah as Jeroboam the son of Nebat had in Israel. It was evidently the link of idolatry between Israel and Judah. There is no record of this in the historical books of the Old Testament, although it has been suggested that the horses given to the sun (2 Ki 23:11) related to idolatry were kept there. The same condemning sin of idolatry of the Northern Kingdom was found in Lachish, so she must bear the same punishment.

Verse 14 has been variously interpreted. Some have held that Moresheth-gath was to be filled with gifts for the enemy; others have maintained that she would be given for help wanted; while still others understand that the city itself (its name means possession or inheritance) would become the inheritance of the enemy by going into captivity. The last is probably the best view. The parting gift was the gift that a father gave his daughter on the occasion of her marriage. Here the home of the prophet Micah would fall into the hands of the Assyrian adversary when he invaded the land.

The houses of Achzib (meaning "lie," probably a site southwest of Adullam) would disappoint the hopes of the kings of Israel, the Judean dynasty, who would be looking to her for help.

The *achzabim* of the Old Testament are brooks that are dry in summer, thus deceiving the thirsty traveler. (See Jer 15:18.)

The Assyrian power would be brought to Mareshah by the Lord to possess her, and the nobility of Israel, the glory of the nation, would be compelled to flee to Adullam (Jos 15:35; 1 Sa 22:1). The Assyrian foe will inherit all that is before him in the land.

ZION'S MOURNING

After mentioning twelve cities, Micah turns to address Israel herself. She is exhorted of the prophet to make herself bald and cut off her hair for her beloved children of whom she is suddenly bereaved.

The custom of shaving the head was prohibited in Deuteronomy 14:1, but it was carried on among the people nevertheless. It was a mourning custom. (See Is 15:2 and Jer 16:6.) Their baldness is compared to that of the bald eagle or vulture whose neck and head are without feathers.

The cause of this mourning is the captivity of Zion's children. This was hardly applicable to the invasion of Sennacherib in the days of Hezekiah, but it does look on to the time of the doom of the Babylonian Exile.

Thus chapter 1 ends with the picture of unrelieved judgment and doom upon the cities of God's people for their incurable sin and transgression of idolatry. Their punishment that awaits them is indelibly impressed in the very names they bear. The most disastrous activity known to man is that of sin. Its consequences are dire and are writ large throughout the pages of the sacred Scriptures.

THE GREATER MOURNING NOW

There are some ten expressions in the first chapter of Micah that point out the mournful and distressing condition of the cities of Judah and Israel. The prophet Micah was unable to view the scene of destruction and havoc dispassionately. His grief was inconsolable. Yet he was only looking at a temporary invasion of Sennacherib and a Babylonian captivity which lasted but seventy, though bitter and weary, years. But how much greater is the mourning that characterizes Israel now? If Rachel mourned for her children at the time of the Babylonian captivity (Jer 31:15) and by Herod's slaughter of the innocents (Mt 2:18) was caused to weep without comfort, how much more is her grief heightened in this our day? Betrayed by friends and harassed by foes, her heart is consumed with grief. And this grief can be assuaged. You and I have in our possession that glorious Good News of a finished redemption through the Messiah of Israel for all her sins and transgressions, that can cause the most sorrowful heart among Israel to leap with joy and to exult in God the Saviour.

UNIVERSAL UNGODLINESS

ISRAEL'S GLARING SINS

If chapter 1 boldly assails the sins of God's people against the Lord, chapter 2 rebukes just as clearly and fearlessly crimes against man. Violence and oppression are indicated as the moral reasons for the judgment of God.

The prophet Micah pronounces woe upon the nobility of the land (see Is 5:8) because at night upon their beds they occupy themselves with premeditating evil, with conceiving the plan, then with working out the fuller scheme or arranging ways and means, and finally with the putting of the device into operation with the coming of morning. (Contrast their action with that of the righteous in Ps 4:4.) The ungodly are successful in their plottings because they have the power to carry out their desires. With them, might is right. (Cp. Gen 31:29 and Pr 3:27 for the same expression.)

Verse 2 makes clear what the evil plottings of the wicked have in view. They covet the fields and property of others and by violence and oppression they seize them, as did wicked Ahab and Jezebel the rightful heritage of Naboth. (See 1 Ki 21.) Whenever the rights of God are lightly treated, the rights of man can fare no better. As in the days of Noah, when the ways of men are corrupt before the Lord, they fill the earth with violence. It requires no superior insight to draw the parallel for our own day.

THE NATION EXILED

In contrast to the wicked devisings of the ungodly, the righteous God warns the nation, with special reference to those who perpetrate the deeds of verses 1 and 2, that He is devising an evil against them. He will place upon them a yoke from which they will not be able to remove their necks. This God-imposed yoke is the invasion of the land by the enemy and the exile of the people from their land. No longer will the great of the land walk haughtily, for they will be prevented from doing so because of the yoke upon their necks. It will be an evil hour, the time of their captivity. (Note Amos 5:13.)

To add to the misery of Israel in the hour of her calamity, her enemies will take up a parable to deride and mock her. They will evidently use Israel's own words. The three Hebrew words (*nahah, nehi, nihyah,* an expressive play on words) give the impression of a monotonous wail: "lament with a lament of lamentation." Then those undergoing the judgment in Israel will bewail the fact that God has given their land to the nations about them. The land is taken from them as a punishment for their plunder of the inheritance of the poor of the nation. Their fields will be given to the rebellious, the nations who are their enemies.

Verse 5 has been variously interpreted. It is claimed that there would be none remaining in Israel with the authority to divide the land and set the landmarks. The suggestion has also been made that reference is to the apportionment of a man's property among his children after his death; the ungodly in Israel will have none to receive the inheritance. The probable meaning of the passage is this: because of the sins of verses 1 and 2, no one will have an inheritance or possession apportioned out to him. (See for the first division of the land by lot, using a line for measurement, Jos 13:6.) The division of Israel's land was now to be made by Israel's foes, not by herself. She will be completely at the mercy of her enemies, so that she will not be allowed to divide parts of the land for inheritance. The ungodly among the leaders of the people will have no further share in the inheritance of the Lord's people. In seizing the portion of others, they lose their own.

THE FALSE PROPHETS

Evil devisings, covetousness, oppression, and pride are accompanied by a hardness of heart that will not hear the message and word that come from the prophet of God. It is not only the false prophets who would prohibit the true prophets from foretelling the coming judgments of the Lord, but Israel as such so commands the true prophet when he preaches to her an unwelcome message from the Lord. (See Is 30:10; Amos 2:12; 7:16.) God takes the people at their word and in judgment gives them their evil desire. They will have no prophets to prophesy to them. But by the same token there will be no removal of their shame. If the true prophets do not prophesy to the unrighteous (vv. 1 and 2) because of their sins, then the reproach and shame of the nation will not depart, but destruction will fall upon them. When man is given his desire, a desire not born of the Lord, then leanness of soul always accompanies it.

Now the prophet Micah meets the charge as to whether the absence of prophecies of blessing can be laid to a lack on the part of the Spirit of the Lord. Is His compassion less than it has been in the past? They need not ask whether such threats from the prophet of God are in keeping with the mercy and grace of God. Does the Lord find pleasure in His predictions of judgment? It is because of Israel's sin that the punishments foretold by the prophets were necessary in the first place. Repeatedly the Scriptures make it plain that the heart of God does not delight in afflicting His creatures; punishment results only when His loving entreaties are spurned and not heeded.

Moreover, if their ways had been pleasing to the Lord and they had done His will, His words would not have come to them in the form of threatenings. If they would but walk uprightly, the Lord would ever delight to do them good. God would have noted repentance if it had been present, and He would have wrought on behalf of the godly. There was, then, no constraint in the Lord in His dealings with them, but the fault lay with them.

UNGODLINESS OF GOD'S PEOPLE

And in order to reveal how blameworthy they were, the prophet again turns to picture their multiplied sins which are so grievous in the sight of the Lord. Even in recent times their oppressions have increased, so that they are likened to an enemy and an invading foe. In robbing the helpless and defenseless they are not only enemies of their victims, but of the Lord as well. (Cp. Ex 22:25-27 and Deu 27:18.)

The garment mentioned may be the covering of the poor at night. It is suggested that the wicked rob their own countrymen who are returning victorious from battle and consider themselves secure. The ones who are the objects of the plundering are probably peaceful and innocent passers-by. Life is made insecure for those who have no intentions of harm toward their fellowcountrymen. (See Ps 120:7.)

The women who are cast out of their pleasant houses are doubtless widows, unprotected and unsuspecting. And their orphan children are spoiled of their sustenance also. (Note Is 10:2 for a portrayal of conditions of the same period in the history of Israel.) The pleasant houses are the homes inherited from their husbands to which memories cling. Their properties are seized heartlessly, and they are evicted.

The glory spoken of with reference to the young children is the sustenance given them of God, a proof of the blessing of God on them. Sex nor age made any difference to the oppressors of the people. Nor was there contrition on the part of those responsible for these outrages, for the passage indicates they intended to continue such actions "for ever."

That society is indeed in a low state of morality when even widows and orphans are not spared. These are set forth throughout the Bible as the special charges of the Lord, and he who deals with them perversely does not do so with impunity. Therefore, the Lord commands peremptorily: "Arise ye, and depart."

Some students of this passage understand the command to be addressed to the godly who could not find rest in the midst of such pollution. We understand it, however, to be directed to the ungodly who will be dispossessed of their inheritances as they go into the already predicted exile.

God is threatening them again with a removal from their own land. The land cannot abide their outrages any longer.

God had intended Canaan to be a resting place (Deu 12:9-10) for His people, and in times of obedience and blessing it was such. But now because of the pollution of the land by their infamous deeds, the land was to cast out its inhabitants. (See Lev 18:25, 28 for the warning given through Moses.) The terms of the Palestinian covenant (Deu 28-30) promised blessing and continuance in the land upon the sole ground of obedience; in case of disobedience there was but one alternative: exile. Micah, therefore, is pronouncing the breach of this covenant, or its nonfulfillment, and the exile which inevitably followed.

Since the people of God refused the order of prophets who spoke the word of God truthfully from the Lord, they were all the more ready to receive and harbor the false prophets. Since these false messengers, who ran when they were not sent, spoke from their own minds and hearts, they are said to walk after wind (so the Hebrew text) and to traffic in lies. (Cp. for this phenomenon Jer 5:31; Eze 13:3; and Ho 9:7.) Those things that delude and are unstable satisfy the heart of the one who has turned a deaf ear to the word and revelation of God. When men turn from the truth, they do not occupy themselves with some higher substitute but with downright fables.

But why is the false prophet so popular? He tells the people what they like to hear. With no concern for the truth, he is at liberty to flatter the people in their every whim. Only those prophets who indulged their sinful pleasures could hope to be agreeable to them. Even the most false prophet, who flattered them, was acceptable to the contemporaries of the prophet Micah. Gratification of earthly pleasures was the theme of the message of the wicked prophets. Yet the people had so departed from the truth of God and their spiritual sensibilities had become so hardened, that they gladly accepted the ministry of such miserable charlatans and frauds.

It cannot be emphasized too strongly that the primary reason for the rise of the order of false prophets was the unpopular character of the message of the true prophet. Every age has those who are more eager for the plaudits of men rather than the praise that comes from God, and our age is surely no exception.

THE GATHERING OF THE REMNANT

After such vivid denunciations of the sins of Israel, one would hardly expect Micah to close this portion of his prophecy with a promise of future blessing and restoration, so some have understood the last two verses of chapter 2 to be an announcement of punishment and not a promise of deliverance. But sudden transitions in the prophets are not unknown. (See Ho 2:2; 6:1; 11:9.) Such instances could be multiplied throughout the prophetic writings. The abrupt change here, then, is entirely in keeping with the method of the prophets.

We need always to be reminded, also, that God delights in showing mercy and is ever seeking to bless. With emphatic language the prophet predicts the restoration of Israel after her dispersion. Both Jacob and Israel, the ten tribes and Judah, will be assembled and regathered. The restoration from Babylon through Cyrus cannot exhaust the promise, for it was partial and our prophet includes "all of thee." The regathered nation will be brought to one place for rich pasture.

Bozrah was noted for its rich pastures (note 2 Ki 3:4), and the sheep of Bozrah may have been as famous as the kine of Bashan (Amos 4:1) and the rams of Nebaioth (Is 60:7). In the time of their regathering they will make a loud noise as is common in a large crowd of people.

The promise in verse 12 is heartwarming indeed, but the best of the prediction is yet to come. The people of God will not come together again as sheep without a leader. The breaker, the one who clears the way and removes the obstacles, will go before them.

This is none other than the Messiah of Israel who breaks down every obstacle in the path of His people. Three times in this verse we have the blessed assurance that, as He went before them when they went out of Egypt (Ex 13:21 and Deu 1:30, 33), so the Lord will go before them in the coming day and He will be at the head of them (Is 52:12). When the Messiah clears the way, they will break forth from the enemies' cities where they have been held captive and will pass through the gates. No one will be able to hinder their restoration, for the work of their promised Messiah will be effective on their behalf. He is seen here in a threefold fullness: Breaker, King, and Jehovah. All Israel's blessings for all time are inseparably bound up with the blessed One of the Lord, the Lord Christ.

GUILTY RULERS, PRIESTS, PROPHETS

UNJUST RULERS

Just as chapters 1 and 2 form the first portion of the prophecy of Micah, chapters 3 to 5 constitute the second division of the book.

The section begins with the same charge to hear the words of the commissioned messenger of God. Chapter 3 is an expansion of the judgment set forth in 2:1-2.

It is nothing short of remarkable how the indictment of God can be set forth in such varied fashion, thus avoiding painful monotony. The twelve verses of our chapter divide equally into three paragraphs. Verses 1 to 4 are addressed to the rulers; verses 5 to 8 are spoken to the prophets; then rulers, priests, and prophets are all included in verses 9 to 12.

The heads of Jacob and the rulers of Israel are the judges and magistrates. The same group is in view in Isaiah 1:10. Micah asks them, intending thus to awaken them to serious reflection on their evil ways, whether they are not the very ones who should know in a practical way the demands and characteristics of justice. Was it not their special duty and responsibility to know justice? Since they were accustomed to sitting in judgment on others, they should be aware of the judgment that awaits them for their evil deeds. (See Ro 2:1 for an enunciation of this great principle.) Their condemnation is the greater when their deliberate failure lies in the very realm of their special duty.

Now the prophet Micah sets forth in vivid and strong language the moral and spiritual conditions which prevailed in his day. Those who should have been examples in their love for good and their hatred for evil were characterized by their habitual (so the verbs in the original) hatred of the good and love of the evil. Their barbarous conduct against the poor and innocent is likened to the brutal slaying and eating of animals. All the processes in the transaction are outlined for us with the frankest portrayal of the merciless ways of the exploiters of the people of God. (For similar, though not so full, expressions cp. Ps 14:4 and Pr 30:14.)

Every variety of cruel oppression seems to have been resorted to in order that these ungodly judges might rob their fellowmen of their goods. When will unprincipled rulers realize how sorely they invoke the wrath of God by their glaring misdeeds? Only when God's judgment is upon them will they perceive the extent and enormity of their abominable ways. If the reader would see how fully this theme enters into the pronouncements and predictions of the prophets of God, we suggest that even a casual perusal of the prophets will suffice. What a contrast these leaders were to the Shepherd of 2:12. (Note the condemnation in Eze 34:1-10 with the glorious prediction in 34:23-24.)

The offenders against justice are not left to surmise what the judgment of God will be; their plight in the time of God's wrath is declared to them. Then they will cry to the Lord but He will refuse to hear. Theirs will be a cry for deliverance from anguish only and not one that arises from true repentance over sin. Since they refused to heed the cries of the needy, the Lord will recompense them in like kind. (See Jer 11:11 and Pr 21:13.) When the hour of God's judgment arrives, the time of grace and longsuffering is over. The Lord will hide His face from them (what unspeakable punishment is this, for it is of the essence of the punishment of hell) and allow them to perish in their iniquities. As blessed as is the grace of God, so terrifying is the wrath of God.

LYING PROPHETS

If the conduct of the rulers was blameworthy and reprehensible, that of the prophets, false messengers not sent of God, was no better. The second portion of the chapter answers to the subject matter of 2:6, 11, where the charges are made against the lying prophets. The prophets mislead the people purposely by not denouncing their sins which call forth the displeasure of God. They lull the people of God into complacency and carnal security instead of declaring fearlessly the truth and will of God. They flatter and encourage the people in their sins. And as long as they are well provided for with food and material necessities, they can be counted on to prophesy peace and prosperity to the nation. However, when they are not so provided for, they predict war and calamity. They are adept at shaping their messages to suit their own selfish interests. When they do not have their way and are not given what they demand, they prepare (lit., sanctify) war against their opponents. They announce an impending war as a holy judgment from God, as though to vindicate the honor of the Lord against His foes. (Note Is 13:3 and Jer 6:4.)

Because these deceivers have so outraged the sacred office of prophet, the Lord states in four different ways in verse 6 the calamities that will press heavily upon them. A common figure for calamity and distress is darkness. (See Is 8:22; Amos 5:18; 8:9.) Those who blinded the eyes and minds of the people will be smitten with night and darkness and blackness. The practice of deception is always disastrous to the one who indulges himself in it. The light which was formerly present becomes darkness indeed.

Now the prophet classifies the seers and diviners with the false prophets, for just as their works have the same objective in view, namely, the practice of deceit and hypocrisy, so their end will be the same and their punishment identical. Like the prophets of Baal in the days of Elijah, the lying prophets of Micah's generation will be put to shame. They will cover their lips. In the Orient men prided themselves on their moustache and beard. To cover them was a token of shame and silent mourning. (Cp. Lev 13:45.) Their shame will be manifest to all, for there will be no answer from God. They will no longer pretend to have answers from God, because they will be confronted with the stubborn reality of the calamities sent upon them by God. The Lord will not bring to pass any of their predictions. They will then appear in their true light as those whom God never sent.

Micah now sets himself in contrast to the false prophets and seers, and in doing so gives us clearly the distinguishing features of the messenger of God. Every detail of the description is of great importance. Micah was full of power by the Spirit of the Lord. He spoke by the leading of the Holy Spirit while the false prophets prophesied of their own spirits. Their message originated with themselves and their own fallible human faculties and powers; his word was ever energized and controlled by the Spirit of God. (See Jer 5:13 and Eze 13:3.)

Since the prophet of God was full of the Spirit, he was also empowered to set forth in an impartial manner God's holy judgment. Moreover, he was filled with might or moral courage, holy boldness, to proclaim the truth regardless of the desires of the people. On the contrary, the false prophets had no regard for the demands of the truth and were ever eager to please the whims and consult the pleasures of their hearers. The true prophets (for what was true of Micah was descriptive of the ministry of all God's prophets) were not to be bribed by anticipated favors from the people. Such preparation was needed by the messenger of the Lord in order to declare to Jacob his transgression and to Israel her sin. The prophet had to declare what the people may not have wanted to hear, but needed to nonetheless.

In this eighth verse of chapter 3 we have a pen portrait of the preparation and equipment of the prophet of God. All who speak for God in any age do well to measure themselves by this God-given standard. Less than this will never satisfy the heart of our God. With such definite contrasts between the true and the false prophet, how could Israel ever have failed to recognize the spurious from the genuine? Their luxurious living, their low moral conditions, and their unconcern for the things of God served to blind their eyes and dull their sensibilities to these vital issues. The hour in which we live is a tragic commentary on the same conditions in professing Christendom. Note carefully the description and warning in 2 Timothy 4:1-4.

THE JUDGMENT IMPENDING

After the prophet Micah has flayed the godless in Israel, he turns now to sum up the charge leveled at the heads of the nation in verse 1. He is putting into practice his commission of verse 8 to declare the sin and transgression of the people to them. It will be noticed throughout these denunciations that there is no word against the king himself (so also in the prophecies of Isaiah), for the king at this time was the God-fearing Hezekiah. But he was evidently powerless to curb the greedy and rapacious leaders.

The heads and rulers of the nation, by their hatred of justice and perversion of all right, were building Zion with blood and Jerusalem with iniquity. The thought here is not that they were giving sacrificially of their lifeblood to build the city, but that they were building by extortion and robbery. At the cost of human misery, woe, and murder they were erecting for themselves grand dwellings. Wealth gained by the blood of the rightful owners was used to entrench the selfish and wicked interests of the leaders of Israel. (See also Jer 22:13; Eze 22:27; and Hab 2:12.)

In a grand indictment of the three classes—judges, priests, and prophets —Micah particularizes the chief sins of each group. The magistrates were making judicial pronouncements for reward. This practice was distinctly forbidden by the Law of Moses (Ex 23:8 and Deu 16:19). Impartial meting out of justice is impossible when once a bribe has been received.

The priests were no better, for they taught the people for hire, for the payment of a fee. Priests were appointed of God to instruct the people of God in the Law, and that without wage. When they did it for hire, it took the keen edge from their impartiality. The portion of the priests was assigned them of the Lord; thus they were commanded by the Law to teach gratis. (The following Scriptures are in point here: Num 18:20; Deu 17:8-11; 18:2; 21:5; Lev 10:11; Eze 44:23, 24; and Mal 2:7.)

The sins of the judges and the priests are matched by the misdeeds of the prophets. They divine for money, showing that they are false prophets. The word *divine* is never used in the Old Testament in a good sense. Like Balaam and other heathen prophets, they were willing to make favorable pronouncements for their patrons for a price.

Sad picture indeed we have of the leadership of Israel in the days of Micah! Wherever one looked for guidance or leadership, whether to judge, priest, or prophet, one dominant consideration held sway: reward, hire, or money. And worst of all, there was a proud and unfounded confidence in the presence of the Lord. (See Jer 7:4, 8-11.) They boasted that because the Lord was in their midst, no evil could befall them. This was tantamount to claiming that God was blessing them in their wicked ways. Consider how offensive it must have been to the Lord to have those who claimed to be His people (and were) glory in His presence with them in order by this pretense to provide a cloak for their wicked ways and selfish interests.

The cup of their wickedness is full, so God must pour out His wrath and judgment upon them. Micah predicts that for their sins, Zion will be plowed as a field, Jerusalem will become heaps, and Moriah would be as an overgrown forest.

The reference to Zion has in mind the city of David to the south of the capital; Jerusalem includes the portions in the center and to the north of the city; and Moriah denotes the temple on the east.

The prophet is predicting the complete desolation of the city of Jerusalem. The prophecy is quoted in Jeremiah 26:18. Passages like Nehemiah 2:17; 4:2; and Lamentations 5:18 indicate the fulfillment in literal manner of these words of Micah. The Talmud records (Jerome noticed it and the Jewish philosopher Maimonides repeated it) that at the destruction of Jerusalem by the Roman Titus in AD 70, Rufus, an officer in the Roman army, plowed up the foundations of the temple with a ploughshare. Little credence is given the story. The invasion and destruction by Nebuchadnezzar fulfill the prophecy with sad accuracy. Truly the wages of sin is death, and death in every realm and sphere of life.

NIGHT FOR ISRAEL

The words of Micah to the prophets of his day in their sin are applicable to God's ancient people Israel in our day. It is spiritual night for them. They have no vision and turn to the plans of their fallible leaders. Their spiritual state is dark indeed. But God has provided for this very situation. He has graciously sent the promised Messiah, the Lord Jesus Christ, as the Light of the world to give light to this people sitting in darkness (Is 9:2). His death and redemptive work for them can display God's love for them and can dispel all gloom, darkness, and night from their sad hearts.

MESSIAH AND MILLENNIAL GLORY

MICAH OR ISAIAH?

When the three opening verses of chapter 4 are compared with Isaiah 2:2-4, it will be seen that the passages are practically identical. This has raised the question as to the original source of the material. Did Isaiah quote Micah or vice versa? Or did both of them quote a still earlier prophecy?

Orthodox and reverent expositors are divided on the issue: some claim Micah quoted from Isaiah, while others feel that Isaiah utilized Micah's material which fits better into the context of the minor prophet's predictions. Frankly, it is difficult to be dogmatic in the matter. The context in Micah appears to favor the prophecy, but we can multiply examples where the prophets make a quick shift in their outlook. This could not be said to militate against Isaiah's uttering the prediction first. In any event it is the inspiration of the Holy Spirit which insures us that we have the mind of God in both cases.

Chapter 4 in the main discusses the restoration of blessing and glory to Zion. The third chapter closed with a word of stern punishment upon Israel; now we are given the reversal of the judgment indicated in 3:12. God interposes a word of mercy and grace after He has pictured for them the chastisement then threatening the people and the land.

The phrase "in the latter days" is one well known in the prophetic writings. Reference is thus made throughout the Scriptures to the period which ushers in the Messianic age as well as the Messianic age itself. Here we have a clear reference to the time of the Messiah's reign over restored and regathered Israel. The majestic and blessed kingdom of the Messiah will excel all rule and sovereignty the world over. Zion will be the governmental and spiritual center of the whole world.

Some understand the passage to teach, not an elevation of physical height but an elevation of moral and spiritual dignity alone. If we understand Zechariah 14:9-10 correctly, there will be definite physical changes that will bring about vast changes.

But this kingdom will not be restricted to the godly in Israel; peoples and nations throughout the earth will be attracted and irresistibly drawn to the center of Messiah's kingdom. The movement will be a spontaneous (the meaning of the original in the word *flow*) one, springing from the hearts of the redeemed nations. Mutually encouraging they will resort to the place of Messiah's rule to receive constant instruction in the ways of God. The Word of God and all teaching of His will are to be carried on by the Lord Himself. (For a similar prophecy of the same time, see Zec 8:20-23.)

Imagine for a moment, if you will, Washington, London, Paris, Berlin, Moscow, and others proceeding to Jerusalem to learn the will of God! Could these things apply to our day? No, they will and must take place in the era of the personal and visible reign of the Messiah, the Lord Jesus Christ, on the throne of His father David. But the Messiah will not only be King and Teacher in this time indicated, but He will be final Arbiter in all disputes between nations. Even powerful nations far off from the seat of His government will obey His authoritative pronouncements. Should insubordination arise, it will be dealt with in summary fashion. (Note Rev 2:27; 12:5.)

In that day there will be no need to resort to force to settle disputes: the effect of Messiah's reign will be peace. Former instruments of warfare and carnage will now be utilized for peaceful pursuits. Weapons which were used for destructive purposes will be transformed into instruments of usefulness and productivity. Nations will cease to practice war and will study military science and strategy no longer.

What a glorious day! But it must be accomplished by God Himself in His plan; the United (?) Nations is powerless to bring about such conditions. They are seldom at peace in their own deliberations.

Verse 4 of chapter 4 is not found in Isaiah, but it continues the picture of prosperity and complete security. (Cp. 1 Ki 4:25; 2 Ki 18:31; and Zec 3:10.) The vine and the fig tree were native to Palestine. Vineyards were very common as can be seen from the laws concerning them (Ex 23:11; Lev 19:10; 25:3-4; Deu 20:6). The vine came to be the symbol of the nation Israel among the prophets and psalmists (Is 5:1; Jer 2:21; Ho 10:1; Ps 80:8). In later times it was frequently found on Jewish coins. The fig tree is mentioned among other places in Deuteronomy 8:8 and 2 Kings 8:31. Both the vine and the fig tree form natural arbors. The thought of the prophet Micah is that men will be secure without the customary dwelling places. They will be safe living in the open fields. There will be no poverty, none to grasp property not his own, no war to dispossess or to terrify the even tenor of life.

Though this seems beyond belief it is true, nonetheless, because God has said it. Were man to promise this we might well disbelieve, but God can perform as well as predict.

The fifth verse has puzzled interpreters in view of the prophecy of verse 2. The suggestion has been made that the words are spoken by the Jews during their dispersion. Because they see the devotion of the heathen nations to their gods, they determine that they will never forsake the true worship of the Lord. Certainly the prophet does not mean that every nation will worship the true God under the name of its own god. There is a contrast here between the transient worship of idols and the eternal worship of God. Micah is declaring that, although the heathen peoples worship their own particular gods now, Israel, in the time of peace and glory just described, will be in a state of spiritual blessing, because she will be worshiping the eternal God and walking in His power and strength.

RESTORATION OF THE DAVIDIC KINGDOM

Before Israel can enjoy the glories of the Messianic kingdom, she must be regathered from her worldwide dispersion and settled in her own land. This Micah now indicates. For, preparatory to the reign of the Lord Jesus Christ, the Lord will assemble His flock, the lame, the driven ones, and the afflicted. The time is that indicated in the first verse of chapter 4.

The figure of the scattered flock resumes the picture used in 2:12-13 of Israel's restoration. The sheep are in such pitiful condition because the Lord has afflicted them for their sins. But of such ones will the Lord make up His remnant; He will increase them and empower them, and He will rule over them in Mount Zion forever. (Cp. Is 9:6-7; Dan 7:14, 27; Lk 1:33; Rev 11:15.)

The prophet now addresses two places, Migdal-eder, or tower of the flock, and Ophel, which was the southeast slope of the Temple hill. Genesis 35:21 mentions the tower of Eder as a place near Bethlehem. According to Jerome (who lived in Bethlehem in the fourth century after Christ) the Tower of Ader was about a mile from Bethlehem. Thus the first place stands for the birthplace of David (the Messiah also, as our next chapter in Micah will indicate), and the second represents Jerusalem where he ruled. These places are now apprised of the fact that unto them will be restored the former dominion, that of David and Solomon, but greatly expanded and magnified in the reign of the Lord Jesus Christ, the Messiah of Israel.

BABYLON CONQUERS JUDAH

From the vision of the coming incomparable glory of the millennial reign, the prophet now turns to the dark future immediately before the nation. Though the stroke did not fall until a century after Micah's day, he clearly foretells the Babylonian siege and invasion of Judah.

The near future holds the exile of the people to Babylon. The nation is seen as crying aloud in terror over the approach of the Chaldeans. The prophet asks her why she does not turn to her king or counsellor.

The question has been understood by some to contain a taunt in her distress. It is more likely given to indicate to Israel her helpless condition when her king has been taken captive by the Babylonians, as was the case with Zedekiah. (See Jer 52:9; Lam 4:20; and Eze 12:13.) By the term *counsellor* reference may be made here to the king also (Is 9:6). Before the blessed day of the coming of the great King, Judah will lose all kingly rule.

Continuing with the figure of a woman in travail, Micah predicts that the daughter of Zion will be in great sorrow and distress before the hour of her glad deliverance. The details of her calamity are vividly brought out. With the capture of the city, its people will be compelled to leave it. Without defense and without a fortified city, they will have to live in the field. Ultimately they will be brought to Babylon. Micah, like Isaiah, looks beyond the present world power of Assyria to the coming might of Babylonia.

But the same verse that foretells the captivity predicts the deliverance from it. By the repetition of the word *there*, we are informed that where they will be oppressed will be the place of their deliverance. The Lord was to redeem them through the hand of Cyrus. (Note Is 43:14; 44:28; 45:1-4; and 48:20.) Babylon will be the scourge in the hand of God to punish His people, but they in turn will be visited in judgment through Cyrus. The import of the message of the prophet in verse 10 is: you must suffer but the suffering will end in joy. Travail is difficult but there is joy at the time of birth; so Israel's suffering will issue in the day of her deliverance.

WORLD SIEGE OF JERUSALEM

There are expositors who believe Micah is continuing the theme of the Babylonian invasion in verse 11. The mention of nations, then, would have reference to the different peoples in Nebuchadnezzar's armies.

It is not explained why these different groups in the armies should be so particularly singled out in this instance. Was it not the custom of rulers on their military campaigns to fill their ranks from many sources? With many others we believe that the prophet has in mind a different siege from that of verse 9.

From the contemplation of the Babylonian siege his mind is carried on by the Spirit of God to the last great attack of the nations of the world against Israel. The events are those of Joel 3, Zechariah 12 and 14, Ezekiel 38 and 39, and other prophetic portions of the Old Testament Scriptures.

In verse 2 we learned of a great confluence of peoples and nations to Jerusalem to hear the Law and the Word of God, but that day will be preceded by one in which the nations will attempt their final onslaught against the beloved city and people of God. Their purpose will be to defile Zion. The figure is taken from a virgin and means here that Zion will be defiled by the wanton slaughter of the people of her land and the profanation of her holy places. The besiegers will look with delight on the calamities of the Jews. They will gaze insultingly when she is in her pain and shame. Her distress will afford her enemies the greatest pleasure. They do not comprehend the love, wisdom, and grace of God which will overrule Israel's calamities for good. In their venomous hatred against Zion the nations will believe that they have hit upon a plan which will successfully deliver to Israel a death-dealing blow.

Their blindness is evident, when we realize that their coming together thus in a world confederacy against Israel is nothing less than the Lord's assembling of them as sheaves to the threshing floor. The figure of sheaves and threshing floor is one for complete destruction of a people. (See Is 41:15, 16 and Jer 51:33.)

Who will do the threshing? God has appointed that the beleaguered daughter of Zion shall thresh the godless nations. Like an ox treading out the corn, her horn will be made strong as iron and her hoofs of brass will inflict terrifying punishment upon the rebellious hordes that have come against the congregation of the Lord.

This whole sad transaction will not be one of wreaking vengeance on inveterate enemies. All will be done for the glory of God (Is 60:1-9). Heathen conquerors used to set apart a portion of their spoils to the gods in their temples. Victorious Israel will devote the wealth gained from her triumphs to adorn the Temple of the Lord. He will be known in that day as the Lord of the whole earth. Marvelous God is ours who can bring ultimate glory to His praiseworthy-name from the carnage and wreckage and rebellion of sinful man.

THE PERSON AND WORK OF MESSIAH

HUMILIATION OF ISRAEL

The first verse of our English text of chapter 5 is the last verse of the fourth chapter in the Hebrew text. Probably the division of chapters in the Hebrew text is better, because there is a return here to the thought in verse 9 of chapter 4.

Zion is exhorted to gather together in troops to withstand the enemy. She is designated as daughter of troops, not only because of those stationed within her and in the outlying districts, but because she is in a beleaguered condition.

The enemy has laid siege against Jerusalem. In the course of the siege, the enemy smites the judge of Israel with a rod upon the cheek. The judge indicated here is probably the king. (See Amos 2:3; Mic 3:1, 9, 11.) Such smiting was one of the greatest insults to an Oriental (1 Ki 22:24 and Job 16:10). The siege ends in conquest because only thus could their leader be subjected to such indignity.

What invasion of Jerusalem is referred to here and who is the king thus humiliated? Some students of this passage, judging in part from the second verse of chapter 5, think the person intended is the Lord Jesus Christ. Though there may be a foreshadowing here of the humiliation of Christ, the reference cannot have Him in view primarily, for three reasons. First, Christ was not smitten in any siege. Second, He was not smitten with a rod. (Cp Is 50:6; Mt 26:67-68; 27:30.) Finally, He was smitten by His own people, while the besieger here is an alien enemy.

Micah is predicting the shameful treatment of King Zedekiah at the time of the Babylonian invasion of the Southern Kingdom of Judah. Any siege of Jerusalem after that time would not fulfill all the requirements of our passage. In the smiting of her king, Israel was thus bearing the reproach of her sins which occasioned the Babylonian captivity.

BIRTH AND MINISTRY OF MESSIAH

The degradation of the judge of Israel is contrasted with the greatness of the future Ruler of Israel. Micah first indicates the birthplace of the Messiah of Israel. Bethlehem Ephratah was about six Roman miles southwest of Jerusalem and was the birthplace of David. (Note Ru 1:1-2; 4:11.)

There were two cities by the name of Bethlehem, so this one in Judah is distinguished by the added name from the Bethlehem which belonged to the tribe of Zebulun (Jos 19:15). Bethlehem means "House of Bread" and Ephratah comes from a root meaning "fruitful"; thus both names refer to the fertility of the region.

The birthplace of the King is indicated as being too little to be reckoned among the thousands of Judah. The tribes were divided into families, clans, or thousands with a head or prince over each. (See Ex 18:25 and 1 Sa 10:19.) The prophet is indicating the insignificant character of the village, for we know that it is not mentioned among the cities of Judah in Joshua 15 nor is it in the list of cities of Nehemiah 11. John 7:42 speaks of it as a village or hamlet. The low condition of the Davidic dynasty is also indicated here. From this small village will come forth unto the Lord the Ruler of Israel.

The words *unto me* are significant in that they show the coming of the Ruler is to carry out the purposes of God. He comes in the will of the Father to accomplish the plan of the Father. (Cp. 2 Sa 23:3 and Jer 30:21 as commentaries on this passage.)

This Ruler comes forth from Bethlehem in time, but He is not circumscribed by time. His goings forth have been from old, from everlasting. These goings forth were in creation, in His appearances to the patriarchs, and throughout the Old Testament history of redemption. The phrases of this text are the strongest possible statement of infinite duration in the Hebrew language (Ps 90:2; Pr 8:22-23). The preexistence of the Messiah is being taught here, as well as His active participation in ancient times in the purposes of God.

Isaiah, a contemporary of Micah, had already (9:6-7) set forth the fact of the divine nature of the Messiah. To whom did the Jewish scholars refer this ruler? Rabbinical interpreters understood it of the Messiah, though they differed as to who He was to be. In the time of Herod there was no question in the minds of the chief priests and scribes as to the birthplace of the Messiah (Mt 2:4-6).

Just as united as interpretation is on verse 2, so divided is it with regard to verse 3. One view would connect verse 3 with verse 1 and show the result of smiting the judge of Israel on the cheek, connecting all this with the judgment on Israel for the rejection of their Messiah. Another suggestion is that God gives up Israel to suffering under the Chaldeans because of her sins. She will not be restored till about the time of the Messiah's birth. With many others we hold that because of what was predicted in verse 2, it is clear that Messiah's birth in Bethlehem instead of Jerusalem, which was the capital of the kingdom, could only mean that the family of David had fallen on evil days, that Israel had been given up into the power of her enemies.

So it was. When the Messiah was born in Bethlehem, Israel was writhing under the firm and galling yoke of Roman domination and oppression. The woman who travails to bring forth is the nation in general and the virgin Mary in particular. Isaiah already had foretold of the virgin birth (Is 7:14; see also Rev 12:1-6).

The latter part of our verse is not stating that foreign Jews out of the land were to be gathered together to those in the land to receive the Messiah when He appeared. The thought of the prophet, in keeping with numerous passages throughout the Old Testament prophetic Scriptures, is that Judeans of the tribe of the Messiah will be joined with the members of the other tribes in their own land before the ministry set forth in the next verse. It foretells the regathering from worldwide dispersion of the Jews scattered by the judgment of God.

The second coming of the Messiah is in view in verses 4-6. The rejected One becomes the Shepherd of Israel. He will stand, will endure, as He feeds His flock. He shall have the needs of His people at heart.

There is no more beautiful nor expressive designation of Christ in the Old Testament or the New than that of Shepherd of His flock. The office of shepherd expresses well His royal care and protection. (Cp. 2 Sa 5:2 and 7:7.) The concept of feeding has in it the thought of rule as well (Is 40:11). All His ministry He will perform in the strength of the Lord and in the majesty of the name of the Lord His God. Though He subordinates Himself to the Father (Jn 20:17), the majesty spoken of will be more than divine endowment of a human earthly ruler.

During His rule and government Israel will abide; she will dwell in peace and security. It is the same thought as that which has been before us in 4:4. At the time which the prophet sees for the fulfillment of the prediction, the Messiah will be great, for His rule and power will be worldwide. (From the many passages on this theme see Ps 2:8; 72:8; and Mal 1:11, 14.)

What the Messiah's coming will mean for His people and the world is summed up under the thought of peace. He will be peace. He will have it in Himself and will bestow it on His people. (Note carefully Eph 2:14; Is 9:6-7.) He will be such to Israel in a threefold sense: (1) He will defend her against her enemies (vv. 5 and 6); (2) He will empower her to overcome her enemies (vv. 7-9); and (3) He will destroy all weapons of warfare, and idolatry also (vv. 10-15), so that warfare will no longer be a possibility. (For the same elements, cp. Is 9:4-6 and Zec 12:1–13:1.)

Shiloh will be the Author of peace and will be able to maintain it as well. How this will be carried out is revealed next. The Assyrian of verse 5 has been explained by some as an indication of an Assyrian foe in the end time before the earthly rule of the Messiah. The majority of expositors understand the reference to be representative or typical; that is, they take it as a type of the nations, because this was the one which threatened Israel in Micah's time. The enemy of that day is representative of all Israel's enemies. From Joel 3, Zechariah 12 and 14, and other portions, it is clear that there will be a confederated movement on the part of the nations of the earth at the end of the Great Tribulation to blot out God's chosen people Israel. All Anti-Semitism from Pharaoh's day to our day and beyond is leading to this colossal attack.

But the Messiah is the Champion of the cause of Israel in that hour. He raises a sufficient bulwark, referred to here as seven shepherds and eight princes among men, against the onslaughts of the enemy. (For the numerals see Pr 6:16 and Ec 11:2.) They will effectively stem the attack of the enemy. Then the battle will be carried into enemy territory. As the foe invaded the territory of Israel, so would their own borders be entered.

Nimrod is mentioned, because in him both Babylonia and Assyria may be said to be united (Gen 10:10). The deliverance will come through the Messiah who will use His own to waste (lit. to eat up) the enemy's land.

The revelation of the Messiah in this portion is indeed full. He is first seen as the Babe born in Bethlehem; He is indicated as the everlasting One, whose activities have been from eternity; His Shepherd rule is set forth next; His character as Peace-bringer is next before us; and finally, He is disclosed as the great Deliverer of His people. No one was ever as humble as He, and no one ever so majestic. How satisfying a portion He is continually for His own.

ISRAEL IN BLESSING UNDER MESSIAH

In two striking figures the remnant of the Lord's people is set forth as they enjoy the bounty of Messiah's reign. They are first compared to dew from the Lord and showers. Since rain does not fall in Palestine from the beginning of May to the latter part of October, the dew, the night-mist of the summer months, is essential to the summer crops.

The dew speaks of Israel's abundant, refreshing, and fertilizing ministry among the nations. The idea of abundance is conveyed both by the dew and the rain. It will be granted from the Lord, all of grace, in no sense dependent upon the wish or will of man.

The righteous among the nations will enjoy this phase of the service of Israel, but there will be rebellious ones as well. To these, Israel will appear as a ravening and irresistible lion. Israel will serve in a twofold character: as a source of refreshing (dew, showers) and as a source of power and judgment (lion) in God's hand. She will prevail over every enemy; for when her hand is lifted up in power and victory above her adversaries, then all her foes will be routed.

How different is this picture from the one with which chapter 5 began. The difference lies in Israel's attitude toward the will of God: when contrary to that will, she is in distress and oppression and humiliation; when in the center of that will, she is a source of refreshing, power, and blessing in the hand of God.

PURGING OF ISRAEL

In order that Israel may be usable in the hand of the Lord, He will remove all carnal supports in which she trusted. Evil of every kind must be uprooted and done away with. (Cp. Is 47:6-22 for a striking parallel passage.) Horses and chariots, in which Israel often placed her confidence, will be destroyed. They had been forbidden even in the time of Moses. (Deu 17:16). Her fortified cities will be demolished. Witchcrafts manipulated by hand will be abolished and soothsayers will be no more. Pillars, which were heathen symbols of the Canaanite worship, will be destroyed. Asherim will be utterly exterminated from her midst with the cities where these services were performed. The Asherim were trees or posts set up as idols and dedicated to the Canaanite goddess of nature. They were prohibited (Deu 16:21) and to be destroyed (Ex 34:13), but the ungodly in Israel had them nevertheless (2 Ki 13:6 and 23:6).

God's Controversy with Israel
ISRAEL'S INGRATITUDE

Chapters 6 and 7 make up the third division of this great prophecy and the call to hear heads the section as in 1:2 and 3:1.

Chapter 6 is set forth in the form of a controversy between the Lord and His erring people. The same method is employed in Isaiah 1 and in the first chapter of this prophecy. The chapter now before us gives a contrast between the fitness and justice of God's requirements and the ingratitude and superstition of Israel which were the cause of her ruin and judgment.

The prophet is not looking at the future full of blessing but at Israel's present, which is full of sin. Micah pleads with the people of God regarding their moral condition; he appeals both to their heart and their conscience as to why they are against the Lord.

The mountains and the hills are called upon by the prophet to witness the Lord's complaint against His people. The Lord has a controversy with Israel. Calling inanimate nature—the mountains and the enduring foundations of the earth—as witnesses was a method with the prophets whereby they demonstrated the greatness of human sin. (See Deu 32:1; Is 1:2; and Jer 2:12-13.)

What should strike us most in this is God's amazing condescension in thus reasoning with His creatures. Mark how the prophet speaks of Israel as "his people"; in verses 3 and 5 they are addressed directly in the words "O my people." They are pointed out and addressed as God's people with emphasis to indicate their relationship to the Lord in spite of their sin, as well as to quicken their consciences in the matter at hand.

God asks the people of Israel to accuse Him if they have any complaint. What had He done to them and wherein had He wearied them that they had so grievously departed from Him? Had He wearied them by unusual requirements and excessive demands (Is 43:23) or by unfulfilled promises (Jer 2:31)? (Cp. Is 43:24, where they are said to have wearied the Lord. For a similar complaint, see Is 5:4.) There is a tone of tenderness and yearning in the Lord's pleas with them. The Lord assumes for the moment the position of defendant.

On the contrary, instead of wearying them the Lord has heaped blessings and tokens of His favor upon them. He has repeatedly wrought wonderful acts of deliverance on their behalf. The unforgettable act of God's goodness to them was His redemption of them from unbearable bondage in Egypt. With mighty signs and a strong hand and an outstretched arm He had manifested His power in Egypt and delivered them from their oppressors.

Even then the Lord was not done with His mercies: He sent Moses, Aaron, and Miriam before them. God provided them with the great lawgiver; He placed over them a high priest; and He sent Miriam the prophetess (Ex 15:20) to lead the dance of triumph at the Red Sea. All these remind us of the gracious dealings of God with His people Israel. (See Jer 2:6-7; Ho 11:1; 12:13; and Amos 2:10.)

But there was yet more. Balak, king of Moab, devised a wicked plan to curse Israel and hired the heathen prophet, Balaam the son of Beor, to call down imprecations upon them. The record in Numbers 22 to 24 reveals how God sovereignly turned the curse into rich blessing. The curse of Balaam in itself could not have harmed them, but it might have given courage to the enemies of God's people and struck terror into the hearts of Israel. God will allow no man to curse His people (Ps 105:14-15). Before the words "from Shittim to Gilgal," we must supply the words like, "remember what happened." Balaam did not cross over the Jordan to Gilgal, but was slain in the land of Midian. (Note Num 31:8.)

The suggestion has been made to remove the place names from the text, but there is no authority for doing so. The words are meant to include the subsequent march to Canaan. Shittim was the first camping place after Israel met Balaam (Num 25:1). Gilgal, located between Jericho and Jordan, was the first stop in Canaan. The settlement in the land was the climax of the favors bestowed by God from the time of the Exodus. Such recollections would serve to show Israel in Micah's day the miraculous displays of God's power on Israel's behalf. By inquiry and entreaty the Lord would show Israel the baseless ingratitude of her heart for all His manifold mercies.

GOD'S REQUIREMENTS

Now Israel is seen as convicted and eager to obtain God's favor at all costs but ignorant of the means. The answer of the penitent people shows how little they really understand the kind of worship and service that is pleasing to the Lord. Israel's answer in the form of specific questions is directed toward the prophet, not toward the Lord.

The first question inquires how the penitent is to meet the Lord as one does a friend with gifts, and how this one can suitably appear in true submission before the august God. The natural recourse which the Law provided in case of sin was burnt-offerings. Shall the convicted Israelite now appear before God with such offerings and the best of sacrificial animals (Lev 9:3)?

Or is it a question of quantity with the Lord? Would thousands of rams or ten thousand rivers of oil be more suitable? Oil was added as a libation to certain offerings. (See Lev 2:1, 15; 7:12; Eze 45:24.)

The last question is the most desperate of all; it reveals to what lengths men are willing to go to gain the favor of God. Shall the penitent one offer up his firstborn for his transgression, thus delivering up the fruit of his body for the sin of his soul? This last inquiry is so important that it requires clarification. First of all, we must remember that the Law stated that the firstborn of both man and beast belonged to the Lord. (Cp. Ex 13:2, 12.) Second, the sacrifice of children was forbidden under penalty of death (Lev 18:21; 20:2-5; Deu 12:31; and 18:10). Furthermore, there is an indication here of the manner in which the heathen people began their practice of human sacrifice.

It is wrong to infer from this passage that in Israel, human sacrifice was common. For this there is no proof. (Note Eze 20:25-26.) Those who departed from the worship of the Lord did commit this outrage, as in the cases of ungodly Ahaz (2 Ki 16:3) and the godless Manasseh (2 Ki 21:6). Moabites and Phoenicians especially used such methods and efforts to appease their gods, as their literature clearly attests. (See also 2 Ki 3:27.)

Though this practice was not common in Israel, it was nevertheless practiced by those who went into idolatry (Jer 19:5 and 32:35). The underlying principle of all such offerings is erroneous, because God desires the giving up of the spirit in surrender and not the flesh. God could not be seeking such gifts, for He wants above all else inward conformity to His blessed will.

A word of caution needs to be given here. There are those who point to this passage as a proof that God never desired animal sacrifices. But the books of Moses are clear that God instituted the Levitical system. Nevertheless the sacrifices were worthless when not accompanied by the proper attitude of heart and spirit (Is 1:10-18; Ps 50:7-23).

Will the prophet Micah answer clearly and concisely for the individual Israelite these vital and burning questions of his soul? Does God want all men of all ages to know what pleases His heart? Yes, and that we have before us in verse 8. The verse is surpassingly beautiful and has even been called extravagantly "the greatest saying of the Old Testament." But it has its roots in the will of God already revealed even in Moses' time.

The prophet first calls attention to the ignorance of his people. Their ignorance is culpable, because they could have known from God's previous revelations of His will that sacrifices in themselves have no moral power or virtue.

They are addressed as "man" to show the universal application and validity of this truth. Micah's answer sets forth the moral demands of the Lord. The piety that God approves consists of three elements: a strict adherence to that which is equitable in all dealings with our fellowmen; a heart determined to do them good; and diligent care to live in close and intimate fellowship with God. When such piety is compared to the mere offering of sacrifices, how woefully lacking does the latter procedure appear. (Among many passages on this important theme see the classic passages: 1 Sa 15:22; Is 1:11-20; Jer 7:21-23; Ho 6:6; Amos 4:5; 5:15, 22-24.)

We have here an epitome of the whole Law (Deu 10:12, 18).

The three features of our text embrace both tables of the Law. God requires not some outward things, but certain qualities of the heart: righteousness, love, and humility (humble piety). Liberals who love to make a religion out of this verse fail to realize that these requirements of the Law are impossible of fulfillment by the unregenerate man. Only the Spirit of God can enable any man to fulfill the righteous ordinance set forth in the Law (Ro 8:3, 4; Phil 2:13).

FLAGRANT SINS

Instead of the presence of such piety as just set forth, Israel is marked on every side by glaring sins. Israel lacks the very virtues just outlined, therefore God must punish. The city addressed is probably Jerusalem which is the center of the sinful practices (1:5).

The second sentence in verse 9 has received various translations: "the man of wisdom shall see thy name" (shall regard God in His revelations of Himself); "the man of wisdom shall fear thy name" (shall reverence the Lord); "wisdom has thy name in its eye" (has God's glory in view); and "there is deliverance for those who fear thy name." Only slight changes in the original Hebrew are required for these different readings. The thought is that when the voice of the Lord is lifted to speak forth judgment, the man of wisdom sees the dealings of God that reveal His righteous character. Therefore, let all Israel similarly note the chastisement of God and who it is that has brought it about.

The rod is the emblem of punishment (Is 10:5, 24). When the Lord's chastening is so near, it is wise to give heed to what is said in His name. The beginning of blessing has come when the soul admits the justice and righteousness of God's disciplinary dealings. From verse 13 on the prophet will reveal what that rod is and means.

Verses 10-12 indicate some sins which are examples of others. In spite of repeated warnings the wicked still accumulate unjust gain in their houses to continue to provoke God's wrath. This they do by giving scant measure and using deceitful weights. God's hatred of these practices is set forth in Leviticus 19:35-36; Deuteronmy 25:13-16; and Amos 8:5.

How do they expect to be considered pure and guiltless when they give themselves to these abominations? The rich men of that day practiced fraud and violence; lying was the constant companion of their cheating. They filled their homes with the proceeds of their wicked dealings. What a catalog in contrast to verse 8: sins of covetousness, false balances, violence, lying, deceit, and other unrighteous business dealings. No wonder it is that the wrath of God was ready to fall upon them.

PUNISHMENT INESCAPABLE

For the sins already cataloged, the hand of the Lord has been heavily upon them. But the future holds more chastisement. They will have no satisfaction from the labor of their hands. Emptiness and famine will be in their midst. Attempts to save goods by removing them from the path of the enemy will be unavailing. Famine will stalk the land. There will be no oil with which to anoint themselves. The warm climate of Palestine necessitates the application of oil to the skin for comfort and pleasure (2 Sa 12:20). All these threatenings were in perfect keeping with the warnings of Leviticus 26:26 and Deuteronomy 28:38-40; see also Haggai 1:6.

Thus far it is clear they have not followed the explicit commands and statutes of the Lord. Whose statutes, then, have they kept? They have perversely followed the wicked ways of Omri and Ahab. Omri is singled out because he was the founder of Samaria and the idolatrous house of Ahab, as well as a sponsor of the wicked deeds of Jeroboam (1 Ki 16:16-28, especially verse 25).

The godless rule of Omri was climaxed in Ahab who was in the Northern Kingdom the standing example of a government hateful to God. The works and counsels of Ahab were the introduction of the Baal and Asherah cults (1 Ki 16:31); the persecution of the prophets of God (1 Ki 18:4); and robbery and murder (1 Ki 21). From Israel idolatry entered the Southern Kingdom (2 Ki 16:3), so that both Jerusalem and Samaria are now guilty and will be made an astonishment, a hissing, and a reproach among their enemies. There is no bright side to the picture of sin. God sees it as it is and has prepared its punishment beforehand.

GOD'S GRACE PROMISED

CONFESSION OF UNIVERSAL CORRUPTION

The sixth chapter closed with an indictment of the nation and a prediction of the certain judgment. Now in chapter 7 Micah, voicing the confession of the godly, describes most vividly the universal corruption in Israel. His soliloquy of penitence is peculiarly pointed and touching.

Invoking woe upon himself, he points out that the nation is comparable to an orchard after the harvest of the summer fruits and as a vineyard after the vintage. There is neither a cluster to eat nor a first-ripe fig. The latter was especially desirable and considered a delicacy. (See Is 28:4 and Ho 9:10.)

What is the meaning of the prophet? He is declaring that Israel is as lacking in good men as an orchard or vineyard after the fruit has been gathered with only gleaning left. One looks for a righteous man but cannot find him.

To what time or period were these conditions applicable? It has been suggested that these facts were especially true in the wicked reign of Ahaz. Another opinion is that the spirit and language of the passage resemble the prayers of the exile. Still another view would place the description in the terrible days of the Antichrist. Such conditions as Micah points out must have been present in Israel in more than one period, and they were certainly in evidence in the prophet's own day, as his prophecy throughout so graphically delineates.

The imagery of verse 1 is explained in the following verse. The godly man seems to be an individual of the past; he cannot be seen among the nation now. On the contrary, there is bloodshed on every hand, and every man is intent on compassing the destruction of his brother. Civil strife is the order of the day. It is as though each were hunting his brother with a net. Nets were used in the East for hunting as well as fishing. (For the thought of this verse, see the portrayals in Ps 12:1; 14:2; and Is 57:1.)

From this general condemnation of the nation, the Lord now turns to specify the particular wickedness of the governors and judges. Both hands are intent upon doing evil earnestly and diligently. With might and main they give themselves to accomplish their nefarious deeds. They are wholehearted in their ungodliness, and they are wicked successfully.

Their method of operation is this: the prince asks for the condemnation of an innocent man; the judge accedes to this request for a bribe, being ready to prevent justice at the desire of the influential; the great man, who is the rich man with influence, desires to bring about the ruin and destruction of another. Thus the prince, judge, and great man weave their plots and conspire together. An example of such schemes is to be found in the case of Naboth (1 Ki 21:11).

The best of them is as piercing, hard, and injurious as a brier; the most upright is more sharp and crooked than a thorn hedge. They injure and plague all who come in touch with them. (Cp. 2 Sa 23:6-7.) The corruption is, indeed, so widespread and outbroken that judgment must follow.

The day of visitation predicted by Israel's watchmen, the true prophets, was at hand. (Note Is 21:6 and Eze 33:2.) When the trouble strikes, they will not know what to do because as a nation they have not hearkened to the warnings of the prophets of God.

Sin works such havoc that all normal relationships are out of joint. Sin breaks every bond of nature, friendship, kinship, and gratitude. Neither neighbor, nor confidant, nor wife even is to be trusted. All are treacherous and not to be trusted. Jeremiah complained in a similar vein (Jer 9:2-6), and the Lord Jesus Christ warned of the enmity provoked by the truth of the Gospel (Mt 10:35-36; Lk 12:53). Unnatural feeling will replace the normal affection that should exist in the home. Sons will condemn their fathers, and daughters will be at strife with their mothers; parental honor and love will be lacking. Even servants in the home (not relatives) will turn in treachery against their masters. The holiest relations and the closest ties mean nothing to the wicked.

It was a sad picture socially and spiritually which Micah viewed: confusion, disloyalty, and suspicion reigned on every hand. When God is not honored as He should be, no human bond can survive.

CONFIDENT HOPE

In the days of general moral and spiritual declension when all others are faithless, God alone can be counted upon to remain faithful. The confidence of the godly must be in the Lord. As for the prophet, speaking representatively for the godly remnant, he would turn his eyes to God and wait for the hour of His deliverance and saving grace. Such confidence the Lord will never disappoint; He will hear the cry and hope of the godly. The restoration of the Lord's favor is assured His people.

Micah now views the nation in exile and distress with her enemy triumphant over her. This enemy, under the figure of a woman, is addressed and dissuaded from rejoicing over the forlorn condition of Israel. The hope of Israel is certain that, as the Lord has brought about her punishment and affliction, He will raise her up and give her both deliverance and joy.

Who is the enemy indicated here? The answers have been various, and it has been suggested that it cannot be definitely decided. Assyria, Babylon, Edom, and the heathen world power (any hostile to God's people) have been advanced. Since the Babylonian captivity lay directly ahead for the nation in the time of Micah, we should refer it to that hour in the first instance.

However, in view of verses 11 and 12 we must recognize a later and final fulfillment of the prophecy. The Jews understand Rome to be the enemy, but a time after ancient imperial Rome's sway is called for.

Verse 9 moves in a beautiful way into the realm of confession and submission. Here we find submissive endurance of the Lord's chastening hand because of conviction of sin committed. Humility and submission to the

will of God are evident. The Lord will yet plead the cause of His downtrodden people.

Though chosen of God as His instruments of punishment upon Israel,
the nations have exceeded all bounds and are bent on Israel's annihilation.
Israel is guilty before God, but she does not deserve the injuries her foes
inflict upon her. (See Zec 1:2, 15.) The hope of the godly is that the Lord
will bring about their physical and spiritual deliverance. In keeping with
His many promises, God will restore Israel to His favor. His righteousness in maintaining His covenants will be made manifest.

But the deliverance of Israel is but one phase of the Lord's dealings; the
other is God's vindication of His righteousness in the destruction of her
enemies. No longer will the enemy taunt Israel as to the impotence of her
God; the foe will have abundant testimony borne to the power of God
when she is trodden under. (For the figure see Is 10:6.) This will be
retribution in kind (4:11). It is a fearful thing to fall into the chastening
hand of God. Israel will be vindicated; this was Micah's confident hope,
and it is ours as well.

From the scene of destruction where Israel's enemies are set at nought,
we now turn to a day of Israel's upbuilding and expansion. The next
verses have been called ambiguous and very difficult, but there are many
parallels in the prophetic Scriptures of what is predicted here.

Zion is addressed as a city, and she is compared to a vineyard. (Cp. Is
5:1-7 and Ps 80:8-9.) The walls spoken of are those around a vineyard.
The hour has now come in the providence of God when Zion's walls are
to be built. Could this refer to the time of the return from Babylonian
captivity? There are those who think so, but the next verse has a distinct
time in view. In that day the decree will be far removed.

Students of the passage have found difficulty in identifying this decree.
One suggests that since the walls were built under Cyrus, the decree refers
to the rule of Babylon which will be removed. Another would connect the
decree with the decree of God which had to do with the political changes
about to take place in Babylon and all the countries about Judea, whereby
great numbers would join themselves in faith to Israel. One view would
relate the decree to Jeremiah 31:31-34, regarding the new covenant and
the removal of the old Law order. Still another suggestion understands
the decree to be the limit which God established to separate Israel from
the nations, which bound will be done away with so that peoples from all
lands can come to Zion (4:1-2).

The true meaning of the passage seems to be along the lines suggested
by the last view. In the glorious period when Zion's walls are built, her
boundary (so the word in the original may be translated) will be greatly

enlarged. (Note in this regard the passage in Zec 2.) The Assyrians and Egyptians, as in Zechariah 10:11 for the inveterate enemies of Israel, will be joined to the Lord's people finally in blessing (Is 19:23-25). From Egypt to the Euphrates will the multitudes come to restored Zion.

Indeed, the hordes will come from sea to sea and from mountain to mountain. There are those who make these designations apply to the Mediterranean and Persian Seas and Sinai in the south to Lebanon in the north. A comparison with Psalm 72:8 and Zechariah 9:10 will show that the prophet is speaking of all lands and all countries. The geographical notations are of the most general kind. In harmony with all the prophets, Micah predicts that Zion will be rebuilt and all nations will be joined to her in spiritual blessing. This our prophet has already foretold in 4:1-4.

But before the glorious future is realized, a time of punishment must first intervene with the desolation of the land because of the sins of her people. God's promises never invalidate His warnings of punishment for sin. This explains why the prophets move so quickly from punishment to blessing and then back to punishment. They would give the ungodly no ground for baseless hope and the godly no basis for unnecessary despair.

PRAYER FOR GOD'S CARE

In his closing prayer, the godly Micah commits his people to their Great Shepherd's care. On the basis of the promise in 5:4, the prophet prays representing again the godly in Israel. The prayer is prophetic in its outlook. The Lord is entreated to feed His people with His rod, not that of punishment as in 6:9, but now that of tender care and protection (Ps 23:4). God is to feed the flock of His heritage as they dwell alone in security and without harm in the forest in the midst of Carmel. (See Num 23:9 and Deu 33:28.) Carmel, Bashan, and Gilead stand for the whole land (for a similar designation of the land see Zec 11:1-3), and were noted for their rich pastures. For this reason they were chosen by the tribes of Reuben, Gad, and the half tribe of Manasseh (Deu 3:12-17; cp. also Jer 50:19).

The security of that restored condition is likened to that of ancient times. The days of old are not the times of Moses and Joshua, when Israel came into possession of the land, for those were troublous times. The reference is to the days of David and more especially those of Solomon (1 Ki 4:25 with Mic 4:4).

THE ANSWER OF GOD

The answer to the prophet's prayer in verse 14 is set forth in verses 15-17. God promises His help and intervention on behalf of His people;

as He showed His miraculous power (Ex 15:11) at the exodus from Egypt, so again He will work wonders. There were no miracles at the return from Babylonian captivity, great things but not miracles (Ps 126:1-3).

The predictions relate definitely to the time of the return of the Messiah to set up His kingdom. At that time the nations will be defeated through the power of God. They will be ashamed of their might, because it will be so unavailing in opposition to God's. They shall be astounded at Israel's deliverance, so that they shall be silenced. Their ears shall be deaf not to hear of Israel's triumphs. See Isaiah 52:15. Licking the dust like a serpent means utter routing and subjection. There is an allusion here to Genesis 3:14. Compare Psalm 72:9 (with reference to the Messiah) and Isaiah 49:23 (with reference to Israel). Contemptuously the prophet speaks of the ungodly nations coming out of their hiding places as crawling things to surrender themselves because of fear of the Lord and Israel.

PRAISE FOR GOD'S GRACE

The coming more glorious redemption calls forth praise of God's character and grace, just as the deliverance of Israel from Egypt did. Here we have a description of God's grace unsurpassed in Scripture.

In adoration at the goodness of the Lord, Micah cries out, "Who is a God like unto thee?" The allusion to Micah's own name is clear. The question was first asked at the Red Sea (Ex 15:11). God is He who pardons iniquity and forgives the transgression of the remnant of Israel. He does not delight in chastisement, but loves to bestow His mercy and grace (Ps 103:9-10 and Is 57:16). He treads the iniquity of the godly under foot, and casts all their sins into the depths of the sea, an allusion to Exodus 15:4, 10. Their sins will be cast into eternal oblivion. See Jeremiah 50:20 for the same thought.

Thus the Lord will make good His truth, His promise, made to Abraham, Isaac, and Jacob. (To Abraham, Gen 12:2-3; to Isaac, 26:24; to Jacob, 28:13-14.) The return from captivity could only be a foretaste of the greater display of God's grace in the coming reign of the Messiah. The purpose of all God's dealings with Israel is the accomplishment of God's promise to Abraham and his seed.

The last three verses of this book are joined to the book of Jonah for reading in the synagogue on the afternoon of the Day of Atonement. Once a year on the afternoon of New Year, the orthodox Jew goes to a running stream or river and symbolically empties his pockets of his sins into the water, while he recites verses 18-20. The service is called "Tashlich" after the Hebrew word meaning "thou wilt cast."

By God's grace to us, you and I know this is not God's way of casting our sins into the depths of the sea. He does this for us only because of the work of the Lord Jesus Christ on Calvary where He bore those sins for us. Because He was punished for them, God can pass over the transgression of any sinner.

10

NAHUM
JUDGMENT ON NINEVEH

GOD'S HOLY VENGEANCE

THE PROPHET AND HIS BOOK

THE NAME OF THE PROPHET NAHUM means "consolation." Apart from the fact that he is designated as an Elkoshite, nothing is known of his personal history. Even Elkosh, the place of his birth, is not known with certainty. The name occurs nowhere else in the Bible.

Three suggestions have been advanced: (1) that it was a town about twenty-four miles north of Nineveh. The tomb of Nahum is shown at Elkosh in Assyria. But we cannot credit this view, because the tradition dates from the sixteenth century. (2) According to Jerome, translator of the Vulgate, it was a small village in Galilee. This position has much to commend it, though we cannot affirm that Capernaum (lit., the village of Nahum) received its name from our prophet. The name was not uncommon in Israel. (3) A third suggestion would place Elkosh in the south of Judah.

We are probably correct in believing that the prophet was born in Galilee and moved to Judea where he ministered in the Word of the Lord. The vivid character of the description of the invasion of Sennacherib (1:9-13) would seem to call for Jerusalem as the place of Nahum's prophetic ministry. It is a matter of rather general agreement that the one spoken of in 1:11 is Sennacherib, king of Assyria, who invaded Judah in the fourteenth year of the reign of Hezekiah. (See 2 Ki 18:13—19:37 and Is 36 and 37.)

Thus Nahum is a contemporary of both Isaiah and Micah. Note his parallels with Isaiah's prophecy: compare 1:8-9 with Isaiah 8:8 and 10:23; 2:10 with Isaiah 24:1; 2:10 with Isaiah 21:3; 1:15 with Isaiah 52:7.

The style of Nahum's book is lyric poetry of a high order. It has been indicated that his style is the most impassioned of all the prophets. All will agree that Nahum has a vividness and forcefulness of style all his own.

The message of Nahum deals solely with Nineveh and her destruction. Jonah prophesied about a century and a half before Nahum. The prophecy before us is the sequel to Jonah's book.

Nineveh was for some hundreds of years the dread of western Asia. It was an immense city by the Tigris River. The city was strongly fortified and was a great commercial center enriched by numerous military campaigns. Having been warned of God in Jonah's day and having repented only temporarily (in that generation), Nineveh is now to suffer final and complete destruction. Chronicles outside the Bible relate that this visitation took place in 612 BC by the hand of the Medes and Babylonians.

The first chapter of Nahum presents God as the great source of strength and sustaining power of His people. The second and third are given over to a most vivid portrayal of the desolation of Nineveh. Because the book is so largely a threatening prophecy of judgment, it is entitled a "burden."

OUR MAJESTIC GOD

The invasion of Sennacherib was probably the occasion of this prophecy. Over against the ruthless invader the prophet places before the eyes of his people their own majestic and omnipotent God.

Nahum's description of the character of God is unsurpassed for grandeur and majesty. Whenever God is spoken of in the Scriptures as jealous, we are not to conceive of this quality in the light of its earthly, human, and petty limitations. It conveys the idea of burning zeal. The thought is that of a feeling of injured justice and a strong desire to see the right accomplished. Nahum has in mind the desolation caused by the Assyrians when they took the ten tribes captive (722 BC) and now when they invaded the land, capturing the fortified cities of Judah. The source of God's jealousy is His great love for His people, and He will vindicate the wrongs done them. (Cp Ex 20:5; Num 25:11, 13; Deu 4:24; 5:9; and 1 Ki 19:10.)

Thrice over the prophet declares the vengeance of God upon His enemies. Little do the thoughtless nations consider how they evoke the wrath of God when they mistreat His people. The repetition of the thought of vengeance and of the name of the Lord lends solemnity to the declaration.

It is not to be inferred from these statements that God is quick to anger, for He is long-suffering, but not from a lack of power. By no means will the Lord treat the guilty as though innocent. The power of God, which can be exerted in the affairs of men, is already seen in the workings of nature, in the whirlwind and the storm. (Note the manifestations at Sinai, Ex 19:16-18.) As for the clouds, though they be large, God treads on them as one would on dust.

But the prophet has not exhausted the omnipotence of God. By the rebuke of the Lord, both rivers and seas are dried up. God manifested this power at the drying up of the Red Sea and the Jordan; Christ did as much to the Sea of Galilee (Is 50:2; Mt 8:26).

Through drought the Lord makes Bashan to languish. Ordinarily it was very rich in pasturage. Carmel was famous for its vineyards and Lebanon for its forests. But the Lord can remove from both their beauty. (See Is 33:9 and Ho 14:7.)

All nature and human beings must acknowledge and recognize His manifestations in the realm of nature.

If God can so affect the hills, the mountains, the earth, and the world with its inhabitants, it is clear that no man can successfully withstand the indignation of the Lord. To ask the question is to have its evident answer (Joel 2:11; Mal 3:2; and Rev 6:17). The Lord in His power controls the volcanoes and breaks the rocks asunder. The power and might of the Lord are unsearchable, and they are committed to the accomplishment of His holy and perfect will. Foolish is that man who thinks he can stand even a moment before the indignation and fierceness of the anger of the Lord. It is the portion of wisdom to make peace with God through the work of His well-beloved Son, the Lord Jesus Christ.

GOD'S GOODNESS AND WRATH

The prophet has been dwelling at length on the wrath and vengeance of God, but this cannot imply that the Lord is any the less good. The previous description was intended to assure Israel of safety in the Lord when the armies of Sennacherib swept into the land (701 BC). The Lord is ever and always good (and oh, how good!) and infinitely holy. He is the refuge and fortress for the troubled one in the hour of crisis.

Hezekiah found Him so in that calamitous hour, and unnumbered hosts can bear similar testimony. The knowing of His own is one of kindness and love. (See Ps 1:6; 144:3; Amos 3:2.) He ever cares for His own.

But the Lord has another portion for those who oppose Him and His truth. The Assyrian invaders will be overwhelmed of the Lord. They will be destroyed and their place not found. Nahum is anticipating here what is fully described concerning Nineveh in the later chapters. A river overflowing its banks and carrying devastation in its path is a figure for an invading army. (Note Is 8:8 and 10:5-19.) The account of Ctesias (Greek historian of the fifth century BC) relates that during a drunken feast the floodgates of the city were swept away by a sudden overflowing of the river (the Tigris), and the foundations of the palace were washed away. The Babylonian army, then besieging the city, entered by the breach and burned the city. The Lord knows how to reserve wrath for the time of judgment upon the ungodly. (For the goodness and severity of the Lord see Ro 11:22.)

THE JUDGMENT DECREED

From verse 9 through 14 the prophet foretells the defeat of the Assyrians. Abruptly Nahum turns to address the Assyrian invaders to show them their brazenness in opposing God and the futility of their feeble efforts. In short, he asks them, "Can you cope with such a God as Israel has?" For the historical account see Isaiah 37:23-29. The Assyrian power will be completely destroyed, never to threaten them again. As when a serpent's head is crushed so that it cannot lift itself up, so Judah's distress through the Assyrian invasion will never be repeated by that world power. (Note v. 12.)

The proud Assyrian army is described as entangled thorns. Such thorns are not easily loosed (2 Sa 23:6-7) and so are cast together into the fire. Their armies presented a supposedly impenetrable front, but like stubble fully dry, they are powerless to resist the oncoming fire. What makes them an easier prey than ordinarily is the fact that they are saturated with their carousings. Such are easily handled and overthrown. The one who has gone forth from Nineveh devising evil against the Lord is Sennacherib himself. He has counselled wickedness (lit., Belial), worthlessness, and in the moral realm, wickedness.

The same truths that have just been before us are now approached from a different viewpoint. The Assyrian king had come with a great and formidable host (2 Ch 32:7), yet they would not be able to prevail against the people of God. They may be sound, unharmed, perfect in all that is needful for the battle, but they themselves would be cut down. Just as Assyria was a razor (Is 7:20) to others, so she was to be cut down (lit., shorn). The army of Sennacherib was to be destroyed and he was to return home.

To be sure, this prophecy was fulfilled to the very letter. We read that in one night the angel of the Lord went forth among the besieging Assyrians and slew in their camp 185,000 men. This was the hand of the Lord and not some bubonic plague as some would have it. Dismayed and discouraged, Sennacherib lifted the siege of Jerusalem and returned to his capital city, Nineveh. (For the historical facts, see 2 Ki 19:35-36 and Is 37:36-37.)

The latter portion of verse 12 has been taken by some to refer still to Nineveh, but the better sense sees a reference to Judah now. God turns now to comfort those who are the victims of the Assyrian siege. It is clear that the punishment of the Assyrian is final; that of Judah was meant to be corrective. The sense is that Judah was not to be afflicted any more by the Assyrians, and not that God's judgments would never be visited upon them by others.

As in verses 7 and 8, so in this passage we have a coupling of the severity of God upon His adversaries and the blessing of God upon His own people. The yoke imposed by the king of Assyria will be completely removed and broken from Israel and the foreign bonds will be torn asunder. (Note Is 10:27.) The yoke certainly included the tribute imposed on Hezekiah by the Assyrian king (2 Ki 18:14).

The prophet has not yet concluded his word of threatening to the God-defying Sennacherib. It is not a general word of judgment upon Assyria and Nineveh, but directly addressed to the king of Assyria. The Lord pronounces through Nahum the extinction of Sennacherib's dynasty. No future rulers will bear the name of his ruling house. Not only would the dynasty be cut off, but the temple worship with its many idols would be done away with. The Medes under Cyaxares (the founder of the Median empire), who destroyed Nineveh together with the Babylonians, despised idolatry and were glad to destroy the idols of the Assyrians.

Even the place of Sennacherib's death is here indicated: the temple of his gods. While worshiping his gods, his sons slew him (2 Ki 19:37 and Is 37:38). In the balances of God he was vile (lit., light; see Dan 5:27) and rejected. Sennacherib proved in his life, as so many others did before him and have experienced since him, the truth and reality of God's chastisements in His wrath. He is indeed a jealous God and takes vengeance on His enemies.

DELIVERANCE ANNOUNCED

In the Hebrew text, verse 15 of chapter 1 begins chapter 2. This is the announcement of a deliverance gladly heralded by welcome messengers. The text is almost the same as Isaiah 52:7. Nahum is speaking of deliverance from Assyria; Isaiah, from Babylon. Some understand this of the joyous announcement of the destruction of Nineveh already described in verse 14, which took place in 612 BC. It is probably better to take it as referring to the miraculous deliverance of Jerusalem in the reign of Hezekiah in 701 BC. To be sure, neither view excludes the other.

Judah is called upon to keep her feasts. During the Assyrian invasion the people were hindered from going to the capital city to keep the feasts. They are also to perform their vows, made while the Assyrian was invading. The wicked one noted here is undoubtedly Sennacherib; he will no longer trouble the people of God. Paul in Romans 10:15 applies our passage to the glorious deliverance wrought by the Messiah.

THE SIEGE PORTRAYED

THE ADDRESS TO NINEVEH

At the close of the first chapter of our prophecy, the Lord had announced to Judah the cutting off of the oppressor and the reestablishment of her feasts; now in chapter 2 Nineveh herself is addressed.

The suggestion has been made that the opening words are directed to Hezekiah and Jerusalem to encourage them to withstand the Assyrian attack. If such were the case, then the one who dashes in pieces would be the king of Assyria. However, since chapters 2 and 3 are both occupied in detail with the desolation of Assyria, it is better to understand the verse as referring to Assyria, who is ironically advised to strengthen herself and every fortification against the approaching Medo-Babylonian army under Cyaxares and Nabopolassar.

The words of Nahum are ironic because God has decreed her destruction for her sins. Every defense will be in vain. Try as she may, her every effort will be fruitless. Nineveh's time has come because the Lord has sufficiently judged His own people and has purposed to bring about their restoration.

The designations "Jacob" and "Israel" indicate both kingdoms. As in Psalm 47:4 and Amos 6:8, "excellency" signifies the land of Canaan as distinct from other countries. The restoration was to be brought about partly by the destruction of the Assyrians and more fully by the return from Babylon. The emptiers are those who have plundered Israel, specifically the Assyrians. In the vine branches we have a reference to Israel as in Psalm 80:8-16. Judgment from God upon His enemies always means deliverance for His people, Israel.

THE ATTACK UPON THE ASSYRIANS

The siege and capture of Nineveh are now vividly portrayed for us. The prophet pictures for us the frantic disorder that prevailed in Nineveh when the enemy broke down and penetrated the defenses of the city. The mighty men referred to are those of the armies of the Medes and Babylonians.

They were especially fond of red. (See Eze 23:14.) The shields were made red either by painting them red or overlaying them with copper. Calvin suggested that the ancient warriors dyed their bull's hide shields red to frighten the enemy and especially in order that the blood from their own wounds might not be seen to give confidence to the enemy. In any event the reflection of the rays of the sun upon copper shields would have the same effect as red paint. The military tunics were of scarlet also.

In order for the chariots to flash with steel, scythes were put at right angles to the axles of the chariots and turned downwards. At times they also projected from the ends of the axle. It was one of the most terrifying weapons of antiquity which cut down all who came against them. It is known that the scythed chariots were already in use among warring nations in the time of Nahum. The Medo-Babylonian general would have all these at his service in the time of his preparation for battle. The brandishing of the cypress spears has reference to the custom of the spearmen to wave their weapons before the people to show their readiness and eagerness to engage in combat.

Nahum now describes for us the vain attempts of the Ninevites to defend their city. With unusual speed the war chariots rage in the streets; they rush to and fro in the open areas of the suburbs of the besieged city. The blazing sun strikes the speeding chariots and they appear as flaming torches. Their swift running can only be likened to lightnings.

There have been those students of prophecy recently who have seen in verse 4 of chapter 2 a reference to the modern automobile. Such biblical interpretation is ridiculous and does more harm than good. The expositor of our day should make the Scripture applicable to his own hour but not in the matter of modern inventions. Applications to the full can be made of ethical and spiritual principles.

In the defense of the city, the king of Assyria relies heavily upon his nobles, the military leaders of the land. But they are a sore disappointment, because in the hour of dire need they stumble in their march out of fear and haste. The protection of the wall of the city is of paramount importance in any siege, so the leaders rush to take their place there. Some understand the mantelet to be a covering of the besiegers which they use to approach the wall, but it is rather the protection employed by the defenders. It refers to some kind of breastwork of interwoven boughs and branches of trees put up between the towers on the walls. Diodorus Siculus, a Greek historian of the first century BC, tells us that Nineveh had fifteen hundred towers, each being two hundred feet high.

But the race is not to the swift nor the battle to the strong (Ec 9:11), so we find sinful Nineveh undone. Verse 6 is remarkable both for its brevity and accuracy in describing the manner of the fall of Nineveh.

Cyaxares of the Medes and Nabopolassar of the Babylonians had made an alliance against the Assyrians, cementing their confederacy by the marriage of the daughter of the former to the son of the latter.

Cyaxares surrounded the city on the north. During the early assaults of the invading armies, the Ninevites inflicted heavy losses on the besieging forces. To celebrate these initial successes the Assyrians gave themselves over to carousings and revelings. The besiegers took advantage of this situation and drove the Assyrians behind their walls. A part of the Assyrian troops were put to flight and driven into the Tigris River. The city itself remained safe.

In the third year of the siege, however, heavy rains brought on a flood which broke down the walls about the city. This is exactly the picture given by the prophet. The canals of the great Tigris were opened and the palace was destroyed. Such an end was decreed for her by God Himself.

The word "decreed" (lit., *huzzabh*) has been variously interpreted. Some claim that Huzzab was the Queen of Nineveh; for this there is no proof whatsoever. Others prefer to understand it as a symbolical name of the city of Nineveh. The passage necessitates nothing more than the common rendering of the word, that is, it is set, decreed, or determined.

The remainder of the verse indicates what the whole purpose of God was toward her. She was to be stripped of all her wealth and finery, and annihilated. The people of the city, seen as her handmaids, bewail lamentably her fate and beat upon their breasts for anguish. It is ever thus: the way of the transgressor is hard.

THE SPOILING OF NINEVEH

Though Nahum has set before us the desolation of the city, he has not completed his minute delineation of the end of Nineveh. The ancient city (Gen 10:11) was like a pool of water. The river wall of Nineveh on the Tigris was 4,530 yards long. Dams around the city formed a water barricade. These should have provided security for the people in the siege, but they flee away panic-stricken.

The military leaders of the people command them to stand their ground against the invading forces, but all is confusion. Flight is uppermost in every mind; commands fall on deaf ears.

Now God addresses the conquerors and calls upon them to spoil the city of its wealth, its silver, gold, and furniture. Because of the elevated position of the city (30-150 feet above the Tigris), the flooding of the city would be only temporary. Then the spoilers would do their finishing work.

The prophet indicates there would be no end to the store. Accounts of ancient writers, almost fabulous in their descriptions, narrate the great treasures of metals and vessels accumulated in Nineveh. They exceeded by far the enormous treasures of the Persian Empire. The Medes and the Babylonians, who conquered and plundered Nineveh, furnished Ecbatana and Babylon with gold and silver to a degree unequalled at any period in history.

The city that had been so rich, influential, and populous is now seen as empty, void, and waste. An atmosphere of gloom and despair pervades all.

The three Hebrew words at the beginning of verse 10, having similar sounds (*buqah, mebhuqah, mebhullaqah*), are well chosen synonyms which give much force to the concept of complete destruction. The words imitate the sound of the emptying of a bottle. The city is stripped and its people are helpless. All courage is gone; anguish takes its place; and stark terror is written on every face. Sad picture, indeed, is this of the once magnificent leader among the nations. All power is but for a moment when it is pitted against the omnipotent God.

GOD'S JUDGMENT EXECUTED

The prophet sees the desolation already accomplished and asks the taunting questions of the city which has boasted so in her time. In pride they had asked, "Where?" (2 Ki 18:34), and now it is the Lord's turn to ask the same question.

The figure of lions brings out the ravenous lust of their rulers and people. The symbol is made full and forceful by the mention of the lion, the young lion, the lioness, and the lion's whelp. The comparison is especially fitting because lions of every form, with wings and at times with a man's head, are found frequently in the Assyrian sculptures. The prediction of the prophet of God has been fulfilled so literally, that armies have marched over the city of Nineveh without knowing they were passing over its ruins.

In its day the Assyrian lion tore in pieces, strangled, and filled his caves and dens with prey. The Assyrian relics bear eloquent witness to this description of the rapacious ways of the Assyrian monarchs.

Tiglath-pileser I boasted that he had fought and conquered sixty kings. In the beginning of his reign in combat with five kings he made the blood of the warriors to flow in the valleys and on the high places of the mountains. He cut off the heads of his enemies and piled them up outside their cities like heaps of grain. City after city is reported as having been defeated, burned with fire, devastated, and destroyed. Twenty-five cities of one land were so treated in one campaign. Their troops were cut down like lambs. One boast of this king was that he dyed a mountain red with the blood of the slain. Tiglath-pileser III boasted that he hung warriors on stakes. Sennacherib recorded that he so treated all the corpses of one city he conquered. He found pleasure in cutting off precious lives as one cuts a string—his own expression. And so the monotonous tale goes on. Allowing for a certain amount of exaggeration common to those who are recording their victories, we still have pictures of frightfully cruel carnage and bloodshed. The picture of Nahum is not one whit overdrawn.

The Lord who is against Nineveh will burn her chariots in smoke. The Assyrian sculptures reveal how fully their reliance was upon their chariots. Here they represent all the paraphernalia of warfare. She that was noted for burning the cities of other nations (practically every in- scription of a battle includes such a statement), will be recompensed in kind. Her own people would now be decimated; the sword would now bereave her followers as she had done to other peoples. She will no more carry off the spoil of the nations of the earth. Her enviable position among the nations of the world would be a thing of the past. Her mes- sengers and envoys, conveying the commands of the conquering Assyrian monarch and demanding tribute of vassal nations (2 Ki 19:23), would be silenced to vex the oppressed peoples no more. This is truly a full judgment upon Nineveh, but it was occasioned by the fullness of the cup of her iniquity.

"I AM AGAINST THEE"

These are fearful words when uttered by the living God against those who have incurred His righteous indignation. Nineveh was entrusted of the Lord with a large measure of sovereignty over the people of her day. Instead of ruling in the fear of the Lord, she employed her power and influence to destroy and dominate the nations for her own profit. This was grievous enough in itself, but Assyria must needs lift her armed hand against the little flock of the Lord's pasture, Israel. With this, God declares its iniquity is full and it is time for judgment.

Paul indicates (Ro 8:31) that if God be for us, no one can successfully be against us. The reverse is true also: if God be against an individual or nation by virtue of sin, then no one can successfully be for that person or nation.

When Assyria touched Israel, God said, "Behold, I am against thee!" This is inevitable if God be true to His promise to Abraham. He had solemnly promised that in just such instances He would curse those who cursed the seed of Abraham. The truth of God's dictum is written in the fate of Nineveh. But the first portion of the promise to Abraham is also true. God has also bound Himself to bless those who bless Israel.

Nineveh's Complete Desolation

THE ATTACK DESCRIBED

In this last and longest chapter of his prophecy, Nahum recapitulates the cause of Nineveh's judgment, he vividly portrays its destruction and shame, he announces how thoroughgoing will be her desolation, and he reveals that her stroke will be an incurable one. Woe is pronounced upon the bloody city, for it was full of murders and bloodshed. Her kings were constantly at war. She was full of lies, unreliable and untrustworthy. Promises to other nations for help or protection were never kept. Truce-breaking was common practice with her. Violence and extortion marked the city's life.

It has been suggested that the prophet's reference to the prey's not departing points to the fact that the Assyrians had not restored the ten tribes of the Northern Kingdom of Israel. The verse seems rather to be setting forth a general statement regarding the greed of the doomed city. She never ceases to live by extortion, never refrains from plundering. The later history of Assyria is one of continuous warfare. Thus our verse is a striking description of the cruelty of the Ninevites. The records from Assyria abundantly attest these charges.

Once the condemnation has been set forth, the prophet now describes with the vividness of an eyewitness the attack and storming of the city of Nineveh. This description of the siege of the city has been praised, and rightly so, as an unexcelled account whether in sacred or secular literature. One hears the noise of the whip as the riders urge their war-horses on; the noise of the rattling of the wheels of the war-chariots is almost deafening; the horses leap high; the chariots bound over any and all obstacles in the way; the horsemen spur their steeds on to the encounter; the swords flash; the spears glitter in the brilliant sun; and the result is death everywhere. A great host are slain; the corpses are heaped so high, that it appears as though there is no end to them. The living stumble over the dead; death stalks broadcast over the city. It is ever a fearful thing to fall into the hands of the living God when He arises to execute the sentence of His righteous wrath. Since none can abide His wrath, it is the part of wisdom to avail oneself of the provision of His mercy to sinners.

THE SHAME OF NINEVEH

Nahum outlines the cause of the judgment in verse 4. Nineveh is likened to a well-favored harlot. Her splendor and brilliance dazzled the nations about her. In what did her whoredoms consist? Some students of the passage feel it cannot refer to idolatry, as it does in the case of Israel, because the Ninevites were not in covenant relationship with God. Since witchcrafts are mentioned twice, it is clear that she trafficked in the occult. We may be sure that filthiness of flesh and spirit characterized her. She made other nations subject to her, robbing them of their liberty; thus she sold them through her cunning ways. For such ungodliness the Lord declares that He is against her, and will requite her with the punishment her sin requires.

The treatment she is accorded is the disgrace a woman of shame brings upon herself. Her skirts will be thrown so high as to reach over the face. This is great shame to heap upon a woman in the Orient. (See Is 47:3 and Eze 16:37-41.) The shame of Nineveh will be made as public as possible, and with the casting of abominable filth and refuse upon her she is made to bear the mark of greatest contempt. In her vileness she will be the astonishment and gazing-stock of all the nations. Those that pass by will flee from her out of terror, so that they may not partake of her afflictions. In her wasted condition, she will be an object of both disgust and scorn. She who befriended none will have to bear her misery alone. Her cruel ways left her friendless among the nations. No one will lament her fall or comfort her in it, because she has so well deserved it.

THE EXAMPLE OF NO-AMON

Furthermore, Nineveh was without excuse; she should have learned the way of the ungodly is hard from the fate of No-Amon. God is no respecter of persons: He cannot be partial and still be true to His own holy character. If sin be punished in No-Amon, it will surely be so with the mighty Nineveh.

No-Amon or Thebes was the great capital of Upper Egypt. Students of Egyptian history consider it the first great city of the Near East, describing its ruins as the most magnificent of any ancient civilization anywhere in the world. It was the capital city of the Pharaohs of the Eighteenth to the Twentieth Dynasties, and boasted such architecture as the Greeks and Romans admired. The Greeks called it Diospolis, because the Egyptian counterpart of Jupiter was worshiped there.

It was located on both banks of the river Nile. On the eastern bank were the famous temples at Karnak and Luxor. Homer, the first Greek poet, spoke of it as having one hundred gates. Its ruins cover an area of some twenty-seven miles. Amon, the chief god of the Egyptians, was shown on Egyptian relics as a figure with a human body and a ram's head. The judgment of this godless and idolatrous city was foretold by Jeremiah (46:25) and Ezekiel (30:14-16).

No-Amon was situated favorably among the canals of the Nile with the

Nile itself as a protection. The Nile appears as a sea when it overflows its banks annually.

Nineveh can read her fate in that of No-Amon, for she is no better than the mighty Egyptian capital. As a matter of fact, No-Amon was even better off than Nineveh, for the former had strong allies, whereas the latter had alienated all the nations about her. No-Amon could count on the help of the strong Ethiopians on her south, as well as the large manpower of the entire land of Egypt. This was considerable and is indicated as infinite. Among the confederates were the lands of Put and Lubim also.

The Lubim are the Libyans of North Africa. Some have tried to identify Put with the Libyans, but they are evidently distinguished in this verse. Present opinion relates Put to Punt, the present Somaliland in Africa.

These powerful peoples could be depended upon in the north and south of No-Amon to come to her aid in the hour of need. Despite all this, she suffered defeat and captivity. The historical reference in verse 10 is to the capture of No-Amon by Sargon of Assyria in his campaign against Egypt and Ethiopia. (See Is 20:3-4 for the prophecy.)

The cruelties of the siege which are mentioned here— the dashing of the children to pieces in the streets, the gambling carried on for the choice captives, and the binding in chains of the notables—were common in conquests. (Note 2 Ki 8:12.) The destruction of No-Amon described here was in the recent past of Nahum, and afforded him a striking point of application to the judgment to be visited upon Nineveh for her continued wickedness.

THE DOOM OF ASSYRIA

Now that the fall of No-Amon has been described, Nineveh can the more readily discern what her portion of judgment will be. She too will be drunken. This has been taken to refer to the last drunken orgy of the city of Nineveh on the night of her fall, but it is better understood as a common scriptural figure for those who have drunk of the cup of God's wrath. (Cp. Is 51:17, 21-23; Jer 25:15-28; Lam 4:21; Eze 23:33-34; Ob 16; and Hab 2:16.)

The prophecy that the city would be hidden has been remarkably fulfilled, as is well known. After the destruction of Nineveh it disappeared completely from history. From 1842 on, the Frenchman Botta and the Englishmen Layard and Rawlinson excavated on the site and uncovered remains of this one time magnificent city.

In the hour of trial and defeat she would seek a refuge and stronghold, but none would offer her the needed protection and immunity from the enemy. Nahum uses two figures to indicate the ease with which her foes would overthrow her. Her fortresses would topple as fig trees with first-ripe figs yield their fruit to the one shaking them. Her warriors would not stand in the battle but would become like women through terror. Consequently, the approaches to the city would be left open and easily accessible to the onsurging enemy. The enemy, once having entered into the city, would burn it completely.

THE HOPELESSNESS OF HER FATE

Since God has decreed the punishment of the city, no defense will avail against the enemy. Hence the next exhortations of the prophet to Nineveh are meant ironically. He advises them, in view of the long siege of the city, to take every precaution to withstand the foe. The primary need is water, and she is to lay by in store a goodly supply of this priceless and indispensable commodity.

She is to fortify every position in the city to make it as invulnerable as possible. The enemy will doubtless make breaches in the walls, so sufficient bricks must be ready to repair the holes in the city walls. But in spite of all these preparations the sword and the fire would make an end of the city's greatness.

Ancient historians indicate that Nineveh was destroyed by fire, and modern findings confirm it. The Ninevites will be so completely cut off, as though they had been visited by a destructive locust plague, and that, too, in spite of the fact that the city's population might be as numerous as the locusts.

Commercially the city had been highly favored. Through her canals she was one of the great trade routes of the ancient world. She carried on lucrative trade with the nations of her day, especially the Phoenicians. Through the Tigris River she had access to the sea. Her enterprises were numerous and rewarding. But all that her merchants heaped up in their commerce, will be spoiled and carried away by the enemy. Nineveh will not enjoy it. Instead of Nineveh passing away because of her own decadence, she will be brought to an end through the scourge of the enemy.

Will her princes and military leaders help in the hour of disaster? Great ones that they are, they will be like swarms of locusts (lit., locusts of locusts) whose wings become stiff in the cold, but with the warm rays of the sun become invigorated once more and fly away. So destructive are the locusts that the Hebrew language has almost a dozen names for them. The feature of the locusts touched upon here is their characteristic of fleeing away without leaving a trace. Such will the Assyrian nobles be to Nineveh in the hour when most needed. They will fail her miserably and irrevocably.

When once the smoke of battle and of fire is cleared, the scene is one of death. The Assyrian king's officials or viceroys, his shepherds, will slumber the slumber of death. (See Ps 76:6 for the same thought of sleep.)

The mountains on the north of Assyria will be filled with her scattered people. Who will redress Assyria for the stroke she has suffered? No one will heal her hurt. Addressing the king of Assyria (the masculine is used), the prophet asks who will heal her grievous wound. The answer is that all the nations about her will rejoice over her judgment, clapping their hands with revengeful joy. For a future rejoicing of the world over the fall of mystical Babylon, see Revelation 19.

The nations had suffered so much and so long from her cunning and cruel dealings, that they rejoice now that she has come to her well-deserved end. But we do God an injustice if we think this is what He preferred for Assyria. God delights to bless and only judges when He must. Far rather would God have heaped upon Nineveh blessing and prosperity instead of shame and ruin. But she chose the contrary part and her doom is writ large in the annals of the world's history. The fulfillment of the prophecy took place about a half-century after the prophet Nahum. The Medes entered an alliance with the Lydians (against whom they were fighting) to form a common front with Nabopolassar (at Babylon) against Nineveh. The city fell in 612 BC, a fact definitely confirmed by the Babylonian Chronicle.

A SCATTERED PEOPLE

The prophecy of Nahum, whose chief message is the destruction of wicked Nineveh, closes with the sad word that the people of the city are scattered upon the mountains with none to gather them. This is the sad picture of Israel in the time of our Lord who were as sheep scattered without a shepherd (Mt 9:36). The loving Saviour, the Lord Jesus Christ, longs for us to gather them to Him through the message of the Cross that there may be one flock, one Shepherd.

PART IV

HABAKKUK, ZEPHANIAH, HAGGAI, AND MALACHI

To

the revered memory of

LEOPOLD COHN,

man of God,

missionary pioneer,

personal benefactor,

this volume is gratefully dedicated.

THE PRESENT STUDY is the fourth in the series of five, projected for all the minor prophets. It is impossible for the author to express adequately his gratitude to God for the privilege of scrutinizing these pages of Sacred Writ, or to indicate fully the inexpressible blessing derived from such exercise of heart and mind. Similar and greater experiences of this nature are coveted for each reader.

The hour is later on God's clock than any one of us realizes. Prophecy should be studied, not for mental exercise alone, but to ascertain the will of God now for each life, and to move into the center of that place of blessing. May love for Israel result from such activity.

Grateful thanks are due to my wife; my son, Paul; my daughter, Lois; and my secretary, Mrs. Franceen Smith, for valuable assistance rendered in typing and proofreading the manuscript. The consideration and co-operation of Dr. J. Hoffman Cohn, worthy son of a worthy father to whom this book is dedicated, have been appreciated every step of the way from the publication of these studies in *The Chosen People* to their appearance in this final form.

May the Lord use these pages to His glory in Christ Jesus.

11

HABAKKUK

PROBLEMS OF FAITH

THE PERPLEXITY OF THE PROPHET

THE PROPHET AND HIS TIMES

NOTHING IS KNOWN of the personal history of the prophet Habakkuk. Some have conjectured on the basis of verse 19 of chapter 3 of this prophecy, that Habakkuk was of a priestly family, and so qualified to officiate in the Temple service. No certainty attaches to this view.

His name means "to embrace." Luther thus explained the name of the prophet: "Habakkuk signifies an embracer, or one who embraces another, takes him into his arms. He embraces his people, and takes them to his arms, i.e., he comforts them and holds them up, as one embraces a weeping child, to quiet it with the assurance that, if God wills, it shall soon be better."

There has been difference of opinion as to the time of the prophetic ministry of Habakkuk. Since the heading of the prophecy indicates nothing as to the reign in which he labored, the time of the prophet must be gleaned from the contents of the book itself. Some have referred the prophecy to Manasseh's or even Josiah's (with less reason, I think) days, but the best view is that which places it in the reign of Jehoiakim. This is arrived at from the nature of the sins prevalent in Israel pictured in this book and from the manner in which Habakkuk speaks of the Chaldeans. If this be true, then he was a contemporary of the prophet Jeremiah before the Babylonian invasion. At this time sin was indeed rife in Israel, and the hour of the Babylonian invasion was not far off.

The book of Habakkuk differs from the regular addresses of the prophets who ministered to Israel. His is a record of his own experience of soul with God. Prophets spoke for God to men; he expostulates with God about His dealings with men. We are reminded in this regard of Jonah among the prophets and of Job among the poetic books. Primarily and essentially he is the prophet of faith. The keystone of the whole book is 2:4. His main theme (like Ps 73 and other passages in the Old Testament) was the affliction of the godly and the prosperity of the ungodly. He dwells on the perfect dealings of God and the development of faith in His own.

All concede to Habakkuk a very high place among the Hebrew prophets. The poetry of chapter 3 has been rightly accredited on every hand as the most magnificent Hebrew poetry. The language of the book is very beautiful. The message for the most part is couched in the form of communion with God. Chapter 1 dwells on the invasion of the Chaldeans; chapter 2 predicts the judgment of God upon the Chaldeans; and chapter 3 pictures the coming of the Lord and the destruction of the hostile world powers.

Though the book is short in compass, it is quoted from a number of times in the New Testament. Compare Habakkuk 1:5 with Acts 13:40-41; Habakkuk 2:4 with Romans 1:17; Galatians 3:11; and Hebrews 10:38. See also Habakkuk 3:17-18 and Philippians 4:4, 10-19.

THE COMPLAINT OF THE PROPHET

The prophecy is entitled "a burden" because it predicts judgments upon Israel and her enemies. Habakkuk laments over the sin of his people and then over those of her foes.

The first verse gives no clue as to the time of the prophecy which must be gathered, as we have indicated, from other details of the book.

The man of God has been crying unto the Lord concerning the wickedness and violence in the land, yet the Lord has done nothing about it. He is jealous for God's glory. This is not a personal complaint, but he voices the desire and longing of the godly in the nation.

Here we have unveiled for us at the very outset the exercised heart of the prophet of God. Everything is awry, and God is apparently not intervening in the situation. In verses 9 and 13 of chapter 1, we have similar language to that of verses 2 and 3. The reign of Jehoiakim was full of injustice and bloodshed. (Note Jer 22:3, 13-17; for the same inquiry see Jer 12:1; 20:8; and Job 19:7.) Since the prophet is powerless to alter conditions and the Lord has not, he asks why he is permitted to see such iniquity on every hand and violence and strife going unchecked. What troubles the prophet is that the Lord seems to look on these heartbreaking conditions with indifference.

The silence of God in human affairs, then as now, has ever been difficult to understand. But this does not mean that there is not an answer, and that divine wisdom is incapable of coping with the situation. All is under

His seeing eye and everything is under the control of His mighty hand.

But in the meantime the Law was slacked (lit., chilled), rendered ineffective, paralyzed. It came to be looked upon as being without force or authority. Because of unrighteous judges the Law was set at nought. Since the forms of judgment were corrupted, both life and property were insecure. Justice could not prevail because the wicked knew how to hem the righteous in on all sides, so that he could not receive his just due. Miscarriage of justice was the order of the day. Ensnaring the righteous by fraud, the ungodly perverted all right and honesty. Because God did not punish sin immediately, men thought they could sin on with impunity. (See Ec 8:11.)

THE ANSWER OF GOD

God is far from being an unconcerned spectator in earth's affairs. We can always be certain that, if our hearts are stirred over the prevalence of sin and ungodliness, God is all the more deeply concerned.

He addresses Habakkuk and the people of Judah, directing them to look out on the scene of world history among the nations. The Lord points them to the events transpiring among the surrounding nations: the Assyrian Empire destroyed by Nabopolassar; the founding of the Chaldean rule; and the victory of Nabopolassar (with his son, Nebuchadnezzar) over the Egyptians at Carchemish. As they look they will wonder marvellously, a most emphatic expression.

This power of Babylonia was to be used of God to chastise Israel. He may use others, but He claims it as His own work. Thus, instead of God's being inactive and indifferent, He is emphatically at work, in a way which men will scarcely believe. It will be of such unusual character. (In Ac 13:41, Paul warns the despisers of the Gospel with judgment using this verse.) It has been suggested that probably at this time the Babylonian nation was still friendly (2 Ki 20:12-19). Soon they were to invade the land in three sieges in the time of Jehoiakim, Jehoiachin, and Zedekiah. Our prophet has these invasions in view.

The statement that God will raise up the Chaldeans has reference to their invasion of Judah, because they had already been on the scene of political history for some score of years. (Cp. Is 23:13.) The Chaldeans were the inhabitants of Babylonia and were of Semitic origin from Kesed, son of Nahor, brother of Abraham (Gen 22:22). (They are mentioned in Is 43:14; 47:1; 48:14, 20; Jer 21:9; 32:4, 24; Eze 23:23; their invasion is described in Jer 5:15-18.) The indication is clear that Habakkuk ministered at a time when the Chaldeans were coming to the fore in world politics. The prophet gives a threefold picture of the enemy of Israel:

they are cruel, quick, and impetuous in their ways, and bent on far-flung campaigns, such as were conducted under Nebuchadnezzar.

THE ROD OF GOD'S ANGER

Now the text describes at greater length what was touched upon in the message of verse 6, which is the classic passage for the characteristics of the Chaldeans, as Isaiah 5:26-30 is for the Assyrians. The Chaldeans strike terror into the heart and are a dreadful adversary. Their own desire is their only law and standard of judgment. They make their own rules of conduct. This is Babylon in its old character (Gen 11:4). Their dignity did proceed from themselves, for they assumed the superior place in the Babylonian empire on their own initiative. And nothing is lacking in their preparation for military campaigns. Their horses exceed leopards in their swiftness, and in ferocity they surpass evening wolves. Wolves, hungry from the lack of food during the day, prey on the flock as night comes on (Jer 5:6 and Zep 3:3). The Chaldean horsemen are irresistible in their attack and swoop down as an eagle intent on its prey.

We have here the fulfillment of the warning of Moses in Deuteronomy 28:49. The purpose of the invaders is to perpetrate violence in the land. This was Israel's sin (vv. 2 and 3), and it will be her punishment.

The second part of verse 9 has been variously interpreted and translated. One translation would have it that the set of their faces is forward; another is that their faces shall sup up as the east wind. In either case the thought seems to be clear that the enemy will be formidable and irresistible in their advance.

They will blast everything before them as they go. The innumerable host of their captives can only be compared to sand. The Chaldean is fearless and confident of his power, for he scoffs at kings and their helplessness in the face of his attack. He runs roughshod over every obstacle and opposing fortress. He has been called a hasty nation, and this is clearly seen in the manner of his besieging a city. He needs only to cast up bulwarks before fortified cities in order to lay siege to them, when they capitulate before him and he takes them captive.

Verse 11 has received various treatments at the hands of translators and interpreters. It has been suggested that when the Chaldean is exulting in his victories, his mind will change (he will lose his reason), and he will pass over all restraints to his destruction. This passage would then be a prophecy of the disease that came upon Nebuchadnezzar when his reason was unseated.

The language of Habakkuk has been likened to that of Daniel 4:16, 30-34 where an unforced harmony between the two books is said to exist.

While this position is entirely within the range of the possible, it is not very probable.

All that the prophet is stating here is that the successes of the Chaldean will be multiplied; he will carry all before him, as the wind sweeps over vast stretches of land. In doing so the Chaldean conqueror heaps up guilt before God because of his ungodly ambitions and his subjugation of many helpless peoples. God is given no glory in these successes, because the Babylonian victor praises his own strength. His own might and power are his god. The Assyrian did the same before him (Is 10:13-14) and multiplied others have followed this method since him. For one to make his own strength his god is to commit suicide of the soul. (See Dan 4:30.)

In this section of the prophecy we have had described for us in a remarkable pen portrait the Chaldean invader, his nature, manner of operation, purpose, weapons, attitude toward others, and the basic cause of his ultimate downfall.

THE DEEPER PERPLEXITY OF HABAKKUK

Has the problem of the prophet been answered by the Lord? Or has the difficulty become worse in the mind of Habakkuk? The messenger of God is in greater perplexity now, for he remonstrates with God for inflicting punishment on Judah by a nation less righteous than they.

The prophet directs his appeal to God whom the enemy has treated contemptuously. He speaks representatively for his people and uses the well-known names for God as Jehovah, Holy One, and Rock. In addressing the everlasting God, he declares by faith that God's people will not die. He knows the nature of the covenant-keeping God who will not allow His people to be wiped out. The ground of his confidence and hope is twofold: (1) God has been Israel's God from ancient times; and (2) He is so holy that He must punish ungodliness whether in His own nation or in the enemy.

Since God does not desire the destruction of His people, it is manifest that He has chosen the Chaldean only to chasten and correct His chosen people. But the wound still aches in the heart of Habakkuk. How could the righteous God, who is so pure and cannot abide any form of iniquity, use such a wicked and treacherous people as the Chaldeans? And human life was so cheap to the Babylonians. They treated men as one would the fish of the sea who have no defenses or rights and as worms of the earth who have no ruler to protect them.

In a figurative manner the prophet shows how the Chaldean callously takes captives as a fisherman plies his trade. The angle, net, and drag represent the armies and weapons whereby the Chaldean carried on his military ambitions. His great successes gladdened and rejoiced his heart. But to whom did he give the glory? He worshiped his own military prowess.

There is no indication that the Babylonians worshiped the sword as did some of the ancients. They did boast of their strength in war, however. How perverse can man be when he delights to worship the creature rather than the Creator, the gift rather than the Giver.

In his distress and perplexity of soul, the prophet asks the Lord whether this cruelty and idolatry of the Chaldean will go on without interruption. Will God not bring such rapacity to an end by His power? On this tense note chapter 1 concludes, but the answer of God will appear in the next chapter. There we shall see that the Lord has set a bound to all which displeases Him. All is taken into account, and the remedy is provided. We do well to bring our doubts and perplexities to the Lord, as did Habakkuk, and leave them with Him for final disposition and solution. He never fails.

"WE SHALL NOT DIE"

This is the glad and glorious testimony of any child of God who has been delivered from death in trespasses and sins through the work of the Lord Jesus Christ on Calvary. But it reminds us that those without Christ are dead spiritually and, if they continue thus, will die the second death which is eternal separation from God. The prophets of the Old Testament cried again and again to Israel that she should not die in her sins.

THE ANSWER OF GOD

At the close of the first chapter we found the prophet distressed at the inscrutable dealings of God with His people, Israel. The prophet complained at first of the widespread iniquity in Judah, to which the Lord replied that He was aware of it all and would judge it at the hand of the Chaldean.

When the prophet learns of the rod of God's anger, he is bowed down in greater mental agony that God should use a nation less righteous to afflict and chasten His people. With the problem still unsolved we come to the solution in chapter 2.

Since God has answered the first questionings of the prophet, he feels confident that God will do likewise with his greater problem. Just as a sentinel is set to keep an eye on that which occurs outside a fortified city, so the prophet stations himself in spirit to await God's answer to his inquiry. The thought is not that Habakkuk actually went to a watch-tower, but that he assumed such an attitude of heart, that of anticipation and watchfulness. The majority of interpreters understand the verse in a spiritual sense of inward preparation. The prophets are compared to watchmen. (See Is 21:8, 11; Jer 6:17; and Eze 3:17; 33:2-3.)

In this spirit of alertness the prophet was ready to receive by revelation the response of God. The answer was first to his own mind and heart, then to his people. The rendering of the last part of the verse as "when I am reproved," is not preferable here. There is no indication that any complaint was lodged against the prophet or that he stood in need of reproof. He was expecting the solution to his complaint.

And God did not disappoint His servant in his need. The Lord commanded Habakkuk to write the revelation given him upon tablets. These were the customary ones for writing (Is 8:1). It could have been on such as were shown in the marketplace on which public notices were written (graven in clay) in clear letters.

The letters were to be large and legible enough to be easily read. The prophet was to reduce the vision to writing so the people would have it for the future. (See Dan 12:4 for similar wording.) The one reading it was to run to tell it forth, because it was such a message of joy to Israel, telling her of the ruin of her enemy and her own deliverance.

The deliverance was not to come immediately, but it was surely to come; the godly should wait for it. Delay is only in the heart of man; God is working the details according to His own plan. Patience was needed. The purpose of God cannot be hastened nor can it be delayed. It comes to fulfillment at the appointed time.

The vision hastes (not speaks, but pants) on it its fulfillment. It seeks the accomplishment of the things it predicts. The end spoken of here is not the end of the times of the Gentiles, as has been suggested, but the realization of the prophecy in history. The vision will not deceive nor disappoint, but will assuredly come to pass. (The latter portion of v. 3 is quoted in Heb 10:37.) The passage in Hebrews is clear that the reference is ultimately to the coming again of the Lord Jesus Christ. The attitude of heart enjoined in our text of the prophet is the normal one for the child of God today. We are as men waiting for the return of their Lord.

BASIC DIVINE PRINCIPLES

In verse 4 we have the content of the vision given the prophet which is the answer to his perplexity set forth in 1:12-17. This text, which later became the watchword of Christianity, is the key to the whole book of Habakkuk and is the central theme of all the Scriptures.

It is not treating of two classes in Israel: those who would reject the prophetic message in their pride and those who would humbly believe it. The reference is undoubtedly to the proud Chaldean, but since we have here basic divine principles, these truths can be applied in a secondary sense to any individual who is in unbelief.

The soul of the proud Babylonian is puffed up and is not upright but full of deceit and dishonesty. This' way is the path to destruction. On the other hand, the just or righteous one (referring here primarily to the godly in Israel) shall live by faith. There have been many attempts to interpret the word *faith* as faithfulness or right dealing, but the sense must be trust in God in this context. (See Gen 15:6; 2 Ch 20:20; and Is 7:9.) We have here the cause of life and death. Pride leads to death because it will not receive by faith the grace of God.

Habakkuk now has his answer to his complaint. He is not to doubt that the pride of the Chaldean will be his destruction, while the godly is to continue looking to the Lord unto life. (The second clause of v. 4 is quoted in Ro 1:17; Gal 3:11; and Heb 10:38.) The Talmud with insight declares that here all 613 precepts given by God to Moses on Sinai are summarized.

Moreover, the proud Chaldean has given himself over to the treachery of wine. Ancient writers confirm this statement that the Babylonians were very much addicted to wine. Note the disaster it brought in Daniel 5. A heathen writer said of them: "The Babylonians give themselves wholly to wine, and the things which follow upon drunkenness." What a scourge to any people is drunkenness! How well we do to heed the admonition in our own land.

Filled with pride, drunken with wine, the Chaldean is also thirsty for power and conquest. His restless nature stirs him up to continuous conquests (1:16-17), so his great desire is to go forth to destroy. Like Sheol (in the New Testament, Hades) his desire swallows up all and yet remains unsatisfied.

Sheol was the place of the departed dead. The body was committed to the grave and the soul went to Sheol. From Luke 16 (especially v. 26) we learn that there were two divisions in Sheol before the death and resurrection of the Lord Jesus Christ: a section for the righteous (called also Abraham's bosom or Paradise) and one for the unrighteous. After the resurrection of Christ (Eph 4:8) He removed the righteous souls from Sheol to heaven where Paradise is to be found now. (Cp. carefully Lk 23: 43; 2 Co 5:1-10; and Phil 1:23.) In this day of grace the ungodly still go to Hades (Sheol), while the believer departs to be with the Lord in the third heaven.

We have thus set before us the two ways, the way of life and the way of death. We note two types of character and the manner of God's dealing with each on the basis of fundamental divine principles. The proud, puffed up, dishonest, drunken, dissatisfied Chaldean will have death; the just, godly, righteous Israelite will have life through faith in the living God. God could not make the responsibilities and issues more clear than He has. And they hold good for all time.

THE FIRST WOE

Now follows a fivefold woe upon the wicked Chaldean oppressor. The five woes are presented symmetrically in five stanzas or strophes of three verses each. The woes are taken up and uttered by all the nations and peoples mentioned in verse 5 who have suffered at the hand of the cruel oppressor. In a taunt song they will heap woe on the Babylonian for his rapacious and plundering ways. He sought to heap up for himself that property which was not his. How long did he think he could go on thus with apparent impunity? Furthermore, he loaded himself with pledges (not thick clay as in some versions, which makes no sense here), that is, the wealth of the nations which he has plundered, as an exacting usurer accumulates pledges contrary to the Mosaic law (Deu 24:10), and which must be given up again. Suddenly he would be called upon to relinquish his ill-gotten gain.

We know that the Medes and Persians struck unexpectedly at the Babylonians. The word *bite* forms a play on words with a similar word which means to exact usury. The thought is that since the Chaldeans had spoiled so much goods from others, they were in a sense indebted to the nations: the surrounding peoples were their creditors. The conquerors would not only be bitten by the subject peoples, but would be shaken violently, referring to the forceful seizure of a debtor by his creditor (Mt 18:28). The spoiler will be spoiled; the plunderer will be plundered. All this will come to him for his shedding of blood and violence inflicted upon the lands and cities of the nations.

THE SECOND WOE

The second woe is pronounced upon the Chaldeans for their covetousness and self-exaltation. The basic meaning of "evil gain" is breaking off, as Orientals do with pieces of silver and other metals in money transactions, then it came to refer to those who sought after ungodly gain.

Like Edom, the Chaldean set up his government on a basis where it was secure from attack. The language is not literal but is taken from the imagery of an eagle (Job 39:27; Jer 49:16; and Ob 4). The ungodly oppressor may think his position an impregnable one, but because of his many plunderings, he has sinned against his own soul and caused his own ruin. He has brought the retribution of God upon himself. Even inanimate things, the buildings he has erected to his own glory and for the satisfaction of his own pride, will cry out because of the injustices perpetrated in them. The reference is not to the dissolution of the empire, as though it were falling apart. But the stone and the beam would cry out together to accuse of sin and bloodshed. (See Gen 4:10, and by contrast note Lk 19:40 and Ps 29:9, ASV.)

THE THIRD WOE

For tyrannical oppression of captive peoples, a third woe is called down upon the Chaldean conqueror. Their cities were built with blood, for the wealth by which the king of Babylon built his magnificent buildings was gained from bloody wars. Captive labor was used to build the grand structures of the empire.

But, contrary to the purposes of the proud rulers of Babylon, the Lord had determined that the labor of these subject peoples would not stand. It would all be consumed in the fire that was to bring the Chaldean empire to an end. The work was for nought.

Of old a kingdom had been set up in Babylon to usurp power and glory (Gen 10:10; 11:4), but it must pass away and be replaced by God's kingdom (Rev 11:15). The Babylonian kingdom must give way to the kingdom of the Lord and of His Christ. In order for the earth to be filled with the knowledge of the glory of the Lord, as the waters cover the sea, the kingdoms and rulers of this world must be judged and destroyed. The purpose of God in creating the earth at all was that it might reflect His glory (Num 14:21; Is 11:9).

THE FOURTH WOE

The next woe upon the Chaldean takes into account his shameful treatment of weaker or neighboring nations. Verses 15 and 16 are probably to be taken figuratively. Otherwise, they speak of shameful and immoral corruption. The condition of a drunken man represents in Scripture the overthrow of a conquered nation. (Cp. Nah 3:11.) The thought is that the Chaldeans with their lust for power and conquest enticed other nations into campaigns for spoil and finally left them to suffer loss and shame. For this, foul shame will be upon those who allured the peoples and they will be as the uncircumcised, which indicated to the Hebrews the height of contempt. The cup of retribution in God's wrath will come round in due time to the Babylonian (Jer 25:15).

Judgment is determined against her because of the desolation wrought in the land of Palestine. They had denuded the forests for their military campaigns and in their building enterprises, and had killed the beasts hiding there. From earliest days conquerors cut down the forest of Lebanon and killed its beasts, as is recorded by different kings both of Babylonia and Assyria. The verse also indicates a climax in wickedness from the destruction of the forests and beasts to the desolation of the cities. The land and city of verse 8 refer to all the nations; in verse 17 the reference is to Judah and Jerusalem.

THE FIFTH WOE

The last woe is uttered upon the greatest sin of all, idolatry. To bring out forcefully the utter worthlessness of idols, the prophet asks of what profit it is. It is of no use. (See Is 44:9-10 and Jer 2:11.) The teacher of lies is the idol because of the false oracles connected with its worship. How senseless of the idolater to cry for help to the dumb idol to awake to help him. Ironically and scornfully, the prophet questions whether such can teach. The idol may be overlaid with gold and silver, showing earthly splendor, but there is no life within it.

The prophets of the Old Testament are at their best when they expose the delusion and senselessness of idol worship. Idols are nothing, but there is a living, all-seeing, ruling God in the heavens. He is not hidden under gold and silver, but alive in heaven, ready and willing to help His people. He is the invisible God inhabiting His heavenly temple and all-powerful, therefore it behooves all nations to be solemnly and humbly reverent before Him. (Ps 76:8-9; Zep 1:7; and Zec 2:13 dwell on the same majestic theme.) The nations do well, as well as individuals, to submit silently to Him waiting for His judgment.

"THE JUST SHALL LIVE BY FAITH"

How Israel needs to hear and heed his word of priceless counsel. The just does not live by works or the merits of the fathers. It is by faith alone in the sacrifice of the Messiah, the Lord Jesus Christ. The Jews are beloved for the father's sake (Ro 11:29), but they are not saved for their sake, but for Jesus' sake who died for them.

THE TRIUMPHANT FAITH OF THE PROPHET

POEM OF PRAYER AND PRAISE

After perceiving the promises and warnings of chapters 1 and 2, the prophet concludes his book with prayer and praise. He recalls past manifestations of God's power and grace; he prays for the speedy deliverance of God's people; and he expresses a firm confidence in God which is un-changeable. Parallels to this poem are to be found in Deuteronomy 33:2-5; Judges 5:4-5; Psalm 68:7-8; 77:13-20; 114; and Isaiah 63:11-14.

This ode was designed for public worship as is seen from the inscription, subscription, and the musical notation "Selah" in verses 3, 9, 13. It is admittedly one of the most majestic and sublime portions of the Word of God. The chapter is entitled a prayer, a designation used for "psalm" in Psalm 102:1. It was used in referring to devotional portions in general. The poem was set to shigionoth which is found (in the singular) in Psalm 7 also. We are certain that it refers to the kind of music which accompanied the song, although the translations of the word have been varied, such as "after the manner of elegies"; "a song"; "a reeling"; or "a triumphal song." Since the word comes from a verb meaning to err, the thought is one of a song sung in great excitement, a triumphal song.

It is interesting to note how Habakkuk lays bare his heart at the beginning of each chapter of his prophecy. He was no passive spectator of the sad spiritual decline of Judah, nor was he a passive recipient of the telling solution of God as he waited on his watch. These disclosures stirred him deeply, as they should do for all of us.

What God had revealed of the Chaldean attack on Judah and God's retribution on Chaldea, that is, the answer of God in chapter 2 especially, had disturbed the prophet and filled his heart with terror and awe. He finds his outlet in prayer and calls upon God to revive His work in the midst of the years. The prophet of God would have Him manifest His grace to Israel and judgment upon her enemies by renewing the displays of His mighty power as of old in intervening on behalf of His people.

While the years yet run their course and Israel still undergoes suffering, God is supplicated to make known by experimental proof the reenactment of His deeds of power. In God's wrath upon both Judah and the Chaldeans, He is besought to remember mercy. Judgment is to be tempered with mercy. In this verse we have before us the theme of the psalm and the heart of the prayer. In short, Habakkuk prays that God will do for His people as He has in the past, and while inflicting punishment will remember to deliver also.

GOD IN HIS MAJESTY

In a sublime manner the prophet now pictures a future redemption under figures taken from past events. The background here is the memory of the events of the Exodus and Sinai. Just as the Lord manifested Himself when He redeemed Israel from Egypt, He will appear again to deliver the godly among His people from their oppressors among the nations and will judge their foes as He did the land of Egypt.

Some critics of this passage have shown a lack of spiritual insight when they see in this section only a description of a storm sweeping from the desert, instead of a glorious appearance of God, a Theophany.

The first verb of 3:3 (and so all the verbs through v. 15) should not be translated as a past, as though Habakkuk were placing himself back at the time of the events of Israel's deliverance from Egypt. It should rather be rendered "cometh" with a future sense, for as the Lord once came to His people at Sinai to do wonders among them and for them and establish a covenant, so He will come again to liberate them from their enemies.

Teman was one of the great cities of Edom; it was probably the capital of the country and was the southernmost large city of Edom. Here it is used representatively for all Idumea. Paran was opposite Teman and only separated from it by the valley of the Ghor (1 Ki 11:18 indicates it was between Midian and Egypt).

Selah indicates a heightening of the musical accompaniment, the musical *forte*. It would allow for a pause and meditation. This notation occurs seventy times in the Psalms and three times in this chapter.

The manifested excellence of the Lord covers the heavens and His praise filled the earth. Verse 3 deals with the extent of God's coming; verse 4 with its effects. All creation reflects His splendor; light is His garment (Ps 104:2). His brightness is as the light of the sun and rays of light encircle Him. The word *rays* means "horns" by comparison of the rays of the rising sun above the horizon to the horns or antlers of the gazelle, found also in Arabic poetry. And there, in the brightness, is the hiding of His power. The splendor actually conceals the glorious, invisible God. Our God is a God that hides Himself (Is 45:15, but how gloriously revealed in Christ, Jn 1:18 and 2 Co 4:6), but it is with excess of light. Glorious God is ours!

GOD IN HIS POWER

As plagues were visited upon Israel's enemies and burning pestilence went before the Lord in the desert, so the Lord will accomplish in His future manifestations. According to Revelation 6, definite plagues and visitations will precede the coming of the Lord visibly to earth.

Now Habakkuk pictures the Lord as stopping in His march and causing great upheavals in the earth. The Lord stood and measured the earth with His all-seeing glance. With irresistible power, His hand drove asunder the nations and overpowered them. Even the mountains, those lofty objects of God's creative power, were scattered as dust, and the ancient hills bowed as though in reverence and submission. All was leveled before His august presence. His ways are everlasting: He works in time and in all creation but transcends all. His goings are ever accompanied with power as of old.

THE FEAR OF THE NATIONS

When God accompanied Israel's entrance into Canaan, the nations were struck with fear. This same pattern of events will exist in prophetic times. The people of Cushan were thrown into consternation. Calvin refers the name to Cushan-rishathaim, king of Mesopotamia, of Judges 3:8, 10, but undoubtedly the reference is to the people of Cush or the Ethiopians.

Trembling seized the land of Midian, those of the Arabian coast of the Red Sea opposite the Ethiopians. Tents and curtains indicate their nomadic life and stand for the people of these lands.

The prophet at this place addresses God directly for vividness and emphasis. When God marches forth, the rivers and the sea retreat. The Red Sea and the Jordan were dried up to allow Israel to pass over dryshod. What God has done to one river and one sea, He can do to all.

The poetic questions reveal how powerful were the ways of the Lord with the sea as with the land. The horses and chariots of salvation upon which the Lord is pictured as riding are not the angels, but the elements— the clouds and the winds. (See Ps 104:4.)

The bow of the Lord was drawn from its cover, and the arrows fell fast upon the heads and penetrated far into the hearts of the Lord's adversaries. By an emphatic expression Habakkuk shows how completely unsheathed was the bow of the Lord to accomplish His purpose.

As it was then, so it shall be again. Just as clear as the first clause of verse 9 is, so obscure is the second. There are but three words in the Hebrew, but as yet they have not been explained satisfactorily. One eminent Old Testament scholar counted more than one hundred translations of these words. With such diversity of opinion, it is foolhardy to be dogmatic at this point. We can only suggest a preference and leave it with that. If we take the rendering of the ASV, the thought is that God's supernatural interventions for His people are not for one period alone, but His oaths secure them for Israel in the future. Such a statement is true, although it does make an abrupt change from the description of God's chastisements upon the enemies of Israel. The marginal rendering of this same version may be somewhat better. "Sworn were the chastisements of thy word" would convey the meaning that according to God's solemn oath, He had foretold vengeance upon His enemies. (Cp. Deu 32:40-42.)

The earth itself in consequence of the wrath of God trembles and waters gush forth from beneath, or at the quaking of the earth the sea empties its waters on the land into rivers. Verse 10 continues the thought of an earthquake caused by the mighty advance of the Lord of Hosts. The prophet repeats in different form what was stated in verse 6, because the mountains are so prominent on the earth. The loud roarings of the waters of the deep are likened to the utterances of a voice. The waves of the sea are spoken of as the lifting up of its hands. In this power-mad age we do well to remember that power belongs only to God.

GOD'S INTERVENTION FOR HIS PEOPLE

The miracle at Gibeon is referred to in verse 11 when the sun and moon stood still in their respective places in the heavens (Jos 10:12). God wrought wonders on earth, among the nations, in the seas, and in the heavens as well.

The arrows spoken of may well refer to lightnings, instruments of the wrath of God, as the bow of verse 9. The Lord marched through the land in His indignation and threshed the nations in His anger. (For a similar figure see Is 63:1-6.)

Lest by this time anyone be in doubt as to the purpose of these manifestations of the power and wrath of God, Habakkuk states expressly that God had in mind the salvation of His own people. There are two interpretations of "thine anointed." One sees here a reference to Israel, thus paralleling the thought of "thy people." The other holds that the anointed is God's King, the Messiah, through whose instrumentality and agency God effects salvation for His people.

Many passages confirm this latter position, while the first view finds support in Psalm 105:15. If the reference be to a past event (as a pattern) in the head out of the house of the wicked man, allusion may be to one of the kings of Canaan. However, if the prophet is speaking of the future, and this is the more probable, then the king of the Chaldeans is meant. The description of laying bare the foundations up to the neck is allegorical, the house standing for the Chaldean dynasty.

Habakkuk identifies himself with Israel in verse 14 and depicts the treatment God offers the invaders of His land. By mutual destruction (as in the cases of 1 Sa 14:20 and 2 Ch 20:23-24), the enemy will fall by their own weapons, those who, like robbers, delight to prey upon the defenseless. The poor here are Israel.

Bringing his recital of God's marvelous acts to a close, the prophet recalls the crossing of the Red Sea (Ex 14), when the Lord trod the seas and mighty waters. Is there a God like our God?

THE TERROR AND TRUST OF HABAKKUK

A cycle of thought is completed in verse 16 which reverts to the subject of verse 2. He is still filled with fear and dread at the coming anguish for his people. He knows his homeland is to be overrun by the Chaldean invaders, and he feels it deeply. It is hard indeed to stand by and see the inevitable stroke fall upon God's people. But his communion and meditation upon God and His ways, as well as His promises, have wrought in him trust as well as terror.

It has not been a fruitless spiritual exercise, this looking to God for His own answer to the knotty problems of life. Out of it has come unswerving trust in spite of coming trouble. Though the enemy come in and destroy the fig tree, the vines, the olive trees, mar the fields, and carry off the flock from the fold and the herd from the stalls, yet Habakkuk will rejoice in the Lord and joy in the God of His salvation. The Lord God Himself will be his strength and sustaining power, enabling him to surmount all obstacles with abundance of vitality as he freely moves about in his own land.

What desolations the Chaldeans were to carry out but what consolations God grants His servant to carry him through. Not only will he have calm in the hour of trial, but joy in spite of all desolations of the land. This is one of the most forceful manifestations of faith's power recorded in the Bible. With renewed and joyous strength, the prophet will be as the gazelle which is so swift that greyhounds are in danger of dropping from overexertion in the chase.

The musical signs suggest that the psalm was used in the liturgy in the Temple; it is not so certain from the use of "my" in the subscription that Habakkuk performed this Levitical function himself.

Note what a contrast the conclusion of this prophecy is to the perplexity that overwhelmed the prophet at the beginning of the book. He finds the all-sufficient answer to all his problems in God Himself. He will trust God though all blessings fail. What a word for the times in which we now live.

"FOR THE SALVATION OF THY PEOPLE"

How full of meaning are these words and how well they summarize God's purpose in His dealings with Israel, His chosen. God has done so much for this purpose in past ages—out of Egypt, through the wilderness, in the land, out of captivities, in the midst of persecutions—but above all at Calvary when the Messiah of Israel, the Lord Jesus Christ, gave Himself for their sins.

12

ZEPHANIAH
THE DAY OF THE LORD

GLOBAL JUDGMENT

THE MAN AND THE MESSAGE

THE NAME "ZEPHANIAH" means "the Lord hides" or "he whom the Lord hides." Nothing beyond 1:1 is definitely known of the prophet's life. The genealogy in the superscription of the prophecy is given for four generations. No other prophet has his pedigree carried back so far. It is not usual in Old Testament usage to note a man's ancestry beyond his grandfather unless for special purpose. He was of royal blood and was the great-great-grandson of the godly King Hezekiah. The arguments that have been advanced against this view are not convincing.

Our prophet ministered about a half-century after Nahum, in the reign of Josiah. Manasseh and Amon had been godless kings but Josiah was a God-fearing ruler (2 Ki 22 and 23). Most students of the book think the reformation of Josiah had already begun. (See 2 Ch 34:3-7.)

The reformation in Judah in 621 BC (the ten tribes were already in captivity for a century) touched only the small remnant; the mass in Israel were in the condition pictured here in chapter 1 and in Jeremiah's prophecy. With the latter group all was outward and external, and a strong reaction followed the reformation. The people were ripe for judgment. It is strange that Zephaniah does not mention Josiah's reforms.

Our prophet has been considered as one of the most difficult in the prophetic canon, but his message has a definite focal point, namely, the Day of the Lord. He uses the expression more often than any other prophet of the Old Testament. In the first chapter he announces his word of judgment, centering particularly upon Judah; in the second chapter he predicts judgment on several peoples after an exhortation to repentance; in the last chapter, after a short word concerning judgment on Jerusalem, he promises future glory for Israel's restored remnant in the latter days. His prophecies of world judgment and final salvation for God's own people are comprehensive.

A sixteenth-century writer indicated: "If any one wishes all the secret oracles of the prophets to be given in a brief compendium, let him read through this brief Zephaniah." He has affinities in his prophecy with the message of earlier prophets. Similar expressions are found between Isaiah and Zephaniah and even more between Jeremiah and Zephaniah. In the time of Zephaniah the enemy of Israel was the Chaldean, rather than the Assyrian as with Nahum and others.

UNIVERSAL JUDGMENT

The prophet begins his book with a declaration of universal destruction. God will consume and destroy everything on the face of the earth, whether man or beast. The birds of the heavens and the fishes of the sea will be included in the same visitation. Beasts, birds, and fishes have common interests with man and suffer with him. The detailed enumeration is intended to express both the terror and universality of the punishment. God will utterly destroy all. Universal destruction because of man's sin has occurred before in the history of the world. (Note Gen 6:7.) Especially will the Lord punish the wicked with their stumblingblocks, the objects and rites of their idolatrous worship. (See Eze 14:3-4, 7.)

Thus far the pronouncement of judgment has been of a universal nature, now it is restricted to favored Judah and Jerusalem, who had the revelation of the will of God. The judgment on the whole earth will fall ultimately on Judah and Jerusalem.

Verses 4 to 6 show an advance from crude, external, to developed, internal idolatry. When the Lord predicts that He will stretch out His hand upon Judah and Jerusalem, He is indicating some special work of chastisement (Is 5:25; 9:12, 17, 21). Baal worship will be uprooted and destroyed. Baal was the god of the Canaanites, already worshiped by Israel in her apostasy in the time of the Judges (2:13).

Manasseh's reign was notorious for this worship (2 Ki 21:3, 5, 7; 2 Ch 33:3, 7). The godly Josiah destroyed them (2 Ch 34:4). The feminine deity usually associated with Baal was Ashtoreth. It was a nature worship and full of immoral practices. The remnant of Baal has reference to all that was left of Baal and idolatry generally. It has been inferred from this verse that the reformation of Josiah had already begun, and a curb had been imposed upon the flagrant idolatries of the nation. To the very last trace the godless worship of Baal was to be exterminated. This was fulfilled in Judah after the Babylonian captivity.

The very name of the Chemarim would disappear also. They were the idol priests (Ho 10:5), whom Josiah put down (2 Ki 23:5). The Hebrew root means "black" (from the black garments they wore) or "zealous" (for their fanaticism in idolatry). The other priests mentioned in verse 4 are outwardly priests of God, but careless about the spiritual laxity of the people.

Another class designated in Judah for judgment were those that worshiped the host of heaven upon the housetops. It was carried out on the flat housetops to afford a clearer view of the sky and chiefly by altars for burning incense. (Cp. Jer 8:2; 19:13; and 32:29.) This worship was called Sabeanism, and prevailed quite early in the East. Moses warned against it in Deuteronomy 4:19. Nevertheless, it was widely practiced in Israel, thus virtually making every home an idol sanctuary. (See 2 Ki 21:3, 5; 23:5-6; Jer 7:17-18; 44:17-19, 25.)

Still others in Judah had a compromise system of worship which included the worship of God and of Malcam, the same as Moloch (Amos 5:26) and Milcom, god of Ammon (1 Ki 11:33).

Finally, there are singled out those who at first heeded the exhortation of Josiah to repentance and then turned back and those who were indifferent to it all from the beginning. Such is the bill of particulars of the living God in His righteous wrath against the wickedness of Judah. Every type of iniquity is noted and set forth. All things are laid bare before Him with whom we have to do.

VISITATION UPON JUDAH

Before the prophet elaborates upon the judgment just indicated, he calls all to silence before the Lord. (See Hab 2:20.) He announces that the Day of the Lord, the day of judgment, is at hand. That final Day of the Lord is led up to by preliminary judgments as stages in the process.

Zephaniah is speaking of the same ultimate Day of the Lord which Joel prophesied (Joel 1:15 and Ob 15). The particular sacrifice in view here is the judgment on God's people, Judah. The consecrated guests are the Chaldeans. (Note Is 13:3; 34:6; Jer 46:10; and Eze 39:17.) The final picture is given in Revelation 19:17-18. How galling must be the judgment when God sanctifies the heathen Babylonians as His priests to slay the sacrifices.

The first punishment is set forth for the princes who follow the customs of the heathen. They should have been leaders in righteousness instead of evil. Judgment will fall on the royal family because they followed after foreign customs and oppressed the people.

By "the king's sons" are not meant the sons of Josiah. He could not have had sons old enough to have incurred such guilt. Those in view are either princes of the royal house or children of the king who would be ruling when the prophecy came to fulfillment. (Cp. 2 Ki 25:7 and Jer 39:6, where Zedekiah's sons were slain and he was blinded.) Josiah the king is not included because he was to be spared the judgment because of his godly life.

Some think the reference to foreign apparel points to the strange vestments brought in from the pagan lands abroad in which the ungodly in Israel worshiped idols. With foreign dress came foreign manners and worship, especially idolatry.

Verse 9 points out judgment upon those who plunder and rob their fellow citizens. According to 1 Samuel 5:5 it was a practice in Dagon worship at Ashdod to leap over the threshold, so some have thought the prophet is denouncing here an idolatrous rite. The end of the verse shows this view to be untenable. What is referred to is the zeal with which the servants of the rich hastened from their homes to plunder the property of others to enrich their masters. The homes of the poor were entered by force to spoil their goods. Thus the homes of the rich were filled with that which had been gained by violence and deceit.

In verses 10 and 11 the dishonest merchants who have grown wealthy through their wicked practices are warned.

The agony of Jerusalem in the invasion of Nebuchadnezzar is pictured for us. All parts of the city will be affected. The fish gate was on the north side of the city which was susceptible to attack. Nebuchadnezzar entered through this gate. It received its name from its proximity to the fish market where fish was brought from the Lake of Tiberias and the Jordan River. It answers to what is now called the Damascus Gate. The second quarter was the second district of the city on the hill Acra, where Huldah the prophetess lived (2 Ki 22:14). Along with the crying from the fish gate and the wailing from the second quarter will be joined a crashing from the hills, Zion, Moriah, and Ophel, within the walls. The verse indicates the progress of the enemy until they occupy the prominent positions of the city.

The word translated *Maktesh* is mortar and is not a proper name. Recent atlases indicate the place is unknown. It is thought to be a section of Jerusalem located in the hollow—some make it the Tyropoeon Valley in the city—where the merchants carried on their business.

The Lord will judge His people as corn is pounded in a mortar. The people of Canaan mentioned here are the merchants of Judah who transacted their affairs like the Canaanites or Phoenicians. Hosea 12:7 uses the same designation. Their riches will perish with them.

The wickedly indifferent ones among them are arraigned next. The prophet predicts that the Lord will search out very minutely, as a man does with lamps, the most concealed wickedness. The punishment will fall after such a search upon those settled on their lees, a figure which is proverbial for indifference and slothfulness (Jer 48:11). Hard crust forms on the surface of fermented liquors when they are not disturbed over a period of time. Thus settled in their carelessness, they deny God's governing providence in the universe, His activity and agency in the world, as though He brought about neither good nor calamity. For such wickedness and impudence God will bring upon them the curses of the Law: they would enjoy neither their wealth nor their houses and vineyards. (See Lev 26:32-33; Deu 28:30, 39; Amos 5:11; and Mic 6:15.)

THE DAY OF THE LORD

Every calamity in the godless reigns of Josiah's successors was one more step or prefiguring of the final one in the Day of the Lord. For further details on this day in the minor prophets the reader is referred to the book of Joel. The day is called great because of its tremendous effects (Joel 2:11). So deadly would be the Chaldean attack that even the mighty would despair and give themselves over to hopeless grief (Is 66:6). In verses 15 and 16 we have a most emphatic description of the gloominess and terror of the day.

Thomas of Celano in 1250 wrote his famous judgment hymn from verse 15, "Dies irae, dies illa," meaning "That day is a day of wrath." The day is one of wrath, trouble, distress, wasteness, desolation (the Hebrew words for wasteness and desolation—*sho'ah* and *umesho'ah*—are alike in sound to convey the monotony of the destruction), darkness, gloominess, clouds, thick darkness, trumpet, alarm against fortified cities and high towers.

Unable to find a way of escape out of their distressing calamity, the people of Judah will walk like blind men (Deu 28:29). As though worthless, their blood and flesh will be poured out as dust and refuse. In that hour of catastrophe neither silver nor gold will avail to preserve from the wrath of the holy God. God's fiery judgment will consume the whole land and bring to a sad end all who dwell in the land. The judgments of God are terrible, but how ineffably sweet is His grace which He has manifested to guilty sinners.

THOSE WHO SEEK NOT THE LORD

In the days of Josiah and the prophet Zephaniah, there were those in Judah who sought not the Lord because of wicked indifference. But it is also possible not to seek the Lord because the message of His redeeming grace has not been plainly and lovingly given. Paul indicates in Romans 10 that there can be no seeking of the Lord until the gospel message has been heard.

THE STROKE FALLS ON ALL

CALL TO REPENT

After that fearful setting forth of judgment in chapter 1, the reader may be inclined to feel that nothing more can be said, that the whole story has been told out.

God does not announce coming judgment without indicating at the same time the means of escape from the visitation. Thus we find the second chapter opening with an urgent exhortation to God's people to repent. From this call to repentance the prophet proceeds to foretell judgment on the nations surrounding Israel and especially those who have afflicted her.

Zephaniah calls upon the nation to gather themselves together. The thought is emphasized by the double use of the same verb. The gathering together is not meant to encourage them to collect themselves together or to collect their thoughts, as has been suggested, but to come together to a religious assembly to entreat the favor of the Lord in order that by prayer He may turn away His judgment. (See Joel 2:16.) The word translated "gather together" ordinarily means to gather stubble or fuel for burning, here to crowd together.

The nation is addressed in a derogatory manner because of their sin and called a nation that has no shame. They shrank not from continuous sinning. It is not that they were not desired, as some suppose, or that there was nothing in the nation to commend it to God, but that they were dead to shame. Sin ever hardens the sensibilities.

But there is no time for delay, for the decree hastens nearer as though going on to a birth. The decree is that which God has determined, in this instance, to do with the sinners of the nation. The day of repentance is a glorious opportunity, but it passes away as rapidly as the chaff is suddenly blown away by a strong gust of wind. They must avail themselves of it immediately. After it comes the day of the Lord's fierce anger. Thrice over comes the call to seek the Lord, righteousness, and meekness.

Apparently the remnant of the nation is now addressed, for they are called the meek of the earth (land) who have kept the ordinances of the Lord. It will be remembered that Nebuzaradan left the poor of the land to be vinedressers and husbandmen in the time of the captivity. (Note 2 Ki 25:12.) Though they are meek, they are to seek to grow in this blessed trait. Having diligently followed the requirements of the law of the Lord, they are encouraged to pursue righteousness further. If it please the Lord, they may be hid, preserved, in the day of the Lord's wrath (Is 26:20). It has been suggested that we have a play on the name of the prophet Zephaniah in the word *hid*. The door of repentance was even then wide open for any to enter.

JUDGMENT ON PHILISTIA

If the anger of the Lord sweeps as a storm through the land of His people, we may be certain that He will not wink at sin elsewhere. God cannot overlook sin in His people, but He will not allow the nations to afflict them without punishment. Nations from the four points of the globe are included to indicate again the universality of the judgment. The God of Israel is and always has been the God of the universe, the God of the nations.

Verse 4 begins with the reason why the ungodly should repent and the meek should take courage. The land of Philistia to the west comes first into view for judgment. Four of the five Philistine cities—Gaza, Ashkelon, Ashdod, and Ekron—are mentioned, while Gath is omitted. Amos 1:6-8 omits the fifth also. Uzziah and Hezekiah had kept Gath in subjection (2 Ki 18:8 and 2 Ch 26:6).

In English it is impossible to recapture the play on the Hebrew words for Gaza's forsaking and Ekron's uprooting. Ashdod will be driven out at a most unusual time, at noonday. It is the hottest time of the day and is usually spent in sleep in the Orient, so not a likely time for an invasion to be attempted. When they least expect it, the blow will fall upon them. (See 2 Sa 4:5 and Jer 6:4.)

Woe is pronounced against the Philistines who lived on the coast in the region of the sea. They are called Cherethites, or people of the Cretans, because some of their number had come from Crete (Caphtor of Amos 9:7). David's bodyguard was made up of Cherethites and Pelethites (2 Sa 8:18; 1 Ki 1:38, 44), considered the twofold origin of the Philistine people.

The name Philistine itself properly means emigrant. The name Canaan originally signified the flat coast land. This portion of the land was to be left without inhabitant. Instead of being thickly populated, the region will be fit only for pasture land for nomads. All this has been literally fulfilled upon Philistia. But it was not to remain in this uninhabited condition permanently: the remnant of the house of Judah (Israel had long been exiled, as we saw in chapter 1) were to inherit the land of Philistia when its people were dispossessed in judgment. God was to visit His people with mercy and return them from their captivity to enjoy the homes and land of Philistia. This portion was included in the original grant of the land by the Lord to Abraham. He will faithfully keep His covenant.

JUDGMENT ON MOAB AND AMMON

The origin of the children of Moab and the children of Ammon is important and can be found in the account in Genesis 19:30-38. Though of incestuous and shameful descent, these peoples were characterized by great arrogance. Because of the fall of the Northern Kingdom and the decline of the southern monarchy, the pride of these nations east of Israel was increased greatly. They reproached and reviled the people of God. After each calamity of Israel, these nations sought to profit for themselves by seizure of some of Israel's land. These peoples showed their enmity toward God's people on every opportunity. (Read carefully Num 22; 24:17; Judg 3; 10; 1 Sa 11:1-5; and 2 Sa 12:26-31.) Thus their revilings were not restricted to the time of the captivity, but must cover many occasions when Israel was in distress. Their pride is condemned by the prophets Isaiah and Jeremiah. (Cp. Is 16:6; 25:11; and Jer 48:29-30.)

That the final fulfillment of these predictions is yet future to our day can be seen from the connection of verses 8 to 10 with verse 11. Moab and Ammon will become like Sodom and Gomorrah. Their own territory will suffer as the cities which were destroyed in the days of their ancestor Lot. The land of these nations will be converted into a possession of nettles and into salt pits, indicating sterility and desolation. They have been desolate ever since (Jer 17:6) like the regions on the Dead Sea.

Salt is used in the Old Testament as a figure for sterility and ruin (Job 39:6). This portion of shame and reproach shall they have because of their pride which led them to reproach Israel and magnify themselves against the chosen of the Lord. The nations are exceedingly dull in learning how greatly they displease the Lord when they deal in pride against the nation whom He has chosen as His medium for worldwide blessing.

UNIVERSAL WORSHIP OF THE LORD

We cannot stress too strongly that God's ultimate object and purpose are not to punish and destroy but to overrule evil for good and to bring peace out of hopeless chaos. In His wrath He will be terrible to the sinning nations, thus dealing summarily with the gods they worshiped.

The Lord is said to famish all the gods of the earth; that is, He will make lean, diminish, or destroy them. The Lord is the destroyer of their gods when He brings judgment on the nations who worshiped them. Idols have no real existence apart from the people who serve them (1 Co 8:4-6).

Along with the complete destruction of the idolatrous nations will go idol worship from all the earth. Then will men worship the one true God, each from his place, that is, each in the place where he lives, thus making the worship of the Lord universal.

This Scripture is not fulfilled in our age when some worship the Lord from every nation. (See Jn 4:21-24 and 1 Co 1:2.) The prophet is speaking of that time when the world of nations will be converted to the worship of the true and living God. A similar thought is strongly expressed in Malachi 1:11. The picture refers to the latter days of Israel's history and brings us directly into Messianic times and millennial conditions.

Indeed, it is the other side of the picture given in some prophetic passages, such as Isaiah 2:2; Micah 4:1-2; and Zechariah 8:22-23; 14:16. These portions should be studied in their contexts to give the true chronological framework. After the second coming of the Lord Jesus Christ to the earth, these conditions will exist. All nations in that day will be united, not to do their own wills nor to worship the works of their own wicked hands, but to worship and serve the only God. It is the hour for which the waiting believer devoutly hopes and the one toward which he labors in his day.

JUDGMENT ON ETHIOPIA AND ASSYRIA

Thus far Zephaniah has foretold God's judgment upon nations east and west of Judah; now he directs our attention to Ethiopia and Assyria, nations to the south and north of the Holy Land. The Ethiopians are warned of slaughter by the sword of the Lord. Much is said in the prophetic books of the Old Testament concerning the sword of the Lord, and it is a subject which will repay study. Ethiopia (Cush) is south of the First Cataract of the Nile and ruled Egypt from about 720 to 654 BC (Cp. Is 11:11 and 18:1.) A fulfillment of this prophecy has been seen in Nebuchadnezzar's invasion and conquest of Egypt. The fortunes of Ethiopia were bound up with those of Egypt, which was subject to Ethiopic dynasties. (Note Jer 46:9 and Eze 30:5, 9.) There is reason to believe that Egypt itself is meant under the term *Ethiopians*.

From Ethiopia the word of judgment proceeds to Assyria. At the time of this prophecy the nation had not fallen. The recital of woe and judgment climaxes with Assyria, which was the strongest political factor of the day.

For a fuller treatment of the doom of Assyria, the reader is referred to the prophecy of Nahum. Here it is briefly and pointedly stated that the Lord will destroy Assyria and desolate Nineveh, making her as dry as the wilderness. This is all the more remarkable when we realize that at the very time of the prophet's prediction, the plentiful irrigation of the mighty city was its great boast and joy.

Zephaniah now elaborates on the desolate condition of the ruined city. The once populous and renowned city will be fit only for beasts and herds. The pelican and porcupine (or hedgehog) will make their abode in the ruins of the city. These creatures are found in another picture of desolation given by Isaiah in 34:11. They will lodge in capitals which are the ornaments of magnificent buildings now thrown down and affording hiding and lodging place. The doleful singing of some lonely bird will be heard from the windows of palaces and homes. The homes will be deserted of man and none will pass over the thresholds any more. The beautiful wainscoting and fine carved work of the walls and ceilings of the houses will be ripped apart and laid bare.

The prophet, in concluding this message of doom, takes up a satire such as was sung over a defeated enemy. Nineveh is characterized as the joyous city that had lived carelessly.

The greatness and glory of Assyria were known the world over. About 225 years before this, Israel felt the iron hand of Assyria in the Battle of Karkar (854-853 BC). More than one hundred years before this her armies overran Palestine and for more than a half-century dominated Judah. Now she herself was ripe for the most appropriate punishment.

In her godless self-sufficient boasting, she had claimed that there was none beside her. This was the claim of Babylon also, as recorded in Isaiah 47:8. (See Laodicea in Rev 3:17.) Such self-sufficiency is the very attribute of God (Is 45:21-22). For this arrogance she is brought down to the basest desolation, a place for beasts only. The magnitude and suddenness of her destruction will make her the object of the scorn and contempt of all that pass by. They will wag their hand, implying that she has brought her judgment on herself.

When the Greek Xenophon passed the site of Nineveh in 401 BC, he was able to find out only that a great city had once stood on the site and had been destroyed because Zeus had deprived her people of their wits. What folly and insanity for puny man to arrogate to himself divine prerogatives and attributes!

THE LORD WILL VISIT THEM

The promise of the prophet foretold that the Lord would turn in mercy to His people and bring them back from captivity. All this will be accomplished for Israel in prophetic times. It is that God has already visited His people in grace by the coming of their Messiah in Jesus of Nazareth, foretold by the prophets. By simple faith in the sufficient work of the Redeemer, the Spirit of God visits the willing heart to regenerate and impart new life forevermore. This is Israel's greatest need in the light of which all others pale in significance.

WRATH AND BLESSING

WOE UPON GODLESS JERUSALEM

After the series of woes on the nations in chapter 2, the prophet returns in chapter 3 to his message to Jerusalem. Because she was so highly favored and privileged, much more was to be expected of her in the way of faith and obedience to the Lord.

Although the city addressed in verse 1 is not named, it is abundantly clear from verse 2 that Jerusalem is meant. She is accused of rebellion, pollution, and oppression. She was rebellious because she would not submit to the known will of God; she was polluted because of long continuance in sin in spite of her outward ceremonial exactness; she was oppressing because she regarded not the rights of the poor, the orphans, and the widows.

The nation seen corporately has four distinct charges laid against her. She obeyed not the voice of God in the Law and by the mouth of the prophets; she received not correction—when God's chastisements were upon her, she did not learn the lessons intended; she trusted not in the Lord, but in herself, her idols, and her allies; and she drew not near to her God in faith, worship, and repentance, estranging herself from Him, though He sought to be nigh her (Deu 4:7).

As the people, so were the leaders. Three classes in the nation—the princes, the prophets, and the priests—are singled out for special condemnation. There is no denunciation of the godly king, Josiah. The princes, however, were like roaring lions in the midst of her. They were ever on the search for more prey.

Those who should have shepherded the flock were devouring them. (See 1:8-9; Mic 2:2; Zec 11:4.) The judges of the people were filled with insatiable greed, devouring all at once in their ravenous hunger. They left nothing till the morning.

In verse 4 we have the only denunciation of the prophets in this book. They were guilty of levity, trifling with the weightiest matters. There was no gravity or steadfastness in their life or teaching. They were treacherous because they were unfaithful to Him whom they claimed to represent, rather encouraging the people in their apostasy from the Lord. By their unholy deeds they profaned the sanctuary; they made the sacred profane. They did violence to the Law by distorting its plain intent and meaning when they were teaching the people. (Cp. for a similar charge Eze 22:26.) Princes, prophets, and priests were alike guilty of polluting the nation by their wicked example and ways.

THE CHASTENINGS AND WARNINGS OF GOD

In spite of Jerusalem's iniquities and corruptions, the righteous Lord is in her midst. His presence in her midst makes all the more certain her judgment for sin. He is never implicated with iniquity.

The morning is the time in the East for the administering of justice, so every morning the Lord brings His justice to light. His righteous conduct is made known through His true prophets who exhort to godliness, and through His judgments on the ungodly in the nation.

By chastisements and warnings He continues to manifest His justice. He does not fail or miss, but the ungodly have no shame such as would lead them to repentance. God had meant that by His judgments on other nations His own people would have been warned and turned to Him.

During Josiah's reign, Judea enjoyed peace though wars troubled other peoples. She was spared during the ravaging invasion of the Scythians into western Asia. Even the fate of the ten tribes did not deter the Southern Kingdom from sin.

Verse 6 describes the desolations the Lord wrought among the nations surrounding Judea, and these were meant as warnings to her. But she did not heed the example of other nations in their judgment. God intended by these visitations that Judah would learn to fear Him and receive correction, so that her dwelling place would not be destroyed.

Howsoever the Lord had marked them out for punishment because of their sins, yet if they had repented, He would pardon and not cut off the city. But they, in defiance of the Lord and His displeasure, rose early, indicating the deliberateness of their sinning, and corrupted their ways. The early morning in the Orient is the best for doing business. With great zeal and earnestness they pursued their sinful course. Great is the enticement of sin and great is the penalty it incurs, but man rushes headlong into it, nevertheless.

WRATH UPON THE NATIONS

In order to complete the entire cycle of prophecies of God's wrath, Zephaniah reverts in verse 8 to the theme of chapter 1, the judgment of God upon all the nations. The godly among the Lord's people are exhorted to wait for Him, to trust Him. As the beast ready for plunder the Lord will yet rise up to the prey.

The prey has been understood as those among the nations who will fall to Him as His portion in salvation. (Cp. Is 53:12 with 52:15; 49:7.) But there must be destruction and extermination before this can be realized.

The godly are to await the judgment of God upon the nations, for it will ultimately issue in their redemption. The Lord is determined to gather the nations (Zec 14:2) and kingdoms to pour out upon them in one great act of judgment His indignation, His fierce anger, and the fire of His jealousy. The words are vivid and portray a scene of great prophetic importance. See also Joel 3:1-3 and 3:12-16. (According to the Massoretic scholars, who labored faithfully on the text of the Old Testament, verse 8 is the only verse of the Old Testament in which all the letters of the Hebrew alphabet, even the final letters, occur.)

THE CONVERSION OF THE NATIONS

The remainder of chapter 3 treats of Messianic times. In these verses we have glowing promises of blessing and restoration for God's people and the nations. Zephaniah now outlines what the results will be of God's judgments on the nations. After His wrath is poured out upon the ungodly among the nations, then in the program of His mercies, He will bestow upon the Gentiles a pure language in order that they may call upon the name of the Lord and serve Him unitedly.

The prophet is not predicting a universal language (some say Hebrew, as though we have here a reversal of Babel), but that the impure speech of the nations will be cleansed. It will be a purified, uncontaminated speech, rather than clear, easily understood speech. (Note Is 6:5 for the opposite thought.) The impurity of which they were formerly guilty arose from their swearing by and praying to false gods.

The remnant of the nations is thus indicated as converted to the Lord. The nations learn righteousness through judgment. All will call upon the name of the Lord, a restoration of the conditions indicated in Genesis 4:26. They will not only worship the Lord by word of mouth, but will also serve Him with one consent (lit., shoulder).

The figure is taken from the yoke or burden borne by two, helping one another. Compare this expression with that found in 1 Kings 22:13, "with one mouth." There is no basis here for teaching a restoration of Pentecostal gifts. The verse does not have this in view. In their converted condition, the nations will show their willingness to be used of the Lord in behalf of Israel. From beyond the rivers of Ethiopia they shall bring the dispersed of Israel to their own land as an offering to the Lord (Is 49:22-23; 60:4-9; and 66:20).

The rivers of Ethiopia are the branches of the Nile: the Atbara, the Astasobas, the Blue Nile, and the White Nile. The land is Ethiopia itself (Is 18:1).

There are some who suggest that the ones meant by the suppliants are Jews dispersed in Ethiopia. They point to the west of Abyssinia where the well-known Falashas (the word is from the same Semitic root as Philistine, meaning emigrant) live. They are said to trace their origin to Palestine and the Jewish religion. It is thought that the Abyssinian Christians were originally in part Hebrew believers. We prefer with others to understand the words "my suppliants, even the daughter of my dispersed" as the object of the verb and not the subject. In other words, the Lord's people dispersed in Ethiopia will be brought by the Gentiles to their homeland as an offering to the Lord. The passages from Isaiah indicated above amply attest this truth. Such is the meaning rather than that the dispersed ones bring an offering to the Lord. The effect of the conversion of the Gentiles will be to place them in alignment with the purpose of God for Israel in their restoration to Palestine.

THE REMNANT IN ISRAEL

Now the prophet describes for us the condition of the people of Israel as cleansed, restored, and rejoicing in their land. When they are gathered out of the nations, they will have no cause for shame, because the Lord will have removed from them the ungodly and impious ones. Every shameful deed will have been cleansed. Former transgressions will be put away. Especially will pride be dealt with. Pharisaic pride will be a thing of the past. The Temple mountain will not be subjected to the haughtiness that was found there at one time. Instead of proud ones the Lord will leave in the midst of the land such as are afflicted and poor, the meek and humble, those who truly find their refuge in the name of the Lord alone. Iniquity, falsehood, and deceit will be purged from the remnant of Israel. In that condition spiritually, they will find physical prosperity and peace as well. Neither home nor foreign oppressor will then harass them. They will enjoy the rich blessing of God unmolested and undisturbed. See parallel passages in Micah 4:4 and 7:14. They will fulfill their divine calling (Ex 19:6).

MILLENNIAL GLORY AND JOY

But the full story of blessing and restoration has not been recounted. The prophet now describes it in fuller detail. In view of the glad day that is coming they are exhorted to sing, shout, be glad, and rejoice. God never multiplies words like these without intending an emphatic declaration.

The reason for the rejoicing is given in verse 15. Israel's day of judgment and chastisement is past; every adversary has been cast out; and the Lord, the King of Israel, is in her midst. No wonder then that she has no further cause for fear. Slackness of hands from anxiety and fear will be an experience of the past.

The promises seem to reach a climax with verse 17. The Lord's presence in her midst is repeated (v. 15); this is the source of all the blessedness. He is the mighty Saviour. As the bridegroom rejoices over the bride, so the Lord rejoices over His people. The marriage contract between the Lord and Israel will be restored (Is 62:5; 65:19; and Ho 2:19-20). Then He will rest (lit., be silent) in His love.

This is one of the boldest statements in the Bible. It is stated that God will rest in silent ecstasy over His people, Israel. What assurance for Israel! The love is too great for words to express. The Lord will rest complacently in it. The idea that God will no longer have occasion to rebuke and denounce can only be a secondary one here. He has quiet joy in His love. Then the silence is broken with singing. Read what the Word of God says of the voice of the Lord in Psalm 29:3-9 and imagine, if you can, what that singing with joy will be.

Because they could not celebrate the feasts of the Lord in exile, the godly sorrowed for the solemn festal assembly. These the Lord will gather back to the land of their inheritance. They belonged to the land as its rightful citizens. They had felt keenly as a burden the reproach that had fallen upon God's people. Regathered and restored, the nation will be a source of blessing to all the world.

At that time, in the millennial day, preceded first by the judgment on the enemies of Israel, the Lord will deal with those who afflicted Israel. He will recompense them as they have deserved. Those who are lame and those who were driven away stand for all in the dispersion; all will be redeemed and restored. God will give them a celebrated name in all the earth, whereas formerly they were the objects of shame and derision among all the nations. She will fulfill that which was her destiny from the beginning. (See Deu 26:19.) The Lord will exercise His pastoral care over them by bringing them in and gathering them to Himself from captivity. It will be so wonderful that they will scarcely believe it, yet it will materialize in their sight. Blessed and glad day for tempest-tossed Israel!

THE KING OF ISRAEL IN HER MIDST

Zephaniah's message centers about judgment and especially that of the fearful Day of the Lord. No nation is exempt. But we do him an injustice if we think of him only in the light of chastisement. He concludes his prophecy with words of blessing and promise for the nations and Israel. But these promises to the nations can only be realized when the blessings of God are upon the nation Israel. The King of Israel in the midst of Israel is the Lord God Himself. Would God that were already fulfilled! Every day that the salvation of Israel draws nearer, that of the world's salvation draws nearer also (Ps 67).

13

HAGGAI
REBUILDING THE TEMPLE

Arise and Build

THE PROPHET AND HIS TIMES

OUR PROPHET is the only person in the Old Testament with the name "Haggai." The name means "festal one," and it has been suggested that the name was given him because he was born on some feast.

Haggai is one of the prophets whose personal history is unknown. He is mentioned in Ezra 5:1 and 6:14. He is the first of the postcaptivity prophets, those who ministered after the return of Israel from Babylonian Exile. (Note Ezra 4 and 5 for the historical background.)

It is good to read Ezra, Nehemiah, and Esther in the study of Haggai, Zechariah, and Malachi. They refer to the same period in the history of Israel. The king is Darius Hystaspes, and the time is 520 BC.

The prophecy covers the short space of but four months. Haggai 2:3 does not necessarily imply that Haggai lived in the time of the first temple. He was probably born in exile.

The historical background may be summarized conveniently thus: the remnant had returned from Babylon; the feasts were reinstituted; the foundation of the new Temple had been laid; then the work on the restoration Temple was stopped because of the opposition of hostile neighbors and national indifference; Darius Hystaspes favored the work when he came to the Persian throne; Haggai and Zechariah exhorted the people to the work of rebuilding in their prophetic messages to the nation. The commission of Haggai from the Lord was to rouse the people to rebuild the Temple destroyed by Nebuchadnezzar in 586 BC. He begins with the rebuilding of the temple, but goes on to speak of the shaking of all nations, the coming of the Lord, and the glory of His millennial reign.

Some find four addresses in the prophecy while others find five. Probably the former position is the correct one, the divisions being 1:1-15; 2:1-9; 2:10-19; 2:20-23. The main sections of the book are indicated by dates. The ministry of Haggai preceded Zechariah's by about two months.

He begins his message with reproof and warning and then passes on to the promise of God's presence with Israel in the renewed work. The next outlines the glory of the temple in the future. After setting forth clearly the principles of sin and holiness, he predicts God's continued protection and blessing upon His people. The style of Haggai is simple prose which is given force by frequent use of questions.

THE REBUKE

The prophet dates all his messages, the first falling in the second year, the sixth month, the first day of the month of the reign of Darius. The first day of every month was the new moon when the people were gathered for worship. This was an appropriate time for the declaration of the message of Haggai.

The sixth month is Elul, about our September. Darius began to reign in 521 BC, and this word came in the second year of his rule. The dating of the prophecy (so Zechariah also) according to the reign of a Gentile king reveals clearly that the times of the Gentiles were in progress. (See Lk 21:24.) The date of verse 1 harmonizes with Ezra 4:24. Because of the enemies of the Jews the rebuilding of God's house ceased till the second year of Darius of Persia.

The prophecy is addressed to Zerubbabel and Joshua, civil and religious leaders of the day, but is intended for the whole nation as the contents show. *Zerubbabel* means "begotten in Babylon." He is called Sheshbazzar in Ezra 1:8 and 5:14, 16. He was the grandson of Jehoiachin (1 Ch 3:17, 19) and was appointed by Cyrus to be governor of Judah (Ezra 5:14). Joshua was the son of Jehozadak who was the high priest at the time of the Babylonian invasion (1 Ch 6:15).

Haggai begins with a rebuke of the people's indifference. He sets forth their excuse for not rebuilding the Temple. They were saying it was just not time to come and rebuild the house of the Lord. It was a complaint that the time was not proper nor auspicious. The root of the difficulty was coldness in them toward the things of God. How easy it is to camouflage that dread condition in any of us with an abundance of excuses, evasions, and subterfuges. If faith had been present, the decree of Artaxerxes would have been no deterrent in the work. Since Persian decrees could not be altered, it has been suggested that the decree of Cyrus could not have been repealed by another.

God speaks of Israel as "This people" and not "My people," not so much in contempt as in displeasure. Note that they were not saying the building should not be done; only that it was not time yet to do it. And all this in the face of the fact that the work had been interrupted for fifteen years.

To the dilatory plea of the people, the Lord makes reply by the prophet, asking whether the hour was suitable for them to dwell in their ceiled houses while the Lord's Temple lay waste. Their selfishness, indifference, and ingratitude are laid bare at once by the inquiry. They were moved only by selfish interests in all that they did. Ceiled houses indicate homes that were panelled, luxuriously fitted, not confined to the ceiling, but including the walls also, an overlaying with boards or panels. Wainscoting with cedar was common in the residences of the kings. (Cp. 1 Ki 7:7 and Jer 22:14.)

They had shifted the most important thing out of the picture. First things must be placed first. It was not merely a physical building or structure that was the issue; all revolved around the question of the worship of the Lord.

How blessed it is to have the clear vision given of God to place the preeminent things first. Note Paul's "first of all" in relation to the Gospel (1 Co 15:3). The blameworthy attitude of Israel in this particular may well be compared with David's concern as given in 2 Samuel 7:2. The blessing of God rests upon an outlook such as his; only the displeasure of the Lord can be expected by the course taken by Israel.

THE CALAMITY

The exhortation of the Lord to Israel in her sin was to consider (lit., set the heart) her ways. This call is a favorite one with Haggai; he employs it again in verse 7 of chapter 1 and twice in 2:18.

It is a command to self-judgment. They were to judge the nature of their deeds (or excuses) by the results which followed them. They sowed bountifully but harvested little; they ate but were never satisfied (Lev 26:26; Ho 4:10; Mic 6:14); they drank but did not have enough; they clothed themselves but were not warm; they earned wages but they were soon spent. God disappointed them in all their expectations. The visitations continued as long as the negligence lasted. All the while they were blind to the issues involved and to the chastening hand of God. Their self-seeking had gotten them nowhere. It had brought loss instead of gain. Their necessities were so expensive that their wages left no surplus. A selfish and self-centered people needed to be shown what loss it was to neglect the work of the Lord for their own material gain.

There is no contradiction between verse 6 (also vv. 9-11) which depicts conditions of poverty, with verse 4, which mentions their ceiled houses, because there were surely wealthy members of the nation as well as the poorer class. The principle of Matthew 6:33 still holds good for every age. He that labors without the Lord labors without benefit or profit (Zec 8:10).

THE CHARGE

In view of what the prophet has disclosed of the displeasure of the Lord, Israel is again called upon to consider her ways. The repetition indicates greater urgency to do so. With verse 8 the people are informed of the remedy for their trouble. They were to betake themselves to the mountains, any wooded area, to fetch timber to build the house of the Lord. Thus would the Lord be pleased and be glorified.

He had been displeased with the desolate condition of His house and had surely gotten no glory from their lack of obedience and concern for the things of God.

The blessed results of obedience are here noted. In short, Haggai is saying, "Give God the supreme place in your life." God would then be honored in the worship of His people. A heart attitude of obedience would have shown worship and gratitude on their part, thus glorifying God. God made it quite plain just how He could be glorified. The Babylonian Talmud indicated that five things were lacking in the Temple of Zerubbabel which were present in the Temple of Solomon: (1) the Ark of the Covenant; (2) the holy fire; (3) the Shekinah glory; (4) the spirit of prophecy (the Holy Spirit); and (5) the Urim and Thummim. Whatever may have been lacking, God promises His blessing will be present.

GOD'S VISITATIONS

The prophet reverts to the thought of God's judgments on the people of Israel because of their disobedience (see v. 6). When they labored much and looked for large harvests, there was little to repay their toil. When that little was brought home, God blew upon it. They were not to lay the unproductiveness of the soil to the long neglect of the land during the period of the exile. It was distinctly God's chastening hand upon them. He tells them the reason for it all.

It could well have been that each year at the harvest time, when the crops had been brought into the barns, that the Lord had sent strong winds which leveled the barns and scattered the grain. God scattered it and blighted it. How could God's action be explained? Why did He do it? The answer is simply that they allowed the Lord's house to lie in ruins, while each ran to his own house.

The word *run* reveals the zeal they showed in pursuing their own affairs and interests, while they disregarded the work on the Temple. There is a contrast between "my house" and "his own house."

Because of their sin, the heavens withheld the dew which replaces the rain in the dry summer months. There was no fruit from the earth. The Lord brought drought upon the land and the mountains that affected the grain, the new wine, the oil, all the produce of the ground, and all the labor of man and cattle. Famine is indicated in the Scriptures as an instrument of God's wrath. (See 2 Ki 8:1 and Ps 105:16.) The grain, wine, and oil were the chief crops of the land. (Cp. Deu 11:14 and 18:4.) The cattle are included here because they had to suffer the fortunes of man. The Law had foretold such visitations for disobedience. (Note Lev 26:19-20; Deu 28:23-24.)

THE OBEDIENCE OF THE PEOPLE

The message and reasonings of Haggai with the people fell upon good soil. In verse 12 we have the effect of Haggai's first sermon. Zerubbabel, Joshua, and all the remnant who had returned from exile took the message to heart. There was no dissension nor division. The people recognized the word of Haggai for what it really was—the message of God through His servant. Their purpose to obey is stated in verse 12, just as the fulfillment is given in verse 14. Upon their obedience the Lord grants them an all-sufficient word of encouragement for the task that lay yet before them.

Haggai is designated as the Lord's messenger in the Lord's message. Simply stated, the words mean that the prophet was invested with divine authority. Our prophet is the only one in the Bible who is called the "Lord's messenger," though all the true prophets were also such. The word, in fact, is not exclusively applied to prophets. It is used of priests in Malachi 2:7. It does not have the significance here of angel, as many of the Church fathers in the early Church held, although the Hebrew word legitimately has both meanings, as does the corresponding Greek word in the New Testament.

The word of encouragement was that the Lord would be with them. Short message it was but all that was needed for that hour or any other. What more could any man need or hope for? The promise indicates that their repentance was genuine. It guaranteed them the presence of the Lord for help, protection, and blessing. It was the greatest of all blessings, because it includes all others. This is the all-sufficient assurance of their

future success. (See Ro 8:31.) The favor of God was now to rest abundantly upon them in the place of His former displeasure.

THE RESUMPTION OF THE BUILDING

It was the Lord who energized leaders and people alike and inclined
their hearts to the work (Phil 2:13) . They were encouraged of God from
their previous discouragement.

There was a lapse of twenty-three days between verse 15 and verse 1;
the interval had been spent, doubtless, in planning and preparing for the
work by way of removal of debris, gathering of material, and the like.
Blessed is the lot of that people that yields to the leading of the Lord to
do His work in His appointed time. Blessing must follow.

THE COMING GLORY

THE ENCOURAGEMENT OF THE LORD

Haggai dates his second message on the twenty-first day of the seventh
month. Reference to Leviticus 23:39-44 will show that this was the seventh
day of the Feast of Tabernacles, the final feast of ingathering.

Work had now gone on for almost a month on the rebuilding of the
Temple. Many were making comparisons between this Temple and
Solomon's. The people needed hope and encouragement now to guard
against despondency after they had resumed the work in answer to the
exhortation of the Lord through the prophet.

In the first chapter of this prophecy the nation needed a word directed
to their consciences because of their coldness and indifference; now they
stood in need of a word of cheer and comfort to strengthen their hands
and purposes as they pursued the task in obedience to the Lord.

Again the message is addressed to the civil and religious leaders of the
nation and the remnant that had returned from captivity. The Lord
Himself draws a contrast between the Temple of Solomon and the one
then in process of construction. He asks who among them remembers the
glory of the first Temple and inquires whether they do not find this Temple as nothing in comparison.

Ezra 3:8-13 gives us the historical background for the question of the
Lord. There it is recorded that at the time the second Temple was
founded, the priests accompanied the laying of the foundation with appropriate psalms of praise and with singing and blowing of trumpets.
While the younger generation shouted with joy and exultation over the
achievement, the older men who had seen the first Temple in its glory
wept because of the evident contrast between the two buildings. It is to
this latter group especially that the words of our prophet are now directed.

God speaks of the former glory of His (this) house. From God's viewpoint there was only one house of the Lord on Mt. Zion, whether it was the Temple built by Solomon, Zerubbabel, or Herod later. Because of the limited means of the people (see 1:6, 9-11) and the absence of such treasures as the Ark, the Temple of Zerubbabel must truly have appeared as "nothing" in the estimation of many.

Should this disparity be the occasion for discouragement and further stoppage of the work? No, there is a threefold word to be strong to Zerubbabel, Joshua, and all the people. The same God who draws the contrast in all its vividness is the one who offers the needed spiritual stimulus for the ongoing of the building. Thus the comparison of verse 3 was not introduced to dishearten them, but to urge them to rely heavily on their God. Moreover, God's estimates differ widely from ours. They are charged to continue the work with the repeated assurance (1:13) that the Lord will be with them. And they have ample reason to know that the Lord will keep His promise. He kept the word which He covenanted (lit., cut, with reference to the sacrificial victims cut to ratify a covenant) with His people when He brought them from Egypt.

The covenant at Sinai is referred to here. (See Ex 6:7; 19:5; and especially 33:12-14.) If the Lord kept His promise in this regard through all the intervening centuries, He can be depended upon now to maintain His promise. Yea, and His Spirit was still abiding (the participle is used signifying "abideth") with them at that very moment. Surely they have nothing to fear. God is for them; who can successfully be against them?

THE GREATER GLORY

The ensuing four verses of chapter 2 are distinctly Messianic with a blending, as in so many other passages like Zechariah 9:9-10; Isaiah 61:1-3; and Daniel 9:24-27, of the first and second comings of the Lord Jesus Christ, Israel's King and Messiah.

The Lord predicts that in a little while He would shake the heavens, the earth, the sea, and all the nations of the earth. There are some who see here only a startling display of God's power in the realm of nature. This is to see too little where much is intended.

What is the connection of these statements with the promise of the Lord uttered in verses 4 and 5? It is after this manner: the Jews are encouraged to continue the work of the Temple by the assurance that the Lord, who is God of the nations, would in a brief period of time manifest His infinite power to bring about an overturning in the kingdoms of the world in preparation for the setting up of Messiah's kingdom.

The passage has been referred to the revolutions in the Persian and

Greek empires. There were such shakings in these governments, but they can only be considered as initial and preparatory steps in the long process where the kingdoms are shaken from their position of rule, and finally the kingdom of the Lord Christ is realized upon earth. (Note Rev 11:15; also Heb 12:26-27.)

Much difference of opinion has centered about the interpretation of verse 7, especially the words translated "the desire of all nations" (KJV) or "the precious things of all nations" (ASV). Some of the translations offered are: "the precious possessions of the heathen" or "the Gentiles shall come with their delightful things" or "the choicest of all nations will come." The interpretation in these renderings is pretty much this: the lack in this Temple by way of outward adornment would be more than compensated for by the precious gifts which all the nations would yet bring to make the Temple of the Lord glorious. This they would do in homage to the true God.

This interpretation is supposed to square with the fact that the feminine singular subject has a plural verb. It is suggested that reference is being made to "the good things to come" of the new covenant. We do well to remember that from earliest times the majority of Christian interpreters have referred this passage to the coming of Christ. Jewish tradition also referred it to the Messiah. Without being dogmatic we should like to point out that the desire of all nations can only refer to the longing of all nations for the Deliverer, whether they realize it or not.

In Hebrew an abstract noun is often placed for the concrete, so this could refer to the Messiah. The plural verb is no argument against the Messianic interpretation, because the verb sometimes agrees with the second of two nouns. The first Temple was filled with a cloud of glory (1 Ki 8:10-11; 2 Ch 5:13-14); this Temple was yet to be filled with the divine glory in Christ (Jn 1:14); but the prophecy relates to the glory of His second coming (Mal 3:1). The Lord promises that the nations will be shaken (not converted); that shaking began preparatory to the first coming and it will be finished at the second. See Daniel 2:35, 44 and Matthew 21:44.

Thus will the Lord fill His house with glory inexpressible. Says the prophet in verse 8: "Do not be disturbed over the absence of the precious metals (it has been estimated that in Solomon's Temple over $20,000,000 worth of gold went to overlay the Holy of Holies) in the Temple now in building, for the Lord could supply that easily (Ps 50:12), but He intends to beautify it by the glory of His Son in His first coming and second coming, first veiled, then revealed."

The poor remnant of that day had little to ornament and decorate the rebuilt Temple, but silver and gold are the Lord's. Moreover, the latter glory of this house will excel the former, and the Lord will grant peace there. For "latter glory" see the contrast of verse 3 with its statement "in its former glory."

The Temple of the Lord in Jerusalem is conceived of as one existing under different forms. Through the presence of Christ in the second Temple its glory would exceed even that of Solomon's Temple. The opinion has been given that the latter glory has reference to the millennial glory of the Temple described in Ezekiel 40 to 48. We have just noted how Scripture sees a continuity between the Temple in its different stages, so this position cannot be ruled out. Though Zerubbabel's Temple was leveled to the foundations by Herod when he renovated it, his Temple was considered still the second Temple.

The peace noted here is not only that spiritual peace which He wrought out in Jerusalem (Col 1:20) and grants to believers now (Ro 5:1; Phil 4:7), but is also that ultimate external peace which He will effect as the Prince of Peace (Is 9:6-7). Thus we have the sufficient answer to the discouraging appearances of verse 3. God has the best reserved for the future. The eye of faith alone can discern it.

CAUSE AND EFFECT

The second section of chapter 2 comprises a message delivered some two months after the preceding message. It seeks to show that since blessing was withheld because of disobedience, now that they are obedient, it will surely be granted. The cause and effect can be stated thus: their former disobedience was to their former chastisements and trials as their present obedience is to their coming blessings.

The people are instructed by Haggai to seek legal counsel from the priests of the day. The priests were the teachers of the people in matters of the Mosaic law. (See Deu 17:8-9.) The priests perform their function when they interpret the Law (vv. 11-13); the prophet does his duty by applying it (v. 14). Verses 11 to 13 describe the nation as it had been, a condition not to be repeated.

There were two distinct questions: (1) If a man were carrying sacrificial (holy) flesh and happened to touch another object, would the object touched thereby become holy or set apart to the Lord? (2) If a man who was unclean by reason of contact with a corpse should touch any such object, would the object become unclean because of the man's uncleanness? The answer to the first question is negative; to the second it is affirmative. The passages bearing on the subject should be read carefully. (Note Lev 22:4-6; Num 19:11; and Lev 6:18.) Moral cleanness cannot be transmitted, said the Mosaic law, but moral uncleanness can. Legal impurity is more easily transmitted than legal purity. A healthy man cannot communicate his health to his sick child, but the sick child can communicate its disease to the father.

In spite of their poverty the people were still bringing their offerings ("which they offer" of v. 14; it was on the altar at Jerusalem probably in view of the people, see Ezra 3:3), even though they had been previously neglecting the work of the Temple. These offerings had not been acceptable, a fact clear from the withholding of the divine blessing, and now the prophet explains the reason. Just as the one who was ceremonially unclean polluted all he touched, so they, under the displeasure of the Lord for their long disobedience, transmitted the results of their lack of obedience to the work of their hands which made it unprofitable. And since holy flesh of the sacrifices could not communicate its consecration to anything beyond those objects in the sacrificial service, so their external good works, even their offerings on God's altar, could not avail beyond the carrying out of outward ceremonies, thus being unable to secure the blessings of God and the joy of holiness. All their former work partook of their spiritual uncleanness. They are not to return to their former disobedient ways; they are warned to desist from their past experience. Haggai is explaining cause and effect here from the angle of the Mosaic law, just as he briefly explained it from the viewpoint of sowing and reaping in 1:6, 9-11. That the same time past is in view is clear from the use of "This people" in 1:2 and "this people . . . this nation" in 2:14.

Their condition when indifferent to the Lord's house is reviewed in verses 15-19. They are asked again to consider their plight while they had interrupted the work on the Temple. In those trying days when one came to a heap from which he expected twenty measures, he found it yielded after threshing only ten measures. The winevat that was supposed to have fifty measures of wine had only twenty.

God dealt with them further in chastisement. As in the time of Amos (4:9), the Lord smote them with blasting, caused by excessive drought, and by mildew, caused by excessive moisture. What was left was smitten with hail.

In spite of these evident tokens of the Lord's displeasure, the people did not turn to Him in repentance and faith. The call of the prophet is to consider and to consider. How little thought men give to the vital and important relationships of life, especially those which they sustain toward the Lord of all. The proof of all the prophet has been stating can be very easily found in an examination of the barns and granaries. There was no seed in the barn, and the vines and trees had not brought forth. But from the day of their obedience the Lord promises to bless them. He who withheld the blessing can as sovereignly bestow it in answer to faith and obedience.

ZERUBBABEL AND MESSIAH

The last message of Haggai is directed to Zerubbabel personally and is uttered on the same day as the message on the people's uncleanness and lack of blessing. The message of the prophet to the governor of the day merges with God's future judgments on the nations.

The end time is in view and the person of the Messiah is prefigured. The shaking referred to here and the overthrowing of rule in earth is the same as indicated in verses 6 and 7. The passage has been assigned to the time of the overthrow and revolt of peoples and provinces (Persians, Babylonians, Medes, Armenians, and others) who sought to destroy the Persian Empire when Darius began to reign in 521 BC. We take it as definitely prophetic.

Notice that it is "throne" in the singular and not the plural. There is one supreme rule over the earth, permitted of God and carried out by Satan, and it will be replaced by that of our Lord Jesus Christ. (See Rev 11:15.)

The strength of the nations will be destroyed when the Lord overthrows chariots, charioteers, horses, and horsemen. Chariots and cavalry were the chief strength (Zec 10:5) of the armies of the East. The destruction will be completed when each turns against his brother (Eze 38:21 and Zec 14:13). This will take place in the War of Armageddon.

But Zerubbabel is not appointed to wrath but for a special mission. God elevates and honors him. The promise actually applied to the office he held as ruler in Judah, because it could not have reference to Zerubbabel's own lifetime. In his day there were no such revolutions as indicated here. Also note "in that day" and not "in this day." The Messianic line was to come through Zerubbabel just as through David. David's throne is here in vivid contrast to the doomed dynasties of the world. Zerubbabel was honored by a place in both genealogies of the Messiah (Mt 1:12 and Lk 3:27). Christ is truly the Son of Zerubbabel as well as Son of David.

Jewish commentators have referred this passage to the Messiah also. The title of servant is one well known for the Messiah (Is 42:1; 52:13; and others).

God promises to make Zerubbabel as a signet for He has chosen him. The signet was a mark of honor and authority. It was the object of care and pleasure. (See Song 8:6 and Jer 22:24.) It was much valued and constantly in view. The signet was used by the owner to sign letters or documents, thus it represented him. The owner rarely parted with it but wore it always (Gen 38:18; Jer 22:24). It came to stand for one's most prized possession. All this prefigures the precious Christ.

14

MALACHI

FORMAL WORSHIP

The Pollution of the Priesthood

MALACHI AND HIS DAY

MALACHI is the last of the great succession of prophets who foretold the coming of Messiah for over one thousand years. Nothing is known of the personal history of the prophet. Some think "Malachi," which means "my messenger," is not a proper name at all. Liberal critics generally claim that the book was originally anonymous. Because the Hebrew (so the Greek also) has one word for "messenger" and "angel," several Church fathers took the prophet for an incarnate angel.

Since the priesthood is prominent in the book, some have thought Malachi was a priest. The Aramaic Targum of Jonathan considers that Ezra the scribe was Malachi. It is claimed that nothing is said of the prophet's lineage or place of birth. The same holds true for Obadiah and Habakkuk. Jewish tradition makes Malachi (with Haggai and Zechariah) a member of the Great Synagogue. No prophetic book of the Old Testament has come down to us anonymously, so we can hold with assurance that Malachi was the name of the last prophet in Israel.

Our prophet ministered in the time of the governorship of Nehemiah. It is clear that he ministered after the captivity: the Temple was rebuilt; the priestly worship was carried on; and the people had fallen into spiritual decline. He prophesied about a century after Haggai and Zechariah; he sustained the same relation to Nehemiah that they did to Zerubbabel and Joshua. The time would be near the end of the fifth century BC.

Malachi's message is, for the most part, rebuke and condemnation. The spirit of the people manifested in his day developed later into the sects of the Pharisees and Sadducees. The moral and spiritual conditions of Israel in his day are those of professing Christendom today.

249

The spiritual life of the remnant who had returned from Babylonian captivity is fully portrayed. They were insensible to the great love of God displayed toward them. They were unaware of the enormity of their departure from the will and the way of the Lord. They lacked reverence for the Lord and actually despised Him. They were so lacking in spiritual perception that, when their deeds were pointed out to them (and this is not mere literary device), they saw no harm in them. Their attitude toward the Lord is revealed in the oft-repeated "Wherein?"

The sins of Israel that provoked Nehemiah were the same that stirred up Malachi. The failures were: (1) the defilement of the priesthood; (2) foreign marriages with divorce of their Israelitish wives; and (3) neglect of the tithe and offerings. The prophet also indicates the place and outlook of the godly remnant in the nation.

The book is a continuous discourse. The prophet employs a direct, forceful, and pointed prose style. There is the introduction of a dialectic form of instruction which became very popular in later Judaism. The eightfold controversy of the Lord with His people is stated in 1:2, 6, 7; 2:14, 17; 3:7, 8, 13. In each instance when they are accused of sin, they contradict the Lord and ask for evidences of these charges.

GOD'S LOVE FOR JACOB

The designation of the prophecy as a burden indicates that the message is one of rebuke rather than comfort or encouragement. The word is found here and in Zechariah 9:1 and 12:1. The prophet directs his word to Israel, all the twelve tribes which had returned. As indicated above, analogy with the titles of other prophetic books would show that Malachi is a proper name and not merely a designation of public office.

The prophecy begins on the glorious and heartwarming note of God's love for Jacob. In the very last prophecy of the Old Testament and, as it were, on the last page of the sacred Word, God reiterates the persistence of His love for Israel. (See Deu 10:15; 33:3; and Amos 3:2.)

The choice of Jacob was by undeserved love (Ro 9:13). The doctrine of God's electing love is neither capricious nor arbitrary, nor does it minimize one whit man's repsonsibility before God. We cannot restrict this love to the temporal advantages of Palestine over Idumea, in that the former had been restored from exile, while the latter had not. For the whole prophecy of Malachi reveals God in several relationships to His people: as Father, Lord, God, and Judge.

In response to this love, Israel asks with ungodly boldness, "Wherein hast thou loved us?" The root of all her sins was her unawareness of God's love and her own sin. Replying in infinite patience, God repeats the fact of His love for Jacob rather than for Esau.

Over against the love of God for Jacob is set His hatred of Esau. Many interpreters of the book see the word *hate* in a comparative sense and point for this usage to Genesis 29:30-31; Deuteronomy 21:15, 16; Proverbs 13:24; Matthew 6:24; Luke 14:26 with Matthew 10:37, where the thought is love less or love more. This statement of God's hatred of Esau is quoted in Romans 9 from this prophecy and not from Genesis.

God does not exercise His sovereignty to reprobate any creature. The hatred of Esau had been well deserved after the continued opposition to God through the centuries; it is mentioned at the end of Old Testament history and not in Genesis.

There is no room here for the position of reprobation, which is not taught in Scripture. The instance chosen to reveal the hatred of God for Esau is the desolation of his mountainous land and the wasting of his heritage to make it a place for the jackals of the wilderness.

Some understand the reference to be the conquest of Edom by the Nabateans; others, the wars between the Persians and Egypt; and still others, the desolation by the Babylonians. The Chaldeans had invaded their country five years after the destruction of Jerusalem in 586 BC. The word translated "jackals," the same as in Isaiah 13:22, cannot be rendered "abodes" to preserve the parallelism with "desolation," because such a translation would be meaningless in the Isaiah passage and the word *abodes* is of uncertain origin.

Though Esau, in his pride, should attempt to rebuild his waste places, God says He will throw down their building. Every attempt to rebuild the land will meet with defeat.

The threat here shows that God will never allow Edom to regain its former position and power. That which was properly and formerly known as the border of Edom, the territory of Edom, will be called the border of wickedness. Men will realize that the desolate condition of Edom is because of his sins.

We do not need to assume that the prophet is speaking of a blotting out of the name of Edom entirely. The degradation of Edom will be added proof to Israel of the goodness and love of God extended to her. Then she will bear witness that the Lord's rule over her land is indeed a gracious one. The goodness and greatness of the Lord will be manifest upon His own people.

POLLUTED SACRIFICES

How did Israel requite the Lord for His gracious love? From the love of

God the prophet now turns to the ingratitude of His people. God has treated the people of Israel as a son; have they honored Him as Father? They have sustained the relationship of servant to Him as Master; have they rendered Him due reverence? The rightful respect due God has been withheld, due mainly to the ungodliness of the priests against whom the charge is directed.

The first sin of the Levites was the neglect of their duties in the Temple. In this they were despising the name of the Lord.

The nature of the offense is stated in the next verses. The priests were offering blemished sacrifices on God's altar. Deuteronomy 15:21 forbade them explicitly. That Malachi is referring to sacrifices, that is, animal flesh, in the word *bread* is clear from three considerations: (1) their connection with the altar; (2) the mention of blind, lame, and sick in verse 8; and (3) the use of "bread" for sacrifices in Leviticus 21:6, 8, 17. If the bread be the sacrifices, then the table is the altar of sacrifice rather than the table of showbread. (Cp. Eze 41:22.)

Contempt for God's appointed service implies contempt of Him ("thee"). They were offering the blind, the lame, and the sick which were forbidden by Mosaic law. (See Lev 22:20-25 and Deu 15:21.)

The repetition that such were no evil is in rebuke and irony. It has been suggested that the stronger rendering would be, "Is it not evil?" They were always willing to modify God's requirements and laws by circumstances. They had the audacity to offer to God what they would not have dared to present to their governor, probably the Persian governor. The prophet is appealing to their sense of propriety which is more sensitive on the human plane than it is toward God. There are always those who love the praise of men better than the praise of God.

THE DISPLEASURE OF GOD

At first sight the charge to the people to entreat the favor of God that He may be gracious to them, appears to be a serious exhortation to repentance. But it is best taken as ironical suggestion. The prophet is saying, "Do you think that with such unacceptable offerings God will be pleased with you?" Their prayers could never avail as long as they were presenting such sacrifices. It was the doing of the priests, and Malachi places the blame squarely upon them. As a result God could not regard them or respect their offerings.

The wish is expressed that someone would shut the doors of the Temple, so that fire might not be kindled upon the altar in vain. The word translated "in vain" can also mean "gratis." There are those who believe that the priests were so greedy and covetous that they demanded a price for the smallest exertion, even the closing of doors. Others think the priests were so lazy and careless that they might not close the Temple doors at the right time. The best explanation is that, since the worship was outward and insincere, God would rather it ceased. (See Is 1:11-15.) It is better to have no sacrifices, than vain ones. The Lord had no pleasure in priests or sacrifices.

ACCEPTABLE WORSHIP

But there is a well-defined worship which is acceptable to the Lord; it will be revealed and carried on throughout the whole earth. From the rising of the sun to its setting is an expression for the extremities of the earth. (See Ps 103:12 and Zec 8:7.) This is not the accomplishment of this present age, but a prophecy relating to the millennial era. The last chapters of Ezekiel (40-48) show that in millennial worship in the rebuilt Temple, incense and offerings will be present. There is no reference here that God regards the worship of the heathen as pure worship of Him, nor that the prophet is speaking of conditions in Malachi's own day (for which some writers contend), but of the future time we have outlined.

Because the Lord will receive pure worship throughout the world, as His name is recognized and honored in every place, is given as the reason why He will not really be pleased with the polluted and heartless service of Israel. God will not accept the blemished offerings (v. 10) of His people, because He is the great God to be worshiped by incense and pure offering throughout the nations. Strangely enough, the Roman Church rests its practice of the mass on this passage among others. No more applicable to the prophecy is the view of the Church fathers who understood the passage to be a prediction of the Eucharist (the Communion) in the Church.

PROFANING HOLY THINGS

Malachi returns to the theme of the sin of the priests and their contempt for the majesty of the Lord. The reproof of verse 7 is repeated. They were profaning the name of the Lord not in actual words, but their deeds testified so. The use of the participle in "profane" indicates they were habitually doing so. The altar and sacrifice of the Lord were considered contemptible. The whole service was burdensome and wearisome to them, because their hearts were not in it. (Note Is 43:22-24 and Mic 6:3 for similar thoughts.) They disparaged and disdained the offering of the Lord; they snuffed at it, that is, they snorted and sniffed at it, treating it with utmost contempt. The priests cared little what they presented to God, so they offered that taken by violence, the lame, and the sick.

How could God accept such a sham and insult as satisfactory to Him? And it was not because of poverty, but the difficulty was greed. The curse is pronounced upon the deceiver who thinks he can vow—in such cases the best was promised to God—a proper sacrifice, and then fulfill the vow with an unsuitable animal. Such offerings were an insult to the majesty of God, for He is a great King whose name despised (v. 6) and profaned (v. 12) by Israel, and yet to be exalted (v. 11) among the nations, is even now terrible and awful among the Gentiles. What an exalted God is our blessed portion, blessed be His name!

"I LOVED JACOB"

This is a beautiful declaration of the supreme love of God for unworthy Jacob. Many speak of him as though he were the object of God's discipline and displeasure, and nothing more. No, God dearly loves him and that people that have sprung from him, the nation Israel. In this love God provided heaven's richest treasure, the Messiah and King of Israel, the Redeemer of men.

MARRIAGE AND DIVORCE

THE GUILTY PRIEST

Chapter 2 continues God's rebuke of the priests begun in the first chapter, especially in 1:6. The prophet elaborates on the sinful condition of the priests who were supposed to know the will of God and teach it to the people.

Malachi now sets forth the punishment awaiting them in case of impenitence. The commandment referred to is the decree, sentence, or threat of punishment stated in verses 2 and 3. For the priests refusing to give heed to God's warning and failing to glorify Him, there is pronounced the curse of Deuteronomy 27:15-26 and 28:15-68. The blessings spoken of are not to be restricted to the revenues of the priests only, but must include all the benefits of God's gracious hand, those promised the people by the priests by virtue of their office. (See Num 6:24-26.)

Included here also are the blessings of life and peace noted in verse 5. These God had withheld because they had consistently denied Him their obedience. Moreover, He threatens to rebuke their seed. The word should not be translated "arm" as parallel to "faces" in the same verse. What is meant is the seed of their land, for since the priests were dependent on the increase of the harvest for their tithes, they would inevitably suffer if God cursed the seed.

Furthermore, God warns them that He will spread the dung of their feasts upon their faces. This would be disgraceful treatment indeed. The maw was the assigned portion of the priests (Deu 18:3), but the dung in the maw of the sacrifices on feast days would be cast upon their faces. The priests would then have to be taken away with the refuse as an abhorrent thing. They would know by actual experience the nature of the admonition being sent to them. The implication is that there will be obedience or the Levitical covenant could scarcely remain in force. By their giving heed to the declaration of judgment, God could continue His covenant which He made with Levi in the beginning.

GODLY LEVI

Malachi here contrasts the culpable conduct of the ungodly priests of his day with the godly character and manner of life of their ancestor with whom the Lord had made the priestly covenant. The reference need not be limited to Phinehas (note the wording of Num 25:12-13), for at Sinai, Levi was faithful in spite of the sin of Israel at the golden calf. For this fidelity to God's honor the Lord made a covenant with Levi and his descendants. (See Ex 32:25-29 and Deu 33:8-11.)

The nature of the covenant was such that it guaranteed him life and peace (salvation). The Lord intended that His name should be feared, and Levi walked before Him in godly fear and reverence. The prophet continues his beautiful description of the true piety of Levi. His interpretation of the Law, for the priest was the teacher of the people in the Law of God, was not according to partiality or for selfish ends, but according to the strict norm of truth. His speech was in righteousness. He worshiped God and lived in the will of God. The expression "walked with" indicates a more intimate fellowship with the Lord than is implied in "walk after" as in 2 Kings 23:3.

The result of such life and ministry was that many were led from sin to the fear of God. (Cp. Dan 12:3.) Verse 7 indicates the intended ministry of the priests in Israel: they were the regularly appointed teachers of the Law of Moses to the nation. They are called messengers of the Lord. The word ordinarily refers to angelic beings, but is employed here of the priest as it was of the prophet in Haggai 1:13.

UNGODLY LEVITES

But what a contrast there was between Levi of Israel's early history and the careless priests of Malachi's day. They departed radically from the way just outlined in verses 6 and 7. By false interpretation of the Law and by their bad example, they induced others to violate the Law as well as they. They corrupted the covenant of Levi by making it inoperative through their inattention to its obligations. (See Neh 13:29.) Because

they treated the worship and service of the Lord as contemptible (1:7, 12),
the Lord made them base before the people. Their degradation in the
eyes of the nation was retribution in kind. They were partial in the performance of their duties, which included bribery as well as other methods
of circumventing the just administration of the Law.

ABOMINABLE MARRIAGES

The offenses of the priests would have been sufficient if they had included only the ones already mentioned. But in addition to these the
priests and the people had committed grievous sins against their fellow
countrymen, especially their wives. They were offenders in the matter of
unholy and unsanctioned marriages.

The prophet introduces the subject by asking whether they had not all
one father, whether one God had not created them. The obvious answer
is in the affirmative. The father spoken of must be God and not Abraham
or Jacob. The force of the parallelism shows that a human ancestor could
scarcely be meant here, when in the second part of the verse God is mentioned. The ultimate reference is to God as Father of all men by virtue
of creation, but the primary reference here is to God as the Father of all
Israel as the covenant people.

If the verse is referred to God, it brings it into agreement with 1:6 ("a
father"). Israel is being taught that men and women stand in the same
relation before God as Father and Creator. Too, God had created them
not only physically, but had made them His covenant people. (Note Is
43:1 and 60:21.)

Since God had made this unity, they dare not introduce divisive elements into the national life. The general term *brother* includes the injured
wives. They were violating the covenant which the Lord made with their
fathers to insure their remaining a people separated from all others.
(Cp. Ex 19:5; Lev 20:24, 26; and Deu 7:1-4.) The Law of Moses thus
forbade all marriages with the heathen as a safeguard against the impor-
tation of idolatry into Israel. Judah, Israel, and Jerusalem, the entire
nation, had dealt treacherously with regard to the Jewish wives who were
divorced to contract marriages with heathen wives. These mixed marriages were mentioned in Ezra and Nehemiah (Ezra 9:1, 2; 10:1-4; and
Neh 13:25-27).

Profaning the holiness of the Lord has reference to the people of Israel
themselves. (See Jer 2:3.) This they had done by wrong treatment of
their wives who were also set apart as holy to the Lord. What a high regard we have here for women in contrast to the usual status accorded them
at that time in the Orient. The daughter of a foreign god indicates an

idolatrous woman. A worshiper is regarded in Scripture as a child to a father (Jer 2:27). So grievous and abominable is this sin in the sight of the Lord that He threatens to destroy completely the offender and all his family.

The one who wakes and answers has no connection with the Levites who kept watch in the Temple at night and called and answered each other at certain times, nor with a teacher (Is 50:4) and scholar, but is a proverbial expression stating that no one would be left. The universality of the judgment is meant. Anyone offering an offering could not by this performance clear himself of his guilt in mistreating his wife. How holy does God regard the marriage ties!

THE EVIL OF DIVORCE

The marriage of men of Israel with idolatrous women had another aspect to it. There was a second thing, a second sin. Such marriages involved divorcing their Jewish wives. These forsaken wives came to the altar of the Lord and covered it with their tears. Thus when the former husbands came with their offerings, the Lord would not receive them with goodwill. Because He had regard to the tears from their heartbroken wives, He had no regard for their offerings.

Nowhere in the Old Testament do we have so much said concerning the evil of divorce. We need not press its applicability to our own day; it is a sin which cries out mightily unto God. But the contemporaries of the prophet ask why God should reject their sacrifices. The answer is because God was a witness to the legally contracted marriage where God was called to witness the covenant. Their Israelitish wives were the companions and wives of their youth, their choice in youth sharing both the joys and sorrows of life.

Verse 15 is a strong argument against divorce, but at the same time is considered the most difficult verse in the whole book of Malachi. It has always been a problem to interpreters, Jewish and Christian. Without dogmatizing we shall review the main views and indicate our preference.

We can safely say at the outset that the first portion is as difficult as the latter portion of the verse is simple. The prophet is warning against continued treacherous dealing with their wives by divorcing them and marrying heathen wives. An alternate reading has been proposed for the first part of the verse: "And not one hath done so who had a residue of the spirit." This means that no one had contracted such marriages with foreign women and divorced their former wives, if he had anything of the Spirit of God. If this translation be adopted, it does not go smoothly with the remainder of the passage. The Targum and most rabbis understood the "one' to mean Abraham who might be cited as a case where another wife was taken in addition to the first. The Jews would then in the prophet's day be defending their action by pointing to the example of Abraham who took Hagar after he had Sarah to wife. The view holds further that Abraham still had the Spirit of God, because his aim was not selfish pleasure but to obtain the godly promised seed. Thus the case of Abraham and the contemporaries of Malachi were not analogous. This appears to us to be too strained an exposition.

It is most natural to see, since the prophet is speaking of divorce, a reference here to the original institution of marriage by God Himself. Compare Genesis 2:24: "one flesh" with "one" here. In the marriage relationship God made two into one. One wife was provided for one man, though God had the residue of the Spirit, He still had the creative power of the Spirit, to have made Adam a number of wives. But why did God make just one woman for the man? He was seeking a godly seed; He wanted to carry on a godly remnant.

Polygamy and divorce are not conducive to nurturing children in the fear of God. And ultimately these practices were not helpful to obtain the godly seed in the stock of the promised Messiah. The purpose of God in a godly seed was being counteracted and set aside by their intermarriage and divorce. In view of all this, Malachi warns them to take heed diligently to themselves that they refrain from such godless deeds.

In short, God declares unequivocally that He hates divorce, the putting away of wives. This verse is not at variance with Deuteronomy 24:1, where divorce is allowed. This was countenanced because of the hardness of their hearts. (See Mt 19:3-8.)

The hatred of God is also expressed against the one who covers his garment with violence. The reference is to the old custom of putting a garment over a woman to claim her as wife. (Note particularly Deu 22:30; Ruth 3:9; and Eze 16:8.) Instead of spreading their garment to protect their wives, they covered their garment with violence toward their wives. The garment symbolized wedded trust and protection. Again they are warned to take heed to themselves in this vital matter.

WEARYING GOD

The third offense of the ungodly in Israel was an evil skepticism. By their ungodliness and unbelief they had wearied God; they had exhausted His patience. They brought forward the old argument against the providence of God from the prosperity of the wicked and the suffering of the righteous. They had endured so many trials in exilic and postexilic times, that they were ready to believe that God delighted in and favored the cause of the wicked, the heathen who enjoyed prosperity, over against the godly.

They complained that God did not judge wickedness severely enough. And if such were not the case, where indeed is the God of justice of whom they heard continually. Many connect this verse with the next chapter (and it is related in thought), because the answer to 2:17 is found in 3:1. God never fails to answer such a question put forth in such skeptical spirit. It rounded out the tale of their misdeeds and revealed them to be ripe for judgment.

CURSING THE BLESSINGS

How the heart of man delights in the blessings and benefits he receives from the hand of God, even when he does not thank God for them. Israel, too, took these blessings for granted. She did not realize her continuance was conditioned upon faith and obedience. As a result her blessings were replaced by curses. And is it not so all too often in the lives of believers also? They forget that the blessings of God are dependent upon our walking in obedience and upon our making Christ known to Jew and Gentile alike. God will withhold these blessings if we walk in self-will.

MESSIAH AND HIS FORERUNNER

GOD'S TWO MESSENGERS

Chapters 3 and 4 of this prophecy are undoubtedly better known than the first two chapters of the book. These last chapters are full of prophetic disclosure concerning the first coming of the Messiah and His second coming.

As in so many other Old Testament passages, we have both appearances joined together. The chapter begins with the alerting word, *Behold.* The Lord promises that He will send His messenger. This is God's answer to their brazen and skeptical question of 2:17.

In the words *my messenger,* we have a play on the name of the prophet Malachi.

But who is this messenger? It has been suggested that in the light of 4:5 this may be Elijah the prophet, but the whole matter is too uncertain in this view. The possibility has been advanced that the prophet may not have had any specific person in mind. This is scarcely tenable. Most students of the prophecy have rightly seen here the prediction of the coming of the forerunner of the Messiah from the nature of his ministry indicated in the verse under consideration. The messenger is undoubtedly John the Baptist. (Note carefully Mt 3:3; 11:10; Mk 1:2-3; Lk 1:76; 3:4; 7:26, 27; Jn 1:23.) These passages show unequivocally that the one prophesied of is John the Baptist. His work is described as preparing the way before the Lord. This prediction rests on the prophecy in Isaiah 40:3-5. Reference is to the custom of Eastern kings to send men before them to remove every barrier and obstacle in their path. In this instance it meant removal of opposition to the Lord by the preaching of repentance and the conversion of sinners to Him. Such was the objective in the ministry of John.

The ungodly in the nation had asked, "Where is the God of justice?" The answer is that the God whom they sought will suddenly come to His Temple and the messenger of the covenant whom they professed to desire. When the passage states that the Lord would suddenly come to His Temple, it is not implied that this was to occur in Malachi's day but rather unexpectedly, in the appointed time of His coming. This was partially fulfilled in the first coming of Christ and will be completely accomplished in His second advent to the earth.

Who is meant by "the messenger (or angel) of the covenant?" Is it the same person as the messenger already mentioned in the first clause of the verse? The expression occurs only here, and some think the meaning cannot be determined. But the case is not so hopeless. A comparatvie study of the Old Testament Scriptures bearing on the subject will reveal that this person is the Angel of the covenant of Exodus 23:20-23; 33:15; and Isaiah 63:9. The Angel is God's Self-revelation. He is the Lord Himself, the Angel of the Lord of Old Testament history, the preincarnate Christ of the many theophanies (appearances of God in human form) in the books of the Old Testament.

Jewish commentators like Abenezra and Kimchi make this person the Lord, and the latter commentator even refers both "the Lord" and "the Messenger of the covenant" to the Messiah. We dare not miss the three undeniable proofs of the deity of the Messiah given here: (1) He is identified with the Lord; "he shall prepare the way before me . . . saith the Lord of hosts"; (2) He is indicated as the owner of the Temple: "to his temple"; and (3) He is called "the Lord" whom they sought.

What covenant is meant in the phrase "messenger of the covenant?" Some interpreters understand this designation of the new covenant of Hebrews 9:15. It is rather the one already in force in the Old Testament, as seen in the many manifestations of God throughout the old economy. It is the one already made with Israel. (See Ex 25:8; Lev 26:9-12; and Deu 4:23.) The mass in Israel in the time of Malachi and in the days of Christ were seeking and desiring a temporal deliverer. To them this promise would be ironic; but the desire of the godly was sincere. Mark well that the Gospel began with Israel in the first coming, and so it will be in the second advent. Israel is central in the purpose of God in both comings of the Lord Jesus Christ to the earth.

MESSIAH THE REFINER

Just as the first verse blends the first and second coming of Christ— a feature known in Old Testament prophecy as in Isaiah 61:1-3—so the second verse combines elements of both appearances of the Messiah to His people Israel. The prophet had indicated they were desiring the presence of the Lord, but he asks now who among them could abide the day of His coming? The expected answer, in view of the ungodly in the nation, is no one will abide that day. It was certainly true in Malachi's day; it was eminently applicable in the day of Christ's first coming when He scrutinized all and then decreed the destruction of Jerusalem and the scattering of Israel; and it will be true when He comes again. (Cp. Joel 2:11; Mal 4:1; Mt 3:10-12; and Rev 6:15.) The coming will be in judgment to purge out the dross, that is, the iniquity, from Israel.

The refiner's fire is a vivid figure from the field of metallurgy to show that the Messenger of the covenant would not come merely as an earthly monarch and liberator to bestow temporal benefits, but as the Searcher of hearts and lives. (For the same figure of refining see Zec 13:8-9.) The thought of cleansing is further brought out by the figure of the fullers' soap.

The Lord is seen sitting as Judge. The refiner sits with the crucible before him watching both the intensity of the fire and the metal being purified of its dross. When judgment comes, it truly begins at the house of God (1 Pe 4:17).

The entire nation will be purged, beginning with the sons of Levi (Eze 48:11). These are specified because their offerings had been unacceptable on account of their godlessness. They will be cleansed of the sins described in chapters 1 and 2. Then they will present to the Lord offerings in righteousness, as in 2:6 and not as in 1:7-14. They will be righteous offerings, because they will be given from hearts in the right condition before the Lord.

Most Roman Catholic commentators think this is a prophecy of the offering of the Eucharist, but it actually refers to millennial conditions when He shall have returned and have set up His righteous kingdom on the earth.

In the days of cleansed and restored Israel their offering will indeed be acceptable to God as an offering in righteousness. The offerings of millennial days (Eze 40-46) will commemorate the sacrifice at Calvary, as the Lord's Supper does now. Many believers forget that, although the Church has remembered the death of the Lord Jesus Christ on Calvary for sinners in the Lord's Supper, Israel has thus far had no such memorial of His work in the centuries of their unbelief.

The millennial sacrifices will perform the function of such a memorial for the redeemed nation. It cannot be argued against them that they would not be efficacious sacrifices in the millennial kingdom, for even in Old Testament times the sacrifices had no real efficacy. (See Heb 10:4.) In the Old Testament economy sacrifices were signposts; in the millennial day they will be memorials looking back to the central event of Calvary. The days of old mentioned by Malachi are the times of Moses or perhaps also the times of David and the early part of the reign of Solomon. At that time the offerings were indicated as pleasing to the Lord.

JUDGMENT FORETOLD

The prophet now speaks to his contemporaries, threatening them with the judgment of God. Evil doers must still be judged. This is still the answer of God to their insolent challenge of 2:17. The first to come under the chastisement of God will be the sorcerers. (Note Ex 22:18.) Magic prevailed in Israel in postcaptivity days, a sin into which the men were probably led because of their foreign idolatrous wives, and which continued even down to New Testament times (Ac 8:9).

Adulterers will also experience the rod of God's displeasure. This term probably applies to those who were living with foreign wives, after divorcing their Hebrew wives, those of 2:16.

The judgment will also be directed against the false swearers, those who practiced false witnessing. Perjury is condemned in Exodus 20:16; Leviticus 19:12; Deuteronomy 19:16-20; Jeremiah 29:23; and Proverbs 19:5. Those who deal falsely in the wages of a hired servant are classed with the foregoing.

Finally, those under sentence are the oppressors of the widow, the fatherless, and the sojourners, classes which are the special objects of God's care and love.

And all their defections are traced to their source; they all stemmed from their lack of fear of God. But because God is the unchanging and steadfast Lord, who has purposes of mercy toward them which He must accomplish, He will carry out to fruition His purposes of grace in spite of their wayward ways. The Lord is declaring that, though He must punish them, yet He will not utterly destroy them, because He is unchanging in His covenant promises.

The nation is called "sons of Jacob" in relation to the Lord's covenant with the patriarch. In short, Israel owes its existence in spite of its sins to the unchanging purpose of the Lord to grant her abundant grace and mercy. All the nations' hope, as ours as well, is grounded in the never-failing, unchangeable character of our covenant-keeping God.

ROBBING GOD

But just as God is unchangeable in His goodness, so they have not changed from their evil ways. For a long while now, even from the time of their fathers, they have gone astray from the commandments of the Lord. This is no novel action with them; it is one in which they have had much evil experience. The call of God to them is to return to Him in penitence and He would return to them in blessing. (See Zec 1:3.) In spite of the length of time involved in their departure from the Lord, He is willing to receive them if they turn to Him in true penitence.

In their self-righteousness the ungodly majority in the nation, satisfied in their careless ways, do not see the need for real turning back to the Lord, and ask wherein they need to mend their ways. The answer is clear enough. Could it be possible that puny man would rob the infinite God? Yet they robbed God. They had robbed Him in tithes and offerings. In all probability, they had decreased their tithes and offerings because of adverse conditions, which is labeled here as robbery of God. (Cp. Deu 14:22-29 and 26:12-15.)

The offerings in Israel were the firstfruits, not less than one-sixtieth of the corn, wine, and oil (Deu 18:4). There were several kinds of tithes: (1) the tenth of the remainder after the firstfruits were taken, this amount going to the Levites for their livelihood (Lev 27:30-33); (2) the tenth paid by the Levites to the priests (Num 18:26-28); (3) the second tenth paid by the congregation for the needs of the Levites and their own families at the tabernacle (Deu 12:18); and (4) another tithe every third year for the poor (Deu 14:28-29). These tithes were not being properly given by the people in the days of Nehemiah and Malachi (Neh 13:10), so the people are rightly accused of robbing God. In seeking to rob God they robbed themselves, for they had failure of the harvest and famine, judgments corresponding to their sin. Thus were they cursed with the curse, for they were still defrauding (the participle is used) God. And the evil was being perpetrated by the whole nation.

THE PATHWAY OF BLESSING

However, all is not hopeless. The prophet sets forth the pathway of God's favor. There is an important spiritual principle enunciated here which is applicable in every age: God meets with blessing the heart wholly devoted to Him. If we want God to open His storehouse, we must first open ours. The nation is counselled to bring the whole tithe in the storehouse, that there may be food in the Lord's house.

The storehouse was the chambers in the Temple where the tithes were brought. (See Neh 10:38 and 13:12.) In obedience to this exhortation they would find by practical test that the Lord would open the windows of heaven and pour them out such a blessing, that there would not be room enough to contain it.

God loves to be put to the practical test as in 2 Chronicles 31:10. God would send them abundant rains; abundant blessing is compared to rain. Nothing would be withheld in the way of blessing. The land had evidently been suffering from drought as indicated in verse 11. Now there would be a superabundance and not room enough to receive it.

God promises that every injurious thing, the locust or any similar scourge from God, would be withheld for their sakes. When the rain watered the fields, the scourge would not destroy the crop. The locust especially is called the devourer because of its insatiable greed. In the way of obedience and as a result of the blessing of God upon them, all nations would call them blessed. Both God and man would find delight in her. Then would be fulfilled the words of Deuteronomy 33:29; Isaiah 62:4; and Zechariah 8:13.

"RETURN UNTO ME"

This is the pathetic cry of the Lord to Israel throughout the Old Testament. To realize the blessing of God in their national life they need only to return to God through the Saviour, the Lord Jesus Christ. Let us sound forth continually the call to Israel to return unto God!

STOUT WORDS AGAINST GOD

The same type of skepticism displayed by the godless priests in 2:17 is now seen to have infected the remainder of the nation. Their words had been obstinate, unbearable against the Lord. But the insensibility of their conceited and willfully ignorant hearts made them ask what they had spoken amiss against their God.

Actually, they had said it was useless to try to serve God. They claim to have kept His charge and walked mournfully before Him, all to no profit or avail. They were wholly in error with regard to God's service, for they regarded it in a mercenary spirit, as though to be profited thereby were the chief and sole goal. God looks at the motive, however, and not at self-interest. They thought the outward appearance would suffice instead of genuine humiliation, so they walked in sackcloth and ashes pretending to be grieved for their sins. See Isaiah 58:3-8 for the meaning of true worship.

Not satisfied with complaining over their lean lot, they called the proud happy. Since they have not prospered in their half-hearted worship of the Lord, they pronounce the proud the favored of the Lord. Some think the proud are the godless heathen outside of Israel, while others feel they are the godless in Israel.

Neither view excludes the other, and there is no reason why both positions could not be true. They esteemed the proud anywhere as the favorites of the Lord. They made much of the prosperity and flourishing of the wicked, who tempted God by presumptuous words and deeds and yet escaped all judgment.

GOD'S BOOK OF REMEMBRANCE

When the wicked are blatantly mouthing their unspeakable blasphemies against God, then the godly must be forewarned how to meet these accusations against the Lord. In the midst of spiritual failure and corruption on every hand, the godly remnant are drawn together by their mutual spiritual needs and desire, in the fear of the Lord. When gathered together, the godly held mutual converse with reference to truth and godliness, strengthening themselves in their trust in the Lord. The word *often* found in the KJV is not in the original Hebrew text.

While the remnant spoke together of Him, the Lord inclined His ear and heard. Then these acts of communion were written in a book of remembrance before Him. This is the language of appearance, for nothing is past to God to be remembered, and He needs no keeping of books. But it is for the encouragement and assurance of the godly. That books are kept in heaven is attested already in Psalm 56:8.

It is thought that the figure of the book is taken from the custom of Persian kings to keep a record of the names of those who did service for the king with a statement of that service. (Cp. Est 6:1-2.) But this is not necessarily so, for we read of a book in Daniel 12:1 and the passage already cited from the Psalms. God tenderly keeps before Him those that truly reverence Him and think on His name.

He calls them His in a peculiar and special sense, even His own possession. This designates that which is especially valuable. It is applied to Israel in Exodus 19:5; Deuteronomy 7:6; 14:2; and 26:18. They will be particularly remembered in the day God has appointed for the carrying out of His purposes, the day of His judgment when He comes again. God will spare them the doom of the wicked as a loving father does his devoted and dutiful son. (See Ps 103:13.) Then the great chasm between the righteous and the wicked, between those who serve Him and those who do not, will be manifest.

There are those who think the "ye" refers to the wicked murmurers in Israel, but it is better to see here a reference to the righteous. The godly have had ample opportunities to see that God does not treat all alike whether righteous or ungodly; it will be all the more evident when the Lord gloriously delivers the godly and sovereignly destroys the wicked.

"THE SUN OF RIGHTEOUSNESS"

THE DAY OF BURNING WRATH

Most editions of the Hebrew Old Testament and most manuscripts of the original text incorporate the six verses of chapter 4 as a continuation of chapter 3. All the versions have the division as it is found in our English translations. There are those who think the chapter break is unfortunate, but we fail to see that it does violence to the thought of the passage.

We should view these final words with solemnity of heart, for chapter 4 gives us the last message of the Old Testament prophets. After this prophetic word, the heavens were silent for four centuries until the voice of John the Baptist was heard calling Israel to repentance in view of the coming of the Messiah.

The day spoken of is the important Day of the Lord so prominent throughout the Old Testament; it is the time of the wrath of the Lamb revealed in the New Testament.

The language is short and abrupt, which brings out the dread reality of the prediction. Because God's judgment is often likened to fire, the day is said to burn as a furnace. (Among many passages note carefully Is 10:16; 30:27; Jer 21:14; Eze 20:45-48; Amos 1:4; and Zep 1:18; and 3:8.) Before the fire of God's judgment, the wicked will be as stubble to be burned up root and branch. The intensity of the heat sets forth the greatness of the wrath of God.

Notice the end of the proud; it is quite different from their thought expressed in 3:15. Root and branch, as the two extremities of the tree representing the whole, is a proverbial expression for totality. All will be utterly destroyed. All that offends will be purged from the kingdom (Mt 13:41-42).

Annihilationists make much of this verse for their erroneous teaching that the wicked will be blotted out of conscious existence completely. But the passage speaks of judgment on the body of the wicked; the soul and spirit will be judged at the Great White Throne. Scripture knows nothing of souls that go out of existence through the judgment of God. The godly are in conscious bliss eternally, while the wicked are in conscious woe throughout eternity (Rev 20:11-15).

The results of the coming day of judgment for the wicked are indicated in verse 1; in verses 2 and 3 we have the consequences of that day for the righteous. Nothing in Scripture outlines with greater demarcation the vastly different lots of the believing and unbelieving when the Lord comes to judge the earth.

THE SUN OF RIGHTEOUSNESS

Those who fear the name of the Lord (the same as in 3:16) have a blessed portion assigned them. For them there will not be the blasting heat of the furnace, but the genial heat and warmth of the Sun of righteousness with healing in its wings. He who is an oven to the wicked, is like the sun to the righteous.

Some interpreters see no more in the phrase "sun of righteousness" than a period of blessing for the godly. We believe the sun is used here figuratively of God Himself, and specifically of the Lord Jesus Christ, Israel's Messiah. (Note Ps 84:11; see also 2 Sa 23:4 with Is 9:2 and 49:6.) He is called the Sun of righteousness, because He is the Lord our righteousness (Jer 23:5-6 and 1 Co 1:30).

There is spiritual healing in this Sun, for just as the rays of the physical sun give light and heat for the growth of plant and animal life, so the Sun of righteousness will heal the wounds inflicted upon and borne by the righteous.

The beams of the sun are here spoken of as wings because of the speed with which they spread over the earth. Israel's hope is the Sun of righteousness; the hope of the Church is the Morning Star (2 Pe 1:19 and Rev 22:16).

Mark the distinction between the Morning Star, which ushers in the dawn, and the Sun of righteousness, which brings in the bright day. Through the redeeming activity of the Deliverer the godly will go forth, escaping the judgment to come upon the evildoers. Such will be their freedom from outward constraint, their vitality, and their joy, that they will gambol as calves of the stall. And they will tread down the wicked; God will reverse what is usually the condition between the righteous and the wicked. The ungodly are compared to ashes, the result of the fire of God's judgment. All this will transpire in the day that God has appointed.

MOSES AND ELIJAH

Since no prophet was to appear from Malachi's time until the coming of Messiah's forerunner, it was all the more needful that they give closest heed to the Mosaic law. Moses gave the Law, but it was not from himself, for in this as in all his ministry, he was a servant of the Lord. Mark it well that the Law was given for all Israel and not for any others, the vaporizings of the Seventh Dayists to the contrary notwithstanding.

Moses is connected here with Elijah (v. 5), as they were at the mount of transfiguration and, as many believe, they will be in the Great Tribulation (Rev 11:3-12).

In verse 5 we have the third great "Behold" in the latter part of the prophecy of Malachi. (See 3:1 and 4:1.) Compare the wording at the beginning of this verse with 3:1.

Commentators are divided into two distinct camps on the subject of whether Elijah is meant personally or ideally (representatively) through John the Baptist. Those who take the reference ideally of John the Baptist point to passages like Matthew 11:14 and Luke 1:17, where John is said to have come in the spirit and power of Elijah, and where he is spoken of as representing Elijah to them, if they would receive him. This view explains the denial of John 1:21 as referring only to the personal sense of the term, that is, he was denying that he was Elijah literally. Matthew 17:10-13 is also explained in such a way as to give the force that Elijah had come in John the Baptist.

The great and terrible Day of the Lord is explained as the dreadful time of judgment which resulted in the destruction of Jerusalem by the Romans. Actually, there is no such usage of the phrase "day of the Lord" in Old Testament prophecy, as that just noted. Jewish commentators and Christian interpreters generally have taken it to refer literally to Elijah the Tishbite.

With this view we are in agreement. John the Baptist himself testified that he was not Elijah (Jn 1:21). He knew by the Spirit that he was referred to in a sense in Malachi 4:5 (Lk 1:17), yet he knew also by divine illumination that he did not completely fulfill all the conditions and requirements of this prophecy. There is a future fulfillment.

Even after the transfiguration experience, the Lord in Matthew 17:11 speaks of Elijah's coming as still future, although in the person and ministry of John the Baptist he had come in a certain sense. The mention of the Day of the Lord shows that John cannot be meant exclusively here, for his ministry preceded the day of Christ's grace and not the day of His judgment.

As John the Baptist came in the spirit and power of Elijah before the first coming, so Elijah will come in person before the second coming. In short, John the Baptist's coming was a testimony to faith, not the fulfillment of this prophecy.

The ministry of Elijah to Israel had been one of calling apostate Israel back to the Lord whom they had forsaken. He will come again in order to avert the curse of God from Israel. This work John did not accomplish in his ministry. Some believe the two witnesses of Revelation 11 are Moses and Elijah, thus fulfilling this prophecy.

Note there the nature of the miracles performed. The aim of the ministry of Elijah when he comes before the great and terrible Day of the Lord, is to turn the hearts of the fathers to the children and those of the children to their fathers (the very opposite of what took place in the first coming, Mt 10:34-36), lest the Lord come and smite the earth with a curse. The reconciliation worked for is (on the basis of Lk 1:16-17) to be between the unbelieving children and the believing ancestors and forefathers (like Jacob, Levi, Moses, and Elijah, mentioned in 1:2; 2:4-6; 3:3; and 4:4).

If the restoration is not brought about, the coming of the Messiah will be a curse upon the earth and not with a blessing. The curse or ban meant destruction and extermination. (See Lev 27:28-29 and Deu 13:16-17).

It is both interesting and instructive that the final word of the last prophet of the Old Testament should be *curse,* while the first word of the Messiah on the mount was *blessed* (Mt 5:3), and the last word of the New Testament is one of *grace* (Rev 22:21).

The Jews repeat verse 5 after verse 6, because Malachi ends with the pronouncement of a curse. In four Old Testament books the Jewish scholars indicated that the last verse but one was to be repeated in the reading. These are Isaiah, the Twelve (the minor prophets concluding with Malachi), Lamentations, and Ecclesiastes. Compare their last verses.

THE REMEDY FOR THE CURSE

The book of Genesis shows how the curse entered the human race, and Malachi indicates the curse still threatens. The book of Matthew begins with the Son of David, the Son of Abraham who came to be made a curse for us by hanging upon a tree, declared a curse in the Word of God, that we might have blessing, joy, and eternal life through faith in His name. Only through Messiah Jesus the Lord can Israel escape the awful curse.

To

AUGUSTA E. SUSSDORFF,

missionary to Israel for a half-century,

and

BERNHARD SCHATKIN,

missionary to the lost sheep of Israel for more than twoscore years, this section is respectfully and affectionately dedicated.

THIS VOLUME is the last in the series of five covering the major messages of the minor prophets. All five books have been written under the constant pressure of a busy ministry in teaching and preaching and writing, so the author is deeply grateful to the Lord for His grace and strengthening in the task.

Throughout the expositions on the minor prophets, the writer has purposely avoided documentation of any kind. This does not mean that he has not carefully weighed and studied the considered and reverent positions of godly expositors. He has written, however, with the ordinary reader in mind. The aim has been throughout to instill a Bible-based and Spirit-taught love for God's ancient people, Israel.

My grateful thanks are due to my wife for help in proofreading the manuscript and for encouragement all along the way; and to Dr. J. Hoffman Cohn for his kind and thoughtful assistance in every detail from the writing of these studies for *The Chosen People* to their issuance from the press.

God has been pleased to bless the studies in the minor prophets to the hearts of His people according to their expressed testimony, and it is devoutly prayed that He will magnify His Son, the Messiah and Saviour of Israel, through these pages.

15

ZECHARIAH
COMFORTING WORDS

THE MAN AND THE MESSAGE

THE NAME "ZECHARIAH" means "the Lord (Jehovah) remembers." Some twenty-nine different persons in the Old Testament had this name. He is the great prophet of the days of the restoration from Babylonian captivity. With Haggai and Malachi he is a postexilic prophet.

He was born in Babylon of a priestly family that returned to Jerusalem from Babylon when some 50,000 exiles trekked their way home under Cyrus. His father probably died early, so that he is designated as the son of Iddo, who was his grandfather. (See Ezra 5:1; 6:14; Neh 12:4, 16.)

Like Jeremiah and Ezekiel he was both prophet and priest. He is spoken of as a young man in 2:4, though no specific age can be gleaned from this reference. Jewish tradition credits him with being one of the Great Synagogue, a body which is thought to have gathered and preserved the sacred writings and traditions of the Jews after the exile.

Zechariah began his ministry two months after Haggai had commenced his prophetic service. (Cp. Hag 1:1 and Zec 1:1.) It was in the second year of the reign of Darius Hystaspes (521-485 BC) which was the year 520 BC.

The length of his ministry is unknown. His book has three notations of time (1:1; 1:7; and 7:1).

His ministry, like that of Haggai, was to encourage the returned remnant to rebuild the Temple, and to nourish hope in the coming time of victory over every enemy. Zechariah's ministry extends in scope far beyond that of Haggai.

The prophetic horizon of Zechariah is far broader than that of the other minor prophets. His book has been called an apocalypse because of the presence of a number of visions. He dwells on the Person and work of Christ more fully than all the other minor prophets together.

Complaints have been made both by Jewish and Christian interpreters of the difficulty in interpreting the prophecies of Zechariah. It is admitted by them that his visions and oracles are the most Messianic and yet the most difficult of exposition. This difficulty can be overcome in large measure if we keep in mind that Zechariah is a postexilic prophet (so promises of future glory cannot refer to the return from Babylon), and that he draws heavily upon the former prophets, as similarities in style will reveal. Apart from the visions, the language of Zechariah is simple and direct.

The book can be divided into two large divisions: chapters 1-8 and 9-14. In the first section we have a series of eight prophetic visions with the prophet's contemporaries particularly in view; the second portion deals with the events of the end of Israel's age and the Millennium. The Prophet foresaw the completion of the Temple in 516 BC (Ezra 6:15), but went far beyond that in the last chapters of his prophecy.

A simple threefold outline of the prophecy is: (1) visions, chapters 1-6; (2) questions, chapters 7-8; (3) burdens, chapters 9-14. The prophet gives a complete spiritual history of Israel and of the relations of the Gentiles to her from the return from captivity to the end time. Messiah and Jerusalem are the centers about which all the prophetic messages revolve. Zechariah has in view three empires: Persia (with Darius in chaps. 1 and 7); Greece (with Alexander in chap. 9); and Rome (by implication in chaps. 12 and 14).

THE WARNING TO REPENT

The first prophetic message of Zechariah came in the second year of Darius' reign. The designation of a prophecy after the reign of a Gentile monarch shows clearly that the times of the Gentiles (begun in the reign of Nebuchadnezzar) had already commenced and were in progress. (See Lk 21:24.) The exhortation to repentance in verses 1-6 was probably delivered in the audience of all the people.

In strong language Zechariah sets forth the displeasure of the Lord with the fathers of his contemporaries. It was not merely their negligence in building the Temple (Hag 1:4, 5, 7) which called forth this rebuke, but their general spiritual condition. They had come back from exile, but they needed to turn fully and trustingly to the Lord.

The greatness of the Lord's displeasure is readily seen in the destruction of their city and their captivity for seventy years. The path of blessing is clearly indicated by Zechariah: if they return wholeheartedly to the Lord, He will turn unto them in favor and blessing.

Note the title "Lord of Hosts" throughout this passage and the entire prophecy as well. It is the characteristic name for God in Haggai, Zechariah, and Malachi, occurring more than eighty times. The Greek translation of the Old Testament renders it "the Almighty." God is Lord of the stars, the powers of heaven, and all the forces of the universe—a most inclusive and comprehensive name for God.

Because a bad example is so easily followed, the prophet warns his people not to follow in the ways of their ancestors, who had not heeded the words and exhortations of the prophets before the captivity. He appeals to the earlier prophets as authoritative, just as they did to the Law of Moses.

Zechariah points out that both those who preached (the prophets) and those who were ministered to (the fathers), were gone, but the truth of God's message through His servants is abundantly witnessed to by the desolate condition of Jerusalem and her people.

God's words and decrees were fulfilled to the very letter, as those who witnessed the performance of them testified. Prophets and fathers are alike mortal in contrast to God's undying and imperishable Word. The exile had vindicated the truth of the messages of the preexilic prophets; it was now for Zechariah's contemporaries to learn the lessons of history and follow the Lord implicitly.

THE VISION OF THE HORSES

All eight night visions date from the same night, and because of the importance of these revelations the dating is given in detail. It was three months after the first message. All eight visions form a unit, and the first is the key to all of them. Zechariah saw in his vision a man riding upon a red horse in a low place, and red, sorrel, and white horses behind him. The man on the red horse is identified as the Angel of the Lord in verses 11 and 12. This angel in human form is designated again and again in the Old Testament as God. (Cp. carefully His appearances in Gen 16:7-13; 22:11-12; Ex 3:2-6; Judg 6:14, 22; and 13:9-18, 22.) In the Babylonian Talmud the statement is made, "This man is no other than the Holy One, blessed be He; for it is said, 'The Lord is a man of war.'"

The low place was probably a spot well known to the prophet, for there were myrtle-covered glens in the neighborhood of Jerusalem (Neh 8:15). The myrtles in a low place may well represent Israel in her lowliness and degraded position among the nations of the earth as still fragrant to the Lord.

What do the horses symbolize? It is suggested that they represent the hosts of heaven, the angels, but they are rather the symbols of the divine activity in the government of the earth.

Do the colors have significance? From analogy with other prophetic Scriptures, we must conclude that the difference of color suggests a difference in the mission to be carried out by horses and riders. Red signifies war and bloodshed, here vengeance upon Israel's enemies. (See Is 63:1-6 and Rev 6:4.) On such a horse the Angel of the Lord Himself is riding, revealing what the purpose of God is for the then present hour. The sorrel is a mixture of the other colors. White clearly speaks of victory and triumph (Rev 6:2). To make the colors refer to the Medo-Persian war in which Babylon was defeated, the confused state of conditions that resulted from it, and the final setting up of the new dynasty in the Persian Empire is a needless straining for detail.

The angel who spoke with the prophet is the interpreting angel who explains the visions (he does not introduce them). Note the angel in Revelation 1:1 and 22:16. When the prophet asks the angel for the significance of the horses and riders, the Angel of the Lord answers that they have been commissioned of the Lord to reconnoitre. God is actively interested in the conditions of earth, especially as they relate to His earthly people, Israel. (See Job 1:7 and 2:2 for this activity by Satan for a sinister purpose.) The riders report that all the earth is enjoying peace. The early years of Darius' reign were marked by repeated rebellions throughout the Persian Empire, but at this time all was quiet again. Yet Haggai had foretold that the nations would be shaken (Hag 2:21-22). We may be certain that God will not fail in fulfilling His threats and His promises.

THE PRAYER OF THE ANGEL OF JEHOVAH

Since God's people were still under Gentile power and dominion and in an oppressed state, the tranquillity of the rest of the nations was all the greater contrast. Thus the Angel of the Lord is moved by His love for Israel to intercede with the Father on her behalf. He prays the prayer of expectant faith that it will please the Father to have mercy on Jerusalem and the cities of Judah which have now endured the wrath of God for seventy years. From 606 BC (2 Ki 24:1) to 536 BC (the year of Cyrus' decree to rebuild the Temple), the predicted exile had run its course. (Note Jer 25:11 and 29:10.)

The answer of God met the need abundantly; He replied with comforting words which foretold the good of Israel. Verses 14 to 17 indicate what the comforting words are; they give the details of the answer—the blessings in store for Israel. The sevenfold consolation is (1) the uninterrupted jealousy of God for Israel, (2) His vehement displeasure with the nations, (3) His return to Jerusalem with mercies, (4) the rebuilding of the sanctuary, (5) the restoration of the destroyed city, (6) the enlarged prosperity of the cities of the land, and (7) the comfort of Zion and choice of Jerusalem.

How glorious for Israel to know that God was still jealous for her welfare. At the same time He was sorely displeased with the nations; for He intended His wrath against Israel for a brief period, while the nations wanted to annihilate her. (See Is 47:6; Eze 25:3, 8, 12, 15; 26:2; and Ob 10-14.)

It is here revealed that the peace enjoyed by the nations did not mean the blessing of God was upon them. God had evidence of their selfishness and evil intent: the commission to chasten Israel was from the Lord, but they fulfilled it for themselves and not for Him. They were at ease in a bad sense, in careless and unfeeling security. (For the same concept see Amos 6:1; Is 32:9, 11; and Jer 48:11.) The great sin of the nations of the earth has been and is hatred toward God's ancient people, Israel. It is seen here and will culminate in the events of chapters 12 and 14. Let the nations of earth beware how they incur the wrath of Almighty God in their treatment of Israel!

Zion which is the focal point here, is specifically the southeastern hill of the city where David built (1 Ki with 2 Sa 5:9). The name came to be used for the hill to the north where the Temple was situated (Ps 48:2), and finally for the whole capital, becoming thus synonymous with Jerusalem.

The evidence of God's return to Jerusalem with mercies was manifest in the rebuilding of the Temple. As noted before, the Temple was already in building, but for the most part was unfinished; it was completed in the sixth year of Darius (Ezra 6:15).

Just as a line was formerly stretched over the city to destroy (2 Ki 21:13 and Is 34:11), it was now to be extended over Jerusalem preparatory to building (Job 38:5). Moreover, all the cities of Judah were to experience an overflowing prosperity, like an overflowing vessel. According to the historian Josephus, the population of the land had increased greatly by the time of the Maccabees.

By God's comfort (Is 40:1-2) of Zion He was to reveal the unchanging character of His choice. The prophet thus concludes the words of promise for future blessing. That these predictions were fulfilled in a preliminary way even in that time, no one will doubt. But the testimony of Scripture is sure that these words will find their highest fulfillment and greatest expression in the days of the glorious reign of Israel's Messiah, the Lord Jesus Christ.

This has been the cry of faith of many believing hearts for the coming glory of Israel. Her destitute and forlorn condition among the nations is proverbial, but God has promised to do something about it, yes, to do much to remedy it.

THE VISION OF THE HORNS AND WORKMEN

In the Hebrew Old Testament the second vision begins the second chapter of the prophecy; our English versions follow the Greek translation (and the Latin version) of the Old Testament. In either case no harm is done to the sense of the passage.

Zechariah lifts his eyes to see four horns. The horn is a well-known symbol in Scripture for power, the figure being taken from the bulls and other horned animals whose strength is in their horns. (See Mic 4:13; Dan 8:3-4.)

Different interpretations have been given for the presence of four horns. Many feel that the number stands for the four quarters of the earth: Israel's enemies have threatened her on every side. One suggestion would make the enemies specific for that time: the Samaritans on the north, to the east the Ammonites, the Edomites on the south, and to the west the Philistines and Tyrians. Another view would make the reference as broad as possible—all the empires who have had dealings with Judah and Jerusalem, oppressing them until their final deliverance by their Messiah. Judging from the figures in Daniel and Revelation, we conclude with many others that the passage is referring directly to the four world powers of Daniel 2, 7, and 8. The powers that scattered Judah, Israel, and Jerusalem (the entire nation with their capital city) were Babylonia, Persia, Greece, and Rome. It is true that at the time of Zechariah the third and fourth powers were not yet in existence, but it is the prerogative of prophecy to see the entire scheme of events in one broad view. Often events are noted together which are separated in their fulfillment. (For examples, read carefully Is 61:1-3; Dan 9:24-27; and Zec 9:9-10.)

Then the Lord showed the prophet four workmen or artisans. The Hebrew word is used for any skilled workman in wood, metal, or stone. The purpose of the workmen is to strike terror into the hearts of the nations who have trodden down and scattered God's people, and ultimately to bring about the overthrow of Israel's enemies. The workmen are the instruments of God to break the horns to pieces. What means God used to destroy the adversaries of Israel in times past are known to all. Adequate means, both human and above the human, are ever available to

Him to bring about the deserved punishment of the nations involved. It is revealing to note that for every horn, God had an agency to destroy it.

NO MAN LIFTED HIS HEAD

The scattering of Israel has been accomplished with such Satanic fury that the Word indicates no man could lift up his head. This tells fully the prostrate condition of Israel and the injuries suffered at the hands of her foes. The world would do well to learn the lesson that such action does not pass unnoticed by God. He is still awake to Israel's interests.

THE APPLE OF GOD'S EYE

THE MEASURING OF THE CITY

The second chapter of our prophecy brings before us the third vision in the series, which is related to what has gone before. If the second vision be seen as an amplification of the truth of 1:15; then the third vision is an elaboration of the promise in 1:16.

The man with the measuring line whom Zechariah sees is not just an additional figure, but as in the other visions it is an angel in human form. It cannot be the Angel of the Lord, for He would be specified more clearly by some added statement. (The same figure to convey the same prophetic truth is found in Eze 40:3; 41; 42; in another connection it is seen in Rev 11:1-2.)

In answer to the question of the prophet the man informs him that he purposes to measure the city of Jerusalem to ascertain its exact dimensions. It is not the future city, but that of the prophet's own time. Jerusalem is not thought of here as already built. It is being measured in view of its complete restoration. The vision is prophetic of the future Jerusalem and of the accomplishment of the promises of God for her.

THE PROMISE OF GLORY

In order to bring the meaning of the vision to Zechariah for transmission to his people, the interpreting angel went forth to meet another angel—he is too inferior in position to be the Angel of the Lord—to hear the glowing promise for Jerusalem's future. The message to the young prophet assures that Jerusalem will expand to such an extent that it will overflow its bounds and be inhabited as villages without walls. Men and cattle will be multiplied in her.

Dwelling without walls speaks of peace and safety. (See 1 Sa 6:18 and Est 9:19; and Eze 38 and 39 where the enemy from the north seeks to take advantage of this condition.) Such an increase in population as here predicted could not come from the return of a large number of Jews from Babylon; it looks on to a far future day, indicated in verse 5.

Though without physical walls to protect her from her inveterate enemies, Jerusalem will not be without a protecting wall. The Lord promises that He Himself shall be her protection round about and glory in her midst.

Our passage was not meant to discourage the building of Jerusalem's walls, which was done under Nehemiah in 445 BC.

The wall of fire, indicating security and safety, is reminiscent of the pillar of fire in the Exodus. (Note Ex 14:24, also Is 4:5 and Zec 9:8.) God will be her wall of salvation and protection (Is 26:1). The Shekinah glory is promised here. Surely it will not be denied that the fulfillment of this prophecy is in millennial times (Hab 2:14). The theme of the vision is the rebuilding and resettlement of Jerusalem, bearing out the words of 1:16-17, and the full accomplishment of these words will be the establishment of Jerusalem in the earth as the city of God's dwelling. Blessed day for Israel and all the earth that will be.

THE WARNING TO FLEE

After the third vision, Zechariah turns to direct prophetic address to issue a timely warning. The exiled Jews are to flee from the land of the north, which is Babylon (Jer 6:22; 16:16). Though they had been spread abroad there as with the fury and violence of the four winds of heaven, they are admonished now to flee from the doomed land.

The reasons they were to flee from Babylon were: (1) because God had set before them the promises of His sure blessing in their own land; (2) because of the calamity about to fall on Babylon (vv. 7-9). Darius, whose conquering armies would make no difference between Jew and Babylonian, was soon to defeat Babylon and bring it low. (Cp. Is 48:20; Jer 50:8-9; 51:6, 45; and the warning to flee from doomed Babylon in Rev 18 and 19.)

Although dispersed by the power of God, they would have to return of their own free will. Some had already returned, but the majority had not because of unbelief, the waste condition of their homeland, the loss of attachment to the land through long absence from it, and the security and prosperity in Babylon contrasted with Judea, where city and Temple were in a desolate condition. The matter is so urgent that they are exhorted to flee for a second time.

The prophet now assigns the compelling reason for such flight. The words *After glory* are important and have been variously interpreted. A number of students of the passage feel it refers to the time of the glory mentioned in verse 5; that is, after the return of the Lord in glory to dwell in Israel's midst, He will deal summarily with all her foes who have plundered her through the centuries. Two objections to this view make it untenable. First, the glorious appearing and dwelling of the Lord in the midst of His people, the culmination of all their hopes, would not be introduced in such an indefinite manner, for there is no definite article with the word *glory* in the Hebrew text. And second, by comparison of this passage with others in the prophetic Scriptures it will be readily seen that the time element is confused according to this view. The Lord does not visit judgment on Israel's plunderers after He is dwelling in Zion, but before it. (Note the sequence of events in Zec 12 and 14; Rev 16-20.)

It has been suggested as another possibility that the words are a motto or a war cry given by the Lord to His people to encourage them to the task before them, the departure from Babylon. The cry here is compared to that in Judges 5:14: "After thee, Benjamin." This view is not only forced, but gives no meaning to our passage. We hold with others that the Lord is declaring that for the vindication and display of His glory (which is inseparably bound up with the fortunes of His people), He will send the Messiah, not the prophet, to visit the nations that have plundered His people. Babylon, of course, is included here, but the mention of nations shows that God is speaking of the day when He reckons finally with the nations relative to their treatment of His people. (See Mt 25:31-46.) The one sent, mentioned in verses 8 and 9, must be the Messiah, from the character of the mission indicated and because of the power displayed in the deeds performed.

Why is God so eager to vindicate His honor in Israel? The answer is that whoever touches Israel (the thought here is a touching with evil intent) touches the apple of God's eye. As is well known, the eye is one of the most complex and delicate organs in the human body. The pupil is the most tender, most easily injured, and most important part of the eye. The loss of it is irreplaceable. Through it light comes to the retina of the eye for vision. (Note Deu 32:10; Ps 17:8; and Pr 7:2.) What a fit symbol for Israel this is.

To carry out His purposes of judgment on the nations who have oppressed Israel, the Lord will shake His hand over them, so that they will become servants to God's people. The shaking of the hand is a threatening gesture (Is 11:15). It will make servants of former masters and masters of former servants. (See Is 14:2.) When this is fully accomplished, the nation will know by experience that God has sent the Messiah, the Angel of the Lord.

How is it that the prophet continually moves from the then present hour to the far future when Messiah shall consummate the purposes of God? The answer is to be found in the way Scripture views the events in the national life of Israel; they are never viewed as so many different, distinct, and separate occurrences, but as links in a chain or stages in a plan working on to a grand and magnificent finale. Thus it is that the prophets move easily and without a feeling of incompatibility from deliverances and blessings of the moment to the final and concluding ones in Messiah's reign on earth. In the truest sense of the word all previous events are leading up to that blessed time.

It is in point here to ask whether any judgments were carried out at that time against Babylon. On the rock of Behistun at the border of Persia is the record of the two great rebellions of Babylon and of its seizure twice, once by Darius himself and then by his general, Intaphres.

THE COMING OF THE LORD

Pervading all the promises of blessing set forth in the first two chapters of Zechariah, has been the dominant thought that the Lord is to return to His people in the Person of Messiah. The prophet reverts to it here. He calls upon Zion to sing and rejoice over this unfading joy. It is actually Messiah speaking.

No one will mistake the reference to the tabernacling of the Son of God among His people in the first coming (Jn 1:14), but as the passage reads on, the emphasis is definitely on the second coming. What was begun in the appearing of grace is consummated in the appearing of glory (Titus 2:11-15; see also Zec 9:9; Mal 3:1; Is 40:10.) In the reign of Israel's King, many nations shall be drawn to the Lord and joined to Him, an evident proof of the divine commission and ministry of the Messiah of Israel.

In verse 11 we have for the third time in this chapter a word concerning the Lord's dwelling in the midst of His people; the other references are in verses 5 and 10. (Note 8:20-23; Is 14:1.) The word *dwell* is the root from which the word *Shekinah* comes, signifying the dwelling presence of the Lord on earth.

This joining of the nations to the Lord has been mistaken for the influx of proselytes into Judaism as a result of the exile of the Jews in Babylon or the gathering of the Gentiles into the Church. The prophet has in mind the future conversion of the Gentiles to the Lord, the fulfillment of the Abrahamic Covenant in the rule of the Messiah.

However, the blessing of other nations will not detract from Israel's; they will still be the portion of the Lord and His chosen. His grace toward them was hindered for a time, but His covenant abides permanently. (Cp. Ro 11:28-29.)

This passage (v. 12) is the only place where the phrase "holy land" is to be found in the Scriptures.

In conclusion the prophet calls upon all men to hush (Ps 46:10; Hab 2:20) before the Lord; let all people await the hour of God's intervention on behalf of Israel. The Lord is represented as awakened from His holy habitation, that is, heaven (Deu 26:15), to bring about the full counsel of His will. As long as things go on quietly (1:11), it appears as though the Lord is asleep, but His waking is given under the figure of a lion roused from its lair. Let the foes of the Lord and Israel beware!

ISRAEL, THE CLEANSED PRIEST

JOSHUA AND THE ACCUSER

In the first three visions of the prophecy, Zechariah has dwelt on the subjects of the great solicitude of the Lord for His downtrodden people, Israel; the prayer of the Messiah for the blessing of His own; the prediction of judgment upon the nations that have harassed them; and the promise of unlimited enlargement with the presence of God in their midst, attended by their spiritual restoration and the conversion of the Gentiles.

But before these blessings can be Israel's, there must be a spiritual transformation in her. Furthermore, the purpose of this vision was to restore the people's confidence in the priesthood and its service. Since they were rebuilding the Temple, there was need of reassurance that God would once more own and recognize the reinstituted worship there. The priesthood had become polluted and the subject of condemnation in preexilic and exilic times, as Ezekiel 22:26 shows.

The one who introduces the vision to the prophet is not the interpreting angel, who only explains the visions in this prophecy, but the Lord Himself. Zechariah is shown Joshua the son of Jehozadak, the high priest, standing before the Angel of the Lord with Satan at his right hand accusing him. The place where these events transpire is not given; it must be determined from the sense of the passage.

It is necessary to point out at the outset that Joshua is here in his official and representative character, not in a personal and private capacity. The outcome of the vision will ultimately comfort Joshua too, but he is before us in his official position. This can be demonstrated from three facts: (1) emphasis is laid on the fact that he is high priest (vv. 1, 5, and 8); (2) the rebuke is given Satan (v. 2) on the basis of God's unchanging choice of Israel; and (3) the cleansing of Joshua is made to prefigure the removal of the iniquity of the land (v. 9). The issue is, then, of more than casual interest: if Joshua is cleared, the nation is; if he is rejected from priestly service, they are.

In what sense are we to understand Joshua's standing before the Angel of the Lord? The difficulty arises from the fact that the expression "to stand before" has a twofold technical use in Hebrew. It is employed for priestly service, as can be seen in Deuteronomy 10:8; 2 Chronicles 29:11; and Ezekiel 44:15, among a number of passages. The phrase is also used in a court scene (as in Num 35:12; Deu 19:17; Jos 20:6; and 1 Ki 3:16). Thus, there are some who think Joshua was standing in the sanctuary in the performance of his priestly ministry. The high priest in Israel was able to perform all the duties of the ordinary priests in addition to those which were peculiarly his (as on the Day of Atonement, Lev 16). Others suggest that Joshua was accused, or feared an accusation, at the court of Persia. Another view holds that the high priest was standing before the judgment seat of the Angel of the Lord. There is no formal judicial procedure indicated in the vision. The best explanation seems to be a blending of the two meanings of "to stand before." Joshua was engaged in his priestly functions in the Temple, when he found himself the object of the accusations of Satan, the archenemy of God and man, before the Angel of the Lord.

The right hand is the usual position of the prosecutor in a lawsuit (Ps 109:6), but it is also the place of the defender (Ps 109:31). Knowing the deceit of Satan, we cannot deny that he could take the place of defender in order to accuse, but we cannot be dogmatic on the point. Somehow both Jewish and Christian expositors have built up baseless theories on this passage. The Targum and the rabbinic writers indicate that Joshua was accused for allowing his descendants to marry heathen wives as is stated in Ezra (10:18) and Nehemiah (13:28). This view is scarcely valid when we remember the official capacity in which Joshua appears in this vision. Some Christian interpreters have held that our passage is the basis for the reference in Jude 9. The verse in Jude cannot be connected with chapter 3, because "the body of Moses" spoken of there has no parallel in Scripture usage to refer it to the Jewish congregation. The "body of Christ" for the Church rests on an altogether different concept and relationship. Jude is doubtless speaking of the literal body of Moses.

That the Angel of the Lord is Deity is clear from the answer to Satan in verse 2; the Angel is designated as the Lord. The Messiah in a twofold statement calls down the rebuke of the Father upon Satan and his accusations. The repetition is meant to show the certainty that Satan's accusations will be nullified. The thought in "rebuke" is to chide, so as to silence those who are reproved.

The most remarkable feature in the entire transaction is the basis upon which God brings to nought the accusations of Satan. It is not because of the righteousness of God's people, nor because of the baselessness of Satan's claims, nor because the nation has already suffered much for their sins, nor because of a promise to do better in the future. The sole plea for God's people lies in God's sovereign choice in grace. (See Ro 9:16 and 11:5.) It is basically and fundamentally a matter of God's infinite choice. He asserts His right to do as He pleases with the objects of His boundless mercy. Let those who rail at the choice of God note this passage, and let them rejoice that this is their certainty and assurance for eternity also.

Israel is likened to a brand plucked out of the fire. The figure is familiar (Amos 4:11) for that which is thrown into the fire, or has fallen into it, and is then rescued by the owner, because he has future purposes for the brand, thus delivering it from total destruction. God punished Israel in the Babylonian captivity, but through His grace He has spared them from total annihilation.

It is interesting how important events in Israel's history are connected with fire: the covenant with Abraham (Gen 15:17), the revelation to Moses (Ex 3:2), the deliverance at the Exodus (Ex 14:24), the giving of the Law at Sinai (Ex 19:18), the rearing of the tabernacle (Num 9:15), the wilderness journeyings (Deu 1:33), and numerous other instances.

Now the prophet sets before us the actual condition in which Joshua was standing, as accused, before the Angel of the Lord. He was clothed in filthy garments. Filthy garments did not symbolize the criminal in Israel, but one in the pollution of sin. (See Is 4:4 and 64:6.) Though outwardly delivered from Babylonian captivity, it was still possible for them to be defiled as far as acceptable priestly ministry was concerned. It was not merely ritual uncleanness of the priesthood because of their prolonged exile in the unclean land of Babylon, but moral uncleanness. The filth spoken of here is of the worst physical kind, representing moral pollution. Israel was delivered but not cleansed. How telling this description is of her present condition also.

THE CLEANSING OF THE HIGH-PRIEST

Because Joshua was helpless to bring about his own cleansing and purification, the Angel of the Lord sovereignly commanded His attending angels to remove the filthy garments from the high priest. It is clearly God's work without help from man.

Here we have another distinct proof that the Angel of the Lord is God. The removal of the polluted garments signifies (together with the clothing mentioned immediately thereafter) forgiveness, acceptance, and restoration to a position of privilege. The clothing with festive apparel indicates reinstatement into the priestly office. The figure may be taken from Isaiah 61:10.

The prophet, as he views the ceremonies, cannot contain himself longer, so he expresses his longing and prayer for the complete cleansing and clothing of the priesthood. The mitre or turban of the high priest had fastened to it the plate of gold engraved with the words "Holiness to the Lord." (Cp. Ex 28:36-38.) The Angel of the Lord stood by witnessing the proceedings and gracing them by His benign presence.

THE CHARGE TO JOSHUA

A cleansed high priest needs a renewed commission, and we find this in the next verses. In solemn words the Angel of the Lord declared (the additional thought of warning is also present in the word *protested*) His charge to Joshua. He is directed first concerning his personal piety to walk in the ways of the Lord. Then he is enjoined concerning the performance of his official duties; service is to flow out of a godly life. If Joshua will be circumspect in these matters, then he is promised authority to judge the Lord's house. This does not mean a share in the government, as has been suggested by another, as though the house stood for the people of God. It refers to the Temple then in building. The duties of the priests included deciding and judging between clean and unclean. (Note carefully Lev 10:10; Deu 17:9; Eze 44:23; and Mal 2:7.)

The courts, too, had to be guarded from profanation; care had to be exercised as to the kind of persons who were to be allowed to enter. And the highest privilege of all is that the high priest will be granted access (lit., walks, paths), that is, entrance and exit, among the angels of the court of heaven. The promise speaks of direct and immediate communion with the Lord and free and ready access to the Lord. This was possible only to priests who were ritually and morally pure. (See Ex 40:30-32.) Joshua, representing the nation, is placed under responsibility; if found faithful, he is promised a secure place in the presence of the Lord.

MESSIAH'S COMING

But the prophet has a word for the future concerning the perfect High Priest of Israel. The call to hear indicates the importance of what is about to be revealed.

Joshua and his fellow priests are designated as men who are a sign. This does not mean men to whom signs are committed, nor men for whom signs are wrought, nor persons able to interpret the puzzling words of the prophets, but sign-men, typical persons.

The Angel is stating that, apart from all that has been done for the priesthood itself in Israel, the office of priest is itself prophetic, and that of God's Servant, the Branch. The Branch cannot be Zerubbabel, as some would have it, for he was already on the scene of history, while the Branch was yet to appear. The Branch is the Messiah.

Joshua's name is that of the coming Saviour of Israel. He typifies the Messiah the High Priest, while his fellow priests speak of believers. The priesthood will be maintained until the great Antitype comes. "My Servant" is a characteristic designation for the Messiah. (See Is 42:1; 49:3; 50:10; 52:13; 53:11; Eze 34:23-24; also Phil 2:6-8 for the important passages of the Scriptures on this grand theme.) Branch is a proper name for the coming Messiah also, the tender branch from the line of David. (Cp. 6:12; Is 4:2; 11:1; 53:2; Jer 23:5; 33:15; and Lk 1:78, where "dayspring" can be substituted for "branch").

The tenderness, the lowliness, and the humanity of the coming Messiah are in view, and much more. In verse 9 we find the third name of Messiah, "the Stone," thus forming a trilogy or triad. Many are the interpretations given to the stone mentioned here; it is said to be the foundation stone of the Temple, the capstone of the Temple, the jewel in Messiah's crown, all the stones of the Temple in building at the time, Zerubbabel, an altar, a jewel on the breastplate of the high priest or upon a royal crown, and the finished Temple itself.

The manner in which the stone is here introduced, and because of what is stated concerning it, the reference can scarcely be to an ordinary material stone. We have already declared our position that this is the Messiah. Scripture proof will be found in Genesis 49:24; Psalm 118:22; Isaiah 28:16; Matthew 21:42; Acts 4:11; and 1 Peter 2:6.

The seven eyes upon the Stone are not so much the providential care of God over the Messiah (judging from 4:10), but the fullness of knowledge or omniscience of the Stone. (Contrast with this the eyes in the little horn in Daniel 7:8.)

The engraving of the Stone alludes to Messiah's beauty, gifts, graces, and preciousness, as polished stones. Through the Stone, the Branch, God's Servant, the iniquity of Israel's land will be removed in one day.

This has no connection with the day of completion and dedication of the Temple, nor with the national Day of Atonement of Leviticus 23:27. It has to do with the day in which Messiah finished His expiatory work on the cross, making salvation possible for Israel, and even more so with Israel's national Day of Atonement of 12:10 when this salvation becomes actual.

The mention of "one day" signifies there will be no renewal; His work will be once for all. (See Heb 10:10, 12, 14.)

Now it is clear why Joshua and his fellow priests are typical persons: the act of forgiving grace and cleansing look on to that of the Messiah whereby the nation will be not only potentially but actually redeemed, and their iniquity forever removed. When Israel is found in such a spiritual condition—so reads the united testimony of the Old Testament—material prosperity is always promised her. Thus we read of the peace and prosperity of.the time in verse 10. (Cp. 1 Ki 4:25 and Mic 4:4.) May God graciously hasten the day!

ISRAEL, THE WORLD'S LIGHT

THE GOLDEN CANDLESTICK

We have seen that the fourth vision of the book in the third chapter was intended to encourage and reassure Joshua the high priest that the priesthood was cleansed and reinstated in priestly privilege and office. If the religious leader in Israel needed heartening for his duties, the civil head required it also.

For almost a score of years, Zerubbabel the son of Shealtiel, governor of Judah, had been frustrated in his attempts to build the Temple. How could this be understood other than that God was not looking with favor upon his efforts? Assurance is now given by vision and direct prophetic address. God in His strength and power is enough for any task: this is the reliance needed by Zerubbabel and provided for him through the work of the sovereign Holy Spirit Himself.

An interval elapsed between the fourth and fifth vision, after which the interpreting angel returned to the prophet; he had possibly been receiving further instructions from the Lord. The prophet was aroused as a man is awakened out of sleep, because the period when visions are not presented to prophetic messengers is likened to that of sleep. (Cp. Dan 10:9-11.)

This time the angel does not wait to be questioned by the prophet but rather initiates the question himself. The prophet saw in the vision a golden candlestick, or candelabrum, or more properly a lampstand.

The one in the tabernacle of Moses described in Exodus 25:31-40 and 37:17-24 is the basis of this vision. The Romans carried off the one from the Temple in AD 70, as seen on the Arch of Titus at Rome. Interestingly enough, the candelabrum is the symbol of the new state of Israel also.

The one in Zechariah's vision differed in four particulars from that of the tabernacle and Solomon's Temple: it had a bowl, pipes, olive trees, and two golden spouts. The lights themselves were doubtless very simple—small, shallow vessels of shell shape still found in Palestine—with a lip at the outer and narrower end, from which the wick protruded.

Note the number seven in chapter 4; it is the number of fullness or perfection. In verse 2 we find seven lamps and seven pipes; in verse 10, seven eyes.

The lampstand was all of gold, suggesting purity and preciousness. There were seven lamps to the lampstand, and seven pipes to each lamp. Some follow the Latin and Greek translations of the Old Testament in holding that there were but seven lamps with one pipe to each. In the original Hebrew the numeral is repeated; in other words, there were seven pipes apiece or forty-nine in all.

The whole picture is intended to convey the thought of an unlimited supply which needed no human instrumentality for replenishing, as did the lampstands in the tabernacle and the Temple. The larger the number of the oil pipes, the brighter the light of the lampstand. The purpose of the vision is clearly brought out in verse 6.

What does the lampstand represent? It has been suggested that it may symbolize the Temple they were then building. Many who make no distinction between the Church and Israel (a demarcation which is one of the clearest in the Bible), think the figure stands for the Church. It is true that lampstands are used as a figure of the Church in Revelation 1:12, 20, and that the Church is compared to lights in Philippians 2:15, but the Church is not a matter of prophecy in the Old Testament. The Church is first foretold in the New Testament in Matthew 16:18.

The symbol in Zechariah's prophecy refers to Israel when restored to the Lord and the means of light to the world, as God originally intended. God planned to have in them a kingdom of priests (cp. with Zec 3) and a holy nation (cp. with this chapter). See Exodus 19:6. It is thus an ideal picture portraying what is in the mind and will of God for His people. Special mention is made in verse 3 of the two olive trees which supplied the needed oil to the bowl, from which the oil poured forth through the pipes to the several lamps of the lampstand. The abundance of imagery is intended to convey the thoughts of the great importance of the entire process and the unstinted supply to the lamps for light.

THE OMNIPOTENT SPIRIT OF GOD

When the prophet asked this question, found in verse 4, he did not mean that he did not understand what the lampstand was. With this he was familiar through the furniture of the tabernacle and Temple of Solomon. He was inquiring what the whole vision of verses 2 and 3 signified for that special time. What was its definite and needed application to the hour in which he and his contemporaries lived?

The question of the interpreting angel serves to increase the prophet's suspense. There is also the implication that the prophet might have known the meaning of the vision. Apparently he expected Zechariah to know the significance of the vision. The interpreting angel now explains that the vision is the word of the Lord, that is, the vision was a prophecy in symbolic form.

What follows in verse 6 gives us the key to the vision. Some think Zerubbabel had become despondent in his work because of the opposition to it, the greatness of the task, and the small means to carry it out. There were sufficient elements in the situation to make the most energetic despair. Zechariah is told that God's message for that hour for Zerubbabel is that success and completion of the task depend, not on man's might nor power, but on the Holy Spirit Himself. The word *might* may mean "army" also, but it does not make sense here. Actually there is not much difference in meaning between the words *might* and *power*. All kinds of power available to man are meant: physical, mental, or moral. These at their best are insufficient for the task in hand or any work for God. Man's weakness is no hindrance in the work of God, because He supplies the power of the Spirit of God. (Cp. 1 Sa 14:6; Ho 1:7; 2 Co 12:9-10; Heb 11:34; also 2 Co 4:7.) That which was ministered to the nation was the grace and power of the Spirit of God, pictured by the oil.

How timely this message is for our day with its complex and manifold committees, boards, drives, plans, organizations, contests, budgets, sponsors, rallies, groups, and much more. These can never avail in themselves to bring about the accomplishment of the task God has entrusted to us; since it is from first to last a spiritual work, it must be by the omnipotent and unfailing and unerring Spirit of God. The arm of flesh fails; He never does.

THE ENCOURAGEMENT TO ZERUBBABEL

All the encouragement Zerubbabel would ever need was given to him in verse 6, where he is directed to the unfailing supply of the Spirit of God. Now the prophet elaborates on that all-inclusive promise.

The question form he uses makes the statement all the more emphatic. The mountain stands for all the difficulties in the way of the completion of the Temple. For these mountainous obstacles, see Ezra 4 and 5.

Zerubbabel represents the people here, just as Joshua did in the previous chapter. Before the governor and the people, every difficulty would be done away by the power of God. Zerubbabel is promised the honor and joy of finishing the building, as stated in verse 9. He is said to bring forth the capstone, for it was the custom of officials, then as now, both to lay the foundation of a building as well as the capstone. (Note Ezra 3:10.)

Some inject here the idea of God's bringing forth the Messiah, the Stone, but this is forced and destroys the smoothness and unity of the passage. First, it is Zerubbabel who brings forth the stone (capstone here), and not

God. Second, the shouting of grace to the Messiah would be meaningless. And last, verse 9 is clear enough that the matter in hand has to do with the completion of the building of the Temple. Just as shouting of joy attended the laying of the foundation of the Temple, so the consummation of the work would call forth similar shouts of joy. (See Ezra 3:11-13.) The shout of triumph at the completion of the task would doubtless be: "May the grace of God abide on this His house!"

Lest Zerubbabel be minded to become discouraged in the work, the promise is repeated in verse 9: just as he began the building, he was to finish it. This promise was literally fulfilled in the sixth year of Darius' reign (Ezra 6:15).

The words *sent me* cannot refer to Zechariah, because he is addressed as "thou shalt know." Note also verse 8 for the fact that God was directly addressing the prophet. The one meant is the Messiah, as in 2:9, 11.

In chapter 3 the Spirit of God looked beyond Joshua and his cleansing to the sin-absolving work of the blessed Branch. In chapter 4, the Holy Spirit directs the gaze of the prophet beyond Zerubbabel and his building to the same Branch who will build the Temple in His earthly reign. See 6:13. Never be surprised that the Holy Spirit brings the Messiah into the picture; He has no greater delight, and His work in revelation has no greater theme. What could be more heartwarming?

Now we know from Ezra 3:12-13 and Haggai 2:3 that there were not merely among their enemies but among their own number those who in unbelief despised the small beginnings of the restoration Temple. The day of small things was the time since they had begun to rebuild the sanctuary of the Lord. They are informed that God in His fullness of knowledge and omniscience (seven eyes) rejoices in the progress of the work under Zerubbabel and in its completion. It is not that those who formerly despised the small commencement will necessarily rejoice at the strides the work has made. The running of God's eyes throughout the whole earth speaks of God's providential care put forth for the finishing of the Temple. (For the same figure see 2 Ch 16:9.) What further assurances could Zerubbabel and the people of God need in addition to these specific and blessed ones already given?

THE TWO CHANNELS OF GRACE

But not all of the vision has been explained to Zechariah; he asks now concerning the two olive trees. In this chapter the prophet asks three questions, verses 4, 11, and 12. Zerubbabel has been mentioned four times in this chapter, but he could not be referred to by these two trees at the right and left of the bowl which fed the oil into the lampstand.

A common Old Testament comparison is that of a man to a tree. (Note Ps 1:3; 52:8; Jer 17:8; and Dan 4:10 among others.) We know from verse 6 that the golden oil referred to in verse 12 speaks of the Holy Spirit. The figure of oil for the Holy Spirit is clear throughout the Old Testament in the anointings of prophets, priests, and kings for their respective offices. Who, then, are meant by the two olive trees? The interpreting angel brings that matter to a climax and conclusion by indicating that the two olive trees represent the anointed ones (lit., sons of oil) that stand by the Lord of the whole earth.

We have already set forth what persons were anointed in Israel for the execution of their ministry. Their standing before the Lord is the position of servants waiting to receive orders from their masters. "Lord of the whole earth" is the title of God as Creator. The two anointed ones have been taken to refer to the Mosaic system and that of Christ, or to the two natures of Christ, the human and the divine. But the reference must be to two anointed and consecrated individuals. They are Joshua and Zerubbabel in their official capacities as God's channels through whom the Spirit of God manifests His power and grace to the whole nation. These leaders are viewed in their position of favor, privilege, and protection before the Lord.

Thus chapters 3 and 4 are complementary, concluding with a combined word of cheer to both Joshua and Zerubbabel, the high priest and governor in Israel respectively.

An interesting adaptation of the two olive trees is found in Revelation 11:3-4. If these two in Revelation are Moses and Elijah, there are the civil and religious powers represented as with Zerubbabel and Joshua. Contrast them with the Roman beast (civil power) and the false prophet (religious power) of Revelation 13. Needless to say, the ultimate fulfillment of verse 14 is the Messiah, who is both King and Priest (6:11-13). May we ever follow the wisdom of the Spirit of God and ever keep Him in full view.

16

SIN REMOVED

THE VISION OF THE FLYING ROLL

THE REMAINING VISIONS of this prophecy, that is, the two in this chapter and the one in chapter 6, deal with the theme of judgment. The fourth chapter viewed Israel in an ideal position; this one sees her as she actually was. Judgment will fall upon Israel for sin, first individually (vv. 1-4) then nationally (vv. 5-11), and finally it will strike the nations as well (6:1-8). The prophet includes in his area of vision the hour in which he lived and moves from that time to the judgment of the wicked in the last days, just before the setting up of the kingdom of the Messiah on earth.

When Zechariah lifted up his eyes after the fifth vision, he saw a flying roll or scroll. The ancients wrote on the inner bark of trees, on rolls of papyrus and dressed skins of animals; here probably the last type is meant. The roll was seen flying because its pronouncements were swiftly to be visited upon the guilty. It was unfolded or its contents and dimensions could not have been seen. (Similar symbols to convey the thought of judgment and punishment are found in Eze 2:9-10; Rev 5 and 10:2.)

The interpreting angel asked the prophet what he saw, whereupon the prophet described the flying roll. It was a large roll, thirty feet in length and fifteen feet in breadth, to indicate the great number of curses it contained. There are those who think the dimensions are incidental and not intended to convey any truth. However, it will be remembered that the holy place in the tabernacle of Moses and the porch of Solomon's Temple (where the Law was usually read) were of the same dimensions (1 Ki 6:3). The vision would teach us that the holiness of the sanctuary of the Lord is the measure of sin and that judgment must begin at the house of God. (See 1 Pe 4:17-18.)

THE CURSE AND ITS WORKS

The interpreting angel now explains to Zechariah that the roll pronounces a curse as it flies over the land. The commandments God had given Israel by Moses were a covenant with a curse pronounced upon the violator of them.

The word *curse* is used collectively for all the curses contained in the Law (Deu 27:15-26 and 28:15-68). The land referred to is the land of Judah, and not the whole earth, because the Law was given to Israel only (Ex 20:1-2).

After the analogy of the tables of the law, the scroll was written on both sides. (Note Ex 32:15.) The swearing falsely by God's name broke the middle commandment of the first table containing duties toward God; the stealing was an infraction of the middle commandment of the second table, comprising duties toward man.

There are those who think the theft and perjury were committed in connection with their default in the matter of tithes and offerings. (Cp. Neh 13:10 and Mal 3:8.) There is no need to limit the passage thus. As violators of the first table they were false to God; as transgressors of the second table they were false to man. There was a penalty upon any breach of the commandments, but it is thought that these two transgressions are especially emphasized, because they were probably particularly prevalent at this time. The two commandments are actually taken as representing the whole Law of Moses. According to the provisions of the roll, the offenders were to be cut off, that is, purged out, swept away, and cleared away, as in Isaiah 3:26 and Jeremiah 30:11, where the same word occurs.

The Lord outlines in His warning the manner in which the cutting off will take place. God Himself will bring forth the curse, and it will accomplish its devastating work. The sinners cannot shut themselves up in their houses to guard against the curse; it will enter despite their efforts. The destruction will be complete, leaving no trace of the house, as in the case of the house of the leper in Israel. (See Lev 14:45.) The curse lets loose the power that brings about its fulfillment. There is no question here of the effectiveness of the curse, and the consumption of the house includes those who reside there (Amos 3:15).

Sin is an intensely personal thing, and God's visitation upon it is equally personal. The word *abide* means literally "to spend the night," but it also has the meaning of "to remain permanently." Such is the intended sense here. (Note also Ps 49:12.) Be not deceived: nothing is so deadly to us and inescapable, as far as our own powers are concerned, as sin.

It can never triumph ultimately, because it is so diametrically opposite to all that God is and loves. Doubtless, it wrought its havoc in the time of the prophet Zechariah, and the judgments for it were grievous. But the passage looks on into the far future, and sees the final extermination of ungodliness before the righteous reign of the Messiah. Thus it is that this vision naturally and smoothly blends into the next in chapter 5.

THE VISION OF THE WOMAN IN THE EPHAH

The going forth of the interpreting angel indicates that another vision is being presented by the Lord to the prophet, and that the interpretation of it is being called for. Zechariah sees an ephah going forth.

Notice the number of times in this chapter that movement is indicated. Moral forces in the world do not remain stationary or stagnant; there is either progress or retrogression.

When the prophet asked, "What is it?" he was inquiring as to the significance of the ephah. He recognized the ephah but wanted to know what it symbolized, what truth it was meant to convey to him and then through him to the people of God.

The ephah itself was well known, for it was the largest measure in use among the Jews, containing a little over our bushel. The angel explains that the ephah is designed to portray the appearance of the wicked in the land. Just as in an ephah all the separate grains are brought together, so the sinners of the land will be gathered together. The measure signifies the measured judgment for sin appointed of God in His infinite justice.

The view has been advanced by some that the ephah, being the symbol of trade and commerce, points to wickedness in commerce. They point to the prominence of a godless commercialism in James 5 and Revelation 18. But there is no need to restrict the reference thus; just as the offenses in the previous vision were of a representative character, so we have that here which stands for wickedness in general. Again the mention of the land must be taken of the land of Judah. The prophet is receiving the message primarily for his own people and especially those of his own day. They must learn the gravity and tragedy of sin.

A talent of lead lying on the mouth of the ephah as a lid was lifted up in order to allow the prophet to see what was in the ephah. The talent was the heaviest weight used among the Hebrews. When the ephah was uncovered, Zechariah saw a woman, who represented wickedness, sitting in the ephah. The comparison of wickedness to a woman is found also in Proverbs 2:16 and 5:3-4. The reason is clear: in Hebrew the feminine is used to represent abstract ideas.

The context does not require that this woman should be defined as the great harlot of Revelation 17 and 18. Some students of the passage refer it (the wickedness personified) to idolatry (Jer 44:20 and Eze 23). It is true that idolatry is the most hateful type of wickedness in the sight of

God, but such a reference as we have in our passage covers well all types of wickedness, idolatry included.

It is maintained, by citing Ezra 9; Isaiah 57; 65:1-7; and 66:17, that idolatory was practiced even after the exile. The reference in Ezra was true before the reforms of Ezra which brought the people back to God; those in Isaiah have no bearing on postexilic times, for they portray conditions among Isaiah's contemporaries in the eighth century BC.

The personification of wickedness under the figure of a woman should be compared with the presentation of wickedness as headed up in the one known as the man of sin (2 Th 2:3). As the prophet looked on, the angel cast the woman into the midst of the ephah and cast the talent on the mouth of the ephah in order to render impossible her escape from the coming visitation of God.

THE FLIGHT TO SHINAR

We shall now learn the final disposition of wickedness as far as God's people, Israel, are concerned. Two women come forth to carry off the ephah with its burden. It is a striving after too great detail, as well as a failure to realize the full importance of the future reference to prophetic times, to find in these two women the Assyrian and Babylonian nations who were used of God to remove the idolatry of Israel from the land of Palestine.

The women are necessary features to make the vision vivid and complete the revelation of God's plan. They are consistent with the image already before us. There are two because of the weight to be carried between them. The wind does its part in helping them carry their burden with greater speed through the air. The women are provided with wings like those of a stork, a bird very common in Palestine.

The stork has long and wide wings and is a migratory bird (Jer 8:7). Those acquainted with the habits of this bird inform us that in its annual migration, the stork actually traverses a longer distance than that from Judea to Shinar. Every feature of the vision, then, serves to further the deportation of the ephah from the midst of Israel.

The destination of the flight has not been stated, so the prophet asks now concerning it. The answer is indeed full and sufficient: (1) wickedness is to be transported, as it were, to the land of Shinar; (2) a house is to be built for her there; (3) she is to be established in her own place.

The reference in the land of Shinar is to Babylonia. (See Gen 10:10; 11:2; and Is 11:11 among others.) This was the land where man had first united in a universal rebellion against God. It stands throughout Scrip-

ture for confusion in spiritual matters, for idolatry, for spiritual uncleanness (Rev 17:3-5).

The same spirit of Babylon manifested in Genesis 11 will be revealed
in the Babylon of Revelation 18. It was the land where Judah was exiled,
but not because Babylon was working willingly to accomplish the will of
God. The prophet Habakkuk shows clearly that the contrary was true:
she was intent on her own selfish aims. In Babylon culminates all that
is opposed to God and His righteous rule on earth. The vision speaks of
the overthrow and doom of final Babylon.

The land of Shinar cannot refer to Israel's world wide dispersion under
the terms of the already past Babylonian captivity, for there is no parallel
to this in scripture usage. Neither can the passage be speaking of something already fulfilled literally in the exile just accomplished. The trend
of the whole prophecy is future.

The vision was meant to do more than to show them the gravity of the
evil of idolatry. Seventy years in exile had done that well under the tute-
lage of the Lord. God is stating that all wickedness is developing along
well-defined lines and in due course it will be headed up in that place
which has always stood for defiance against God.

Strangely enough, the mention of a house in the land of Shinar has
been understood to mean an imposing temple, common enough in that
country. The permanent abode is interpreted as an idol temple (in
Babylon called ziggurats) to be built for idolatry, because the worship of
other gods was allowable in foreign lands, as in Deuteronomy 4:19 and
29:25-26.

We shall leave it with the reader to decide by even the most superficial
reading of these passages, as well as the many throughout the Old and
New Testament, whether God is revealed as ever sanctioning (and He the
Lord of all the earth and the God of all the nations) the worship of other
gods. No, the prophet is clearly stating that wickedness is to culminate in
a specific and definite place; there it will have its permanent abode.

The building of the house implies a permanent stay, as it meant a long
exile for the Jews in Jeremiah 29:5, 28; see also Isaiah 34:13. Wickedness,
furthermore, will not find it difficult to adjust itself there, for Babylon is
her own place. It is to abide where it originated and where it has always
belonged. The cycle of wickedness, as it were, is complete. Godlessness in
every form has finally come home.

We emphasize that the fulfillment of this prophecy is yet future, to be
accomplished in that time when sin shall be rooted out of Israel, when
the people have turned to the Lord Jesus as their Messiah, Saviour, and
King.

THE CONSUMING POWER OF SIN

Nowhere in the Bible do we have a more faithful depicting of the awful ravages that sin brings into human life, than is given in this chapter. Sin destroys not only all we have, but all that we are or could hope to be. It is an incurable virus. Incurable, we say, by man's means. But, blessed be God, He has provided once for all and so adequately that deliverance and remedy which every sinful heart needs desperately. It avails for Jew as well as Gentile.

MESSIAH, THE KING-PRIEST

THE VISION OF THE CHARIOTS

The vision of the chariots in chapter 6 concludes the visions which Zechariah saw in one night. The eighth and last vision completes in thought what was presented in the first vision.

There the horsemen were bringing back their reports to the Angel of the Lord; here the chariots go forth to carry out the Lord's commission. The chariots put the judgmental decrees of God into operation. Thus the cycle of truth is rounded out.

This vision has been considered by some as perhaps the most obscure, though this is claimed for other visions also. Proceeding upon the principles of interpretation already followed in the previous chapters, it is possible to obtain a harmonious explanation for this one also.

Zechariah sees in vision four chariots issuing from between two mountains of brass. The chariots are war chariots and give an intimation of their ultimate purpose. A goodly number of interpreters of the passage believe there are four chariots to represent the four world kingdoms prophesied by Daniel. Though we hold that the four empires are in view in 1:18, we do not believe they are presented here. With others we hold this position for two reasons: (1) the chariots are distinctly defined as the four winds of heaven, and (2) the four geographical notations do not conform to the four monarchies of Daniel 2 and 7.

We understand the four chariots to represent the different agents of God's providence in judgment toward the nations which have dealt ill with Israel. The two mountains mentioned in the vision are definite ones (the definite article is employed in the Hebrew), but the interpretations offered for them have been various indeed. They have been taken to signify the immovable decrees of God, the ideal mountains before the abode of God, the gates of heaven, or the empire of the Medes and Persians (because from this empire the instruments of God's providence went forth to punish the nations).

Mountains do signify governments in Scripture, but the symbolism of the Bible is not stereotyped. Both Christ (Rev 5:5) and Satan (1 Pe 5:8) are comprehended under the figure of a lion, but with vastly different implications. The mountains are none other than Mt. Moriah and the Mount of Olives; the chariots ran through the Valley of Jehoshaphat. They are of brass, not to make them immovable, nor to indicate the firmness of the place where the Lord dwells, nor the stability of God's people or His government, but to indicate the righteousness of God in judgment. (See Ps 36:6.) Note the use of brass in the tabernacle and Temple and its purpose there.

Just as the colors of the horses were significant for the first vision, so they have importance here. There were red, black, white, and grizzled horses, denoting war and bloodshed; calamity and distress; victory and joy; and plagues and pestilence. The horses of the fourth chariot are further characterized as "strong," as though to call special attention to them and their work. When these agencies have finished their task, though it be judgment for the enemies of the Lord, the result will be the good of God's people and His own glory.

THEIR MISSION DESCRIBED

When the prophet asked the interpreting angel for an explanation of the symbolism of the chariots, he was informed that they represented the four winds of heaven which go forth from before the Lord of all the earth. The word *winds* is often translated "spirits" also, and for this reason some prefer to see here four heavenly spirits or angels. We do not incline to this view, for there is no parallel in the Bible. It would be difficult to see the force of just four angels without any further limiting word. The angels of Revelation 7:1 have a designated purpose. According to Psalm 104:4, the winds are the messengers of God; here they are the agencies of God's judgment, the instruments of the divine wrath.

Both the black and white horses went forth to the north country, which is surely Babylon; the grizzled sped forth to the south country or Egypt. Under these two names are comprised the relentless enemies of the people of Israel, but there is a reason for the emphasis on Babylon. True, the remnant had just been delivered from the rule of Babylon through God's judgment on that land through Cyrus. But though conquered by Cyrus, that nation had revolted in the fifth year of Darius, who devastated and depopulated the country. As for Egypt, it revolted against Darius and was reconquered by Xerxes in 485 BC, then, after continued rebellion, by Ochus in 340 BC. Alexander took it from the Persians in 332 BC.

The red horses are passed over in silence. It has been suggested that there was no use made of them—not much blood was shed in this campaign of Darius. There is a difficulty in the passage, for in verse 3 the grizzled are joined with the strong while they are separated in verses 7 and 8 (v. 6 also). Too, the red horses are sent on no mission at all. It must be that those who walk to and fro through the earth through the permission of the Lord are none other than the red horses of the first chariot.

It cannot be said that the task of these horses is unimportant for it is mentioned three times. Wars and bloodshed were to be the order of the day in all places. Well do the prophetic Scriptures reveal how these conditions look on toward the end time. It is impossible to restrict the reference to "the earth" to the land of Palestine. The context calls for a broader scope. The red horses go on to finish the work begun by the other three teams.

The final word in this vision is given by the Lord Himself or the Angel of the Lord who indicates that those who have traveled to the north country have pacified His wrath there. The use of "spirit" in the sense of "wrath" is well attested in Judges 8:3; Ecclesiastes 10:4; and Isaiah 33:11. It is not, as suggested, that God was to cause His Spirit to rest among the exiles to stir their zeal for the rebuilding of the Temple and for the quickening of their hope for the future. We have a clear and pointed statement that God's punishment has already been visited upon Babylon; that it will rest there ultimately in the last days of Israel's national history we have already seen in the visions of the fifth chapter of our book. Babylon must be and will be judged before Messiah reigns in justice and truth.

THE GIFT FROM BABYLON

The series of eight night visions is beautifully and fittingly concluded by a symbolical act which is introduced by the customary prophetic discourse. The transaction was not carried out in vision, but was performed by Zechariah as a symbolical act. The prophet was charged by the Lord to meet three men who had come as a deputation from Babylon to the home of Josiah the son of Zephaniah with a gift from those still in exile for the building of the Temple then under construction. The day mentioned in verse 10 is the same as that of 1:7 in which the prophet had his visions.

The men had brought with them silver and gold for the work. This gift the prophet was to take and make a crown to be set upon the head of Joshua the high priest. Again, as in chapter 3, Joshua is typical of Messiah both by name and office. The crown was to be a composite one (the verb is singular in v. 14), one set above another. (Note Job 31:36 and Rev 19:12.)

The Levitical priesthood had no such provision. A crown did not properly belong to his office, but a mitre did. Here the high priest symbolizes the double office of the coming Messiah (Ps 110:1, 2, 4). Some interpreters suggest that the text originally read "upon the head of Zerubbabel the son of Shealtiel" or "upon the head of Joshua the son of Jehozadak, the high priest, and upon the head of Zerubbabel the son of Shealtiel"; for all such conjectures there is not the slightest shred of evidence. In fact, to have put the crown upon Zerubbabel at all would have been misleading and could have been misunderstood as an attempted restoration of the Davidic dynasty, which was not the purpose of God then. (Read carefully Jer 22:30 and Eze 21:27.) All of God's purposes and plans, for individuals as for nations and the world, are proceeding according to schedule. With God there is no need for haste or confusion.

MESSIAH THE PRIEST-KING

The picture of the Messiah in verses 12 and 13 has been hailed as the most inclusive and complete portrait of the coming King of Israel to be found in the pages of the Old Testament. It is a prophecy of surpassing beauty and importance. Joshua the high priest, crowned and honored, is typical of Messiah the Branch, the Priest-King, and this delineation of the Redeemer brings us to the culmination and consummation of Israel's history. That which follows upon earth's judgments (seen in vv. 1-8) will be the millennial reign of Christ on earth.

The words of Zechariah spoken to the crowned Joshua—"Behold, the man"—are the very words uttered of Christ by Pontius Pilate centuries later in those tragic hours of redemption history. Joshua the high priest in Israel prefigured in his person and office the Man, the Branch, known to us from the revelation given in the third chapter of this book. The Targum, the Aramaic translation and paraphrase, renders the passage thus: "Behold the Man, Messiah is his name, who is to be revealed."

The growing up of the Branch from His place points to His lowly origin from His native land, rather than to His miraculous conception. The figure of growing up is in keeping with the symbol of the "branch."

After the Person and nature of Messiah are stated, then His work is indicated. He will build the Temple of the Lord. This was not the Temple Zerubbabel was building, but a future one, the millennial Temple set forth in Ezekiel 40-48. The building of that Temple by the Messiah is of such importance that it is repeated for great emphasis.

The "he" at the beginning of verse 13 is emphatic. The Priest-King is to bear the glory. After His blessed work of redemption on Calvary, He has borne a measure of glory. (See Ps 110:1; Phil 2:5-11; and Hebrews 2:9.) But He is to bear the millennial glory of the Son of David on His throne, and this on into eternity. As the true Melchizedek (Heb 5:10)

He shall sit and rule upon His throne. Permanence, security, and a finished redemption are all here in this replete word concerning the Messiah. (See Gen 14:18; Ps 110:4; and Heb 5:10; 6:20; and chap. 7.) Messiah will be a Priest upon His own throne.

He is seated now on the Father's throne; this is made abundantly clear by Psalm 110:1; Hebrews 1:3; 8:1; 10:12; 12:2; Revelation 3:21. He will come whose right it is to rule, and then He will sit and rule upon His own throne.

Glad day for which the world has waited so many long years, not knowing that a reign in peace and righteousness is possible only through the Lord Jesus Christ. Israel must yet learn this truth of God. When Messiah sits as Priest-King on His throne, there will be the counsel of peace between them both.

Various explanations have been given to the words "counsel of peace," and "between them both." The counsel of peace is doubtless that counsel which produces peace, that is, the highest in temporal and spiritual blessings. There is no intimation in Scripture that there was rivalry between Joshua and Zerubbabel, so the last phrase of verse 13 cannot refer to them. Other suggestions are that there will be the counsel of peace between the Lord God and the Messiah or between the kingly and priestly attributes of the Messiah or the two characters of ruler and priest united in the Person of the Messiah. We believe that the prophet is probably referring to the priestly and kingly offices and dignities of the Messiah which will be united in Him to bring about the glorious plan of redemption purposed by God from all eternity.

We do well to pause here for adoration as we contemplate this resplendent portrait of the altogether lovely One, the Messiah of Israel. How glorious is He both in His manifold attributes and His abundant works.

We must reemphasize that the entire transaction in the day of Zechariah was symbolical. The proof of this is seen in these particulars: (1) the royal crown did not pertain to any high priest or descendant of Levi—only to the tribe of Judah and David's dynasty; (2) verse 12 speaks of "the man whose name is the Branch," indicating the Messiah as seen in chapter 3; (3) verse 13 states that He will build the Temple of the Lord, a work true only of Christ in the future; (4) verse 13 indicates that He will bear the glory, a fulfillment seen only in Christ; and (5) verse 13 reveals He will be a priest upon His throne, a reference to Christ exclusively as demonstrated by Psalm 110 and Hebrews 7.

THE MEMORIAL IN THE TEMPLE

After the crowning of Joshua, the crown was to be preserved in the

Temple as a memorial of the godly concern on the part of Helem (another name for Heldai), Tobijah, Jedaiah, and Hen (another name for Josiah), for the things of God.

There are those who believe the crown remained in the Temple till Messiah came, and then all was destroyed by the Romans.

But Zechariah, viewing the delegation that had come from Babylon, sees by the Spirit that in a coming day those afar off from the commonwealth of Israel, namely, the Gentiles, will come and build in the Temple of the Lord, and this will be conclusive proof of the divine mission of the Messiah.

First, there will be the return of the dispersed of Israel (Is 60:9), then the conversion of the Gentiles (Is 60:10-11). The root and source of all Israel's misery and woe has been her failure to recognize aright the mission and ministry of the Messiah. Thus now her recognition of Him will bring about her spiritual blessing and material prosperity. His coming and work were assured and unconditional, but her blessing and benefit in it were conditioned upon her obedience. She is warned of rejection if she disbelieves.

IF YE WILL OBEY

Has God not placed all men in the position where they must respond by faith and obedience to His blessed message of grace and love? Nowhere in the Bible can we find that God has set eternal life before men without their necessary response of faith to it. So it is with Israel. How much of individual blessing now for the individual Jew (as national blessing in a coming day for the whole nation) there is the moment the heart obeys the charge of God to believe and trust in the Redeemer, the King-Priest.

FASTING OR PIETY?

THE QUESTIONS ABOUT FASTING

With the seventh chapter of Zechariah we have come to another and distinct division of the prophecy. In the first portion we noted the call of the prophet to the nation to repent and turn to the Lord for His blessing. Then there was granted to him a remarkable series of eight night visions which took him from the hour in which he ministered to the coronation of Messiah over His people and the world.

Since that memorable night, some two years have elapsed, and we are brought to the fourth year of Darius' reign, the year 518 BC. Through the Spirit-directed ministry of Haggai and Zechariah and the encouragement God offered through them, the people had given themselves wholeheartedly to the building of the Temple of the Lord. Jerusalem itself was beginning to take on new life with the erection of new homes in the city. The old marks and scars of the invasion and destruction of Nebuchadnezzar were being slowly erased and removed.

In the month Chislev (the Babylonian name for the ninth month which corresponds to part of November and a portion of December), the city of Bethel sent a deputation to Jerusalem for a twofold purpose: (1) to entreat the Lord's favor and blessing, and (2) to inquire concerning certain national fasts. The view has been offered that the deputation came to the Temple, reading "Bethel" as the "house of God," which is its basic meaning. However, the Temple is never called "Bethel," though it is spoken of as "the house of Jehovah" or "the house of Elohim."

The well-known city, once filled with idolatry, sent its representatives on this important mission. Many of the city's former inhabitants had returned from exile (Ezra 2:28 and Neh 11:31). The names of the men are Babylonian, showing they were returned from exile. The manner in which they intended to entreat (lit., "to stroke the face") the favor of the Lord is not stated, but it might well have been by a sacrifice. We know that the altar had been set up, though the Temple was not yet finished (Ezra 3:3).

The delegation came to inquire of the priests, because it was their duty to give decisions on points of the Law. (See Deu 17:9; even Herod followed this practice, Mt 2:4.) The prophets consulted were Haggai and Zechariah. The people of Bethel wanted to know whether they should go on fasting and mourning in the fifth month as they had been doing for the years of exile, a period which they termed "so many years." Now that the building of the Temple was making progress, they wanted to know whether to continue the fasts that commemorated the past calamities. The fasting being done was irksome and burdensome. Their weeping and separation from food and normal pursuits were wearisome to them.

The fast on the tenth day of the fifth month recalled the burning of Jerusalem in 586 BC. (Cp Jer 52:12-13.) This fast is still the greatest fast day (apart from that of the Day of Atonement) of the Jews. The features of such a fast are mentioned in Joel 2:12, 13, 16. The fasts had been instituted by the nation and had not been ordered of the Lord, but they now wished to know from the Lord whether they should continue them or abolish them. Men are always looking for rules, but God gives them principles whereby they can conduct their lives under the Spirit's direction.

THE LESSON FROM THE PAST

Though the questions had been asked in the first person, "I," the answer of the Lord through Zechariah came to all the people, for they were all interested in and affected by the same condition. The reply of the Lord with one clear stroke tore away all the sham and hypocrisy in their attitude. The people and the priests (for the latter were weary of the fasts too) are informed that all their fasting and mourning were done solely to gratify themselves. God had never instituted the fasts, and He was not taken into account.

The essence of real piety, taking God into account in every detail of life, was sadly lacking. The meaning of a fast is always of more importance than the time element. It is "Why?" not "When?" Their fasting did not please God at all. He demands reality.

Their question had centered about the fast of the fifth month; Zechariah adds a word in the questions of the Lord concerning the seventh month, and in 8:19 he mentions four fasts. All were related to the fall of Jerusalem in 586 BC. In the tenth month Nebuchadnezzar besieged Jerusalem (2 Ki 25:1); in the fourth month the Chaldeans penetrated into the city (2 Ki 25:3-4; Jer 39:2); in the fifth month Nebuzaradan burnt the temple (2 Ki 25:8-9); and in the seventh month Gedaliah, the Jewish governor of Judea, was slain and the remnant fled (2 Ki 25:23-25; Jer 41:1-3). The third day of the seventh month is still observed in orthodox Judaism as the Fast of Gedaliah.

The expected answer to the question in verse 5 is a strong negation, for all their acts were self-centered. Moreover, the same spirit pervaded their feasting that existed in their fasting. Zechariah's rebuke of hypocritical and formal fasting reminds us of the classic words in Isaiah 58:3-8. Self-righteousness and self-satisfaction can never be pleasing to the holy God.

Do the words of Zechariah appear harsh and unfeeling? He is not the first to speak in this manner. The prophets before the exile did similarly. (Note Is 66:1-3; Jer 7:21-24; 25:3-7; and Amos 5:21-27.) The calamities that occasioned the fasts were the results of their disobedience to God's Word through His prophets. Why concern themselves with what He has not commanded, when they should be heeding what He has clearly and repeatedly charged them to do? They should rather obey the words of the prophets spoken in the days before the exile when the land was settled and inhabited. These are more important than all their self-imposed fasts. God desires obedience more than all else.

The south referred to is the mountains of Judea (Jos 15:21) and the lowland (Shephelah country) is west of Judah (Jos 15:33).

How much better it is to obey the words of the Lord than to ease the conscience by formal observances occasioned by judgments visited upon sin. They fasted because of their calamities, but these were brought upon them by their sins. Therefore, the cause of their fasts was their sins. If these were removed, then the fasting would be unnecessary.

EXHORTATIONS TO GODLINESS

Lest they had forgotten the burden and message of the former prophets, Zechariah outlines the path of godliness set before their fathers. Administration of justice was to be according to truth. God hates unrighteous judgment, for He is the righteous Judge of all the earth (Gen 18:25). Kindness and pity are to be the order of the day between a man and his neighbor. Public and private relationships alike are to conform to the pattern set forth by the compassionate Lord. The Law of Moses and the prophets clearly espouse the cause of the helpless and unfortunate, namely, widows, orphans, strangers, and the poor. They were warned not to store up feelings of resentment and bitterness against their neighbors.

Their relationship to God could not be right as long as their actions were not right one toward another (Mt 5:23-24). Faith without piety is a mockery of both God and man. Religion without morality is useless; morality without true religion is baseless and without proper foundation. God seeks truth in the inward parts and expects it to be manifested to those about us. The prophet Zechariah had no new message to declare to them, for the principles of God's righteous government are eternal. Man need never be in doubt as to the course of life and conduct that pleases God and assures of His favor and blessing.

THE PUNISHMENT FOR DISOBEDIENCE

But though repeatedly warned and lovingly entreated of the Lord, their forefathers in preexilic times refused to hear the all-wise exhortations of their God. Their stubbornness of heart and unwillingness to obey are strongly presented by four different expressions.

First, they would not hear; then they pulled away their shoulder. The turning a stubborn shoulder is a figure from the animal world; it is taken from the manner of the ox who refuses the yoke. (See Neh 9:29.) The more they refused the word of truth, the more earnestly the messengers of the Lord pleaded with them.

Then they stopped their ears that they might not hear the preaching at all. (Cp. Is 6:10 and Jer 7:26.) Such opposition to the will of God would have been sufficient to have incurred His righteous wrath, but they heaped up further impenitence unto the day of wrath and judgment.

Finally, they hardened their hearts like an adamant stone. The climax is reached here. Having refused light repeatedly, their hearts became more and more hardened, cold, and unresponsive.

Spiritual hardening (sclerosis) is as real as physical but infinitely more disastrous. When the citadel of the life, the heart, is infected, the case is sad and desperate indeed. (Note Eze 3:9 and 11:19.) And their opposition was against the Law and the word of God through the prophets by His Spirit.

There is important truth here that we must not pass by. First, you will mark well that Zechariah places the revelation and message of the prophets on exactly the same standing and footing as the venerated Law of Moses. The Bible knows nothing of degrees of authority in the revelation of God; the words of the prophets are as authoritative as those of Moses. Both issued forth from God Himself (2 Ti 3:16-17). Note also the twofold medium for the impartation of the mind and will of God: the Spirit of God and the prophets, the divine and the human elements. By the former prophets are meant (as in 1:4) the prophets before the Babylonian captivity.

For such continued disobedience, there could be but one result, and this was great wrath from the Lord. The greatness of the wrath can be seen in the great punishment inflicted. (See 2 Ch 36:16.) Divine retribution in infinite righteousness overtook His erring people. Just as the Lord had cried unto them by His prophets, so often and so patiently, yet they would not hear, so they would cry to Him in their distress for deliverance, and He would not hear. All know how sad the plight of the little one is who cries for help of its mother and has a deaf ear turned to its need. How much sadder the condition of the rebellious nation who would cry out for help in their desperation, only to find that the Lord had turned His ear from them (Is 1:15 and Mic 3:4; see also Jer 11:11 and 14:12).

Instead of the Lord hearkening to their prayer, He scattered them with the violence of the whirlwind among all the nations whom they had not known. In the day of Zechariah's ministry, the scattering had already taken place to Assyria and Babylonia, and this is the primary reference in the passage.

But the text has a greater dispersion in mind as well, consequent upon their great disobedience in rejecting the promised One, their Messiah. From the Assyrian and Babylonian exiles many of the nation continued on in captivity and wandered to other lands as well. Wrath was come upon them to the full. Nations who had no dealings with them would not be likely to extend kindnesses to them or manifest compassion upon them.

As a result of the Babylonian captivity the land was left desolate. In God's remarkable providence, no foreign powers took possession of it; when the rightful inhabitants were absent, it was preserved against the day of their return after seventy years. Though the judgment was of God and though He used the enemy as His instruments for punishment of His wayward people, yet they, the people of Israel themselves, are charged with having made the land desolate. It was because of their sins. The responsibility for the desolation was theirs. The pleasant land is literally the "land of desire," that land which God delighted to give to His people. (See Jer 3:19.)

Not even man-made instruments of destruction in the way of bombs and the like can be as deadly and desolating as sin. It made a ruin and a desolation of the delightsome land of Canaan. We can learn from this no more important truth than the ruinous work of sin in human life.

SHOULD THEY NOT HEAR THE WORDS?

The theme of fasting with which chapter 7 is occupied is one quite familiar among Jews. Their religious calendar has its abundance of days of fasting. Yet the underlying lesson of them all is that they commemorate disasters and calamities that have come upon them in their national history because of sin. How much wiser would it have been (and would it be now) for them to hearken to and obey the message of God. Should they not rather have heeded diligently the words spoken by the prophets? But the case is sadder still if they heed not the words of the Prophet, their Messiah, the Lord Jesus Christ.

Cheerful Feasts for Fasts

JERUSALEM THE CITY OF TRUTH

Chapter 8 continues the thought of the previous chapter. The prophet emphasized in chapter 7 the need of obedience from the fate of their fathers; now he exhorts them in chapter 8 to the same condition of heart by placing before them promises of God's future blessing. This section parallels that of 1:14-17, just as chapter 7 answered to 1:1-6.

God affirms twice in verse 2 His great jealousy for Zion. The root meaning of the verb is "to glow, burn." God's warm heart seeks the blessing of His people, but must at the same time visit with great wrath those who are their enemies.

These promises remind us of those in the first two chapters of the book. God is so determined to return to Zion in blessing that He speaks of it as though already accomplished. There can be but one result when the Lord thus dwells among His people: it will be holiness and truth. God's ideal for Zion has always been that she should be the city of truth and holiness. (See Is 1:26; contrast with Is 1:10 and Rev 11:8.) Blessed condition is that which conforms to the will of the heart of God.

PEACE AND SECURITY

When the spiritual issues are right in Israel, God always accompanies them with material blessings. Spiritual peace will be the forerunner of physical peace. Old men and old women with staff in hand will be able to sit peacefully and unafraid in the streets of Jerusalem. The streets of the city will be full of playing boys and girls. The intermediate ages are not excluded, but automatically included. Wars will not cut off the lives of her people in their youth. Her population will reach advanced age. The presence of boys and girls playing in the streets indicates both security and many descendants. Long life and abundant offspring are promised for obedience throughout the Old Testament. (Note Ex 20:12; Deu 4:40; 5:16, 33; 6:2; 33:6, 24.)

There are those who think these promises were fulfilled to the letter in the time of the Maccabees. Scripture reveals these features are to be found in the millennial age. (Cp. Is 65:20, 22.)

Zechariah's words portray conditions so different from what Israel has met and known through the centuries that the remnant in the day of fulfillment (and doubtless the contemporaries of the prophet as well) may be inclined to be skeptical of the performance of them. But though these promises may appear impossible with man, nothing is impossible with God (Gen 18:14; Mt 19:26). They dare not limit the power of the Holy One of Israel. (See Ps 78:19, 20, 41.) Ours and theirs is the God of the impossible.

RESTORATION OF THE LAND

Any future and millennial blessing for Israel must be predicated and founded upon her restoration and return to the land. The prophet, therefore, foretells their regathering from dispersion. The east country and west country do not refer to Babylonia and Egypt exclusively, as some would have it, but they represent every quarter of the earth. Dispersion and exile under the Assyrians and Babylonians were to the east, but this is a future and worldwide scattering as confirmed by abundant scripture testimony. (Read carefully Is 11:11-12; 43:5-6; Eze 37:21; and Amos 9:14-15.)

From worldwide dispersion God will bring His people back to the land. We see only a preview of it today. The designation "west" is especially appropriate, because the Jews are mainly found in lands lying to the west of Palestine. But mark well that the return includes spiritual restoration to the Lord. (See Jer 30:22 and 31:33.) The transaction will be done in truth and righteousness, according to the truth of His Word and in agree-

ment with His righteousness. It will mark the mutual relationship between God and Israel.

ENCOURAGEMENT IN THE WORK

We not only rejoice in these prospects for Israel, but we can see the
wisdom of God in presenting them here. There need be no fear that
Zechariah has wandered far afield from the original matter of fasting by
dwelling on the tragedy of the past and looking forward to the glory of the
future; he now brings all this to bear very pointedly on the situation of the
then present hour.

Every part of the truth revealed was meant to fit them better for the task
then in hand. So Zechariah exhorts them to be strong for the work before
them and for the days ahead. In the fourth year of Darius (7:1) the people were in the midst of their work of rebuilding and needed encouragement. The words of the prophets Haggai and Zechariah were directed
toward this very objective; therefore, the people do well to heed them.

The mention of the foundation of the house of the Lord being laid that
the Temple might be built has special reference to the resumption of the
work of building (Hag 1:15) to carry it through to a conclusion. We
know this had not been the result of their first attempts at rebuilding.
Now it was to be different, and the work was to be completed. But they
must be strengthened of the Lord for the task.

They are further reminded of the state of affairs in the nation before
they resumed work on the house of God. Before those days, there was not
sufficient profit or return for their labor; neither man nor beast was bene-
fited from the work. (See Hag 1:6, 9-11; and 2:16-19.) Added to this
distressing condition was internal and civil strife as well as the enemy
from without. Safety and security were to be found nowhere. The oppressing Samaritans (Ezra 4:1-5) were joined by other neighbors who harassed
the small remnant. Too, the expedition of Cambyses to Egypt through
Palestine must have caused them some distress. All in all, life was insecure and uncertain. When God's affairs are not cared for, our own fare
badly.

But now God is ready to bless their obedience to His command to build.
The earth will now yield its increase; the vine, which is here called the
seed of peace because it flourishes in times of peace, will give its fruit. No
longer will the heavens withhold their dew, so needed and helpful in dry
countries where rain is scanty. The Lord will shower His material blessings upon the remnant, just as He withheld them in the time of disobedience. Moreover, they shall be a blessing to the nations instead of a curse

among the nations. It is not said that they were a curse to the nations; their name was used by the nations to utter a curse.

What a reversal this would be in their condition: instead of the nations making their name the formula for a curse, calling down upon their enemies as bad a fate as Israel's (Jer 24:9; 29:18, 22), their name would be the pattern for blessing, men wishing their friends as happy a portion as that of Judah and Israel. (See Gen 48:20; Mic 5:7; and Zep 3:20.)

This all looks on to the fullest accomplishment in the time of the reunited nation at the time of the consummation for Israel of her national hopes and promises. In view of such present and future blessing, she is exhorted (as in v. 9) to be strong and fearless. When the heart is weak through fear, the hands cannot be strong. But how heartening are all God's sure words of promise!

GODLY PRECEPTS

Zechariah reminds them that when their fathers provoked the Lord to wrath and persisted in their sinful ways, the Lord determined to chasten them and carried through His purpose. Will He not assuredly do them good when obedient, when He delights to bless rather than judge? (Cp. Jer 31:28.)

God outlines again the proper moral conditions that must exist among them (7:9-10). Truth must characterize the dealings of a man with his fellowman; they must make equitable judgments which help to bring about peace as they administer the Law in their cities. In Oriental towns the gate or the space near it was the place of customary gathering and the place where justice was to be administered. (See Gen 19:1 and Amos 5:10, 12.) Above all, the heart is to be kept from devising evil against another; no root of hatred is to be allowed to grow.

Since swearing falsely was a sin of the day (5:3-4), the godly are to hate any false oath. Because God hates injustice, evil, and the false oath, they are to hate and avoid them too. Again the prophet joins inseparably piety and morality. Believers of any age or dispensation are expected to maintain good works to commend to others the way of obedience, life, and joy.

FASTS BECOME FEASTS

If the contemporaries of the prophet had come to the conclusion that the Lord was not to answer their question on fasting after all, they were mistaken, for he deals straightforwardly and fully with the issue. The fast of the fourth month for the taking of Jerusalem, the fast of the fifth month for the destruction of the city and Temple, the fast of the seventh month for the assassination of Gedaliah, and the fast of the tenth month for the beginning of the siege of Jerusalem, these all were to be turned into cheerful feasts marked by joy and gladness. And the condition upon which the change can be realized is set forth: love for truth and peace with all this implies.

It is strange that some interpreters have felt that the prophet gave no clear word to abolish the fasts. How could he have made the case more clear? Nor can we judge wholly from Jewish practice in the matter, for their customs did not conform invariably with the clear pronouncements of the Word of God. According to Jewish tradition, when the nation was in peace and prosperity the fasts were suspended; when they were in trouble the fasts were reinstituted. Since AD 70 the Jews keep the principal fasts of the seventeenth day of the fourth month, the ninth day of the fifth month, the third day and the tenth day of the seventh month, and the tenth day of the tenth month.

ISRAEL A BLESSING TO ALL NATIONS

The eye of the prophet looks on to the hour of Israel's greatest joy and blessing in the Millennium, that era in which Israel will fulfill the purpose of God for her which has always been in His heart. Once Israel is restored, world conversion follows. (Read carefully Ps 67.)

Displaying godly zeal and concern for others, the peoples and inhabitants of many cities will invite one another to go up quickly to entreat the favor of the Lord in Jerusalem. They willingly and earnestly leave their own cities to come to God's. There will be many peoples and strong nations, not just the small nation of Israel, who will yearn to worship and entreat the Lord of all the earth in that day. (See Is 2:3; 45:14-15, 23-24; 56:6-7; 60:3; 66:23; Jer 16:19; Mic 4:2-3; Zechariah has already indicated blessing for other nations in 2:11.)

Then Israel will be the head and leader of the nations; this is graphically set forth by our prophet under the picture of ten men (which is the indefinite use to express a large number) of all nations taking hold of the skirt of a Jew and expressing their desire to go with him, for they have heard that God is with Israel. The taking hold of the skirt is not so much a gesture of entreaty or desire for help, or an indication of a feeling of inferiority, but is an expression of their longing to enjoy the blessings and privileges possessed by the Jew.

The skirt (the hem of the garment) of the Jew (see Num 15:38 and Deu 22:12) was distinctive; in a coming day that blessing enjoyed by them in the Lord will be even more distinctive. We need not emphasize that this was scarcely true through Cyrus' deliverance of the Jews from Babylon. In the earthly reign of the Messiah, whom Cyrus prefigured, the Jew will be the missionary to the nations of the earth.

"GOD IS WITH YOU"

There were times in Israel's history when she was living in conformity to His will and it could be rightly said, "God is with you." When the Lord dwelt in such manifest glory and power and blessing in the tabernacle of Moses and then the Temple of Solomon, the nations could have said with warrant, "God is with you." In the days of the earthly sojourn and ministry of the Messiah of Israel, their Immanuel (God with us), it could properly be said of God's ancient people, "God is with you."

But lo, these hundreds of years of exile have passed since she rejected Messiah as King, Saviour, and Lord, and God has not been with her in fullness of blessing as He so desires. But when the individual Jew turns in faith to the Lord Jesus Christ as Saviour and Messiah, that moment he knows the unspeakable joy of the truth, "God is with you," and in truth God the Holy Spirit indwells him also. And whether it pleases us or not, we must remember that God's Word is clear that the restoration of an apostate world to God will be through the agency of Israel. When God is with Israel, the nations will be turned to the Lord.

17

WAR AND THE PRINCE OF PEACE

THE FALL OF SYRIA

LIBERAL AND DESTRUCTIVE CRITICISM of the Bible, adept in its divisive tactics through long practice on the Pentateuch, Isaiah, and Daniel, would have us believe that chapters 9 to 14 were not from the hand of Zechariah, but from some unknown writer. The arguments, when carefully studied, are sometimes far-fetched, sometimes puerile, always baseless.

The testimony of the oldest translation of the Old Testament (which is the Greek) and the compilers of the Jewish canon are in favor of the genuineness of these chapters. The arguments of the liberals are untenable and can be refuted. We can rest assured that the Spirit of God used the one author for all fourteen chapters. A healthy scriptural supernaturalism is the best antidote for all skeptical naturalism.

Chapters 1 to 8 referred in the main, though not exclusively as we have already repeatedly shown, to Zechariah's own time. The goal in view was encouragement for the rebuilding of the Temple. Chapters 9 to 14, which form the second part of the book, deal chiefly with the future, and were probably written a long time after the first eight chapters. Chapters 1-8 deal with Israel when she was under Medo-Persian rule; chapters 9 and 10 when she was governed by Greece; chapter 11 when she was under Roman domination; and chapters 12 to 14 when she shall be in the last days of her national history.

In verses 1 to 8 of chapter 9, the campaign of Alexander the Great is sketched. His successes are recounted in verses 1-7, and verse 8 notes the deliverance of Jerusalem. After the Battle of Issus, Alexander quickly conquered Damascus, Sidon, Tyre (after seven months it was burned), Gaza, Ashkelon, Ashdod, and Ekron. The course of his victories in 332 BC was from northern Syria south by the valley of the Orontes River to Damascus, then along the Phoenician and Philistine coast.

The title of the "burden of the word of the Lord" is unusual and found only in 12:1 and Malachi 1:1. It has been translated "utterance" or "oracle," but "burden" is best to convey the thought of a threatening prediction of coming judgment. (See Is 13:1.)

The prophet foretold punishment against the land of Hadrach first. Some have taken Hadrach as a name for the Persian Empire; others are uncertain as to whether a country, city, or king is meant. It has been identified as Hattarika, a city mentioned several times in the cuneiform inscriptions. It was between Hamath and Aleppo; the cities mentioned with it show its location must have been somewhere in the vicinity of Damascus. The city must have been of some importance, for the Assyrians waged three campaigns against it to conquer it between 772 and 755 BC.

Though the stroke would fall upon Hadrach, its ultimate goal was really the capital city, Damascus. Native rule was never restored to this important city after its capture by Alexander the Great. The effect of Alexander's conquests on Israel and the surrounding nations was to be one of consternation and wonder; their eyes would be turned to the Lord. We know that the Jews under Jaddua the high priest refused to swear allegiance to the conqueror. Jeremiah had prophesied against Damascus and Hamath even after Nebuchadnezzar had invaded Judah (Jer 49:23-27); and Jeremiah (25:20) and Ezekiel (25:15-17) had pronounced judgment on Philistia.

Now Zechariah predicts judgment on them by the hands of the Greeks under Alexander. Hamath also, which bordered on Damascus, was to experience the same fate. Antiochus IV renamed this city Epiphania after himself. It is still an important commercial center, the modern Hamma on the Orontes River about 120 miles north of Damascus. (Cp. Amos 6:14.)

THE DOOM OF PHOENICIA

With Syria subdued, Alexander pressed his campaign southward to the cities of Phoenicia. Tyre is mentioned as the more important of the two cities, for it had outstripped the older Sidon. It was to be taken in 332 BC though it was very wise in its own sight.

Tyrians were famous for their worldly wisdom. (Note Eze 28:3, 4, 5, 12, 17.) The wisdom of the successful merchant had carried over into diplomacy also. Verse 3 shows how she displayed her worldly wisdom. She fortified herself to the best of her ability and accumulated silver and gold.

Tyre was the center of Phoenician commerce and wealth. The word *stronghold* forms in the original Hebrew a play on words with the name Tyre. The Assyrians besieged it unsuccessfully for five years, the Babylonians under Nebuchadnezzar for thirteen years. The pagan historian

Diodorus Siculus wrote: "Tyre had the greatest confidence, owing to her insular position and fortifications, and the abundant stores she had prepared." Though Alexander was the instrument God used for the doom of Tyre, He is declared as dispossessing her, smiting her wealth in the sea, and devouring her with fire. Her people were to be sent into exile. Alexander built a bridge of the ruins of the old city from the mainland to the island, then besieging the island for seven months, he captured it, slew thousands, enslaved others, crucified still others, and finally set the city on fire. Wealth, strong fortifications, and all were cast into the sea (Eze 26:4-12 and 27:27). No power can prosper apart from the living God.

THE CONQUEST OF PHILISTIA

Of the five Philistine cities, Gath alone is omitted in the mention of the judgment that befell them. It has been suggested that Gath was more inland and not on the direct route of the army. Ashkelon and Gaza would realize their helplessness to oppose the invader and would be struck with terror.

Ashkelon lost its population, and Gaza was reduced after a siege of a few months. Ekron, the farthest north of the Philistine cities and nearest to Tyre, had hoped Tyre would successfully withstand Alexander on his way to Egypt, only to have that hope dashed to the ground with the unexpected fall of Tyre.

Special mention is made by a contemporary of Alexander that the king of Gaza was brought alive to the conqueror after the city was taken; the satrap, or petty "king" of the city, was bound to a chariot and dragged around the city to his death. Thus did the city lose its independence. For these cities see Jeremiah 25:20; Amos 1:6-8; and Zephaniah 2:4-7.

Ashdod was to lose its native population during this invasion, being replaced by a bastard or mongrel people. It was Alexander's policy to mingle different conquered peoples. The loss of political independence, the splendor of their cities, and the glory of their temples would mean the crushing blow to Philistine pride. That in which they trusted most and gloried would be cut off.

Now Zechariah foretells the conversion to the Lord of the Philistines in the millennial reign of Christ. They will forsake their idolatrous ways and be a remnant unto God. Idolatrous sacrifices were eaten with the blood (Eze 33:25); this was forbidden by God. (See Gen 9:4; Lev 7:26; 17:10, 12; and Ac 15:29.) The abominations referred to are the things sacrificed to idols. Once cleansed from their idolatrous practices, they will be incorporated into the Jewish commonwealth, as a chieftain in Judah or as the Jebusites. The latter were the ancient inhabitants of Jerusalem who were incorporated into Israel, living with the people of Judah in the capital as equals and not as a conquered nation (Jos 15:63).

During all this turmoil and strife in Syria, Phoenicia, and Philistia, God promises that He will encamp about His house to protect from the army of the enemy and will keep His people under His watchful and preserving eye. The reference to "my house" has been understood as the Temple, the Holy Land, and the people of Israel; the last is preferable, though all are ultimately included. As a matter of fact, Alexander passed by Jerusalem more than once in his campaigns without harming it, though he punished the Samaritans.

Then Zechariah, by the prophetic law of suggestion, passes immediately from the near future to the final deliverance in the far future when Israel would be delivered from every oppressor. This city will be protected against its final enemies and their invasion (chaps. 12 and 14). See Isaiah 60:18 and Ezekiel 28:24. There is no safety comparable to that enjoyed under the gracious eye of our loving God.

MESSIAH AND HIS RULE

The prophet turns his gaze now from contemplating the movements of the ruthless conqueror, Alexander, to view the Person and work in humiliation and then in exaltation of the coming King of Israel. That the reference is to Messiah is abundantly attested by Matthew 21:5 and all the early Jewish writers. Both Jews and Christians have recognized this to be a Messianic prophecy of great importance. (Cp. Is 9:1-7 for a parallel passage.)

Zion and Jerusalem, representing the nation, are called upon to rejoice and exult in the coming of this glorious King. Nations trembled at the coming of Alexander, but the people of Israel are enjoined to rejoice greatly at the presence of King Messiah, for He comes not only to them but for them, for their benefit and salvation.

The Spirit of God dwells lovingly and satisfyingly upon His threefold qualifications for His office. He is just or righteous; this is the basic attribute of the Messiah (Is 45:21; 53:11; and Jer 23:5-6; see also Mal 4:2). The word translated "having salvation" is literally "saved." Most modern commentators take it that He was delivered or saved from the cross after His death by the resurrection from the dead. Others suggest that it be rendered in an active sense, "saving" or "Saviour." We prefer to understand the passive sense of the word as "entrusted with salvation."

The righteous King works out a righteous salvation for His own. His perfect work issues from His perfect Person and purpose. The Grecian Alexander came to break down and destroy; the righteous Messiah comes to save and redeem. The earthly king came with pomp and pride; the Lord from heaven came riding upon a lowly ass. The riding upon an ass reveals lowliness of outward condition and of inward disposition as well. He came in peace, for the ass was the animal of peace (Gen 49:11). Worldly pomp and display were foreign to Him.

Verse 9 covers the first coming of the Messiah; verse 10 indicates His purpose and accomplishments in the second coming. Between these verses come the centuries of the Church age in which we live. This age was not foreseen by the prophet.

When the lowly King comes again, He will inaugurate His rule by putting down all warfare and strife. The chariot, horse, and battle bow represent all instruments and weapons of warfare. Messiah removes these from His people and from all the nations; no reliance is to be placed in these carnal instruments. The way of peace is otherwise.

Once these weapons are done away with, the Messiah speaks peace authoritatively to the nations. He commands it and it is brought to pass. His word of authority accomplishes what man could never bring about by his own schemes. His kingdom of peace will extend throughout the world.

The references in "sea to sea" and "from the river to the ends of the earth" cannot be restricted to the Holy Land. From Psalm 72:8 and other parallel passages, from the absence of the definite article in these phrases of our verse, and from the general force of the prophetic Scriptures, we are driven to the conclusion that the reign of Messiah will be centered in the Holy Land and will extend to the ends of the earth. His will be a universal reign.

THE VICTORIES OF THE MACCABEES

Zechariah passes from the contemplation of the glorious and peaceful reign of the Messiah to another scene of conflict and war, such as was before us in the first portion of chapter 9. He addresses Zion and promises that on the ground of the blood of her covenant, God would set free her prisoners from the waterless pit.

What is the blood of her covenant? It has been suggested that the covenant is the Mosaic, and it does speak of a time when God entered into covenant relationship with His people. That was a legal covenant, and Israel's failure in it caused the forfeiting of blessing. Perhaps the covenant with Abraham is even more in view here. (See Gen 15:9-12, 18-20; for the blood of the Mosaic covenant, note Ex 24:8 and Heb 9:18-20.)

The prisoners are those of Israel who are still in Babylon and have not returned under the permission of Cyrus. Cisterns without water were used as prisons (Gen 37:24, Joseph; and Jeremiah 38:6, Jeremiah). There is no ground here for the restitution heresy with its teaching of a second chance after death for the ungodly consigned to the pit.

The prophet exhorts the exiles, before whom God has placed such promises and hope, to return to the stronghold or Zion, for He will abundantly bless them in place of their former distress. In spite of unpromising conditions He is willing to do this for them even today.

Verses 13 to 17 refer to the conflicts and victories of the Maccabean age when they were successful against Antiochus Epiphanes in the second century BC (Dan 11:32; also Dan 8:9-14). God's gracious protection is promised them. Judah is likened to the Lord's bow and Ephraim to His arrow; with these He destroys the enemy. God's people are also compared to the sword of a mighty man; they shall be irresistible. This was fulfilled in the Maccabean wars. God would appear on their behalf in mighty power: His lightnings, thunder, and whirlwinds of the south (Is 21:1; these were the most violent) would aid them.

Their triumph would be a decisive one, for they would tread down their enemies as weak and contemptible slingstones; in a figure they are seen also as filled with the blood of the enemy as the horns of the altar and the sacrificial bowls in the Temple were (Ex 29:12 and Lev 4:18).

The ultimate benefit to Israel will be spiritual deliverance after physical victory; she will be the flock of the Lord and as a glittering crown (not like the slingstones) on His land. The prophet exclaims over the goodness, beauty, and prosperity which the Lord displays and views the people in a time of peaceful prosperity in the fulfillment of their Messianic promises.

BLESSINGS OF MESSIAH'S RULE

EXHORTATION TO PRAYER

Chapter 10 is closely connected with the previous one: the blessings indicated in 9:17, which will make the people to flourish and rejoice in the Lord, will result from their looking only unto Him. The rain is to be prayed for which will bring about the fulfillment of the bountiful increase of grain and new wine.

The commandment is not so much a rhetorical device to bring the truth more emphatically before those addressed, but it is meant to impress upon them that the Lord will give them the rain in answer to believing prayer (Jer 10:13 and 14:22). They are not to seek rain by magical and forbidden means but from the Lord.

The time of the latter rain is spring (about March or April); this rain ripens the grain (Joel 2:23). God's blessings on Israel are compared to rain (Ho 6:1-3); here are included all material blessings, emblems of the spiritual ones. The lightnings which precede the rain will assure her of the rain, and God will give her torrential rains to supply the need of every heart in Israel. Our God is a bountiful Giver, but He must be entreated and trusted implicitly.

WARNINGS AGAINST IDOLATRY

But Israel has had sad experience in the past in trying to achieve material prosperity by means disallowed of God. She resorted in her sin to the teraphim, the diviners, and the false dreamers. Instead of bringing blessing, these wrought spiritual and material havoc in Israel.

The teraphim were household gods used for the purposes of divination, probably in the form of human beings. They were like the household gods of the Romans. (See Gen 31:19, 30.) They were kept at shrines (Judg 17:5) and in private homes (1 Sa 19:13, 16). Much has been made of the fact that the Jews were not guilty of idolatry after the exile as they had been before that time.

It is thought that their marriages with heathen women presented an ever-present source of danger, hence the warnings here. Note Nehemiah 6:10-14 (false prophets); Malachi 3:5 (sorcerers); and Acts 5:36-37; 13:6 (false prophets).

The passages just cited are not analogous with the one now under study in Zechariah. The prophet is referring to the sins which had brought about their exile. All these unlawful means had led them astray and deceived them with their palpable falsehoods. Their assurances and comfort were empty. For such indulgences both kingdoms of God's people were scattered like sheep; they wandered into exile with the loss of their native kings. These practices are again warned against as those which occasioned their downfall and as those which must be forsaken completely. These could not give the temporal and spiritual blessings they sought, but the Lord could.

How sad indeed was their lot to be without the aid of their rightful shepherds and without the voice of God through His prophets during the weary years of their dispersion. But those shepherds, rulers of God's people, who aided them in their idolatry and were leaders in it were to know only the wrath and displeasure of God for so misleading the sheep.

The he-goats, who head the flock, are the civil leaders who are to blame in all this departure from the Lord. These civil leaders, since the native kings are gone, are those of the nations who oppressed and persecuted the poor flock. God will visit these tyrants with His sore judgment but will be gracious in His dealings with His flock.

The figure of the sheep is replaced by one of a horse richly equipped for the battle. Such a horse is shown special grooming and care; so Israel will be the special object of God's providential care. When she is in the place of obedience, there is no good thing which the Lord will withhold from her. The fulfillment of these things is not to be seen in the victories of the Maccabean warriors, as some have conjectured, but in the days of the rule of the Messiah of Israel, and to this theme the prophet now turns our gaze.

THE PROMISE OF THE MESSIAH

The view has been advanced that this verse 4 is not appropriate here, but it is most fitting in the context where the prophet has just indicated the lack of a king. Moreover, the Aramaic Targum of the Jews referred it to King Messiah. The phrase "from him" occurs four times in the verse to give the strongest possible emphasis. The one referred to is not the Lord, though it is true that all blessings ultimately issue from Him, but Judah who has been before us in the previous verse. Not from the foreign rulers spoken of will the Messiah come, but from the house of Judah.

The cornerstone, the battle bow, and the nail are figures of the Messiah to represent His qualities of stability, dependability, and strength. The cornerstone speaks of the ruler or leader on whom the building of government rests figuratively. (See Judg 20:2; 1 Sa 14:38; and Is 19:13.) It is a well-known symbol of the Messiah. (Cp. 1 Co 3:11 and 1 Pe 2:6, quoting Is 28:16.) The nail refers to the large peg in an Oriental tent on which were hung many valuables. On the Messiah will rest the hope and trust of His people. He will be the worthy support of the nation, the altogether dependable One, the true Eliakim. (Note Is 22:23-24.) The battle-bow stands for all implements of war and might. Messiah is the great military commander of His people; He is the Man of war (Ex 15:3). This will be clearly and openly manifest when He comes to rule (Ps 45:4-5).

A number of interpreters have seen a fourth designation of Messiah in the role of "ruler." This view follows a kindred word in the Ethiopic language, rendered "negus." But this will not hold for the Hebrew; we must translate it "oppressor" or "exactor" as in so many other instances in the Old Testament. It is not another title for the Messiah; rather it sets forth the results of His work and ministry as the One indicated in the previous titles. Because He is the cornerstone, nail, and battle bow, every oppressor and exactor will go forth from the midst of God's people. The addition of the word *together* makes it all the more emphatic. We understand it then, that the work of the Messiah will bring about the removal of every exactor from Israel. The thought is related to that predicted in 9:8.

VICTORY IN THE LORD

Again the prophet looks on to Messianic times and pictures the glorious victory of God's people over their foes. Since the Messiah is so definitely in the midst of all these events, it is difficult for us to agree with those who insist that these victories are only those of the Maccabean era, judging from the fact that this was the theme of the predictions in 9:11-17.

Those who have been before us previously as sheep of the flock, then as a richly adorned horse of battle, are now depicted as invincible warriors. They shall be empowered of the Lord to trample their enemies under foot in the conflict; the Lord's presence with them will be in clear evidence. Oriental armies made much of cavalry (Eze 38:4 and Dan 11:40), but these will not be able to stand against the onslaught of the people of God.

The house of Judah and the house of Joseph speak of the reunited nation. Thus it is clear that a future return from exile after that of Babylon is intended by the prophet.

The name "Joseph" is used in different senses. It is a designation for Joseph individually as in Genesis 49:22-26. In Judges 1:22-23 the name has a tribal connotation; however, there are instances, as in our present passage, where the term is used, like Ephraim, for the tribes of the Northern Kingdom. The promise given is heartwarming indeed, for they are told that they will not only be restored to the land in mercy, but they will be as though God had never cast them off. God knows how to erase the years that the cankerworm has eaten. His ear will be sensitive and attuned to the believing cry as they return to the Lord in obedience.

Ephraim is now pointed out for blessing, for his exile had been longer than that of Judah. Like Judah, he will experience the victory granted of his God and will exult greatly as though with wine. His children also shall experience and witness the God-given victory and rejoice with him. The joy of the Lord will be given to all His people.

THE NATION REGATHERED

As we have already indicated, these manifestations of the power of God on their behalf presuppose their regathering and restoration to the land. This is now elaborated upon by the prophet. The Lord will hiss for His people and will gather and redeem them. This regathering cannot be restricted to the ten tribes, because many of them were still in exile; for the regathering looks far into the future after a worldwide dispersion of Israel. As beekeepers call their bees together by a whistle, so the Lord is represented as signaling for His ancient people. (See Is 5:26 and 7:18.)

Nor will their number be few, for they shall increase in that future day as they multiplied in the time of Egyptian bondage. (Cp. Ex 1:7; Jer 30:19-20; and Eze 36:11.)

Regathering, redemption, and repopulation are all promised here. Our position that the prophet is foretelling more than a return from Assyrian or Babylonian exile, is definitely confirmed by the declaration of verse 9. Zechariah predicts that the Lord will sow His people among the nations, and in those far-off lands they will remember the Lord.

The word *sow* is never used in a bad or judgmental sense. It has the thought of spreading and multiplying. Here it is revealed that God had a special purpose in thus sowing them among the peoples of the earth. In those places they would bring to mind the goodness and blessings of the Lord in former days and return wholeheartedly to God. (Note Deu 30:1-3; Jer 31:27; Ho 2:23; and Mic 5:7.)

Upon their return to the land they will live both politically and spiritually. Their children will survive with them and enter into the good things prepared of the Lord for His people. Fathers and children alike shall witness the restoration to the land. The areas from which they shall return are mentioned as Egypt and Assyria.

Some seek to press these geographical designations here, but they must admit that there is no record of any of the ten tribes in exile in Egypt. They think it probable, therefore, that many fled there at the invasion of Tiglath-pileser at the time of the decline of the Northern Kingdom. Too, they maintain, when Ptolemy tried to conquer Syria and carried away many captives, there must have been some from the north among them. Others believe that many from the ten tribes must have fled to Egypt when their kingdom fell. Of course, those who had remained on in Assyria from their number would also return.

Our position is that these two lands, having been the inveterate enemies of the people of Israel in ancient times, stand now representatively, one in the south and the other in the north, for the nation's dispersion in all lands. God will bring them back and resettle them in Gilead and Lebanon, which formed their original territory on both sides of the Jordan (Jer 50:19 and Mic 7:14-15). All the land is comprehended here. Because of their great numbers (v. 8), no place will be found for them in the land. (See Is 49:20 and 54:3.)

Since Egypt, the typical oppressor of Israel, has been pointed out, Zechariah dwells further on the Exodus as the typical deliverance. (Note Is 11:11-16.) Just as the Lord went before them and smote the waters of the Red Sea, causing them to go over dryshod, so He will dry up every hindrance in the path of their restoration and return to the land of prom-

ise. The pride of Assyria will be abased, and the land of Egypt will lose its
own government.

THE NATION REGENERATED

The prophets are one in declaring that the restoration of the people of
Israel to their own land will be followed by their conversion to the Lord.
Zechariah concludes chapter 10 with a portrayal of their redemption and
conduct. They will be strengthened in the Lord in every spiritual need
and will walk up and down in His name. The whole of their life and
conduct will be permeated with a thought for the glory and honor of the
Lord. They will live constantly under God's gracious and protecting hand
(Mic 4:5) .

The promises of blessing in this chapter, which exist in the reign of
Israel's King, are brought to a close with the record of Israel's redemption and her walk in agreement with His will and character. This is the
climax and goal of prophecy in Israel. Happy is that people whose God
is the Lord.

THEY SHALL LIVE AND RETURN

Truly we are living in momentous days as we view Israel and the preview of the things God has predicted for her. The nation does live again
governmentally and politically and nationally. They are returning by
every mode of conveyance and in astonishingly great numbers. But there
is more to come. This is not the fulfillment of the prophecies of the
prophets of the Old Testament in their highest sense. They predicted
spiritual life and conversion to God for the nation. God will never rest
till this be accomplished (Is 62:1) . We need ever to be admonished that
political prestige and recognition for Israel do not connote the blessing of
God He intends for her. She must rest by faith in Messiah Jesus the Lord
if she is to know the full purpose of God.

The Good Shepherd

DESTRUCTION UPON THE LAND

The predictions of chapter 11 were given probably long after the
completion of the Temple of Zerubbabel. The events themselves concern
the more distant future from the standpoint of the prophet. The chapter
is undoubtedly the darkest of Israel's history. And there has been much
difference of opinion as to which desolation Zechariah has in mind in the
highly poetic words of the first three verses.

One view has it that the passage speaks of the judgment of the land
under the Chaldeans in 586 BC. If so, the prophet is setting forth a historical fact and not a prophetic event of the future. Another position is

that the text refers to the invasion of Palestine in the far distant future by the different confederacies of nations indicated in the prophetic Scriptures and specifically in chapters 12 and 14 of this book. We are frank to admit that, if the verses are taken alone, they are so general that the coming universal conspiracy against Jerusalem could be in view. There are some who are ready to state that it is not certain what invasion is referred to here. However, the context of the rest of the chapter is determining and it points unmistakably to the judgment which resulted from the rejection of the Shepherd of Israel, that destruction which overtook the land and people in AD 70.

Among those who interpret the passage of events after the rejection of Israel's Messiah, there are those who understand the judgment to be described in figurative terms, as well as those who see a portrayal of destruction in literal terms. With the latter position we agree. The figurative view understands the address to Lebanon to refer to the Temple, because the cedars of Lebanon furnished the timber for it (1 Ki 5:6). This is the ancient rabbinical position.

Others who interpret figuratively believe the cedars, firs, and oaks are symbols of power and majesty, and may refer to the principal men of the nation or anything lofty such as the nations who harassed Israel.

If we take the words as literal, we have a most graphic picture of the way God's judgment fell on the land from north to south in AD 70. The opening command makes more vivid what would be stated as a matter of fact. The great forest of Lebanon was to be visited by the fire of God.

What took place there would be duplicated in other parts of the land: Lebanon, Bashan, and Jordan comprehend the whole land in the vision of the prophet. There is to be much wailing for, if the highest are not spared, the lowest in nature cannot escape. The shepherds too will mourn, for their pasture land will be destroyed and their flocks will suffer as a result. The pride of Jordan signifies the thickets on the banks of the river which were lairs for lions. (See Jer 49:19 and 50:44.) Nothing in the world is so disastrous as sin.

THE FLOCK OF SLAUGHTER

In Hebrew style an effect is often stated first, then the cause is presented afterward. So it is here. The cause of the judgment, the rejection of the Messiah by Israel, is now elaborated upon. The charge is to the prophet who performed in vision what was commanded. He acted representatively for the Messiah in whose personal history these transactions took place.

It is actually the commission of the Son of God by the Father. The Messiah is given the task of feeding the flock of slaughter. He was to act as a shepherd to the flock who were yet to be slaughtered. (Note Ps 44:22.) They were doomed to be slaughtered by the Romans for their sin. We have the authority of the historian Josephus that about a million and a half perished in the war with Rome.

The nation was in a miserable enough condition when Christ came to them, but their lot was to be sadder yet. They were as sheep bought and sold unfeelingly in the market. The reference is not to the procedure of collecting taxes in Palestine at that time, but to all the oppressive measures under which they groaned while under foreign domination, especially under the Romans. These foreign oppressors had no scruples in the matter, for they thought they could continue without punishment. They hypocritically credit God for their gain in misusing the sheep.

This was bad enough, but their own shepherds had no pity on them. Their own unprincipled leaders, the Pharisees and others, did not spare them. There was no man to espouse their cause or mitigate their sad plight. But the climax of woe is reached when the Lord states He will no longer pity the people of the land. The thought is not that God was going to punish the nations for their treatment of His people by bringing upon them wars and civil strife; the reference is to the inhabitants of the land of promise. The Lord, in not pitying them, delivered them over to internal strife.

It is well known how many factions existed in Israel during Messiah's earthly ministry and immediately thereafter. Moreover, they were to be delivered into the hand of their king, in this instance the Roman emperor whom they themselves acknowledged as king. (Note the remarkable admission in Jn 19:15.)

The smiting of the land by those who harassed God's people is a summary way of stating that they were subjected to many oppressive measures and burdens. He who is in the bond servitude of sin serves a hard master indeed. Well did the Lord call His own people the flock of slaughter.

THE MINISTRY OF THE SHEPHERD

The omniscient Messiah of Israel knew what the outcome of His ministry among His nation would be, but He faithfully undertook the ministry of the shepherd. Twice in verse 7 it is noted that He did feed the flock.

The prophet saw himself in vision carrying out the transactions which the Messiah would experience in His earthly ministry in the fullness of time. (See Mt 9:36 and Jn 10.) When He fed the flock, He was in truth feeding the poor or the humble of the flock (Zep 3:12). He fed them all for the sake of the remnant among them.

Throughout the passage these are distinguished from the mass of the nation. Two staves are taken because the shepherd in the East carried a staff to protect against wild beasts, another to help the sheep in difficult and dangerous places. The names given to them in this instance indicate the purpose God intended for Israel in the shepherd ministry of the Messiah. The first is called Beauty or favor, or graciousness; the second is called Bands or bonds, or binders. The first indicated God's restraint on the nations from destroying the nation Israel; the second had reference to the brotherly ties within the nation itself. In other words, by the work of the Messiah the Lord meant to preserve for Israel His overruling providences among the nations of the earth whereby they could not and would not work His people harm; by that same benevolent oversight the brotherly bonds in the nation were to be confirmed and strengthened.

We are not left long in doubt as to the results of the shepherd ministry now before us. In one month, in a comparatively short time, the shepherd found it necessary to cut off the three shepherds over the nation. The soul of the shepherd wearied of them and their soul hated him.

Forty different interpretations have been counted on verse 8; the conjectures cover a wide range. It would appear settled that the three shepherds are undershepherds of the flock under the Messiah; also, they must have ministered and had oversight over the people in the life and ministry of the Messiah. For this reason any suggestions involving Old Testament characters are immediately ruled out. The best view is that which sees in the three shepherds three classes of leaders in Israel: the prophet, the priest, and the king (or more properly, the civil magistrates). (See Jer 2:8.)

There was mutual disgust, because they rejected His grace and favor. Now we have the language of one whose patience is finally exhausted. When every means of grace had failed to draw them, the Messiah gives over the nation to its own sinful way. The sheep which are dying of pestilence and famine will die. Those of the flock that are to be cut off by war and bloodshed will be cut off, and the rest will be given over to continuous internal conflict. Light rejected always brings greater night.

THE FIRST STAFF BROKEN

In order to symbolize the severing of certain relationships, the Messiah breaks His staff Beauty. This indicated the breaking of the covenant which God had made with all the peoples. The peoples spoken of here are not the tribes of Israel, as some think, for they are not so designated in the Scriptures. Moreover, this action would be duplicated in the breaking of the second staff which relates to internal conditions in the nation Israel itself.

Zechariah is speaking of the nations of the earth, and he reveals an important truth: God has made a covenant with the peoples of the earth relative to His own people Israel. He has placed them under restraint lest they work Israel harm or ill. (For the same principle see Job 5:23; Eze 34:25; and Ho 2:18.) When the restraint was removed, the Romans destroyed their city and economy. Neither Alexander, nor Antiochus Epiphanes, nor Pompey was allowed to mar their national existence. But when the Messiah broke His staff, neither Titus nor his generals could spare the Temple, nor could Julian the Apostate later restore it.

Anticipating the fulfillment of the prediction, the prophet says the staff was broken in that day. Again it was the poor of the flock, the godly among the nation, that knew that the word from this transaction was the message of God to the nation. The willing heart, then as now, perceived the truth and intent of God through His servant.

THIRTY PIECES OF SILVER

In order to bring to a focal point the condition of the people spiritually and to test their gratitude for the ministry and service of the Messiah, the Messiah asks the nation to give Him His hire or wages for His labors among them. The wage He expected, we know, was their love, their obedience, and their devotion to God and His Shepherd. But it was not to be a matter of compulsion; if they were so minded, they could refrain from any manifestation of their evaluation of His ministry.

They were prepared, however, to indicate their estimate of Messiah and His work. They gave Him thirty pieces of silver (money) for His wage. According to Exodus 21:32 this was the price of a gored slave. A freeman was considered worth twice that amount.

Think of the insult of it! They placed the Messiah on the level of a worthless slave. How will God receive this base ingratitude? The prophet is commanded to cast the sum to the potter in the house of the Lord. This is God's estimate of their evaluation of His Son.

To make the action more solemn and public, it is carried out in the house of the Lord. The price was so disgraceful that it was to be cast to the potter who busied himself with things of little value.

Casting a thing to the potter may have been proverbial for throwing away what was worthless. Sarcastically the prophet refers to the price as a goodly one. Then he casts the sum from him as he was charged by the Lord. This passage is quoted in Matthew 27:7-10 where the evangelist is recording the betrayal of Christ by Judas and the results of the transaction.

The difficulty there is that the prophecy is attributed to Jeremiah, not Zechariah. Many have been the solutions offered to explain the wording of the New Testament passage. It will not do to say the passage did not originally appear in the book of Zechariah. There can be no real doubt that the words were in the prophecy of Zechariah in the days of Matthew, since it is found in place in the Greek translation of the Old Testament, made before New Testament times. It has been suggested that the name of the better known prophet is used, as in Mark 1:2 (the case of Malachi and Isaiah), but it is not an analogous case. The solution is probably to be sought in the fact that the name of Jeremiah stood at the head of the whole collection of the prophets, because his prophecy was placed first. There is evidence in Jewish writings for this position.

Now the prophet acts out the final severing of shepherd relations with Israel. He cut asunder the staff Bands to show the dissolution of the brotherhood between Judah and Israel. This was surely fulfilled in the sad scenes during the siege of Jerusalem by the Romans under Titus. There was a breaking up of the social fabric of the Jewish nation. Internal strife and divisions were prevalent and contributed largely to the downfall of Judea.

THE FOOLISH SHEPHERD

The sad rejection of Messiah has been accomplished, but what is the outlook for the future? We know how God scattered His people throughout the world at that time. When He begins again to deal with them, it will be after the manner spoken of in verses 15 to 17. Since they would not have the Good Shepherd, they shall have the foolish shepherd. This one has been taken to be all the ungodly rulers in Israel between Zechariah's time and the fall of the Jewish nation; Herod the Great; or Ptolemy IV. The one spoken of as the foolish and worthless shepherd is undoubtedly the personal Antichrist of Daniel 11:36-39; John 5:43; 2 Thessalonians 2:1-12; and Revelation 13:11-18.

With reference to verse 7 the prophet is told to take the instruments of such a shepherd. They are the same as those of the true shepherd; the condition of heart makes the difference. This shepherd is a wicked one; wickedness is represented in Scripture under the figure of folly. In the Old Testament foolishness implies moral lack and failure. The Lord allows him full sway, and he neglects the sheep and cruelly mistreats them. He has no heart for the sheep. His greed is his ruling passion. The judgment of God will rest upon this wicked one: his arm (the organ of power) will be withered which cared not for the sheep, and his eye (the organ of intelligence) will be darkened for it did not look after the flock. God's judgment on him will be sure and swift.

18

ISRAEL'S DAY OF ATONEMENT

THE SIEGE OF JERUSALEM

THE FIRST BURDEN of the latter part of Zechariah's prophecy covered chapters 9 to 11; the second burden is found in chapters 12 to 14. From the angle of the light these chapters throw on the consummation of Israel's history, they are among the most important to be found in the prophetic Scriptures.

The great confederacy and conflict spoken of in Zechariah 12 should be compared with the predictions of chapter 14. Strangely enough, this passage has been explained as recording the invasion of Palestine by Nebuchadnezzar in the days before the Babylonian captivity. This is impossible for a number of reasons, particularly because the results of the conflicts were not at all the same. Another student of the text refers verses 1-9 to the Maccabean conquests as in chapter 9. The fact is, no such coalition of nations (not even in the Roman war of the first century) against Israel has ever occurred in the past.

Chapter 12 deals with events before the reign of Messiah when Israel shall be besieged by the nations for their final death blow against God's people. But God is He who puts down their evil designs. The weighty and threatening prophecy concerns Israel in that it speaks of her benefit and ultimate good. It is threatening to her foes but for her permanent benefit. The prophet foretells the destruction of Israel's enemies.

God is first presented as He who stretches forth the heavens, lays the foundation of the earth, and forms the spirit of man within him. The expressions are such that they reveal God sustaining constantly His creation. The majestic picture of the Lord as Creator and Preserver is presented to dispel all doubt and unbelief concerning the things predicted here. God is abundantly able to carry out what He purposes to do. (See Num 16:22; Is 42:5; and Heb 12:9.)

When the nations come against Jerusalem in battle, God will make that city a cup of reeling to their armies. The cup is a well-known symbol of

God's wrath. Israel had drunk this cup too. (Cp. Is 51:17, 22; Jer 13:13; 25:15-28; and 51:7.) The siege will not be confined to the capital, but will be against Judah as well as Jerusalem. The enemy will be given a staggering blow.

The discomfiture of the enemy will be so great that Zechariah now indicates it by another figure. God will make Jerusalem a burdensome stone which will sorely wound the ones who try to lift it. Some think there is a reference here to some athletic game. Jerome, who lived in Palestine, stated that it was a custom there to test the strength of young men by lifting a weighty stone.

Those who would crush God's city and people will be crushed by Jerusalem. A clear example of this in the past had been Sennacherib's siege of Jerusalem in 701 BC.

How great the confederacy will be is indicated in the reference to all the nations of the earth. Since cavalry always formed a large part in Eastern warfare, the enemy will be well supplied; but God will incapacitate them, turning this source of strength into a detriment and weapon of destruction. The horses of the enemy will be smitten with terror then with blindness (to lead their riders to their doom), and the horsemen will be struck with insanity. Such will be the confusion and tumult created by God in the midst of the enemy, while His eyes will be turned toward Jerusalem and her people with great favor and compassion. Little do the nations of earth realize how they incur the wrath of God against them when they touch Israel for harm, let alone seek to wipe them completely from the face of the earth.

GOD-GIVEN VICTORY

God brings about victory in a twofold way: first, He overpowers and deprives the enemies of their strength, and then He empowers and fortifies His people to resist and conquer their foes. The prophet makes it plain that the victory will be supernatural. The Lord will work in the hearts of the leaders of His people, so that they will realize and acknowledge that the support given them from the inhabitants of the land is effective only because the Lord is sustaining and supporting His people. They will not assume that they are responsible for the success of their resistance of the vicious attack of the nations against them. The miraculous intervention of God on their behalf will convince the leaders of God's power exerted for their sake.

The chieftains of Judah are likened to a pan of fire among wood or a burning torch among sheaves of grain. They will consume the enemy on every side. The figures convey the thoughts of the ease and completeness of their victory, as well as their irresistible might under God. The result for God's people will be that the inhabitants of Jerusalem will be enabled to dwell again in safety in their own city of Jerusalem.

THE DELIVERANCE OF JERUSALEM

In order that all may realize that the deliverance is of the Lord, He intervenes in behalf of the tents of Judah first. The tents of Judah are contrasted with the well-fortified capital. The outlying districts of the country, which would be more exposed to attack and thus more helpless, will be delivered first.

God gives priority to the weak and defenseless, so that human glorying may have no basis. The human heart ever seeks self-glory, but God will wipe it out in this triumph. He adds the word of assurance and manner of their defense. The Lord Himself will be their defense, and He will strengthen beyond all their natural abilities or limitations. The one among them who is so weak that he stumbles in his walk will be made like David, the great warrior king who was invincible in battle. He is given as the highest type of strength for conflict on earth. (See 2 Sa 17:8 and 18:3.) Those who are of the lineage of David, for they will be known in that day, will be empowered as the Angel of the Lord, the highest type of power in heaven. He went before Israel in days of old. (See Ex 23:20; 32:34; 33:2; and Jos 5:13.) Thus will the Lord seek to destroy all the godless nations that dare to come against Jerusalem.

The statement in verse 9 is after the manner of man with no implication of weakness, especially after the promise of power in verse 8. God will summarily deal with the nations who seek to thwart His purposes in Israel for world blessing.

THE SPIRIT OF GRACE

God has thus far made known His righteous judgment on the nations, but He has spiritual purposes which must be accomplished in Israel also. The nation is not yet in the place of blessing, not yet in the place of obedience and trust in Messiah the Saviour.

In the remainder of Zechariah 12, the prophet sets forth, as nowhere else in Scripture with such vividness and power, the conversion of Israel to the Lord. Nothing in Israel's past history can be interpreted as the fulfillment of this passage. In that coming day of Israel's national atonement, the Lord will pour upon the royal house and all who dwell in Jerusalem, then throughout the whole nation, the spirit of grace and supplication.

The words *grace* and *supplications* are derived from the same Hebrew root. The reference is not to the disposition to rely on grace and prayer, but to the Holy Spirit of God in all His influences. The outpouring of His conviction upon them will drive them to believing prayer. (Cp. Eze 39:29 and Joel 2:28-29.) They will supplicate the Lord then for His forgiveness and favor.

In this broken-down condition they will look to the One whom they pierced. The looking is with earnest regard and with fixed attention, realizing now what they had never conceived before. (See their confession at this time in Is 52:13 to 53:12.) It presupposes a definite condition of heart. But did they themselves pierce the Messiah? By their unbelief and rejection of Him they have made the actions and deeds of their ancestors their own (Jn 19:37). Just as the pouring out of the Spirit implies the deity of the Messiah, so the piercing indicates His humanity.

Some (after the Greek translation) would like to translate "insulted" for "pierced." It is an impossible rendering, because the word in all other passages where it is used in the Old Testament can have no other meaning than to pierce the body. (See 13:3.) Besides this, it is difficult to conceive the intensity of grief spoken of later for the offense of insulting the Messiah.

The Talmud pronounces peace upon one who refers the passage to Messiah the son of Joseph, yet to be slain. The theory of two Messiahs, one to die and one to reign, is an invention of the rabbis without foundation in Scripture to explain the passages which present the Messiah as suffering and as ruling. The answer is to be found in the two advents of the one Messiah, as proved by this very passage under consideration. It is not some unknown martyr of whom Zechariah is speaking but of the coming Messiah Himself. The oldest interpreters of the passage, both Jewish and Christian, so understood it. Once they view Him as He was rejected, they will manifest their true repentance by mourning.

The great grief is spoken of as the most intense kind of sorrow, like that for an only son. This is especially forceful, because childlessness was considered a curse and dishonor. Their hearts will be smitten with grief like that for the firstborn in the home, a peculiar sorrow to loving parents. The mourning has been compared to the greatest private sorrow; now it is likened to the most intense public grief exhibited in Israel.

The calamity referred to was Pharaoh-Necho's slaying of the godly Josiah, the only ray of hope of the nation between Hezekiah and the fall of the Jewish nation. (See 2 Ki 23:29-30 and 2 Ch 35:22-27.) Even Jeremiah wrote special dirges for the occasion.

The name "Hadadrimmon" is a compound of two names of Syrian gods, Hadad and Rimmon (2 Ki 5:18). It was the name of a site in the great plain of Esdraelon near the fortified city of Megiddo which was on the

southwest side of the plain. It has been famous in Israel's past history
(Judg 5:19 among others) and will be in the future also according to
Revelation 16:16, whence comes the name for the War of Armageddon.

In the early Christian centuries (according to Jerome) the place was
called Maximianopolis. Jerusalem's mourning over that tragedy must
have been great indeed to become the point of comparison with the sorrow of penitent Israel over the sight of their rejected and pierced Messiah.
Thank God for that godly sorrow which worketh repentance.

THE NATIONAL MOURNING

But Zechariah has not concluded what he wishes to reveal concerning
that sorrow. It is of such importance that he elaborates upon it. The manner of the mourning is detailed for us. There will be universal and individual mourning. Seclusion and privacy will be sought at this time of
grief. The prophet outlines for us the way in which the nation will be
divided into family groups and then further into individuals as they pour
out their bitter weeping over their rejection of the Messiah, Jesus of
Nazareth.

The house of David will take part in the mourning, and the house of
Nathan. Some identify this Nathan as the prophet (2 Sa 7:2) while others
think it is the younger son of David (2 Sa 5:14). If the former is intended,
then the royal office and prophetic are included; if the latter is the meaning, then the highest and lowest in the royal house are in view. We cannot prove either view with finality.

The house of Levi speaks of the priestly family; Shimei was of the family of Gershon, son of Levi (Num 3:17, 18, 21). Different priestly classes
are comprehended here. The leaders, who are pointed out, and the common people of the land will engage together in the lamentation, each in
his individual place.

Five times it is mentioned that their wives will mourn apart. It has
been suggested that the reference is to the Jewish custom for wives to live
in separate apartments as well as to worship separately. This is to miss the
inner meaning of the passage. The prophet means that the mourning will
be so intense as to transcend even the closest ties of earth, those between
husband and wife. Each will want to be alone with God in that hour.

"LOOK UNTO ME"

How simple yet how glorious is the way of salvation provided by our
God. It is a looking away from self and man-made plans and endeavors to
the Lamb of God who takes away the sin of the world. In Israel's glad con-

version hour she will come into the knowledge of sins forgiven by looking unto her rejected and pierced Messiah, the crucified Saviour of sinners.

THE LAND PURGED

CLEANSING FOR LAND AND PEOPLE

There exists the closest possible connection between chapter 13 and the previous one. Zechariah continues the theme of Israel's conversion to the Lord. In the day of Israel's glad salvation and restoration to the Lord, a fountain will be opened to all the people for sin and uncleanness.

The figure of the fountain is eminently in place here, for it is ever flowing, not like the laver of the tabernacle and Temple that needed to be filled repeatedly. The cleansing fountain was opened long ago at Calvary potentially, now actually for them. Cowper's well-known hymn, "There is a fountain filled with blood," had this verse for its basis.

Israel now enters into the provision of God at Calvary. (See Ro 11:26-27; also Is 33:24; 59:20-21; 65:19; and Eze 36:25; 39:29.) The provision of God will avail for both sin and uncleanness. Zechariah has in mind moral not ceremonial uncleanness. Justification is here and sanctification as well. Judicial guilt and moral impurity will be removed at the same time. All ranks and classes in the nation will have this blessed provision.

The terms for sin and uncleanness have been used with special reference to idolatry (though the second term has a specific reference to the periodic illness of women), thus forming a transition to the truth stated in the next verse of chapter 13. (Cp. 1 Ki 12:30; Eze 7:19-20.) The cleansing is followed by the abolition of idolatry. Idols, false prophets, and the unclean spirit will all be done away with. To cut off the names of the idols out of the land, so that their names will no more be remembered, is to destroy their authority, power, and influence upon Israel. God's people will cease to acknowledge them. The worship of God will be fully purified and cleansed. God had forbidden long since even the mention of the names of idols. (Cp. Ex 23:13; Deu 13:3; and Ps 16:4.)

False prophets will no longer lead the people astray, prophesying that which proceeds from their own hearts. There will be no true prophets then, because God's revelation will be complete. The unclean spirit, which energizes the false prophets, claims inspiration from God, but is empowered of Satan; indeed, the reference is to his evil activity.

This is the only place in the Old Testament where the expression "unclean spirit" is found, although it occurs often in the New Testament. The unclean spirit contrasts diametrically with the Spirit of grace and supplication of 12:10.

Twice in verse 2 mention is made of the land. It has been maintained that this should be translated "earth," because idolatry had already been wiped out of Israel by the Babylonian captivity. This is a failure to take into account the fact that Scripture reveals the revival of idolatry in Israel after the Church is taken to be with Christ the Lord. (Note carefully Mt 12:43-45 and Rev 13:11-18.)

All idolatry sponsored by and connected with the Roman beast (Rev 13:1-10) and the false prophet or the man of sin (Rev 13:11-18) will be wiped out. The removal of the false prophets will require severe measures. The very measures prescribed by the Mosaic law for the rooting out of false prophecy, wherein the nearest of kin take the first steps to abolish the evil, are indicated here. There the means of death, however, was stoning; here the guilty one will be thrust through with a weapon. Love for God and His truth will transcend the dearest natural bonds. (See Deu 13:6-10 and 18:20.) The glory of the name of the Lord will overshadow every earthly tie and sentiment.

THE FALSE PROPHET

False prophecy was such a snare to God's people through so many centuries, that the final blotting out of this spiritual plague is dwelt upon by Zechariah in further detail. The brazenness of the false prophets in making their lying pronouncements will be replaced in that day by shame; they will seek every means possible to disclaim any connection with false prophesying. They will refrain from wearing the hairy mantle which was one of the distinguishing marks of a prophet.

As wolves in sheep's clothing, the false prophets had donned the apparel of the true messenger of God. The genuine prophets wore this garment to show their frugal manner of life; it was also in keeping with their mournful pronouncements. (Note 1 Ki 19:13, 19; 2 Ki 1:8; 2:8, 13; Mt 3:4; and Mk 1:6.) The false prophets will fear to make known their false revelations and will not be able to deceive the people with the wearing of the garment of the prophet of God. They will not hesitate to cover up their evil activity by resorting to lying.

In verses 5 and 6 we have a description of the detection of one of the false prophets. He is accused by one of the people of being a false prophet and of speaking falsely in the name of the Lord. He knows that such a charge may well result in the forfeiture of his life by those zealous for the name and glory of the Lord. Therefore, he seeks by all means to free himself of any suspicion of connection with false prophecy. He disclaims any relationship with the prophetic office altogether. How could he have exercised the prophetic office, he asks, when he has been kept in a state of slavery from his youth? He claims he has never known freedom from service for others in order to be able to exercise a prophetic ministry. He has always been so occupied with the routine matters of a slave owned by his master that he has not aspired to the office of a prophet.

But he is still under suspicion and is asked what the wounds are between his hands. His answer is that they are the wounds which he received in the house of his devoted friends. Some hold that the scars of the one questioned are on his breast; others believe they are on the back. Surely the first view is correct; else how could they have been visible to the questioner?

It is suggested that we have here an implied admission that he had pretended to prophesy and that his friends had wounded him for it in their zeal for the glory of the Lord. We cannot connect this passage with verse 3 in such a manner, because God's command was to put the false prophet to death, not merely to wound him. The one under suspicion is simply stating that his parents inflicted such punishment on him in their discipline of him.

It is clear from our foregoing remarks that we understand verse 6 to be dealing still with the subject of the false prophet. The view has been advanced that the person in question is the Antichrist. This is scarcely possible.

First, this would be an abrupt way in which to introduce him, for the discussion is in very general terms. Wherever the Antichrist is spoken of in the Scriptures, his person and work are more clearly defined. Note how he is contrasted with the true Messiah and Shepherd in chapter 11 in the last three verses.

Second, in the time of this prophecy of Zechariah 13, the Antichrist will not be in the prophetic program. This is after his appearance on earth and his final doom. For these reasons the person under consideration cannot be the Antichrist.

Some hold that the one in verse 6 is Christ because of the mention of wounds between the arms. This view, though held somewhat generally, has nothing to commend it except a superficial reference to wounds.

It is an untenable position for several reasons. In the first place, Christ was not wounded between His arms with a number of wounds. His wounds, blessed evidences of a finished redemption, were in His hands and feet and the spear wound in His blessed side. It takes some juggling of the wording of the passage to make this wounds between His arms.

Second, He was not wounded in the house of His friends but on a cross of Roman devising.

Third, at what place after His resurrection could He be questioned by an inquirer as indicated in this text? We know from Scripture that He never appeared to the world after His death and resurrection; it was always to His own for confirmation of their faith and instruction (Ac 1) in the truth of God.

Furthermore, there are other reasons which militate against understanding the passage of Christ. Fourth, Christ could not and would not say He was not a prophet. He was not only a prophet, but *the* Prophet, and the Prophet of prophets. (See Deu 18:15-18; Jn 1:18; Ac 3:22; 7:37; and Rev 1:5.)

Fifth, Christ could not and would not say that He was a tiller of the ground. Doubtless, He aided His legal father, Joseph, in the carpenter shop in Nazareth in His youth, but this was not the work of a farmer.

Sixth, Christ could not and would not say that He had been a slave from His youth, or that a man had bought Him for service from the days of His youth. How could any one of the untrue statements already mentioned ever be attributed to the Christ who is the truth?

Finally, the position under discussion pays no attention to the context as to time or circumstances. It stems from the most superficial type of Bible interpretation, yet it lives on because we like to cling to an accepted view. But this one has nothing to commend it, and it does grave injustice to our blessed Lord.

THE SHEPHERD SMITTEN

Whereas verse 6 cannot possibly refer to the Lord Jesus Christ, verse 7 can refer to no other than to Him. The words apply exclusively to the sufferings of Christ. (See Mt 26:31, also the connection with 11:4, 7, 10-14.) Christ referred this prophecy to Himself. The death of the Messiah is here viewed as God's act. (Cp. Jn 3:16; Ac 2:23; 3:18; and 4:28.)

God calls upon the sword to awake against His Shepherd, against the Man, His Fellow. The sword expresses the highest judicial power (Ro 13:4), and represents any means of taking life; here it is employed of divine justice in judgment against sin. (Note Ex 5:21; 2 Sa 12:9; Ps 17:13; and Jer 47:6-7.) The Scriptures have much to say of the sword of of the Lord.

When He addresses the Messiah as "My Shepherd," we have a manifestation of His love for His Son as well as the statement of His justice in the use of the sword. The figure of the Shepherd of Israel is so familiar from the eleventh chapter that we shall not dwell on it further here. But the designation "My Fellow" is both rare in Scripture and filled with much spiritual truth for us. It is found in the Old Testament only here and in

Leviticus 6:2; 18:20; 19:11, 15, 17; 24:19; 25:14, 15, 17. It has reference to persons united in law, rights, and privileges. The word comes from a verb "to bind together." The Hebrew term for "people" (those united in common origin and interest) has the same root.

God is speaking of One as "My Companion, My Associate, My Friend, My Confidant, the One united to Me, the One whom I have associated with Myself, My Equal, My Nearest of Kin." It would not be possible to state in stronger terms the unimpeachable deity of the Messiah of Israel. (See Jn 10:30; 14:10-11; and Phil 2:6.)

The word *Man* denotes His humanity; *Fellow*, His deity. When the Shepherd was smitten, the sheep were to be scattered. The reference is not just to the scattering of the disciples at the arrest of the Lord Jesus (Mt 26:31), but ultimately to the dispersion of Israel as a nation. But God in grace promises that His hand would be turned upon the little ones, a designation of tender affection. The Lord will intervene on their behalf; that is, for the sake of the poor of the flock, the remnant. The Lord will watch over His own.

THE REFINING OF THE REMNANT

Just as in chapter 11, the prophet advances from the rejection of the Messiah by the nation Israel to the judgment of God for this unbelief in the time of the Great Tribulation (11:15-17), so we have the smiting of the Shepherd followed by the time of Jacob's trouble.

A great gap of time exists between verses 7 and 8. In the hour of Israel's national distress, two parts will be cut off by judgment in all the land and die; a third will remain. The third represents the remnant. Mathematical exactness is not in view here, we know, because the remnant is spoken of in Isaiah 6:13 as a tenth. (See Eze 20:34-38 for this remnant.)

The remnant will be brought through trying circumstances and will be refined as silver and gold. This is not the annihilation carried out by the Romans, as some suggest, but the purging brought about by Israel's time of trial when back in the land in the last days. The purpose of the refining is to purify and develop faith in the remnant. Physical deliverance will be followed by conversion. Thus will the new covenant be fulfilled. This will be the full and final renunciation of idolatry. (Note Jer 30:18-22; 31:33; Eze 11:19-20; and Ho 2:23.) Israel the people of the Lord and God their Lord—this is the climax and culmination of Israel's history.

MESSIAH'S RETURN AND REIGN

THE LAST SIEGE OF JERUSALEM

The final chapter of this important prophetic book opens, as did chapter 12, with the last invasion of Jerusalem by the nations of the earth. The time setting in both chapters is the same. Some have claimed that this chapter surpasses all the others in Zechariah in obscurity, and have thought the passage defies historical explanation. On the other hand, the prophecy has been assigned to the invasion of Jerusalem by Nebuchadnezzar in 586 BC or to the siege of the city by Titus in 70 AD with his Roman legions.

Suffice it to say, every feature of this invasion differentiates it from the two just mentioned. We have before us the depiction of the War of Armageddon. It is a day peculiarly the Lord's when Jerusalem's spoil will be divided in the midst of the capital. The day is so designated because in it God means to vindicate His justice and destroy the wicked. It is the day of the Lord as in prophecies of Joel, Zephaniah, Malachi, and elsewhere.

Jerusalem is addressed and informed of the sad tidings of preliminary defeat. The enemy, secure and confident in their conquest, will divide the city's spoil in the midst of her. The prophet has described the result of the siege; now he sets forth the fact and occasion of it.

The Lord says He will gather all nations against Jerusalem to battle. This is the universal confederacy of the armies of the nations described in Psalm 2, Joel 3, Ezekiel 38 and 39, Revelation 16 and 19. In verse 2 Jerusalem is the object of God's judgment, as she is the object of blessing in verses 9 to 11 and 16 to 21.

As an outcome of the invasion the city is captured, the houses are plundered of all spoil, and the women are violated. A deportation takes place, but a remnant of the people continues on in the beleaguered city.

The alignment of the nations at this time is clearly set forth in the prophetic Scriptures. There will be an alliance of the northern powers (Eze 38 and 39); a union of the nations in the south of Europe (the revived Roman Empire of Dan 2 and 7, and Rev 13 and 17); the king of the north (Dan 11); and an entente of the kings of the east or sunrising (Rev 16). And the initial stages of the conflict will witness the success of the arms of the enemies of Israel.

THE RETURN OF MESSIAH

But where Israel is concerned, God is vitally interested. Then in Israel's plight the great Champion of Israel, the Lord Messiah, goes forth, as kings go forth to battle, Himself to fight against those nations, as He fought in many a battle before this time. (See 2 Sa 11:1 and Is 26:21.) The Lord is indeed a Man of war (Ex 15:3).

This is not a description of the providences that overthrew the Roman

Empire; it is a prediction of the visible interposition of the Messiah on behalf of His people in their last conflict of their age. The feet of Messiah, pierced for the salvation of sinners, shall stand in that day on the Mount of Olives, which is eastward of the city.

This prophecy cannot be relegated to the sphere of beautiful poetic description. There is no reason why it cannot be taken literally. Just as the Red Sea was actually divided for the rescue of the children of Israel, so now the Mount of Olives is cleft asunder for their escape from the enemy. In 2 Samuel 15:30 the mountain is called "the ascent of Olives." The place of His departure is the place of His return (Ac 1:11). The scene of the agony will witness the display of His glory. The Mount of Olives will be divided east and west; part of it will move northward, and part will remove southward, causing a great valley.

Because of the judgments in progress in Jerusalem the besieged ones will flee through the valley made by the cleaving of the Mount of Olives. It is an avenue of escape, not a place of refuge. The way of deliverance will reach to Azel, a site probably near the east side of the city.

The flight is likened to that of the people when the earthquake took place in the days of Uzziah, king of Judah. This must have been an unusually severe disturbance, for two centuries had already passed since its occurrence, yet it is set forth here for comparison (Amos 1:1).

Then the gaze of the prophet is directed to the Messiah Himself, coming with His holy ones who are both angels and redeemed humanity. His heart is so filled with the vision that he changes to direct address (Is 25:9). For the constituency of this company see Matthew 24:30-31 (angels) and 1 Corinthians 15:23 and 1 Thessalonians 3:13; 4:14 (redeemed men). Thank God, He that promised to come will come and with great power and glory.

CHANGES IN NATURE

With the coming of the Lord there will be drastic changes in the phenomena of nature. At the time of day there will not be light; the lights of heaven will become congealed or coagulated, thus making darkness. The luminaries of heaven will suffer change. It will be a unique, extraordinary day, the only one of its kind. Only the Lord will know its essential character. It will not be the normal day, for the prophet has just stated that the light will be absent. Neither will it be the usual night, for at evening time there will be an unusual light.

At that time living waters will go forth from Jerusalem toward the Dead Sea and the Mediterranean, thus making fertile and prosperous the whole land. Jerusalem is one of the most arid cities in the world; some think

"Zion" means a dry place. But in that day of blessing, when Messiah is returned to His people, living waters will refresh the land. Waters are a symbol in Scripture of purification, spiritual life, and refreshment. The supply will be constant, in summer and winter, not suffering the drying up of usual bodies of water by the heat of summer. (Cp. Eze 47:1; Joel 3:18; and Rev 22:1-2.) Spiritual power and blessing ever attend the presence of the Messiah of God.

THE REIGN OF MESSIAH

When the Son of David sits on the throne of His father David, the Lord will be King over all the earth; the unity and glory of the Lord will be recognized universally. He alone will be worshiped throughout the universe. (See Is 54:5; Dan 2:44; and Rev 11:15.)

All the land of Palestine will be made like the Arabah to allow the living waters free passage. The Arabah or plain of the Jordan runs from the Sea of Tiberias to the Elanitic gulf of the Red Sea.

Then the prophet gives the exact geographical locations of the changes. Geba is the modern Jeba, six miles northeast of Jerusalem. Rimmon is about thirty-five miles southwest of Jerusalem. Jerusalem itself will be lifted up (Mic 4:1) and dwell securely in her place from Benjamin's gate in the north wall of the city to the first gate, whose location is uncertain though some think it is the old gate, on to the corner gate in the northwest corner of the city; from the tower of Hananel, near the northeast corner of the wall near the gate of Benjamin, to the winepresses of the king, probably southeast of the city near the king's gardens and the pool of Siloam, the city will be rebuilt as in former days. The city will be repopulated, and the curse will be removed because there will be no more sin. Then will the inhabitants of Jerusalem dwell without fear or alarm. How different from the distressing and tense conditions of our own day.

THE DOOM OF THE INVADERS

With verse 12 we return to the theme with which chapter 14 began, namely, the conflict of the last days against Jerusalem. There were details not touched upon there. The Lord will give victory at that time by sending a supernatural plague against the forces of the enemy. The flesh of their bodies will fall away by consumption; their eyes will melt away in their sockets; and their tongue will dissolve in their mouth. It will be a living death. In addition to personal bodily suffering of the severest kind they will be overtaken by supernatural confusion: a tumult from the Lord will send every man raging against his fellow soldier and neighbor. The forces of the enemy will destroy themselves by internal warfare (Eze 38:21).

In the first phase of the conflict the tide of war went against the people of Jerusalem (v. 1), but Israel will win the second and final phase of the battle. All the surrounding country will rally to the defense of the capital against the common foe.

The loss of the enemy will be great in lives and in their possessions. Oriental armies carried large amounts of gold and silver with them on their march (2 Ch 20:25). Apparel is often mentioned in lists of spoil, because it was an important item of wealth in the East. (Note Judg 5:30 and 2 Ki 7:15.)

The plague mentioned in verse 12 is touched upon again to indicate that it will fall upon the horse, mule, camel, ass, and all the beasts in the camp of the enemy. Even the animals of the invading forces will not be exempt from the visitation of God in wrath upon them (12:4).

THE FEAST OF TABERNACLES

When the smoke of the conflict has cleared and the remnant of the nations is delivered, the godly among the Gentiles will go up annually to worship the King, the Lord of Hosts, in Jerusalem and to celebrate the Feast of Tabernacles. The nations will go up representatively, for even all Israel never went up to the feasts to the last man (Lev 23:33-44 and Deu 16:13-17).

The Feast of Tabernacles is the feast of the millennial age. It was the feast of ingathering and rest, of joy, praise, and thanksgiving (Ex 23:16 and 34:2). The other two annual feasts, Passover and Pentecost, are not mentioned, because their antitypes have been fulfilled. The Feast of Tabernacles was celebrated on the return of Israel from exile. (See Neh 8:14-18.) It is preeminently the feast of joy after the ingathering of the harvest. (Cp. Rev 7:9.) When the millennial day dawns, all other feasts will have been fulfilled by their antitypes. Now the Feast of Tabernacles finds its antitype. If any of the families of the earth refuse to go up to Jerusalem to worship the King, then rain will be withheld from their land as punishment.

Much has been made of the supposed difficulty in the coming of the nations to Jerusalem. It is declared to be a physical impossibility. But, as we have seen already, the passage does not require that every person in every nation go to the feast annually. It will be carried out representatively.

Verses 17-19 presuppose that there will be disobedience even in that age. The reason can be found in such a passage as Psalm 66:3 where it is noted that some will give feigned obedience (lit., lie) to the all-powerful King Messiah. The withholding of rain would prevent a harvest in the following year.

In the case of Egypt the threat would have no force, so the prophet declares its punishment. Egypt is not dependent on rain but on the annual overflow of the Nile, hence they may think themselves exempt. But the Lord will have His punishment for them; He will bring upon them the plague, not necessarily the plague mentioned in verse 12. No one will be able to defy then, any more than in any other age or era, the plain command of God and do it with impunity.

"HOLY UNTO THE LORD"

While disobedience outside Israel will be visited with judgment, the Lord's people will be righteous. All will be pervaded with holiness, the great goal and objective of all God's dealings with Israel, the Church, or any individual heart at any time.

How holiness will pervade every department of life and every duty is indicated in the last two verses of this great book of prophecy. The people of God will know in that day the universal holiness which has been the ideal of God for Israel through the centuries. (Cp. Ex 19:6: "a holy nation.") Even the bells of the horses, used for ornament, will be inscribed with the very words which were engraved upon the tiara of the high priest in Israel, "Holy unto the Lord." Horses, usually employed for warfare, will now be dedicated to the Lord and His glory. The pots in the temple were considered the basest objects in the sanctuary, but in the day of Messiah's reign they will be of equal sanctity with the bowls before the altar which caught the blood of the victims for sprinkling before the Lord.

Where holiness prevails, ceremonial sanctity is unnecessary. The last verse of the book states the same truth from another angle. If all the vessels of the sanctuary will be on the same plane of holiness because of universal cleansing, even the ordinary pot throughout the nation will be equally dedicated to the Lord. The vessels of the private homes will be as suitable as those of the Temple for the services of the Lord's house. In that day there will be no more a Canaanite in the house of the Lord. The name stands for the Phoenicians of the north of Canaan, who were the most noted mariners and merchants of the ancient world. They were known for their ungodly ways, and represent here an unholy and ungodly person. (See Ho 12:7.) It is the negative way of stating that all will be holy.

SUBJECT INDEX

SUBJECT INDEX

SCRIPTURE INDEX